MW00397045

The Internationalists

The Internationalists

The Fight to Restore American Foreign Policy After Trump

ALEXANDER WARD

PORTFOLIO • PENGUIN

Portfolio / Penguin
An imprint of Penguin Random House LLC
penguinrandomhouse.com

Copyright © 2024 by Alexander Ward
Penguin Random House supports copyright. Copyright fuels creativity, encourages diverse voices, promotes free speech, and creates a vibrant culture. Thank you for buying an authorized edition of this book and for complying with copyright laws by not reproducing, scanning, or distributing any part of it in any form without permission. You are supporting writers and allowing Penguin Random House to continue to publish books for every reader.

Most Portfolio books are available at a discount when purchased in quantity for sales promotions or corporate use. Special editions, which include personalized covers, excerpts, and corporate imprints, can be created when purchased in large quantities. For more information, please call (212) 572-2232 or e-mail specialmarkets@penguinrandomhouse.com. Your local bookstore can also assist with discounted bulk purchases using the Penguin Random House corporate Business-to-Business program. For assistance in locating a participating retailer, e-mail B2B@penguinrandomhouse.com.

Grateful acknowledgment is made for permission to reprint, in slightly different form, "Why Isn't Biden Pushing Israel Harder?," first published on May 20, 2021, in *Vox* (www.vox.com/22442000/biden-israel-gaza-hamas-history-policy), in Chapter 4. Excerpt used with permission of Vox Media, LLC.

Image credits may be found on page 343.

LIBRARY OF CONGRESS CATALOGING-IN-PUBLICATION DATA
Names: Ward, Alexander, author.
Title: The Internationalists : The Fight to Restore American Foreign Policy After Trump / Alexander Ward.
Description: [New York] : Portfolio/Penguin, [2024] |
Includes bibliographical references and index.
Identifiers: LCCN 2023041007 (print) | LCCN 2023041008 (ebook) |
ISBN 9780593539071 (hardcover) | ISBN 9780593539088 (ebook)
Subjects: LCSH: United States foreign relations specialists. |
Cabinet officers—United States. | Presidents—United States—Staff. |
Culture and globalization—United States. | World politics—21st century. |
United States—Foreign relations—21st century. |
United States—Politics and government—2021–
Classification: LCC JZ1480.A5 W37 2024 (print) | LCC JZ1480.A5 (ebook) |
DDC 327.73009/05—dc23/eng/20231101
LC record available at https://lccn.loc.gov/2023041007
LC ebook record available at https://lccn.loc.gov/2023041008

Printed in the United States of America
1st Printing

Book design by Chris Welch

For Christine,

I love you and I like you.

And in remembrance of Ann Ward,

forever my MVG.

Good and evil both increase at compound interest. That is why the little decisions you and I make every day are of such infinite importance.

—C. S. Lewis, *Mere Christianity*

Contents

Part 3
The Austin Powers Inspiration

Cast of Characters

(in alphabetical order)

Biden Administration, United States

Sam Aronson: Assigned to Hamid Karzai International Airport, Department of State

Lloyd Austin: Secretary of Defense, Department of Defense

John Bass: Assigned to Hamid Karzai International Airport, Department of State

Alex Bick: "Tiger Team" Leader, National Security Council, White House

Joe Biden: President of the United States

Antony Blinken: Secretary of State, Department of State

William Burns: Director, Central Intelligence Agency

Michael Carpenter: Ambassador, U.S. Delegation to the Organization for Security and Cooperation in Europe

Jon Finer: Deputy Assistant to the President for National Security Affairs, National Security Council, White House

Eric Green: Special Assistant to the President and Senior Director for Russia and Central Asia, National Security Council, White House

Avril Haines: Director of National Intelligence, Office of the Director of National Intelligence

Kamala Harris: Vice President of the United States

Emily Horne: Chief Spokesperson, National Security Council, White House

Colin Kahl: Under Secretary of Defense for Policy, Department of Defense

John Kerry: Special Presidential Envoy for Climate Change, Department of State

Zalmay Khalilzad: Special Representative for Afghanistan Reconciliation, Department of State

Ron Klain: Chief of Staff, White House

Gen. Kenneth "Frank" McKenzie, Jr.: Commander, U.S. Central Command

Gen. Scott Miller: Commander of U.S. Forces in Afghanistan, Department of Defense

Gen. Mark Milley: Chairman, Joint Chiefs of Staff

Carlyn Reichel: Senior Director for Speechwriting and Strategic Initiatives, White House

Wendy Sherman: Deputy Secretary of State, Department of State

Elizabeth Sherwood-Randall: Deputy National Security Adviser for Homeland Security, National Security Council, White House

Amanda Sloat: Senior Director, Western Europe, National Security Council, White House

Jake Sullivan: Assistant to the President for National Security Affairs, National Security Council, White House

Linda Thomas-Greenfield: Ambassador, U.S. Delegation to the United Nations

Rear Adm. Peter Vasely: Assigned to Hamid Karzai International Airport, Department of Defense

Ross Wilson: Chargé d'Affaires, U.S. Embassy in Afghanistan, Department of State

Ghani Administration, Afghanistan

Ashraf Ghani: President of Afghanistan

Hamdullah Mohib: National Security Adviser to the President

Zelenskyy Administration, Ukraine

Dmytro Kuleba: Minister of Foreign Affairs, Ministry of Foreign Affairs

Oleksii Reznikov: Minister of Defense, Ministry of Defense

Andriy Yermak: Head, Office of the President

Gen. Valeryy Zaluzhnyy: Commander in Chief of the Armed Forces, Ministry of Defense

Volodymyr Zelenskyy: President of Ukraine

Putin Administration, Russia

Gen. Valery Gerasimov: Chief of the General Staff, Ministry of Defense

Sergey Lavrov: Minister of Foreign Affairs, Ministry of Foreign Affairs

Vladimir Putin: President of Russia

Sergey Shoigu: Minister of Defense, Ministry of Defense

International Leaders

Boris Johnson: Prime Minister of the United Kingdom

Emmanuel Macron: President of France

Angela Merkel: Chancellor of Germany

Benjamin Netanyahu: Prime Minister of Israel

Olaf Scholz: Chancellor of Germany

Jens Stoltenberg: Secretary General, North Atlantic Treaty Organization

Activists

Alexander McCoy: Political Director, Common Defense

Part 1

The Wilderness

Chapter 1

Relearning America

November 2016—January 2021

The location was picked for what it represented. The Javits Center, a large building along the Hudson River in New York City, was wall-to-wall glass—including the ceiling. The metaphor was obvious to the thousands waiting to see Hillary Clinton on November 8, 2016: they would see her shatter the highest obstacle in American politics when she was elected forty-fifth president of the United States that night.

But only hearts were breaking inside the pearl of Hell's Kitchen that night. As Donald Trump won Ohio, and Florida, and Pennsylvania, and Wisconsin, and Michigan, the mood turned as cool as the blustery weather outside. The once jubilant atmosphere—pregnant with promise—had soured. Sobs rang out within the center's cavernous halls. Not until 2:00 a.m. did a member of the Clinton campaign, chairman John Podesta, come out to send the remaining hopefuls home.

"You've been here a long time and it's been a long night and it's been a long campaign," Podesta said, his words beamed across the country and around the world. "We can wait a little longer!"

Jake Sullivan, too, would have to wait. He had worked for Clinton for years, first at the State Department and now as one of her campaign's top policy aides. He was ready to stride back into Washington after leaving the Obama administration two years earlier, playing coy with friends and the media about whether he was plotting a return to politics. He was, and he was the odds-on favorite to be Clinton's national security adviser—which would make him one of the most powerful people in the federal government.

What was supposed to be a dream night for him—a crowning achievement for a man who was days from turning forty—turned into a nightmare. In a Peninsula hotel room two and a half miles from the somber crowd, he watched the TV screens as the American map filled with red, not blue. When the election was called in Trump's favor, Sullivan stood by Clinton's side as she phoned her opponent to concede. hearing the words "Congratulations, Mr. President-Elect," he felt like a truck had run over him.

The former collegiate debater stayed up all night helping to craft Clinton's concession speech, seeking an explanation for the political earthquake he had just witnessed. He grasped for anything, everything, to make sense of the moment.

Many forces combined into a perfect storm, he reasoned with himself. There was a backlash to President Barack Obama's time in office, a demographically changing America, economic pain throughout the country, and a general animosity toward elites, such as Clinton. The inordinate focus on her emails by the media didn't help, elevating to a national scandal what Democrats argued was at most an ill-advised administrative decision.

But in New York City, Trump's hometown and decades-long playground, Sullivan realized that the foreign policy message from Clinton's opponent had played a hand in his victory too. It was by no means the most vital element of Trump's ascendancy to power, but his overall argument—that U.S. foreign policy since the end of World War II hadn't worked out so well for the "forgotten" men and women of America— had clearly hit a nerve.

And when Trump critiqued the elites responsible for forgetting those millions of people, he was unwittingly criticizing Sullivan. The Minnesota boy had allowed the wealthy, glitz-loving real estate developer to beat him at populist politics, and defeat had not been a common event in his charmed and meteoritic rise.

At Southwest High School in Minneapolis, which he graduated from in 1994, Sullivan was named "Most Likely to Succeed." Teachers fawned over his ability to hand in flawlessly written assignments, and he led the student council while winning debate tournaments and quiz bowls. "I thought the idea of grappling with ideas and advocating for positions based on those ideas was an exciting prospect," he told *MinnPost*, an online news organization, in 2016. "I didn't think I would do it anywhere else."

His parents, Dan Sullivan, a University of Minnesota professor, and Jean Sullivan, a guidance counselor at Jake's high school, helped their son rise to the top of the local academic scene. "They made a point of showing us that being on top of what's happening in the world is important to being a good citizen," Jake Sullivan also told the local paper. "By the time I was 10 or 13, I'd learned the world capitals." At dinners, he and his four siblings would spin a globe while racing to the bottom of a pasta bowl. When he wasn't training his brain, he was handling pucks with friends on frozen lakes.

Sullivan left home for Yale University, where he studied political science and international relations and came in third in a national debate championship. He kept amassing knowledge, going to Yale Law School and then Oxford University on a Rhodes Scholarship, attaining there the top seed in the world debating championship.

Despite all his success, and the rarefied air he breathed in the hallowed halls of New Haven and rural England, Sullivan never forgot his roots. "I am a dyed-in-the-wool product of the Minneapolis public school system," he once told Minnesota's *Star Tribune*.

Sullivan even came back to Minnesota for a time following a clerkship under Justice Stephen Breyer at the Supreme Court. He practiced law at

Faegre & Benson, kicking back when not in the courtroom by playing on a curling team in St. Paul. But as much as Sullivan loved his home, he yearned to test himself in the cauldron of Washington, D.C.

He joined Democrat Amy Klobuchar's Senate campaign, impressing the boss and his colleagues with a strong work ethic and an uncanny ability to quote Billy Joel lyrics and *Saved by the Bell* lines. When Klobuchar won, Sullivan joined her in the nation's capital in 2007 as a policy adviser.

It didn't take long—just over a year—before Hillary Clinton hired him as an adviser during her first bid for the presidency. Sullivan, barely five years out of law school, helped the former First Lady prepare for the debates—and when she was knocked out in the primaries, he brought his skills to Barack Obama's successful campaign.

But Clinton didn't let Sullivan leave her orbit for too long, luring him to the State Department as the agency's youngest-ever policy planning director, where he would shape diplomatic strategy and develop long-term plans for U.S. foreign policy.

Even at thirty-four, Sullivan had a manner that impressed Clinton. He was wise beyond his years, she and her team believed, and he had a knack for asking the right questions at the right time. In State's Policy Planning office, the department's think tank, Sullivan could use his skills to prepare the new secretary and the U.S. foreign policy apparatus for what the world had in store for them.

His most impactful role, though, was kept secret for months. Clinton dispatched her little-watched aide to Oman to start talks with Iranian officials over a potential nuclear deal. He'd go on to join five other meetings alongside his colleagues. That someone so young, and so new, was trusted with that responsibility showed that he was the next big thing, not only for the administration but for the Democratic Party. "He's essentially a once-in-a-generation talent," Philippe Reines, a longtime Clinton staffer, said at the time.

Clinton was also Sullivan's champion outside of work. Four years after becoming the policy planning director, Sullivan married Maggie Goodlander at Yale's Battell Chapel in 2015, Clinton read from the Letter of St. Paul to the Romans. In the audience to hear it and see the couple wed was Antony Blinken, the deputy secretary of state who regarded Sullivan as a like-minded peer in the Democratic foreign policy world.

But Sullivan's work was noticed by more than the secretary of state. In 2012, President Obama asked Sullivan to lunch during a trip to Myanmar. Obama wanted to know about the country's history, and it gave the nearly thirty-six-year-old a chance to impress the big boss with his preparation and skill as a briefer. Sullivan passed the test. Later, Obama called Sullivan from Air Force One with a job offer—working not with him but with Vice President Joe Biden. *You should be his national security adviser*, Obama said. Sullivan accepted in early 2013—how could he not?

That late spring, Sullivan told University of Minnesota graduates his own mantra for success. "Reject cynicism. Reject certitude. And don't be a jerk," he said, sporting his trademark parted hair and crisp white shirt. "Now, when I say 'reject certitude,' I don't mean your core principles. You can and must be certain about those. . . . But in public policy, principles simply point the way—they do not provide specific answers about what to do in specific circumstances."

Sullivan's principles were those of the Democratic foreign policy establishment. His and Hillary Clinton's worldviews, for example, were nearly indistinguishable. The United States, alongside allies and partners, had first and foremost to promote and defend the liberal international order—the same post–World War II framework that Trump bashed throughout the campaign—which at its core meant working to maintain the rules and norms that govern global economics and politics. A central objective was a more globalized and interconnected world to lift all nations, making them more prosperous and, over time, more democratic.

But a flaw emerged: while the United States and other global economies flourished over the decades, gains proved unequal not only among countries but also within them. The U.S. didn't escape that problem, opening the space for someone like Trump to blame those defending the liberal international order—like Clinton and her team—for the decimation of steel towns and rural communities.

Trump, indeed, found a receptive audience. Factory workers, mainly in white-majority counties, feared that foreigners were taking their hard-earned jobs and sided with the Republican candidate. Since 1997, after all, the United States had suffered the closure of ninety-one thousand manufacturing plants and the loss of nearly five million manufacturing jobs. Blaming people from abroad and scapegoating elites was a powerful incendiary device for any populist politician.

But now Sullivan, a top aide in Clinton's second bid for the Oval Office, realized he and his cohort had made a grave error. They had failed to connect the high-minded ideals and practice of foreign policy to the very real needs of everyday Americans. Why should NATO matter to a farmer in Iowa? What benefit does a coal miner in Kentucky get from extending the nuclear umbrella to South Korea? How would combating climate change affect workers who rely on fossil fuels to do their work?

Being the smartest guy in the room, writing the perfect policy paper, or forming a team of veteran public servants mattered far less in a campaign than appealing to the id of the voting public. Clinton had experience and accomplishments in the realm of politics and governance. Trump had red hats that read MAKE AMERICA GREAT AGAIN—and he prevailed.

"We were both traumatized in really severe ways from Trump winning," said a close confidant who worked on the Clinton campaign with Sullivan.

The Minnesotan also realized that the wing of the Democratic Party Clinton represented and that he belonged to—the centrists, the pragmatists, the slow-and-steady-change advocates—were losing ground to the progressives. The energy was with Vermont senator Bernie Sanders, an independent who challenged Clinton and painted her as the prototypical Washington insider. Democrats were in large numbers supporting someone willing to fight for government-subsidized health care and college and to spend less time fighting wars abroad. Clinton voted to go to war in Iraq during her time as a senator from New York. Sanders voted against it.

To be relevant, then, the populist elements of the electorate and the bookish orthodoxy of the Democratic foreign policy establishment had to be melded.

Trump articulated one way to do it for the Republicans. Even if he wasn't always coherent, Trump at least wrestled with the questions families across the United States were asking about their leaders. The Democrats and others throughout Washington, D.C.'s professional class didn't even pretend to engage their concerns.

"Jake was heavily influenced by the 2016 campaign," someone close to him noted. "The fact that Trump could win—it had an effect on him, that you really have to be connected to what matters to the American public. You can't adopt a policy that's an elitist policy if that's not where the public is." Later, as Sullivan emptied out his campaign office and left for the last time, someone saw him with a copy of *How the Irish Became White*—a history of race relations between Irish Americans and African Americans—tucked under his arm.

But it was in that New York hotel room less than two blocks from Trump Tower, as he watched Trump and his family revel in the victory on screen, when Sullivan realized he needed to go back to the drawing board. Defeating Trump, a man Sullivan considered a unique danger to the world, in four years, required the next Democrat facing him to be armed with a better lexicon. The candidate would have to articulate a foreign policy vision that most Americans could support.

The next day, as Clinton was set to concede defeat, Sullivan consoled his colleagues, and they consoled him. The man for whom losing was rare made his way home, plotting once again to get back into the halls of power.

He couldn't lose again. Not again. Not to him.

Jake Sullivan found himself in the wilderness professionally, personally, physically. He was in Myanmar in March 2017, two months into Trump's presidency and four months after that devastating night in New York City.

Beside his friend and former colleague Ben Rhodes, he helped train peace negotiators in the war-torn Southeast Asian country. They'd even meet Aung San Suu Kyi, the democratic icon of the country, who only months later would fail to speak up about the ethnic cleansing of Rohingya Muslims.

Rhodes, a national security deputy to Obama for all eight years of his administration, arrived in Myanmar with a nascent plan for the Democratic Party's future. Weeks earlier, another former Obama-era official, Jeffrey Prescott, had come to Rhodes with an idea. Democrats needed an incubator to develop a coherent foreign policy message. It would initially help the handful of lawmakers who cared about global affairs but would prove instrumental once the 2020 primaries got under way.

There was a panoply of think tanks and advocacy groups that worked on foreign policy in the nation's capital, Prescott asserted, but none that were solely focused on creating a winning message to beat Trump in 2016. A new organization could, after victory, serve as the intellectual bedrock for a new administration. Prescott wanted Rhodes to help him start one.

Back in their hotel, aiming to unstick their sweaty clothes from their bodies, Rhodes approached Sullivan about Prescott's pitch. Sullivan's eyes lit up, and as was his way, he asked multiple questions about the group's purpose and how to get it started. Rhodes could see it: his old colleague was interested.

"We both felt obliged to do it," Rhodes would say years later about their conversation, "like someone had to do this, and he was the Clinton guy and I was the Obama guy." They both shuddered at the thought of having to fundraise for such a project, but there was never any doubt that they would do it.

Their conversations about what they hoped to build together continued back in Washington, D.C. During one breakfast meeting at the Four Seasons in Georgetown, Ivanka Trump, the president's daughter, came up to their table to say hello. In tow was Dina Powell, Trump's deputy national security adviser and a former Goldman Sachs investment banker. Little did they know that the two men were actually planning how best to oust them from power. "That was awkward," Rhodes said of the encounter.

Rhodes wasn't a natural fit for the project. He became a lightning rod for right-wing criticism of Obama's handling of foreign policy. A 2016 *New York Times* profile only added to the furor directed at him. "We created an echo chamber," Rhodes said in the story about his efforts to sell the Iran nuclear deal to lawmakers and the public. Of the experts he got to support the administration's views, Rhodes claimed "they were saying things that validated what we had given them to say." He also blasted members of the D.C. foreign policy establishment and the embassies that spin them as "the blob."

But in a way, his all-American story would be a boon to the cause, for Rhodes was raised in elite circles but rejected their ideas whole cloth. He grew up in New York City with a Jewish mother and a Texan father who, once a month, took Rhodes and his brothers to the Episcopal Saint Thomas Church. Young Ben yearned to write, not become a D.C. power player. His practice with the pen paid off: an editor at *Foreign Policy* magazine thought he was too talented for a fact-checking job, so his résumé and writing sample were sent over to Lee Hamilton, the former Indiana representative in Congress, who needed a speechwriter.

It was there, working for Hamilton at the Wilson Center think tank in D.C., that Rhodes became steeped in national security issues. He'd go on to be Hamilton's staffer on the 9/11 Commission and a chief notetaker on the Iraq Study Group, which slammed George W. Bush for the decision to invade the country and overthrow Saddam Hussein. It wasn't a traditional pathway to the White House, but there was more "real America" in his background than most other people in Democratic foreign policy circles could claim.

The two men and their colleagues spent the year raising capital, finding office space, and hiring staff. What they also needed were some heavyweights atop the group to legitimize it. When National Security Action opened up in 2018, it got Antony Blinken and Avril Haines, Obama's deputy national security adviser and his number two at the CIA, to join the advisory board.

It was another mix of establishment and quirk: Blinken was a totem for how to work your way to the top of the party's foreign policy roster. Haines, while well qualified, at one point ran an independent Baltimore bookstore famous for its 1990s "erotica nights." Prescott, whose brainchild NatSec Action ultimately was, signed on to be the day-to-day executive director.

The group also brought in Ned Price, a former CIA official who gained as much notoriety for quitting the Trump administration as for his tweets attacking the Republican president. He went so far as to pen an op-ed in *Politico* ripping Jared Kushner, Trump's son-in-law and a senior White House official, for getting a security clearance despite his ties to senior Russian officials during the campaign.

"Jared Kushner held suspicious meetings with Russians [*sic*] officials and operatives that he failed to disclose when he applied for a security clearance. If he weren't the president's son-in-law, he'd have been frog-marched out of the White House long ago. Why does he still have access to America's biggest secrets?" Price wrote.

In the earliest days, it wasn't clear precisely what NatSec Action would actually do. Should it host public events on foreign policy with key Democrats? Should it assign policy papers to experts and disseminate them to campaigns, hoping staffers would read them and call the authors? Should it be a safe meeting place for all wings of the Democratic Party to discuss national security issues and hammer out their differences?

The answer was yes, yes, and yes. It would be all of the above, and it would have one target: Arm the next Democratic presidential nominee and their staff with everything they need to counter Trump's foreign policy. "From the formation, what was implicit is that these are very likely going to be the people that make up the next administration," Rhodes said years after the organization's founding.

By early 2019, NatSec Action was ready to give a series of off-the-record briefings for reporters who covered national security. Sullivan, Prescott, and Price—the brains, the boss, and the communicator—each updated the press corps on their work and detailed what they hoped to accomplish. Their main pitch was simple: Trump's foreign policy was a profound emergency for the United States, and NatSec Action was the only place working every day to counter it, forging a winning message for the coming presidential election.

They were, in effect, labeling themselves the shadow cabinet of the Trump era. It was a bold claim to stake, especially when an organization like the Center for American Progress had long believed it was the Democratic torchbearer when Republicans were in office. But, NatSec Action argued, there was a void in the party when it came to foreign policy and national security, and only their group was building the infrastructure that Democrats lacked, and would need, when 2020 came around.

An early conundrum for NatSec Action was how to counter the foreign policy story Trump was raring to tell. His administration pounded ISIS into near submission, halted North Korean missile testing, grew close to Israel, confronted rogue regimes in Venezuela and Iran, and fixed long-standing trade problems with China and North American neighbors. What could the Democrats say in response that would resonate during a campaign?

Sullivan's counterargument to the current administration's foreign policy successes was that it had "taken the United States in an undemocratic direction while abandoning our core allies, which makes us weaker," he told a journalist at this time, making specific note of Trump's desire to cozy up to Russian president Vladimir Putin.

Sullivan understood the appeal of Trump's actions: he wanted to look tough while claiming to fight for the little guy. But Sullivan argued that the only way you fight for the little guy is to secure and promote democracy around the world and at home, and work with allies to secure interests so the burden doesn't always fall on America. Sullivan added, "and if you want to counter China, good luck doing it alone. We can't take Beijing militarily, economically, and technologically without our allies aboard."

This response would end up being the core foreign policy argument of a future Biden campaign.

The leaders and members of National Security Action couldn't know Biden would eventually win the Democratic primary. So for months they prepared for any outcome, culminating in a December 2019 retreat in New Mexico to figure out what, exactly, they would present to the nominee ahead of the contest with Trump.

The group invited over one hundred of the Democratic Party's brightest minds for an off-record, four-day session at the Hyatt Regency Tamaya Resort and Spa near Albuquerque, a luxurious and idyllic spot in the desert with a large mountain looming in the background. It was a risky move: the gathering took place as a tense primary season raged on. Fault lines had shown within the party, and while the candidates agreed that Trump had mishandled every element of foreign policy, they hadn't truly offered remedies of their own.

It was also a slightly uncomfortable affair as the large field of candidates had been winnowed down to seven and the first primary votes in Iowa were mere months away. Biden was the standard-bearer for the party, challenged to his left by Sanders and Massachusetts senator Elizabeth Warren while facing upstarts like South Bend, Indiana, mayor Pete Buttigieg and entrepreneur Andrew Yang. Klobuchar, Jake Sullivan's former boss, was still in the mix, as was billionaire Tom Steyer.

The field of hopefuls exposed a party adrift. Clinton, who had loomed large alongside her husband, was firmly out of the picture. Now there was a tension between finding someone who could credibly defeat Trump and someone who could refresh the party. Still, there was an opening. The ideological divides on domestic issues—health care, immigration, how to curb the COVID-19 pandemic—were clear, but there was no real consensus on what to do about the world, save for saying that Trump was ruining America's standing on the global stage.

Sullivan and his cohort hoped that putting together the top representatives of the major campaigns would lead to agreement on at least broad pillars of a new progressive global vision. "Our goal was for whoever the candidate turned out to be, it would be useful to build out their policies. It wasn't just for Biden; we hoped the sessions would prove helpful for Elizabeth Warren or Michael Bennet," said one of the Albuquerque conference's organizers.

In between red-sauce enchiladas and margaritas at community dinners, horseback rides, and spa visits, the participants found time for work. They piled into the Eagle A and B conference rooms on December 6 to find Sullivan waiting for them up front. The intention of that 4:00 p.m. opening session was to answer the private conference's overarching question: "What is the critical challenge facing the United States right now?"

Sullivan didn't answer; instead, he pointed toward the back of the room. "Ned, why don't you start?" Price, by the look on his face, wasn't expecting to go first. He mustered up an answer: polarization at home was the defining national security issue of the moment. "If we're divided internally, we're weaker on the world stage," Price said. Many in the room echoed his sentiment. Distrust and disdain between the parties would make it impossible to form a united front abroad.

Rhodes took it a step further. Polarization wasn't the problem; the radicalization of the Republican Party was. A two-party democracy couldn't function if one party elects someone like Trump and solely aims to block the agenda of the other. America simply couldn't do big things with Republicans in their current state.

Others chimed in. *Climate change! The loss of America's technological edge! Economic competition!* These weren't the collective answers Sullivan and his team thought they'd hear. "We were expecting Russia and China to clearly dominate," one of the organizers told me. "People were really thinking outside their parochial area and trying to come up with something novel, something really innovative." Rhodes told me much later that he was "struck by how many people referenced domestic political issues." It was, after all, a retreat filled with foreign policy minds.

That discussion helped some of the attendees finalize ideas in position papers they were drafting for the group. The documents, commissioned by NatSec Action for a project titled FP2021, would collectively become a foreign policy owner's manual for the eventual nominee.

One paper declared that the United States needed to act fast to compete effectively with China: "China's rapid economic and military modernization have shifted the regional balance of power and eroded America's ability to deter adversaries, reassure allies, and mobilize collective action," it read. Another paper, on U.S. policy toward Europe, recommended that the next president "advance the transatlantic relationship as the foundation of a values-based U.S. foreign policy," partly by developing "a U.S.–Europe climate agenda to meet shared goals" and a "transatlantic approach toward China that creates a strong democratic playing field for competition and cooperation."

As for climate change: "The power of U.S. diplomacy in getting other countries to take serious climate action is dependent in part on what progress the U.S. government makes domestically."

NatSec Action staffers always believed in the importance of their mission. But there was a gnawing feeling that all the effort, all the work, and all the months would amount to little more than an academic exercise. It ultimately didn't mean much if the Democratic nominee failed to use the framework and materials the group placed on a silver platter. Secretly, of course, each NatSec Action member was pulling for their favorite candidate, hoping they'd be the one to receive the fruits of the group's labor.

Any fears of irrelevance dissipated in the spring of 2020. Sullivan phoned Rhodes to tell him he was leaving NatSec Action to be Joe Biden's lead policy adviser in the presidential campaign. Biden was talking about the need to restore the soul of the nation. And with his focus on the middle class, he was the right man for the moment and the right person to beat Trump. Sullivan felt called to help him.

The former vice president was revived at this point, having just won the South Carolina primary handily in February following losses in Iowa and New Hampshire. Biden, who had been left for dead, now emerged as the likely front-runner and eventual nominee.

All of a sudden, the group's work was well-known to one of the most senior people in the top Democratic candidate's campaign. "Once Jake went to Biden to run the show on policy, obviously those [papers] were going to matter," Rhodes told me. "If Bernie Sanders or Elizabeth Warren had won, it wouldn't have been as complete a merger."

A Biden administration official put it more bluntly: "What NatSec Action produced was more influential than anything the Biden foreign policy campaign team came up with."

But Sullivan was thrust more into a domestic policy role in the campaign, not a foreign policy one. That's what he wanted—he was growing tired of national security and felt that problems at home needed to be addressed. If they weren't dealt with, politicians like Trump, or at least Trumpism without the man himself, would be welcomed among the electorate. Sullivan wanted to be where the action was.

He felt qualified to do the work. Sullivan had spent much of 2017 to 2020 speaking with everyday Americans about their problems and about how domestic and foreign policies could help solve them. Those people reminded him of the folks he grew up with in Minnesota and the kinds of conversations he'd had with them as a younger man. He put down his findings in a coauthored report for the Carnegie Endowment for International Peace think tank in D.C. Sullivan and his colleagues were, in effect, trying to translate the language of normal conversation for an elite audience that had long lost the ability to speak plainly.

"After three decades of U.S. primacy on the world stage, America's middle class finds itself in a precarious state. The economic challenges presented by globalization, technological change, financial imbalances, and fiscal strains have gone largely unmet," Sullivan and his coauthors wrote about their findings in the 2020 report. "If the United States stands any chance of renewal at home, it must conceive of its role in the world differently."

What new role might that be? Their proposal was to look at strategic decisions abroad through the lens of how they would affect the economic well-being of Americans at home. It should "better integrate U.S. foreign policy into a national policy agenda aimed at strengthening the middle class and enhancing economic and social mobility," they suggested, breaking down the traditional silos between global and local work.

Easier said than done, though. The average American voter can intuitively grasp how tariffs and other protectionist measures help safeguard their farms and factories. But how do nuclear sanctions against Iran put more dollars into a voter's pocket?

Throughout the campaign, Biden was receptive to what Sullivan conveyed about his reformed worldview, even if it took him a bit by surprise. Sullivan had been a more traditional thinker about the world when he served the then vice president as national security adviser. But between rope lines and restaurant visits, stump speeches and shopping trips, the two spoke at length about the ideas Sullivan had curated at NatSec Action. They matched the candidate's own sensibilities, and helpfully hewed closely to Trump's less adventurous foreign policy.

Biden, too, had gone through an evolution. He arrived in the Senate in 1973, a decade after the Cuban Missile Crisis. Then, the United States and the Soviet Union were duking it out in the Cold War, a battle of ideology and will, a competition to become the world's unquestioned superpower. It was a dangerous time, and in a way a simpler one. There were many threats in the world, but Moscow was the paramount one, and the U.S. government's time and attention focused on that grand, singular problem. The United States, by the early 1990s, proved victorious and emerged as the world's leading nation.

Biden took that win to heart. "We no longer think in Cold War terms, for several reasons. One, no one is our equal. No one is close. Other than being crazy enough to press a button, there is nothing that Putin can do militarily to fundamentally alter American interests," he'd told *The New Yorker*'s Evan Osnos in 2014 as he mulled a presidential run to succeed Obama.

That, at least, is how Biden thought about America's place in the world following thirty-six years in the Senate and nearly eight years as vice president. But he got to that view in meandering and maddeningly contradictory ways.

As a freshman in the Senate, Biden cared less about his nation's moral obligations and more about what he considered to be in the cold, calculated interest of the United States. "I may be the most immoral son of a gun in this room," he said in 1975, arguing against aid to Cambodia. "I'm getting sick and tired of hearing about morality, our moral obligation. There's a point where you are incapable of meeting moral obligations that exist worldwide."

Unlike his future colleague John Kerry, he hadn't been among the millions of people demonstrating to end the war in Vietnam. While he thought the war was "lousy policy," he focused more on life as a married man and wearing "sport coats" than on spilling out into the street to protest. Other people "felt more strongly than I did about the immorality of the war," he told reporters in 1988.

Instead, Biden spent much of his time during the Cold War pushing to broker arms-control deals with the Soviet Union. He traveled back and forth to the country throughout the 1970s, eventually sealing a Strategic Arms Limitations Treaty in 1979. But Republicans and some right-leaning Democrats were skeptical of the pact. When the Soviet Union invaded Afghanistan in late December that year, the prospects for approval in Congress died. Importantly, though, both nations still adhered to the limitations on their strategic forces through the end of 1985.

There were few lawmakers more hopeful that Washington and Moscow could coexist during perilous times, as long as they found ways to cooperate. "I think the prospects of Soviet–American relations are good," Biden told a Soviet television station during a 1979 visit to the USSR. Once the wounds between the two nations started to heal after the invasion, Biden returned to the Soviet Union in 1984 to discuss more arms control, at the behest of President Ronald Reagan.

As he mulled a presidential bid in 1988, Biden was telling reporters in Washington that his foreign policy experience made him a stronger candidate than the others.

The narrative of Biden's foreign policy prowess would take a hit in 1991. President George H. W. Bush wanted to send in forces alongside United Nations member states to push Iraq's military out of Kuwait, and sought congressional approval for the mission. The Delaware senator was skeptical from the start. "What vital interests of the United States justify sending Americans to their deaths in the sands of Saudi Arabia?" he asked rhetorically about the proposed campaign. The war resolution was hotly debated, but it eventually passed the Senate by a close 52–47 vote. Biden was among the 47. His concern was that the United States–led coalition soon heading to the Middle East "has allowed us to take on 95 percent of the sacrifice across the board."

Something changed in Biden once he saw the success of Desert Storm. For six weeks, the coalition flew "more than 116,000 combat air sorties and dropped 88,500 tons of bombs" on enemy positions, according to a U.S. Air Force history. That set the table for the ground campaign, launched on February 24, which lasted only four days once Iraqi forces retreated from Kuwait. Two years later, in 1993, Biden looked back on his opposition to the war: "I think I was proven to be wrong." He'd go on to chastise Bush for not pushing further, saying the president's failure to depose Iraq's Saddam Hussein was a "fundamental mistake."

That experience seemed to turn Biden from a hard-nosed realist into an interventionist, citing human rights and morality as his rallying cries.

In 1992, Serbia and its proxies launched a war in Bosnia, leading the United Nations to place an embargo impacting both Belgrade's military might and Sarajevo's ability to defend itself.

This framework enraged Biden, who blasted American inaction as war crimes were committed in southern Europe. "We have turned our backs on aggression. We have turned our backs on atrocity," he said in 1993 after a trip to the Balkans. "We have turned our backs on conscience." He also penned a stark op-ed in *The New York Times* that summer, urging then president Bill Clinton to act before Serb loyalists traversed the continent like Nazi Germany decades earlier.

"Is this a civil war? Only if you think Austria and Czechoslovakia had civil wars in 1938. Will it be a civil war when Serb fascism rampages into Kosovo and Macedonia, bringing Albania, Bulgaria, Greece and Turkey into the war? If not in Bosnia, will we respond to aggression then? Or anywhere else?" he wrote. Five years later, during the Kosovo crisis, Biden claimed in a Senate Foreign Relations hearing that he had advocated for direct American military action in Bosnia. "I was suggesting we bomb Belgrade. I was suggesting that we send American pilots in and blow up all of the bridges on the Drina," the senator said. U.S. warplanes, on Clinton's orders, began dropping bombs on Serbian nationalist forces in 1994.

Biden's pro-intervention streak continued during another Iraq debate. This time, George W. Bush, like his father, sought a war resolution to send the U.S. military into the country. Following the terrorist attacks of September 11, 2001, perpetrated by Osama Bin Laden's al-Qaeda, the administration's focus shifted in the summer of 2002 to forcing Iraq's Hussein to dismantle his suspected weapons of mass destruction program.

Biden was convinced by the Bush administration's case for war. "In my judgment, President Bush is right to be concerned about Saddam Hussein's relentless pursuit of weapons of mass destruction and the possibility that he may use them or share them with terrorists," Biden said during an August hearing of the Senate Foreign Relations Committee, a panel he chaired. "These weapons must be dislodged from Saddam Hussein, or Saddam Hussein must be dislodged from power," he continued, adding, "President Bush has stated his determination to remove Saddam from power, a view many in Congress share."

While Biden did support a narrower authorization, one that allowed force only for the removal of WMDs, the resolution up for a vote that October was on whether to give the president Congress's full backing to use the military as he "determines to be necessary and appropriate." Biden ended up endorsing the measure. "I do not believe it is a rush to war but a march to peace and security," he said on the Senate floor. "I believe failure to overwhelmingly support this resolution is likely to enhance the prospects that war would occur."

The authorization passed by a vote of 77–23, with 21 Democrats, including Biden, in favor. Biden would later say that he supported the resolution because it would strengthen Bush's hand in diplomatic negotiations to get inspectors to search for WMDs inside Iraq. He'd criticize the administration's handling of the war, insisting that Bush's team sent thousands of U.S. troops into the fight "under funded and under manned."

"We're so woefully unprepared because of judgments made from the failure to plan before we went in of what we were going to do in the aftermath," he said in 2003. Even so, Biden had backed a war that found no weapons of mass destruction and saw 4,500 Americans die—though Saddam Hussein had finally been driven from power, just as Biden had wished a decade earlier.

Despite Biden's complicated foreign policy history, his overall support for American might, and for the nation's ability to underwrite the international liberal order, made Jake Sullivan a natural disciple. But Sullivan had changed during the Trump years after working to define a progressive foreign policy, one that would appeal to denizens of the heartland as well as the well-heeled and well-intentioned urban elites. The Democratic candidate, having watched his opponent in the Oval Office and on the campaign trail, had also come to the conclusion that the usual message on foreign policy needed a first-page rewrite.

It was one thing to have a well-reasoned foreign policy. It would be another to sell it to the American people as Biden debated Trump. Biden and Sullivan hoped the challenger couldn't be painted as some warmongering hawk. That stigma had plagued Hillary Clinton during her bout with Trump, and there was some concern about the former senator's past support for the Iraq War.

Biden added his own flair to Sullivan's framework. Trump's presidency tarnished America's image as the world's leading democracy when he backslapped with strongmen, namely Russia's Vladimir Putin, China's Xi Jinping, North Korea's Kim Jong Un, and Hungary's Viktor Orbán. At home, Trump also wanted troops to quell protests and riots for racial justice in the wake of George Floyd's murder, while his party sought to limit access to the vote.

Biden felt strongly that the way to contrast himself with Trump—and give his presidency an overarching theme—was to say that the world's greatest challenge was one of autocracies versus democracies. Sullivan loved the concept. As the campaign went forward, he and Blinken, Biden's longtime right-hand man, helped pen a July 2020 campaign speech to road test it.

Turning back the tide of rising authoritarianism "means repairing and reinvigorating our own democracy, even as we strengthen the coalition of democracies that stand with us on every continent," Biden said. "I will start by putting our own house in order—remaking our education system so that a child's opportunity in life isn't determined by their zip code or race; reforming our criminal justice system to eliminate inequitable disparities; putting the teeth back in the Voting Rights Act."

This was a wholly different message not just for Biden, not just for Democrats, but for the American foreign policy establishment. It underscored just how successful National Security Action was: it shifted the thinking of one of America's most traditional foreign policy minds, and by his side placed Sullivan, one of the Democratic Party's new intellectual leaders.

"We did pretty well," said a former NatSec Action staffer now in government.

What began as a reaction to, and soul-searching after, the election of Donald Trump had become key talking points for the forty-sixth president of the United States. And in time these tenets would coalesce into a new muscular, Democratic approach to foreign policy. Whether one called it Bidenism or the Biden Doctrine, the new administration would conduct its international relations in a different way than even Barack Obama.

While many of Biden's closest advisers had cut their teeth during the Obama years, they were now embarking on something new, something that could change the way America saw its role in the world. Force would be used only when the foundations of the world that the United States had helped build since 1945 were at risk. Otherwise, the guns would be holstered if the cause was not clearly and directly in the American interest. If Obama was guided by his head, Biden was guided by his gut and by a rock-ribbed belief that the average American needed a champion in Washington.

U.S. foreign policy is never the handiwork of one author. Instead, each of the key players in an administration bring both their ideals and their life experiences to bear. To understand what the Biden Doctrine is, one first has to understand what each of its architects contributed. How would Sullivan's "foreign policy for the middle class" permeate every aspect of the way the administration handled global affairs? What lessons had Antony Blinken learned under Biden in the Senate Foreign Relations Committee, and then in Obama's White House and State Department, to counter great powers like China and Russia?

And how would Biden, a president who came of age in a time when America was the shining city upon a hill, attempt to make it genuinely great again—respected and trusted by its allies, feared by its enemies, and no longer willing to bend to despots?

Doctrines don't just emerge shiny and new off a think tank's assembly line. They need to be road tested, and before Biden would reach the halfway mark of his term, his administration's approach would be faced with a new bloody wave of discontent between Israel and Palestine, a calamitous withdrawal from a decades-long conflict, and the greatest land war in Europe since World War II.

Four years after watching Hillary Clinton lose to Donald Trump, Jake Sullivan was once again watching the television in despair. Moments earlier, an aide had walked into a conference room of the Biden transition's office in Wilmington, Delaware, to tell him that the Capitol in Washington, D.C., was under attack. Donald Trump had incited a mob of supporters to stop the certification of the election result in the Senate. Sullivan completed his video conference with the Mexican foreign minister and watched the scenes on the news.

What he saw—the violence, the anger, the destruction—didn't seem like the country with which he had just gotten reacquainted. The scenes were reminiscent of the political chaos facing other nations, not America. It was otherworldly to him.

Sullivan got in touch with Biden and other colleagues in the wake of the January 6, 2021, insurrection—exactly two weeks before the inauguration. The future national security adviser, with Antony Blinken and others, agreed that the campaign had gotten its broad theme right: the democratic world was under attack, and it was clear that the largest threat to American democracy came from within, even if a small group of extremists didn't reflect the United States as a whole. The job now wasn't just to save the world from Trump. It was also to save America from the forces he had unleashed.

At least this time Sullivan could do something about it.

It helped that transition documents and position papers whizzing around the transition's offices already included language Sullivan had helped cultivate at National Security Action. "They were basically carbon copies," a transition official told me. The shadow cabinet was moving into the White House.

What Biden hadn't expected was that the sitting president would forcibly try to remain the sitting president. That changed the tenor of the transition leading up to the inauguration. Sullivan, Blinken, and other incoming officials offered their thoughts on the address the new president would give to the nation. This was how Biden was going to save the world.

"We can make America, once again, the leading force for good in the world," Biden said from the steps of the recently attacked Capitol as Sullivan watched from the White House's Situation Room. "We will lead not merely by the example of our power but by the power of our example. We will be a strong and trusted partner for peace, progress, and security."

This time, watching a president speak to the country he led, Sullivan didn't watch with horror or despair. He watched with hope.

Chapter 2

Great-Power Competition

January—April 2021

Joe Biden had been in politics long enough to know that 2021 could be the most pivotal year of his presidency. Any new administration had the most flexibility to act in its first twelve months. In the second year, the House would be in midterm-election mode and any goodwill Biden had won from his vote would be long gone. The third year is when the presidential reelection cycle kicks up, and the fourth year is dominated by the election itself. If Biden and his team were going to change the world, they needed to start right away.

There was much to do. China had its sights set on control of the Indo-Pacific region and might be planning to invade the democratic island of Taiwan, but the United States needed to work with China to curb the effects of climate change and avoid a great-power war. Russia had invaded Ukraine's Crimean Peninsula in 2014—when many now in the Biden administration worked for Obama. But the United States and Russia remained the world's foremost nuclear powers. Failing to steady relations with Moscow could destabilize Europe, if not the whole world. On a grander scale, democracy was on the back foot as authoritarians in Beijing, Moscow, and beyond assumed greater power and control. America's own democracy faced a major test following Donald Trump's presidency and the January 6 insurrection he inspired.

To deal with this world, Biden assembled a team of national security A-listers from the Democratic Party—many of whom had either worked for or remained loyal to the president from his time as a senator and vice president. During a November 2020 event, he presented them to the nation, still in the throes of the coronavirus pandemic. Donning masks and standing far apart, the Team of Friends stood proudly behind their familiar new boss, raring to get to work.

It was also clear that their first order of business was to show that the Trump era was over. Stepping up to the podium after a staffer sanitized it, the nominee for secretary of state, Antony Blinken, said the United States must move forward with "humility and confidence." It "needs to be working with other countries" to solve global challenges, he added, a clear rebuke of Trump's disdain for America's traditional friendships. The choice for director of national intelligence, Avril Haines, promised to present Biden with "inconvenient or difficult" information, which Trump had not wanted to hear.

Jake Sullivan, who as national security adviser didn't need Senate confirmation, said he'd fulfill Biden's mandate of "reimagining national security." All actions taken by the administration should be judged by answering a key question: "Will this make life better, easier, safer for families across this country? Our foreign policy has to deliver for these families." This was less a rebuke of Trump than a reframing of his paeans to the everyday American worker. The message was clear: Biden would actually care about the forgotten men and women of the United States—unlike his predecessor.

The bonhomie at the ceremony hid some early differences within the team. For one, Sullivan was more attuned to Trump-style messaging than was Blinken, as the future top diplomat held on to more traditional views of American foreign policy. While friends who agreed on much, the two knew early on that they would tangle over just how much of a "reimagining" of U.S. foreign policy there should be.

There were also questions about how John Kerry, the former secretary of state who had been named as the envoy for climate change, would handle a less glamorous role. Could he work under Blinken, at one point Kerry's deputy during the Obama administration? And how much would he be willing to compromise on issues like human rights in talks with China in order to make progress on climate change?

These were the issues rankling Biden's team as they moved from the transition into the White House. The fear was: Would the minimal but present tensions tear apart a closely knit unit?

Biden sat behind the *Resolute* Desk on January 20, 2021, his first day in office. The glamour of the inauguration was gone, and all that was left was work. To his right sat a pile of thin blue folders, each containing an executive order for him to sign. The moment was orchestrated to show the public that Biden was a man of action, urgency, and leadership.

With a mask on, he reached first and second for COVID-19 and health care–related documents. But the third was about the Paris climate accords, the multinational deal to keep global temperatures from increasing above 2 degrees Celsius this century. Trump had taken the United States out of the 2015 agreement four years earlier, saying that he was "elected to represent the citizens of Pittsburgh, not Paris." During the campaign, Biden promised he would recommit the United States to the accords on his first day in office. Clearly tired from an emotionally charged morning, the president slowly signed his name to the document, a swift change in policy with just a stroke of the pen.

The new president viewed climate change as an existential threat to all Americans, and to the world, elevating the issue to his top national security priority. But reentering the pact was the low-hanging fruit. The hard part was getting China—the world's largest greenhouse gas emitter by volume—to take climate change as seriously as the new administration did. There was a sharp divergence on how to do that from the start, and it exposed a tension within some of Biden's senior-most aides.

One camp, led by John Kerry, argued that Washington could reason with Beijing. The new administration and the Communist Party differed on nearly everything, but a warming planet affected everybody. At some point, Chinese leader Xi Jinping and his coterie would have to work with the United States, and Kerry could broker such an understanding.

That's not how the other side, led by National Security Adviser Jake Sullivan, saw it. China was never going to work with the United States on climate change, or anything, really. America's goal had to be making serious climate-related deals with the rest of the world while boxing China out. That would demonstrate Washington's commitment while painting Beijing as an outsider on the century's biggest issue. Only then would China feel any real pressure to take drastic action on climate change.

Those who agreed with Sullivan feared that Kerry would advise Biden to strike a grand bargain with Beijing. No one could ever outline what exactly that might look like, except to say that the president would be told to "compromise" on issues of human rights or China's regional influence, as much as Kerry would abhor having to suggest it.

But if anyone believed he could pull off the delicate balancing act, it was John Kerry. As Obama's second secretary of state, he felt called to broker the long-sought deal between Israelis and Palestinians, paving the way for both peoples to have their own state. Few in the administration, including Obama, thought it would prove a fruitful endeavor. But Kerry was sure that, if he spent enough time on the problem, he could at least achieve something. History, effectively, would bend to his work ethic.

"Despite the obvious difficulties that I understood when I became secretary of state, I knew that I had to do everything in my power to help end this conflict," Kerry told State Department officials in December 2016, a month before Donald Trump would take the reins of government. But he admitted failure: "The truth is that trends on the ground—violence, terrorism, incitement, settlement expansion and the seemingly endless occupation—they are combining to destroy hopes for peace on both sides and increasingly cementing an irreversible one-state reality that most people do not actually want." Not even he, John Kerry, could break the deadlock.

Whispers of Kerry now seeking a grand U.S.–China bargain on climate change grew louder a month before Biden took office. Kerry's designs appeared in *The Atlantic* by way of three unnamed sources. Thomas Wright, a Brookings Institution scholar who would later join the National Security Council (NSC), wrote that, "Yes, the United States should stand firm when it disagrees with Beijing, as [Kerry] believes it did during his tenure as secretary of state, but everything else, including geopolitical competition with China, is of secondary importance to this overarching threat."

The piece circulated around the capital, and questions about Kerry's intentions swirled. He was asked about them during a White House press conference just one week into the new administration. "Obviously we have serious differences with China," the envoy said, citing Beijing's theft of intellectual property and aggression in the South China Sea as examples. "Those issues will never be traded for anything that has to do with climate. That's not going to happen."

Still, he said, "climate is a critical stand-alone issue that we have to deal on in the sense that China is thirty percent of the emissions of the world; we're about fifteen percent of the emissions of the world. You add the EU to that, and you got three entities that are more than fifty-five percent or so. So it's urgent that we find a way to compartmentalize, to move forward."

But Biden and Blinken believed they could reel in any of Kerry's eccentricities, and not only because the former secretary of state knew what he was signing up for. Biden and Kerry were very close, for example, having served together for years on the Senate Foreign Relations Committee.

Kerry took the gavel when Biden became vice president. Biden was the one to swear Kerry into his role as the nation's top diplomat in February 2013.

Giving the job to Kerry was a true sign of intention—no administration hires a high-profile person for a sideline job. But the problem was that putting Kerry in the role substituted for months of thinking about how to solve climate change. Kerry would execute the president's wishes, but he'd also be trusted with making as much progress as possible. The decision showed a new administration in search of a man more than a policy.

The tentpoles of what would become Bidenism on the world stage emerged early, and it fell to National Security Adviser Jake Sullivan to articulate them in two major concepts.

The first pillar was that foreign policy and domestic policy were intricately linked, and the incoming "A-Team"—which some administration officials called themselves as an homage to the 1980s TV show about a ragtag group of mercenaries in Los Angeles—had to make a "permeable membrane" between them. Trump had questioned America's commitments abroad, from war to alliances, saying that they had to benefit U.S. citizens first and foremost. That reshaped the debate, and forced Biden and his staff to defend why their global actions were necessary to improve the daily lives of Americans. Immediately, the "foreign policy for the middle class" concept Sullivan helped develop became a litmus test for new policy initiatives.

The second pillar was that America's new enemies were really its old ones. The administration was going to be laser-focused on, as one official put it: "Russia, Russia, Russia, and China, China, China." In other words, Biden would continue Trump's emphasis on competition among the super-powers.

This was a marked change from U.S. foreign policy after September 11, 2001. America's national security agencies turned their attention to fighting terrorists and insurgents, caring far less about the threats emanating from whole countries. Al-Qaeda, the Taliban, and ISIS were more immediate concerns than China's and Russia's increased aggressions toward their neighbors.

Trump and his first defense secretary, James Mattis, didn't agree. For the Trump administration, Moscow and Beijing needed to feel a belated American counterpunch. "We are emerging from a period of strategic atrophy, aware that our competitive military advantage has been eroding," the Trump-era Pentagon declared in the unclassified version of the 2018 National Defense Strategy. "Inter-state strategic competition, not terrorism, is now the primary concern in U.S. national security."

The Biden administration disagreed with many elements of what Trump and his team did. But this assessment they agreed with.

Days after Joe Biden won the presidential election, his staff met him in a cramped room at transition headquarters in Wilmington to discuss who would be the next secretary of state. A binder handed to him contained scores of pictures, names, and biographies. Aides expected a drawn-out decision, but Biden immediately put his hands up to stop any debate. Pointing to the salt-and-pepper-haired man across from him, Biden said, "Tony is my secretary of state."

Blinken wasn't surprised; he and Biden had discussed what role the longtime aide might have in a new administration. Biden said he wanted Blinken to be America's senior-most diplomat. Now, as president-elect, Biden had made a decision, and there was little for Blinken to do except to say, "It would be my honor, sir."

Blinken's career—his whole life—had led to that moment. He arrived in Paris at nine years old as the stepson of Samuel Pisar, a Holocaust survivor and later lawyer who had the ear of presidents in the United States and France. Pisar's life story instilled in Blinken the belief that the United States could be a force for good as long as it promoted human rights. "When he has to worry today about poison gas in Syria, he almost inevitably thinks about the gas with which my entire family was eliminated," Pisar said about Blinken in 2013.

Also among Pisar's deeply held beliefs was that there were ways for enemies to coexist and cooperate even as they competed. One way to do that was with increased economic interconnection, an idea that would form the backbone of Richard Nixon's détente with China. Building closer ties, even when there were irreconcilable differences about other global matters, lowered the chance of conflict between great powers, Pisar argued. Even at such a young age, Blinken took in the wisdom of his stepfather, discussing everything from geopolitics to music and art in their spacious home in Paris's 16th arrondissement.

Pisar was not Blinken's only role model—he often labels his biological dad, Donald Blinken, a U.S. ambassador to Hungary, as his "hero." But Pisar instilled in Blinken a set of principles that colored how he saw America's role in the world.

"Looking at his stepfather's life, saved by the United States, attributing that salvation to the United States and, frankly, U.S. military intervention, has reinforced Tony's belief that the United States and U.S. power can do big, important, and moral things in the world," Philip Gordon, a colleague of Blinken's in the Obama and Biden administrations, said in 2021.

Young Tony went to the best schools, ending up at Harvard University in the 1980s for undergraduate studies. He joined the *Crimson*, the famous school paper, as an editor and opinion writer about foreign relations. He wrote often about his left-leaning dispositions, including about an interview with a Nicaraguan trying to convince him that the Sandinistas needed to be overthrown.

"The Nicaraguan's arguments against the ruling Sandinista junta were often convincing and disconcerting for a liberal listener," he wrote. But Blinken ultimately wasn't convinced by the Contra's argument: "Ousting the Sandinistas would in no way ensure a democratic government for Nicaragua. The present opposition is so diverse that there is no telling which of the many factions would take power." Instead, he proposed offering funds to the Sandinistas as long as they "liberalize their rule and schedule elections for the near future."

As he entered his professional life, working for Biden in the Senate and White House, Blinken developed a more moderate, centrist approach to consensus building across the government. He shared the general attitudes toward world affairs that modern-day Democratic leaders from Jimmy Carter to Barack Obama shared: protect the rules-based international order, build economic ties wherever possible, and promote democracy.

What set Blinken apart, though, was his interventionist streak. During the Obama years, he was a lead proponent for U.S. military involvement in stopping the slaughter of civilians in Libya and Syria. But he also believed that "superpowers don't bluff," a statement that American rhetoric couldn't go further than what officials in Washington were really willing to do.

And if America said it was going to lead in the world, it had to actually do it. "American leadership still matters," he told the Senate during his confirmation hearing in January 2021. "The reality is, the world simply does not organize itself. When we're not engaged, when we're not leading, then one of two things is likely to happen. Either some other country tries to take our place, but not in a way that's likely to advance our interests and values, or maybe just as bad, no one does and then you have chaos."

Despite his idealism, Blinken knew how to make a buck. Out of power during the Trump years, he founded WestExec Advisors with fellow Democratic heavyweights. He advised clients such as AT&T, Google, Boeing, and FedEx on national security policy, and helped connect paying customers to the right people in D.C.'s power centers. When he left the firm, Blinken had $1.2 million in guaranteed income. On his first day in charge of the State Department, he had around $10 million in the bank.

None of that mattered to Biden. What mattered was that Blinken was loyal and shared a similar love for corny jokes. Blinken is known to make puns, such as talking about the need to "break the ice" during discussions about the Arctic. He can also be fun, even if his dry, monotone speaking style doesn't automatically suggest that. He plays guitar left-handed for a band called Coalition of the Willing and talks often about his love for classic rock, especially Eric Clapton and the Rolling Stones. "The thread that runs throughout my life is probably music," he said in a 2021 interview.

The other thread was government service—and he had no time to lose as secretary of state, confirmed only six days into the new administration. The last remaining nuclear-arms deal between the United States and Russia was set to expire on February 5. The Strategic Arms Reduction Treaty of 2011, known as New START, put verifiable limits on deployed nuclear-range missiles. It helped the two owners of nearly all the world's nuclear weapons keep calm about each other's arsenals.

The Trump administration knew that the deadline was fast approaching in its final year. But instead of pushing to extend the deal for five years, officials waited, thinking that putting it off might cause Moscow to panic and concede something. Meanwhile, Trump's team hoped to use the opportunity to involve Beijing in the arms-control talks, especially since the number of its nuclear weapons and the sophistication of its missiles were only growing. But Russia didn't cave and China didn't sit at the table—leaving the problem for Biden to solve.

A first test for Blinken would come on the same day as his confirmation, when Biden spoke on the phone with Vladimir Putin. It was a call Putin himself asked for, but one that senior aides like Jake Sullivan thought he could delay. But Biden said to set up the chat. Putin was the leader of a major country, even if it was an American adversary. Leaders had to rise above pettiness when matters of global stability were at stake.

The discussion was "workmanlike and tense," someone familiar with the conversation said, as the two leaders spoke about everything from Russia's hacking of U.S. government agencies to the imprisonment of leading anti-Kremlin activist Alexei Navalny. But the posturing also gave way to progress: they agreed they should extend New START for the maximum five years and would "have their teams work urgently to complete the extension by February 5," per a White House readout of the call.

The good news was that Biden's team had prepared for the moment. "We worked on it during the transition," a senior U.S. official told me at the time. A shorter extension benefited neither Washington nor Moscow, Biden's nuclear experts concluded. There were serious issues to work out with Russia, namely convincing Putin to reverse the 2014 annexation and occupation of Ukraine's Crimean Peninsula and the Donbas region.

The Biden–Putin agreement left Blinken, the newly minted secretary of state, ten days to cross the *t*'s and dot the *i*'s. It was mostly a foregone conclusion that it would get done, but the State Department and White House encountered some sticking points. Nuances remained about how and when to conduct inspections, issues that still had to be brokered with the Kremlin. But after some diplomatic haggling, the deal got done—two days before New START was set to expire.

"Extending the New START Treaty makes the United States, U.S. allies and partners, and the world safer. An unconstrained nuclear competition would endanger us all," Blinken said in a February 3 statement. But, he continued, "we remain clear eyed about the challenges that Russia poses to the United States and the world. Even as we work with Russia to advance U.S. interests, so too will we work to hold Russia to account for adversarial actions as well as its human rights abuses, in close coordination with our allies and partners."

The deal gave administration officials, including Blinken, a sense of relief. Someone who spoke to him during the negotiations said he feared being unable to secure the extension. Not only would that prove a failure, and show that Biden would struggle to reverse Trump-era policies, but it would ruin any chances to improve rock-bottom ties between Washington and Moscow. Blinken was no dove: he despised Putin, what he stood for and what he'd done. But a "stable and predictable" relationship with Russia was better than a consistently plummeting one. That path led only to outcomes that could imperil the world. Getting New START done helped to avoid the worst.

One day after announcing that New START would survive, Biden gave the first major foreign policy address of his presidency. With Blinken's help, Biden set out to explain exactly what he planned to do. While Biden's aides at the White House and across the administration had agonized over the text, it was Blinken who assured the president that the overall message was right.

"The message I want the world to hear today: America is back," Biden began from inside the State Department's Benjamin Franklin Room, standing alongside the secretary of state. After extolling the virtues of extending the arms-control agreement, Biden offered a stern warning to the autocrat in Moscow.

"I made it clear to President Putin, in a manner very different from my predecessor, that the days of the United States rolling over in the face of Russia's aggressive actions—interfering with our elections, cyberattacks, poisoning its citizens—are over. We will not hesitate to raise the cost on Russia and defend our vital interests and our people. And we will be more effective in dealing with Russia when we work in coalition and coordination with other like-minded partners," Biden said.

But the president wasn't done. After calling Russia out, he moved on to another superpower. Even as COVID-19 raged and domestic concerns consumed his time and attention, competing with China would be the defining challenge of Biden's presidency and, he argued, America's fate throughout the twenty-first century.

"We'll confront China's economic abuses; counter its aggressive, coercive action; to push back on China's attack on human rights, intellectual property, and global governance," he said. "We will compete from a position of strength by building back better at home, working with our allies and partners, renewing our role in international institutions, and reclaiming our credibility and moral authority, much of which has been lost."

Internal reviews from Biden's team were mixed. They ran the gamut from "meh, he's basically said all this stuff before" to "wowza, we really laid down a marker."

Just a month later, it was Blinken's turn to deliver a foundational speech for his tenure at State, this one titled "A Foreign Policy for the American People" ("A Foreign Policy for the Middle Class" was, of course, already taken). Within the administration, some didn't fully comprehend why the secretary had to give a similar speech. Part of it was meant to reaffirm the theme about how a sound foreign policy helps Americans—not in a nebulous way but in a concrete way. Another reason was that Blinken and others in the administration felt the China piece had to be hit harder.

He did that.

"China is the only country with the economic, diplomatic, military, and technological power to seriously challenge the stable and open international system—all the rules, values, and relationships that make the world work the way we want it to, because it ultimately serves the interests and reflects the values of the American people," he said. "Our relationship with China will be competitive when it should be, collaborative when it can be, and adversarial when it must be. The common denominator is the need to engage China from a position of strength."

It was only after the speech that the real reason Blinken wanted to outline the administration's view on China came out: he was two weeks away from a major face-to-face meeting in Anchorage, Alaska, with his counterpart Yang Jiechi, China's top diplomat. The administration's first big test with Beijing was literally and figuratively on the horizon.

But first, the administration had some unfinished business to take care of.

• • •

If European diplomacy during the Trump administration was a grocery store, the loudspeaker announcing a spill in aisle one would have been going off with alarming regularity. Blinken had a lot of mopping up to do with NATO allies.

Some of the messes included Trump traveling to Brussels, Belgium, for a NATO summit in May 2017, his greatest opportunity to show support for the alliance after calling it "obsolete" during the 2016 presidential campaign. He did anything but reassure them during his visit. In a made-for-the-internet moment, Trump pushed aside Montenegro's leader so he could stand in front during a group photo. And when it was his turn to speak—to deliver an address that might calm fears about America's place in the organization it leads—Trump shocked his own team by failing to support the entire idea of collective defense.

For weeks, Trump's team had planned for the president to reaffirm America's commitment to Article 5, the NATO provision that says an attack on one member country is an attack on all. Initially crafted to deter aggression from the Soviet Union, the article had been invoked only once in its history: after the attacks of 9/11.

National Security Adviser H. R. McMaster, Defense Secretary James Mattis, and Secretary of State Rex Tillerson had all approved the reaffirmation text for a speech, and Trump's staff confirmed the line in the final version of the draft. "They had the right speech and it was cleared through McMaster," a source familiar with the text told Susan Glasser, then of *Politico*. "As late as that same morning, it was the right one." Trump was supposed to say: "We face many threats, but I stand here before you with a clear message: the U.S. commitment to the NATO alliance and to Article 5 is unwavering." But Trump didn't deliver that sentence. He omitted the line, seemingly all on his own and for reasons that still remain unclear.

It would be two weeks before Trump, standing alongside Romania's president outside the White House and dogged by reporters, reluctantly said what many in the United States and Europe wanted him to say. "I'm committing the United States—and have committed—but I'm committing the United States to Article 5," he asserted.

Two months later, during a gathering of the G20—where leaders of the world's most advanced economies meet at a lavish event to coordinate on trade and finances—Trump and Putin found time to hold a bilateral meeting. In the lead-up to the much-anticipated chat, Trump's team promised that the new president would confront Putin about Russia's interference in the 2016 presidential election. But he didn't. Instead, Trump announced that Putin had denied that his country was involved with the influence campaign, and that he believed him—even though U.S. intelligence openly assessed that the Russian leader had ordered the meddling. Per Russian foreign minister Sergey Lavrov, Trump had told Putin in the meeting that many in the United States were "exaggerating" the extent of Russia's election interference.

As if that weren't enough, Trump chatted with Putin for nearly an hour at a G20 dinner, a conversation the administration didn't disclose for over a week. Trump didn't have staff with him for that conversation, but Putin did, meaning that only Russia would have a transcript of their talk. "Not good," CNN analyst John Kirby said at the time, four years before joining the Biden administration as a top Pentagon and National Security Council spokesperson. "While smaller pull-aside meetings are common, it is strange that a pull-aside with someone like Putin—especially Putin—would not include at least another national security official and a translator."

Late-night comedians in the United States had a field day. "How stupid can you be?" Stephen Colbert joked. "You're in the middle of what could be the worst scandal in U.S. history. People think you colluded with the president of a hostile foreign power. Then you go out of your way to meet with him again and you don't tell anybody? That's like if O.J. does get out on parole and immediately goes glove shopping."

A year later, Trump failed to get along with his colleagues during a G7 meeting. Canadian prime minister Justin Trudeau announced that all the countries had signed on to the pro forma communiqué, proving that the semiformal alliance was aligned on issues like climate change and trade. Instead, Trump bashed Trudeau after the premier noted the American leader's hostility during the meetings. "PM Justin Trudeau acted so meek and mild," Trump tweeted. He left Canada without agreeing to the pro forma communiqué—displaying that America's participation in global cooperation hinged on world leaders treating Trump nicely.

A photo of that event also went viral: Trump sitting down, looking defiant, as world leaders surround him with pained looks on their faces. German chancellor Angela Merkel leaned both her hands on a table, towering over the president, who looked away with his arms crossed. In the background, Japanese prime minister Shinzo Abe stood looking like he was resigned to the fact that Trump—and the America he led—couldn't be dealt with.

It later became clear that the photo misrepresented the moment. Another, for example, showed Trump and Merkel engaged, with the German chancellor smiling at her American counterpart. But the viral reaction to the photo said it all: there was a sense that Trump hated our allies, defied them even, and relished it. It didn't help that on the same day as that meeting, Putin was with Chinese leader Xi Jinping, shoring up that relationship.

Blinken and his colleagues could easily ditch many of Trump's policies toward Russia. But the Biden administration found much more to like in the China plan it inherited, though there were still changes to be made.

"We looked at what the Trump administration did over four years, and found merit in the basic proposition of an intense strategic competition with China and the need for us to engage in that vigorously, systematically across every instrument of our government and every instrument of our power," a senior administration official told reporters on February 10, just moments after Biden held his first call with Xi Jinping. "But we found deep problems with the way in which the Trump administration went about that competition and, in particular, our diagnosis was that the Trump strategy depleted core American sources of strength and put us in a weaker position with which to carry out that competition."

Take one of Trump's signature anti-China initiatives: the trade war. A study commissioned by the U.S.–China Business Council and released in the Biden administration's first month estimated that the Trump-imposed tariffs cost the United States around 245,000 jobs. America's trade deficits with China and much of the rest of the world also grew higher during the Trump years compared with when Obama was in charge. The Tax Foundation said the $80 billion in tariffs—not just on China but also on Europe—was "equivalent to one of the largest tax increases in decades." Keeping them in place would "reduce long-run GDP by 0.21 percent [$55.7 billion] and wages by 0.14 percent."

But that wasn't the only problem, the official said. Trump's questioning of the 2020 election, berating of allies, and disregard for international institutions gave China the opening to fill an America-sized vacuum. Trump, then, had "created a circumstance in which, in a way, our policy was doing China's work for it."

The official wasn't telling the whole story. The Biden administration had already decided not to lift tariffs on China that Trump had placed as part of his unilateral trade war, but the president's aides didn't want to disclose that so early on. They also didn't want to admit that the tariffs helped convey a message to China that the era of free riding was over. At the same time, the United States was able to protect industries in America by making Chinese products more expensive.

The biggest reason for keeping the tariffs, though, was political: lifting the penalties would make it easy for Republicans to paint the new president as weak on China—a charge Trump leveled at Biden throughout the entire campaign. The fear was that it would make it much harder to get important people confirmed at State, Commerce, and the Pentagon. All the nominees would have to make an anti-China pledge so that a fifty-fifty Senate filled with Beijing hawks would greenlight their new jobs. Keeping the sanctions in place, Team Biden assessed early on, was both politically and geopolitically the best thing to do in the moment.

As Blinken flew to Alaska, a domestic bill changed the tenor of his meeting with Yang Jiechi. On March 11, Biden signed into law a $1.9 trillion COVID-19 relief package, giving stimulus checks to millions of Americans, helping small businesses, and putting more money in the pockets of parents. It was the perfect symbol of what Biden hoped to show the world: even in divisive and unprecedented times, democracies could deliver for their people.

"As I stand here tonight, we're proving once again something I have said time and time again until they're probably tired of hearing me say it. I say it [to] foreign leaders and domestic alike: It's never, ever a good bet to bet against the American people. America is coming back," Biden said that evening, commemorating the one-year anniversary of the pandemic-caused shutdown throughout the United States.

The bill turned law gave Blinken and Sullivan the ammunition they needed ahead of their meeting with Chinese colleagues in Alaska. This was the first, best chance for the United States to show China how things would be different with Biden in the Oval Office. Blinken particularly wanted Beijing to leave the meeting understanding that the United States was on the move, swaggering on the world stage once again. A stronger America at home made a stronger America abroad, more confident in pointing out China's human rights abuses, namely the forced detainment of Uyghur Muslims in Xinjiang. Of course, that didn't preclude building a mutually beneficial relationship on global economic and climate change issues, among others.

"We honed and rehoned our message," a top White House official remembered. "It was agonizing." Blinken made sure on a visit to Japan and South Korea—his first foreign visit as secretary, just days before the Anchorage meeting—to coordinate talking points with the two allies.

The administration upped the level of difficulty the day before Blinken and Sullivan landed separately in Alaska. The United States announced that it was sanctioning twenty-four Chinese officials over the crackdown on Hong Kong, which squashed its democracy and accelerated its integration into the mainland. The action came ahead of the city considering a "patriotism test" for those standing for election—a move seen as a way for Beijing to tighten its grip on Hong Kong. Messages from Beijing were privately relayed to the State Department and White House: it's about to get ugly.

"Let's just say we were expecting some fireworks," the White House aide said.

About 999 times out of 1,000, the participants in a bilateral meeting offer forgettable opening platitudes before the real talk happens when the cameras stop whirring. But the exact opposite happened in Alaska. After Blinken and Sullivan's pro forma comments, Yang Jiechi ripped into the United States.

"Wars in this world are launched by some other countries, which have resulted in massive casualties," he said, the tension palpable to anyone in the room or watching on a computer screen. "The challenges facing the United States in human rights are deep-seated. They did not just emerge over the past four years, such as Black Lives Matter," he continued as part of his sixteen-minute diatribe.

Blinken and Sullivan realized what was happening: an official doesn't just riff for that long without preparation. This was a premeditated troll that Beijing knew would be carried live around the world. "Our impression was the Chinese came to Anchorage wanting to make a very clear point," a source in the administration said. "It was north of the acrimony we were expecting."

In the room that frigid March day in Alaska, Blinken moved quickly to counter the rhetorical attack. He motioned the cameras to stay in the room and keep rolling.

"There's one more hallmark of our leadership here at home, and that's a constant quest to, as we say, form a more perfect union. And that quest, by definition, acknowledges our imperfections, acknowledges that we're not perfect, we make mistakes, we have reversals, we take steps back. But what we've done throughout our history is to confront those challenges openly, publicly, transparently, not trying to ignore them, not trying to pretend they don't exist, not trying to sweep them under a rug. And sometimes it's painful, sometimes it's ugly, but each and every time, we have come out stronger, better, more united as a country," he responded, staring daggers at Yang throughout the rebuttal.

Off the cuff, Blinken had expounded on what Biden hoped to make a central theme of his presidency: while America had ills to cure, it could still lead the world—the world that America had made—with unflinching confidence. Blinken hadn't planned on making those remarks, but by making them at all, he showed how deeply he, Sullivan, and Biden believed in those concepts.

The private sessions over the next two days, however, were professional and devoid of drama. "They weren't warm, cordial meetings, but there was no animosity behind closed doors," the official said. That seemed to confirm to Biden's team that Yang's comments were mostly political theater.

Blinken and Sullivan divided the agenda. Sullivan took on issues of the economy and the COVID recovery plan. Betting that the United States couldn't revitalize itself and defend its interests and promote its values wasn't a wise decision, he said. Blinken dove deep on Taiwan, saying that the United States would do whatever it took to deter Beijing from seizing the democratic island by force. Yang likened that to America interfering in China's internal politics. Blinken didn't buy the argument: the United States wasn't trying to hold China back by speaking out on Taiwan or the Uyghurs or Hong Kong, but it was trying to encourage Beijing to abide by the rules-based order.

Biden's great-power competition strategy was coming into view: cooperate when possible, pounce when necessary. China and Russia were wholly different problems, but in the end the goal wasn't to start a Cold War against either of them. It was to convince Beijing and Moscow that it was better to work with Washington than against it. *Never bet against America,* as Biden liked to say.

Russia would soon get a taste of that plan in action—even as it showed muscle of its own.

In August 2020, Russian opposition leader Alexei Navalny was on a flight from Siberia to Moscow. It nearly killed him.

He was poisoned with Novichok, a nerve agent developed in the Soviet Union that Russia had used on a double agent in Britain two years earlier. The attempted murder weapon signaled that Putin authorized the operation to eliminate his fiercest political rival.

On March 2, 2021, Blinken officialy laid blame. He determined that Russia had used a chemical weapon against one of its own—the nation's most prominent dissident, no less—and that this required the United States to place restrictions on any financial support for the Kremlin, including foreign assistance and money for weapons. Seven senior members of the Russian government were also personally sanctioned.

Two weeks later, the administration targeted Moscow again, but this time to make up for something that Trump had failed to do. Trump had spent the entirety of his presidency denying that Russia interfered in the 2016 election that he won (and later denying that he lost the 2020 election). The United States couldn't uphold global democracy if it didn't come clean about what happened during its elections, and doing so certainly would give Biden a leg to stand on when he criticized Trump about his anti-democratic actions.

On March 15, Director of National Intelligence Avril Haines declassified an intelligence report titled "Foreign Threats to the 2020 US Federal Elections." The conclusion was straightforward: Russia and Iran had interfered in the contest, but analysts assessed that no votes were altered and that the final tabulation was not changed in any way. It did say, however, that Putin had ordered an influence operation on the American election, with operators favoring Trump's incumbency over Biden's candidacy.

Yes, Biden and his aides sought a predictable and stable relationship with Russia, but it wasn't going to stop the administration from calling out Moscow's bad behavior. Holding Putin to account came directly from Biden: Putin gets away with nothing while this administration runs things.

Putin tested the limits of that order. Starting in March, he amassed tens of thousands of troops on Ukraine's border. Tanks rolled up to the frontier and scores of warplanes showed up in Crimea, the Russian-annexed peninsula. Biden, Sullivan, and Blinken wondered: Was Putin going to launch the next phase in the war he'd already started?

"We're now seeing the largest concentration of Russian forces on Ukraine's borders since 2014," Blinken said on April 13 at NATO headquarters in Brussels. "That is a deep concern not only to Ukraine, but to the United States."

Sullivan and Blinken were watching the intelligence flow in, receiving briefings from their counterparts at the Pentagon, the CIA, and the Office of the Director of National Intelligence. Movements like these weren't for an exercise, they concluded; they were for an invasion. "That was deeply alarming, because it was out of historical norms. There was no other credible explanation for what they were up to," Sullivan said, recalling that time.

But, surprisingly, almost none of the intelligence showed that Putin had any plans to send the military streaming over the border. It was, Sullivan advised Biden, likely a way for Putin to show strength after so many U.S.-imposed sanctions. The United States had embarrassed him, and Biden wasn't showing signs of giving the dictator any leeway. The Kremlin was simply lashing out.

The U.S. still took the threat seriously. Top administration officials were in constant touch with their Ukrainian counterparts, just as Secretary of State Antony Blinken was with Ukrainian foreign minister Dmytro Kuleba. In a March 31 call, Blinken reaffirmed America's "unwavering support" for Ukraine as Russia threatened its sovereignty.

As messages of solidarity were continuously relayed, information reached Washington about four thousand armed Russian troops moving into Crimea. And just a day earlier, NATO had to scramble fighter jets ten times to intercept six different groups of Russian bombers and warplanes encroaching into allied airspace.

Kyiv started demanding advanced weapons from the United States in case war broke out and, as early as it could be organized, a call between Volodymyr Zelenskyy and Biden. American journalists noticed that the Ukrainian president's call sheet was missing the White House's number. "Bizarrely, President Biden has still not spoken—not even once—with the Ukrainian President Zelensky. This while Russia is escalating and menacing Ukraine," Jonathan Swan, then of *Axios,* tweeted on April 1. "Not to mention . . . President Biden didn't invite Ukraine to the climate summit. Notable invitees included one Vladimir Putin. . . . Extraordinary snub for a supposed ally at a time Russia is escalating."

Zelenskyy wasn't rated highly by the new Biden team. He was a political novice, having made his name on a comedy show in which he played an accidental president. Ukrainians also weren't fully behind his leadership. Polls showed that in March 2021, 68 percent of Ukrainians believed the country was going in the wrong direction.

Kyiv eventually got its wish: Biden and Zelenskyy had their first call on April 2. It got a little testy, with the Ukrainian president asking about the state of a potential weapons package. The United States and Ukraine had been in conversations about sending millions in weaponry to Kyiv to fend off the renewed Russian threat. For a while, it seemed like the U.S. would provide ammunition, rifles, and other materials through presidential drawdown authority, taking what was in current American military stocks to hand over to the Ukrainians. Andriy Yermak, a top aide to Zelenskyy, firmly believed it was a done deal and told his boss that. After all, Biden as vice president was committed to Ukrainian sovereignty, and he was looking to distinguish his foreign policy from Trump's. An early commitment of arms might do the trick.

Zelenskyy, the former comedian, tried to convey the seriousness of the threat. He reminded Biden of what he told Jonathan Swan just three days into the new American administration: ties between Washington and Kyiv could be revived now that Biden, and not Trump, was in office.

"I would like us to enter a new phase, go on a new path. And the path for me is an open conversation," Zelenskyy said in that interview. "I would really like the United States to succeed in what President Biden was talking about. He said he cares and will continue caring and working on the security of Europe. That's of the utmost importance, because the security of Europe—this is us. There is the war in the east of Ukraine, there is the aggression by the Russian Federation, the annexation of Crimea. So, maybe it's kind of selfish, but first of all we address his words to Ukraine.

"I would like the United States and personally President Biden, who, by the way, is very familiar with Ukraine, to help us exit this truly tragic situation. I call it a tragedy when the war in civilized Europe takes place in the twenty-first century," Zelenskyy added.

But on the April call, Biden didn't commit to a weapons package. He did, however, reiterate how much his administration would support Ukraine during such trying times. Zelenskyy was annoyed but didn't press the matter much further, except to say that Ukraine was a democracy in peril. History would remember where Biden and the country he led stood regarding the war. It would be great to discuss these issues in Washington at some point, Zelenskyy concluded. Biden said they'd talk again soon.

Two weeks later, Biden tried to talk Putin down from doing the worst. On the April 13 phone call, Biden said it was good that the United States and Russia had worked closely together on extending New START. As the countries with the world's largest arsenals, it was important for the world that the U.S. and Russia could cooperate when times got tough.

This was one of those times, Biden said. The military buildup was unacceptable. It wasn't how responsible nations behaved. Plus, this wasn't 2014, Biden made sure to mention. Publicly available images from commercial satellites show the world exactly what Russia is up to—there's no hiding this time. But if Putin wanted to talk about the rise in tensions between the U.S. and Russia, then maybe it was time for a face-to-face meeting, Biden proposed. In a few months' time, in some third country, Biden suggested, it'd be good to sit down for a chat and hash out these issues, great-power leader to great-power leader.

Putin didn't respond much to the comments about the increased military presence on Ukraine's border. He deflected, talking about how Ukraine really belonged in Russia's sphere of influence. The U.S. was poisoning the minds of officials in Kyiv, tricking them into thinking it was a Western nation. It's not Western, Putin said. It's still Soviet.

But, yes, an in-person summit would be a good idea, Putin said. He'd have his people in Moscow contact Biden's people in Washington.

Biden had one more point to make before hanging up the phone. The United States had determined that the major hack a year earlier, which reached the Pentagon, as well as the State, Treasury, and other departments, was launched by Russians. His administration had to hold the Kremlin responsible for SolarWinds, as the hack was known, due to the software the hackers used to penetrate federal systems. Expect an announcement in the coming days about crushing sanctions and punishments on your government. Biden reiterated his main point: if you come after the United States, then this administration will make sure you suffer the consequences.

Putin denied responsibility for the massive cyberespionage operation and brushed off Biden's bravado. Okay, he effectively said, I'll still see you soon.

The line went silent. The dismissiveness at the other end of the call didn't deter Biden. "We've got a ball game," he said.

Volodymyr Zelenskyy was beside himself when word of the impending summit reached Kyiv. Biden was going to award Putin—the man with troops perched on Ukraine's border—with a summit. Making matters worse, Biden's desire to meet Putin one-on-one would surely kill the weapons package. The fear was well founded: American officials determined that it was too provocative and might scuttle any chance for a constructive dialogue between the two world leaders.

The meeting was, in Zelenskyy's mind, a betrayal. "The feeling was the Biden administration was prioritizing the relationship with Russia," said someone familiar with the Ukrainian government's views at the time. The United States was trying to put the Russia challenge on the backburner so Washington could focus on China, COVID, and rebuilding the domestic economy. Biden viewed Ukraine as expendable in service of that goal, Zelenskyy and his team felt. "Raging disappointment would be an understatement."

It didn't help optics that Biden would meet with Putin without having first sat down with Zelenskyy. That couldn't possibly be an oversight, the Ukrainian leader told aides, it had to be an intentional snub. Biden, for all his talk about supporting the liberal world order and global democracy, was willing to let a democracy die.

By April, the frozen conflict in the eastern Ukrainian region known as the Donbas had intensified. The deadliest skirmish of the year happened near the end of March, when Russia-backed forces killed four Ukrainian soldiers. The escalation led U.S. European Command to elevate its watch level from possible crisis to imminent crisis. That was the command's highest level, a sign of how serious the U.S. military took the situation. But to Zelenskyy's mind, Biden didn't see the situation as similarly dangerous.

Any goodwill Ukraine might have had toward the United States in the first few months was gone. Long gone. "The bubble," said the person in touch with Ukrainian officials at the time, "had burst."

Chapter 3

Ending the Forever War

January—April 2021

The first big test of the Biden team's mettle would be on Afghanistan. Sullivan and Blinken, veterans of the Obama years, remembered what happened when the then president wanted to end the war. Generals and civilians at the Pentagon leaked their dire assessments about an imminent collapse of the capital, Kabul, and eventually the whole of the country. The Taliban, the Islamist militants the United States had deposed, would return to power and resubjugate a people who were growing accustomed a more Western lifestyle. All the United States and its allies had fought for would quickly, and inevitably, be lost.

Now this adminsitration had to match up against a Pentagon that had convinced Donald Trump—who railed against the war in Afghanistan—to keep a few thousand troops in the country. What Biden's aides knew, though, was that the president had walked into the Oval Office with an immovable sense that it was time to end America's adventure in Central Asia.

During the last Democratic presidency, Vice President Joe Biden found himself the loneliest voice in the room when discussion turned to a war that had begun in the aftermath of the terrorist attacks of September 11, 2001. Obama came to office in 2009 with the war raging more than seven years, with the Taliban overthrown but intense fighting and slow-moving nation building under way. Despite Obama's campaign promises to bring American involvement in the war to a close, it had not been the president pushing hardest to wind down the mission. It was his number two.

During a National Security Council meeting on January 23, 2009—just three days into the new Obama administration—the head of U.S. Central Command, Gen. David Petraeus, recommended that Obama send thirty thousand troops to Afghanistan, adding to the nearly forty thousand already there. Biden exploded: "We have not thought through our strategic goals!" Biden wanted to wait until a policy review had been completed before making any major military decisions. He was also skeptical that U.S. troops could do much if the Afghan government was corrupt and unable to lead.

But Biden kept getting rebuffed. Military and civilian officials at the Pentagon wanted more troops and resources sent to Afghanistan and worked tirelessly to convince the new president to accept their recommendations. Obama remained skeptical of an escalation, but he had yet to hear an alternative he liked.

On September 12, 2009, Biden worked with his top national security aide, Antony Blinken, to provide the president with one. Called "counterterrorism plus," the plan was to focus on killing al-Qaeda leaders and deterring a 9/11-style attack on the United States. America's military presence in the country could scale down dramatically under that plan, allowing the U.S. government to focus on larger projects at home instead of building a legitimate state in Afghanistan.

As he made his case, Biden railed against the leading option other officials wanted Obama to approve: expanding a counterinsurgency mission in Afghanistan. "This isn't an easy call. The military's done a hell of a job.

But nationwide, reinforced counterinsurgency will only expand costs and demand extra resources," he told Obama during a September 13 National Security Council meeting.

Then, on Thanksgiving 2009, a few days ahead of Obama making his final decision, Biden made his last and most impassioned case. While with his family in Nantucket for the holiday, Biden took out a legal pad and jotted down five main points he wanted the president to consider.

The first point was that the United States would be led astray if it followed a counterinsurgency strategy. The second was that America needed to get out of the nation-building business. The third was that the administration should use force to break al-Qaeda, not to keep the Taliban out of power. The final two points were that whatever the U.S. military captured should be transferred to Afghan authorities, and that Washington should pursue the goal of degrading the Taliban with an eye toward reconciliation.

Biden then put those handwritten pages into a classified fax machine for Obama to read. Obama didn't. Instead he announced on December 1 that he'd send thirty thousand more troops to Afghanistan. By the time he and Biden left office, nearly ten thousand U.S. troops remained engaged in what, by that point, was a fifteen-year war.

Biden believed the military had "boxed in" Obama. Give them the thousands of troops they want, and they'll soon come back and ask for many thousands more, Biden warned the president. When Gen. Stanley McChrystal, who was leading U.S. forces in Afghanistan, considered asking for more troops to avoid "mission failure," the White House privately seethed. Somehow, McChrystal's request made it into the hands of *The Washington Post*'s Bob Woodward in September 2009. If Obama didn't follow McChrystal's advice, the novice president would look like he was disregarding the counsel of his seasoned generals.

Biden wasn't a novice, and he concluded that following the Pentagon's recommendations would lead only to more war, death, and bloodshed without securing America's interests in Afghanistan. He would not be boxed in.

He would not make the same mistake. He would not back down, because he had been right before.

President Joe Biden was ready to end America's role in the Afghanistan war. He told anyone and everyone that he intended to do so. His chief of staff, Ron Klain, said Biden's mind had been made up ever since he returned from a trip to Afghanistan as vice president in 2009. The military leaders said that, in order for the United States to leave safely, Afghanistan had to have a viable government that could serve the people. Without it, the mission was fruitless. "When he came back," author Chris Whipple quotes Klain as saying, "he reached the conclusion that there was no way to build a nationwide pluralistic democracy based in Kabul."

It was a message that Biden repeated again and again on the campaign trail. "I would bring American combat troops in Afghanistan home during my first term. Any residual U.S. military presence in Afghanistan would be focused only on counterterrorism operations," he answered in a Council on Foreign Relations questionnaire during the 2020 presidential campaign. "Americans are rightly weary of our longest war; I am, too."

But President Trump had made the same promise and came close to fulfilling it too. After initially sending in three thousand more troops—pushed to do so by his national security adviser, active-duty three-star general H. R. McMaster—his administration brokered a deal with the Taliban in 2020. The United States would withdraw its troops completely by May 1, 2021, in either Trump's second term or a Democrat's first, as long as the militants didn't target or kill Americans.

So in Biden's first days, senior officials wanted to know: What will the president decide ahead of the May 1 deadline?

In a way, administration officials told me, the Trump-era deal left few choices: end the war or continue it and risk the Taliban killing U.S. troops again. "We weren't playing an abstract hand. We were playing a hand we were dealt. That narrowed the aperture of possible outcomes," a senior

White House official told me. But few were under any illusions as to what the ultimate outcome would be. "The withdrawal is going to happen, so prepare. We were told from the beginning," a Pentagon official told me.

No one in or outside the government was willing to sit still. Left- and right-leaning antiwar advocates met regularly with administration officials to ensure that Biden didn't waver from the withdrawal option. The State Department's view on the issue changed after conversations with allies. Top Pentagon figures—from the secretary of defense to the Joint Chiefs chair to the head of U.S. troops in the Middle East—advocated for an indefinite military presence. What ensued was months of wrangling over a decision that was thought to be a foregone conclusion but was actually more up in the air than many believed.

"Biden was adamant, and I think he lived up to it, that he wanted all of us to engage in a real process," a senior administration official told me. "There was no meeting where he said, 'I made up my mind.'" Still, "It was always clear that his lean was to get out unless convinced otherwise."

Even before Biden became president, top officials in Afghanistan wanted to speak with him. Hamdullah Mohib, the country's national security adviser and former ambassador to the United States, hoped to shape and influence the policy review he knew was coming.

Ross Wilson, the U.S. chargé d'affaires at the embassy in the Afghan capital, relayed Mohib's message to the White House. But quickly a response came back: it was too soon. Not because a review wasn't planned or even under way. The National Security Council needed time to find the light switches, learn the route to the bathroom, know where to get pencils and pens. There was also a pandemic to curb, and U.S. officials were barely meeting with one another. A face-to-face meeting with the representative of a foreign government just wasn't going to happen.

Mohib's instinct was to meet instead with his counterpart, Jake Sullivan. The job of running the process on the stay-or-leave decision fell squarely on his shoulders. As the U.S. national security adviser, it was Sullivan's responsibility to run meetings, gather the best information, and give Biden the tools he needed to make the final call. To do that, he first had to rebuild something Donald Trump had broken: the decision-making process itself.

Since its creation in 1947, the National Security Council has been charged with coordinating foreign policy across the sprawling government. What typically happens is that lower-level officials, who have more granular expertise on an issue, give their best advice to their bosses. Then their bosses' bosses whittle down the advice even more, and on and on it goes until the head of an agency comes to a meeting with the national security adviser and the president with a full-fledged recommendation. This not only keeps everybody in the loop about what's going on but ensures that the president is receiving all the necessary data.

That's not really how it worked when Trump was president. "It was an absolute joke," said Olivia Troye, who served as an adviser to Vice President Mike Pence before publicly breaking with the administration over its botched COVID-19 response. "Trump's whims would outweigh the actual process." Sometimes, he'd give an order via Twitter, sending officials throughout the government scrambling to retrofit developing policy to his needs. It didn't help that some senior officials often freelanced and took matters into their own hands, whether on immigration or overthrowing regimes in Latin America.

After four years of procedural chaos during the Trump administration, Sullivan had to revive the interagency process. He aimed to do so in two ways. First, ensure that everyone around the table felt their voice was heard and their advice seriously considered. Second, he rarely, if ever, let his true opinions on an issue be known when he was chairing an NSC meeting. In effect, Sullivan tried to be an "honest broker" during any discussions, a model popularized by Brent Scowcroft as the national security adviser to Gerald Ford and George H. W. Bush. Only that way could he get the best out of the Cabinet and their teams and, thus, be of most service to the president.

For Sullivan, the youngest person to hold the national security adviser role since John F. Kennedy appointed Harvard academic McGeorge Bundy to the job in 1961, this was all terribly important to how he'd be perceived in the job. "Jake was very conscious that people were going to be watching him very closely," a person in his inner circle told me. How he handled the Afghanistan debate would reflect how the administration handled any major national security decision in the years to come. Sullivan needed to prove himself to the Cabinet, the hundreds of people in the NSC, and, most of all, the president.

So as Sullivan started working on the Afghanistan issue during the transition, he held conversations with Biden to make sure the people for and against continuing the war had a fair shot to make their cases. Sullivan would probe and prod, putting his years as a collegiate debater to use, questioning assertions by those from the CIA, the Pentagon, State, or elsewhere. And, importantly, he'd never say what his true view on Afghanistan was. If the president wanted to hear it privately, then of course he'd share it, but never in the Situation Room.

Ross Wilson, the top U.S. diplomat in Afghanistan, was relieved that a serious interagency process on Afghanistan was revving up. He'd been in his position since January 2020 but had yet to participate in one Afghanistan-related meeting with his colleagues back in Washington. If anyone was making Afghanistan policy during Trump's last year, Wilson didn't hear about it. The U.S. embassy in Kabul and the American civilians most in harm's way were left completely shut out.

During the first full Afghanistan review meeting in February, Biden and Sullivan laid out their expectations for the forthcoming months of debate. This was an opportunity to leave no stone unturned. *We want to hear your take. Show us the evidence for why your point of view is the right one. Be honest about the second- and third-order effects of what you're proposing.*

The mood immediately turned serious in the hallowed Situation Room. The future of a war, and America's role in it, would be decided during these conversations.

The president made a final point. Yes, his views on the Afghanistan war were well known and documented, but he was open to changing his mind—as long as he was presented with an irrefutable case for keeping U.S. troops and diplomats in danger. With the preamble out of the way, the Biden administration's Afghanistan war review commenced.

"We came in with a healthy degree of suspicion about the argument for staying in Afghanistan," a senior U.S. official told me, "but we needed to and we wanted to test the assumption, because we hadn't been in government."

The earliest meetings—chaired by Sullivan; his deputy, Jon Finer; or the homeland security adviser Elizabeth Sherwood-Randall—focused more on the history. What happened over the last twenty years? What worked and didn't work in both the diplomatic and the military effort? Was there anything not written down in the Trump–Taliban agreement that both sides were following?

Even in those gatherings, the argument from the Pentagon was made crystal clear: don't withdraw troops; keep them in Afghanistan indefinitely.

Gen. Kenneth "Frank" McKenzie, Jr. then the chief of U.S. Central Command, sent multiple letters to civilian leadership at the Defense Department and the White House arguing that Biden should keep at least twenty-five hundred troops in the country. "I know the criticism: the Taliban are going to come after you and you're going to have to beef up your forces. The commander on the ground and I didn't believe that was necessarily the case. For one thing, at twenty-five hundred we were down to a pretty lean combat capability, not a lot of attack surface there for the Taliban to get at. Two, we would have coupled the twenty-five-hundred presence with a strong diplomatic campaign to put pressure on the Taliban," Gen. McKenzie told *Politico*'s Lara Seligman in August 2022. "What would have happened if we stayed at twenty-five hundred? It's just difficult to know that. Here's what we do know as a matter of history—if you go to zero, they collapse."

How hard the Defense Department fought to remain in the war became unmistakably clear during a February meeting in the Situation Room. The Cabinet-level officials, including Defense Secretary Lloyd Austin and Secretary of State Blinken, were there to discuss which of three broad options to recommend to the president. Option 1: Stick to the Trump-era timeline. Option 2: Negotiate an extension to the deal with the Taliban, permitting American forces to stay beyond the set deadline. And Option 3: Rip up the pact altogether and push for the victory that had eluded the United States and its allies for two decades.

Gen. Mark Milley, the Joint Chiefs chair, said the United States should stay and fight. The onetime deputy commanding general of U.S. forces in Afghanistan made an "emotional" pitch, according to multiple people in the room, that withdrawing American forces would make it easy for the Taliban to regain control of the country. The lives of millions of people would quickly get worse.

Women's rights "will go back to the Stone Age," and it wasn't worth leaving after "all the blood and treasure spent" in the war. As a result, the U.S. needed to keep twenty-five hundred troops in Afghanistan. But if the decision eventually was for a full military withdrawal, then the country would most likely fall to the Taliban between Thanksgiving and Christmas. If Afghan forces played their cards right, they might hold out until the following spring, but surely not later than the summer.

"He went on for a while," said a White House official, "and everyone was sort of like, 'Whoa.'"

But for Milley, this was all straightforward. Once U.S. and Western troops started to pack up, local Afghan commanders would make deals with the Taliban to either join their ranks or be left alone. They and their cadres would fight for their own survival, not the survival of a country that was barely pieced together.

Milley had made similar outbursts before. He grew up in a Catholic military family north of Boston. A great athlete with a sharp mind, Milley knew how to speak casually but with authority. His frame—nearly six feet, barrel-chested—made him an imposing figure in meetings. And he was a general's general, capable of discussing everything from the history of World War II to tactics against insurgents, which gave him further credibility when discussing wartime operations.

He was, however, controversial. He walked alongside President Donald Trump across Lafayette Square on June 1, 2020, for a photo opportunity at a church, just moments after authorities forcibly dispersed Black Lives Matter protesters. He cared deeply about keeping the military away from politics but often failed to do that. As protesters continued to clash with federal authorities and the National Guard in the summer of 2020, Milley walked around the streets of Washington, D.C., in his military uniform, making him seem like a general checking on his troops in a war zone.

Milley would later apologize for his role in the Lafayette Square walk, but that did little to dispel early fears among some in Biden's orbit that he was "Trump's guy."

Austin, the Pentagon chief, heard Milley's appeals in the Situation Room but tried to lower the tension. "We're not going to make decisions based on emotion," he said, noting that feelings run rampant when the topic is about a twenty-year war that many in the room—including the defense secretary—had fought in. Austin later checked in with his chief of staff, Kelly Magsamen, to ask if he had been too harsh with Milley. Magsamen didn't think so, assuring her boss that he was reinforcing for the whole room that the goal of the monthslong review was to reach a dispassionate conclusion.

It was a rough moment for Austin, the first African American to lead the Pentagon, who was trying to balance standing up for the department he led and serving the president. The scene was a reminder of the reasons that Biden had brought in Austin as his secretary of defense. The first was that Austin was a known quantity, someone Biden had dealt with during his time as vice president, and Austin had gotten to know Biden's son Beau while they were both in Iraq and attended Mass together. The second was that Austin had spent time with grieving families who had lost loved ones in war. President Biden was still reeling from Beau's death following a bout with cancer. And the third reason, but one that Biden didn't tell Austin when offering him the job, was that the former four-star army general shied away from the spotlight.

Austin, for example, was scheduled to speak during a 2014 event at the Atlantic Council think tank in Washington, D.C. Such events are common, and they provide flag officers like Austin a chance to engage with the public about what they're up to. Interest was high in what Austin—then chief of U.S. Central Command, the military organization that oversees operations in the Middle East—had to say.

But the day before he was to speak, CENTCOM asked the Atlantic Council to bar media cameras from the event. It was meant to be an "academic discussion," Austin's team said, not a media availability. It was a highly unusual request, as four-stars and senior Obama officials often spoke on camera about what they were doing. But Austin, not the most natural speaker, didn't want to make comments that could be splashed on cable news and possibly get him in trouble with the White House. He was a quiet warrior: he'd say his piece in private, not out in the open.

After Biden's experience watching generals trying to box in Obama, the new commander in chief wanted a defense secretary who would never be a bureaucratic infighter and who had shown loyalty to the Biden family. Austin was the only choice.

After Austin's remark in the Situation Room, Biden took back control of the meeting by pressing Milley. The Taliban will start attacking U.S. troops the moment we announce our decision to keep fighting the war. "That will happen," Biden said. Was it reasonable to ask American sons and daughters to die for a war the United States hadn't won in twenty years?

Milley responded that the Taliban would be hard pressed to kill the few thousand American troops. They wouldn't be on the front lines but would, in fact, be relatively safe in their bases. The option to stay carried few risks and would allow the U.S. to keep supporting the Afghan military against the militants and open the space for diplomacy. It was an argument he'd return to often over the coming months.

Blinken, representing the State Department, had a more bureaucratic argument, which some took as his subtle way of disagreeing with Biden without provoking the president's ire. Any decision to leave Afghanistan would severely impact thousands of government officials who'd spent the last two decades living and breathing the perils and promise of Afghanistan. Working to build a better Afghanistan was effectively an organizing principle for many at the State Department and other agencies. Ending the war would rob them of their chance to see the job through. They'd then have to move on to something else, perhaps with less faith in America's role as a global beacon for good.

Whatever the decision, Blinken continued, it would be good to keep the U.S. embassy in Kabul open. This raised Milley's hackles. "But if the decision is to withdraw troops to zero, then that means zero, right?" he asked openly to the room. In other words, there couldn't even be U.S. Marines stationed at the mission. And who would want to keep the outpost open anyway, especially if the country would inevitably be run by the Taliban? Blinken replied that until the militants took the capital, there was no reason to shutter the embassy. "This was always a friction point in discussions" between the Pentagon and State Department, a senior defense official told me about the deliberations.

The Pentagon's resistance helped kick-start another conversation: Would the U.S. troops in Afghanistan be better used elsewhere? How about beefing up America's military presence near Russia or China? "There were opportunity and cost discussions we might not have had without the Pentagon's push on where our troops were most needed," a senior U.S. official told me.

Biden, in that and other meetings on Afghanistan, was more interested in the effect staying or leaving would have on the country's neighbors. Not just Iran or Pakistan but also Russia and China. Wouldn't both Moscow and Beijing love to see the United States bogged down for another decade in the war? Or would officials in those capitals surmise that U.S. troops packing and going home meant America was a paper tiger, unable to see a hard fight through? Perhaps leaving would embolden America's greatest adversaries? These were great questions, Sullivan would say, and he tasked officials around the table to come up with the best answers for them.

Some of the most important memos weren't about the best reasons for staying or leaving Afghanistan but about how to execute whichever option the president chose. If America stayed: Where do the twenty-five hundred troops go? Will they need more security if the Taliban comes after them? What about the embassy's security? Will Congress, increasingly skeptical about the need for the war, authorize more funds for a continued military presence? What kind of political risk does the president expose himself to if soldiers come home in body bags?

If America left: How quickly should the troops withdraw? Which service members go first? How do you shutter bases safely? Could the Taliban shoot at U.S. forces as they leave? And again: What kind of political risk does the president expose himself to if soldiers come home in coffins?

"I felt all along that the president faced a difficult decision, each fraught with a lot of problems," a U.S. official deeply involved in the review told me.

Ultimately, the war-skeptical president needed to be convinced of one question in particular: Was it in the national interest of the United States to stay in the war? In those early stages, Biden hadn't heard anything to make him think "yes."

One group that wasn't dispassionate about the Afghanistan war was the coalition of antiwar groups. After years of being shunned by previous administrations, progressives gained access they'd never had before, thanks to Biden's political need to play nice and his looming decision on the war. "It was a new situation for us to have a White House that took our calls," one of the activists told me in the early part of 2021.

The organizations, some of them led by veterans, held informal conversations with Biden's team during the transition and at the start of his term in office. They were barely substantive, participants told me—they were more about everyone checking one another's temperature. The White House wanted to see if the groups were people they could work with, and the activists wanted to assess how serious Biden's team was about engaging with them.

One of the leading people in those meetings was Alex McCoy, a Marine veteran who led the liberal antiwar group Common Defense. The black-haired McCoy, who in uniform had guarded embassies in Latin America and the Middle East, acted like a disillusioned service member. His voice rang with a dour tone, though it would liven when he spoke about ending the "forever wars."

He lobbied Democrats to pull the United States out of the war in Afghanistan. His operation got him access to senior figures running campaigns for the 2020 presidential candidates. Now with Biden in office, McCoy had the contacts he needed to organize virtual meetings about the thing he wanted most.

McCoy was someone who'd learned to despise war—and American policymakers who always turned to military action as a solution—while he wore the uniform of the United States.

"There are some people who fucking hate America and want to kill Americans," he told me. But the problem, he felt, was that the U.S. government sent young Americans in uniform to solve the problem. "It's unprepared twenty-two-, twenty-three-year-old corporals who are being put in these situations where if we screw up, people die, and even if we do it right, people may die," he said.

McCoy learned that lesson again and again in 2012 as he watched from the U.S. embassy in Honduras while the deadly events unfolded in Benghazi, Libya—where four Americans, including Ambassador Christopher Stevens, were killed. He got alerts about "dozens" of American embassies under fire around the world. He also saw the images from Tunis of Marines running to the roof to fight off protesters slamming cars into the embassy door, which underscored just how poorly the whole effort to change regional politics by force was going.

In the immediate aftermath, McCoy's superiors tasked him with writing an after-action report on the lessons learned from these attacks. It included ideas for new training and security procedures he hoped the military and State Department staff would take to heart. But the most important assessment the young Marine made, a much more personal assessment, was that the United States was accomplishing very little for the amount of resources it was expending.

What is all this about? What is all this for? he began asking himself.

"Clearly a lot of people didn't see us as the good guys," he told me about his feelings at the time. McCoy couldn't help but realize how American embassies were built like fortresses, hiding staff away from the people they were meant to interact with. Other Western nations, like the United Kingdom and Germany, didn't need modern-day castles to conduct diplomacy.

The Benghazi attack, along with other stormings of U.S. embassies, "was the key politicizing moment" for McCoy, he told me. He seethed as he watched congressional Republicans block more funding for embassies while they blamed President Obama and Secretary of State Clinton for the tragedy. "This whole thing is bullshit," McCoy sensed. "Republicans who say they care about the troops are full of shit."

Now out of uniform, and helping lead a small but influential group, McCoy hoped to end America's ways of war—starting with Afghanistan.

The first formal meeting between Common Defense and the White House was on March 5, 2020. About a dozen people from the organization, including McCoy, hopped on a Zoom call to speak with Tanya Bradsher, who was set to leave the National Security Council to be chief of staff at the Department of Veterans Affairs, and other aides.

Common Defense personnel immediately told their own stories of suffering injuries while serving in Afghanistan, everything from posttraumatic stress disorder to problems walking. Some even revealed that friends they served with had died by suicide. "Don't condemn more young Americans to be like us," one of the veterans on the call said.

Bradsher, a twenty-year army veteran, responded that she felt their pain. She and some White House colleagues had also served in the military, she said, and would never take a decision like whether to extend the war in Afghanistan lightly. "It remains an open issue," she told the group. "I can make no promises, but this is actively being debated internally."

McCoy replied with a thinly veiled threat. "This isn't a concession we want to make," he said. "We're standing ready to fully support the president" if he pulls the U.S. out of the war, "and we're standing ready to fight him if he doesn't."

Two days later, on March 7, news broke that shook the Washington–Kabul relationship to its core. A letter that Secretary of State Antony Blinken wrote to Afghan president Ashraf Ghani leaked to the press, providing the first real indication of where the administration was headed. Such letters are usually sent through secure channels to ensure they don't leak—but someone clearly wanted this one to get out.

"Although we have not yet completed our review of the way ahead, we have reached an initial conclusion that the best way to advance our shared interests is to do all we can to accelerate peace talks and to bring all parties into compliance with their commitments," Blinken wrote. The secretary said that the effort would include United Nations–brokered meetings; having America's top Afghanistan envoy, Zalmay Khalilzad, prepare a proposal for both the Afghan government and the Taliban to discuss; and having Turkey host a high-level meeting to finalize the pact.

Then came the warning: "I must also make clear to you, Mr. President, that as our policy process continues in Washington, the United States has not ruled out any option. We are considering the full withdrawal of our forces by May 1st, as we consider other options," Blinken wrote. "I am making this clear to you so that you understand the urgency of my tone regarding the collective work outlined in this letter."

The letter was embarrassing for the Afghan leader, who not only realized his power was slipping but now had to contend with the world knowing how the Americans spoke to him.

A senior administration official I interviewed shortly after the leak swore they didn't mean for the letter to get out.

"That was not something that we put out there intentionally," this person told me. "The intention was to tell Ghani that this was his last best chance for diplomacy. It was not something that we thought would get out there, because we didn't want to box Ghani in—and with the leak, that's what happened." But, the official later admitted, "we expected some part of the letter to leak, just not the whole thing."

Despite the certainty of the Blinken letter, the truth was that Biden still wasn't close to making a final call about Afghanistan. On March 17, nearly two months into Biden's presidency, ABC News's George Stephanopoulos asked him if he would abide by former president Donald Trump's deal with the Taliban to withdraw all U.S. troops by May 1. "I'm in the process of making that decision now as to when they'll leave," he said. Would they stay longer than that deadline? Stephanopoulos asked. "I don't think a lot longer," Biden replied.

Up to that point, foreign officials were telling their administration counterparts there was deep skepticism that the United States would actually send its troops home from Afghanistan. It was a bluff, a negotiating position, a pressure tactic—it wasn't a reflection of actual thinking in the Oval Office. Biden's comments, which weren't a strategic leak, helped his aides make the case that the withdrawal option was a serious one.

"I can't tell you how many times a foreign counterpart brushed off the idea that Biden would actually pull all U.S. troops out," a senior U.S. official told me. "That helped us tell them directly, 'You should prepare for us to leave.'"

Biden, despite his inclinations, still hadn't dismissed the idea of keeping twenty-five hundred troops in Afghanistan. He saw merit in the argument that they could serve as the backstop for the still-improving Afghan National Defense and Security Forces and assist with the counterterrorism mission. He was also continuing to get advice from trusted aides that the withdrawal position wasn't without serious risks.

On March 21, Defense Secretary Lloyd Austin made a surprise visit to Kabul, becoming the first Cabinet member of the new administration to set foot in Afghanistan. He came armed with a message for Ghani: His leadership was weakening the nation's forces. Ghani kept appointing loyalist generals for political purposes, not because they were the right people to lead troops into battle. This is having a "deleterious effect" on Afghanistan's ability to defend itself from the Taliban, Austin told Ghani during a meeting in the Arg, the presidential palace.

Austin also held a meeting with Gen. Scott Miller, the head of American and NATO troops in Afghanistan. During their discussions, Miller revealed to the secretary that he had developed a rudimentary plan for withdrawal after President Donald Trump sought to end U.S. involvement in the war. It outlined how the U.S. needed to move quickly to leave safely—a slow withdrawal would only put American service members in danger. As they left, troops needed to close outposts and bases from Afghanistan's periphery before moving to Kabul, shuttering installations around the capital ahead of the last cargo plane taking off. Austin told Miller the plan had good bones—it just needed some meat.

Blinken traveled to Brussels on March 22 as part of a four-day jaunt. Officially, the secretary went to attend a meeting of NATO foreign ministers, a perfect opportunity to show how the Biden administration valued the alliance and its European partners, unlike the previous administration. Blinken spent much of the time in a "listening session" about how, or if, to wind down the war in Afghanistan.

"Everyone expected that the president was leaning in the direction of a withdrawal at that point," a senior administration official told me; some

European officials specifically referred to Biden's ABC News interview. Yet what Blinken heard loud and clear, mainly from the Germans, British, and Italians, was that the United States should continue the war. The administration shouldn't peg a withdrawal to the Trump-brokered deadline but to actual conditions on the ground. The best outcome, which America's allies felt was still possible, would be for U.S. and NATO troops to leave once Kabul and the Taliban struck a power-sharing deal.

The Germans were the strongest on this point. In February, just a month before the meetings in Brussels, German foreign minister Heiko Maas said, "We don't have to hang on slavishly to the date of the end of April—these things must be linked and when the peace negotiations are concluded successfully, the time will have come to withdraw foreign troops." He made sure to convey that message to Blinken privately, too, but also emphasized that whatever the U.S. decided to do, it had to be in agreement with European allies. Blinken made that promise.

The secretary came away from the meetings convinced. He called Biden after the first day of consultations, March 23, and recommended that he try the European conditions-based approach. Biden didn't commit to anything in the phone call. Instead, he told his longtime staffer to write up the new recommendation in a memo for him to read. The secretary and his team started drafting the document on the plane ride home two days later. Blinken wanted to make sure one key takeaway from his meetings was reflected in the final version that made its way to the White House: the Europeans might not stand with the United States if America withdraws without their buy-in.

There was a competing alternative: Austin recommended that the United States withdraw, but in "gated" stages—multiple waves—that both showed the Taliban that America was serious about leaving and maintained the pressure for a political settlement.

The president responded positively to Blinken's memo, but not to the Pentagon's plan. The State Department heard from the White House that it was authorized to negotiate with the Taliban. "Raise it with them," a senior administration official said about the White House's message, "and see what they say." Blinken wasn't optimistic that a deal could get done, but the chance of a new arrangement was zero percent if he didn't try. It was slightly above that if he did.

Blinken tasked Zalmay Khalilzad with conveying the administration's proposal to the militants. Khalilzad, the Afghan-born American diplomat, had believed for years that he could broker a deal between the Afghan government and the Taliban. He'd spent time in the United States as a high school exchange student and again when he was studying for his doctorate at the University of Chicago. During his last semester there, in April 1978, a coup overthrew Afghan president Mohammed Daoud Khan. The People's Democratic Party of Afghanistan (PDPA) took control of the country, angering Khalilzad. "I was astonished to hear American experts argue that the leaders of the PDPA were just 'agrarian reformers'—not Soviet-backed Communists."

In the spring of 1979, he published an article in the journal *Orbis* under the pseudonym Hannah Negaran (to protect his family's identity back home), in which "I argued that Afghans were likely to rise up against the new Communist government and that the Soviet Union would eventually face a decision: letting the PDPA fall or intervening militarily. At the time, my views were considered alarmist." His work attracted the attention of the Carter administration; an aide to National Security Adviser Zbigniew Brzezinski called Khalilzad in December 1979 asking him to help out on Afghanistan. Khalilzad, now teaching at Columbia University, declined because his family was still in danger back in his home country.

Still, Khalilzad's analysis for several publications made him a star after the Soviet Union invaded Afghanistan. He called it right. In a conversation with Defense Secretary James Schlesinger shortly after Soviet tanks rolled in, Khalilzad said the Afghans would eventually push the invaders out. Schlesinger wasn't so sure. "Once the Soviets are in, they will not go out," he said. Khalilzad had learned early and often in his career that he saw trends others didn't and that often those without his innate expertise were missing the bigger picture.

Khalilzad later served in the State Department under President Ronald Reagan, formulating strategy for how the U.S. should handle the Soviet invasion of Afghanistan. Despite his bona fides, Khalilzad was greeted skeptically by officials in Kabul, especially President Ghani, because many suspected that the envoy wanted eventually to lead the country. But few knew the issues and the players and the sensitivity of the talks to come better than he did. Khalilzad, he himself believed, was the man for the job.

"We want to explore with you something that might look slightly different from what's on paper from Doha" was Khalilzad's main message to the Taliban. To Blinken's surprise, the militants were initially receptive to the talks, though he was never sure if the Taliban were serious about negotiations or were stalling for time. But a few weeks into the negotiations, he heard back from Khalilzad: no deal. "If you go a day beyond May 1, all bets are off," the Taliban told the envoy, a U.S. official recounted to me later. "No wiggle room."

The message was expected but unwelcome. It didn't please Biden when Blinken and Jake Sullivan briefed him of the Taliban's stance. The president told his aides that the choice was even clearer than before: leave or risk more dead American service members. What's more, the president knew where the Defense Department stood. McKenzie, the Central Command chief, said that if any of the twenty-five hundred troops were attacked by the Taliban after May 1, it would only be prudent to surge more military personnel into Afghanistan to protect them.

But Biden knew there was a problem. It was late March. Even if he ordered all thirty-five hundred U.S. troops out of Afghanistan right then, it would be nearly impossible to bring them home safely by the deadline. In conversations with Sullivan, Blinken, and Austin, the president agonized over the well-being of the service members still active in the war.

Biden also showed his frustrations in public. During a March 25 news conference, his first as president, a reporter asked if there would be no U.S. troops in Afghanistan on May 2. "The answer is that it's going to be hard to meet the May 1 deadline. Just in terms of tactical reasons, it's hard to get those troops out," he said. "And if we leave, we're going to do so in a safe and orderly way."

Prodded further, the president said "we will leave"—it was a question of when, not if. Would the United States be in Afghanistan at any point in 2022? "I can't picture that being the case," Biden replied. It was as blunt as Biden had been on the issue.

But even then, others in the administration weren't convinced that America's departure from Afghanistan was a done deal. Many of Biden's top aides—Sullivan, Blinken, Finer, and more—had worked in the Obama administration. They were disillusioned when a president who so clearly wanted to end America's war in that country not only continued it but escalated it. Biden may be saying the twenty-year mission is finally coming to a close, but he hadn't made the decision yet. That made some of the president's top aides nervous.

"There was always the chance of kicking the can," one person told me. "Nobody thought it was a done deal until it was announced."

McCoy, the Marine veteran who led the antiwar Common Defense group, pounced on Biden's comments. *We're getting out of Afghanistan,* he thought to himself. *It's over.*

It wasn't.

McCoy joined a call with the White House on March 30, expecting to hear that Biden had made up his mind. Now he and others would get advice on how they could best defend the president's decision in the press. But Carlyn Reichel, Biden's chief foreign affairs speechwriter and a longtime confidante on matters of global politics, said not to get too excited yet.

"He hasn't made up his mind," she told the group. "We want him to make it just as much as you do."

McCoy was steaming. There was no cohesive messaging coming out of the White House, he thought to himself. It was misleading and scattershot. It was unconscionable to play with the emotions of people who had served in that godforsaken war. He spoke up.

Look, McCoy told Reichel, at some point not making a decision is a decision. The closer we all get to May 1, the less likely Biden can order troops to withdraw, because he won't be able to get them out in time. It sounds like the president is stalling for time until the point he can claim the calendar forced his hand.

No, Reichel replied. It was a major decision, and Biden wanted to make sure he made the right call.

He knows what the right call is, McCoy fired back. "He should make it."

The debate continued within the administration, but it was nearing a conclusion. The threat of dead American sons and daughters sharpened the discussion. Biden wanted to know if there was any chance, twenty years on, that thirty-five hundred American service members could help usher in a democratic Afghanistan. After weeks of discussion, it was clear the president hadn't heard a convincing argument to dissuade him from his yearslong views. "There was never a moment when anyone was able to say with any clarity, 'This is a viable alternative to what you want, Mr. President,'" a U.S. official told me.

Austin and Milley continued to say that it would still be a good idea to keep twenty-five hundred U.S. troops in Afghanistan. But Biden kept pushing back, asking if they could defend themselves while helping to usher in a stable, democratic Afghanistan. Keeping service members safe would be difficult, they'd tell the president, but noted they could likely hold out for five to ten years. "If the situation deteriorates, you can always ask for more troops," Milley said in one of the many briefings.

"Okay, let me think about it," Biden would say after nearly every session.

It helped Biden reach a final decision when key aides expressed the same skepticism he did. Blinken, after failing to bring the Taliban along on the middle option—returned to the position he'd held before the trip to Brussels. "We should leave Afghanistan," he finally recommended. Austin, despite leading an agency that strongly opposed withdrawal, was now on the side of ending America's fight. They both saw the writing on the wall, and the last thing they wanted was news stories about how the president ignored their advice. In Washington, always appearing to be on the boss's side is the coin of the realm.

Sitting in the Oval Office on April 6 at 11:15 a.m., Biden knew how important the next few words he planned to say would be. The president went quiet for a moment during his morning briefing, and Blinken, Austin, and Milley waited as tension filled the room.

"It's time to bring the troops home," Biden said, breaking the silence with an earthquake. Milley wanted to make sure he understood what the president had just said. "I take what you said as a decision, sir," the Joint Chiefs chair said, reverting back to his military training of repeating what a commander had ordered. "Is that correct, Mr. President?"

"Yes," Biden replied. "Bring them home."

"And zero means zero, Mr. President," Milley checked.

"Yes, zero means zero," the president said. "There's an easy way here and there's a reason we still have troops in Afghanistan. The easier call is just to punt," he continued. "I didn't become president to do the easy thing."

"We'll bring you a plan and then execute," Austin said.

No official paper came from the president. He made his decision and expected his team to carry out his will. It was their job to get it done—and to plan for the worst. Biden believed in his decision, but he was made aware of the potential consequences. "Work to mitigate them" was the general order administration officials heard from the White House.

Word began to spread within the administration and out to its allies. Austin gathered Milley, Gen. Frank McKenzie, and Gen. Scott Miller for a meeting. He delivered the news straight to his people, the same people who had fought against the call the president had just made. "This is not the decision that we wanted, but this is what we got. Now we have to execute it," he said.

Wilson, the top U.S. official at the Kabul embassy, didn't hear about the decision until April 12, when Brian McKeon, a senior State Department official who was close to Biden, called to tell him. "This is a big, big, big decision," Wilson replied. Now that a withdrawal had changed from theory to reality, he switched modes to ensuring the embassy could still operate in the new environment.

One thing he thought about: There was a large blimp at the headquarters of NATO's mission in Afghanistan. It provided the U.S. and its allies excellent visibility as to what was going on in the city and its outskirts. Could they keep that capability with the military gone? And what about having a quick reaction force if there's a serious security situation at the embassy? Could someone who's injured or sick be medevaced in time? Wilson's mind raced well after he hung up the phone. He had a job to do.

A day later, Carlyn Reichel called McCoy. "The president has made his decision, and we will be withdrawing our troops over the next several months," she told him. Stunned and surprised, McCoy spilled his coffee. The ultimate goal, she continued, "is President Biden ending the longest war and honoring the service of our troops," adding "there's no military solution to Afghanistan." Instead of fighting further, the United States would seek a diplomatic end to the war.

"Sorry, I got tears in my eyes. This is incredible," McCoy said in response, promising that his organization and others would back the administration.

Reichel then offered the strategic reason behind Biden's forthcoming announcement: "This is a big decision for the United States. It's about reorienting our foreign policy so that we're taking on the real challenges of the future."

My phone buzzed nonstop the day it happened, once the news leaked first to *The Washington Post*, which added the detail that all the troops would leave no later than September 11, 2021—the twentieth anniversary of the terrorist attack. Sources couldn't wait to confirm the decision with me, and others just wanted to dwell in the moment with someone. "Holy shit," a Democratic Senate staffer closely following the process said to me on the phone about the news. "He did it. He actually did it."

Gen. Mark Milley thought it was appropriate to inform former military leaders who served during the twenty-year war. Sitting at his side table, adorned with at least a hundred military challenge coins covered by a circular glass top, he spoke with around ten people, including retired admiral Mike Mullen and retired general Joe Dunford, two men who once sat in the same seat Milley was occupying. "I wanted to be the one to tell you what the president decided," he told both men.

As Biden walked up to the lectern on April 14, the somber look on his face was discernible even with the dark mask he wore. The moment he had long waited for had come, but the occasion didn't call for a celebration—too many had died, too little had been gained.

"I have concluded that it's time to end America's longest war. It's time for American troops to come home," Biden said. "We cannot continue the cycle of extending or expanding our military presence in Afghanistan, hoping to create ideal conditions for the withdrawal and expecting a different result."

Biden acknowledged that he wouldn't have made the deal Trump did, namely giving the Taliban a firm date for America's departure. But it was a deal the American government made, whether he liked it or not, and so as president he had to honor it. Still, withdrawing all of America's troops out of Afghanistan also provided the United States other benefits.

"Rather than return to war with the Taliban, we have to focus on the challenges that are in front of us," such as combating terrorism, competing with China, and curbing the pandemic. "We'll be much more formidable to our adversaries and competitors over the long term if we fight the battles for the next twenty years, not the last twenty."

There was also a personal element to the president's thinking that he didn't let on about until later at Arlington National Cemetery: his late son

Beau. Beau, who served in Iraq from 2008 to 2009, died in 2015 from a brain tumor. He was the apple of his father's eye, and the president's intimate experience with the fears of sending a child into war weighed on his mind throughout the Afghanistan policy review.

"I have trouble these days even showing up at a veterans' cemetery and not thinking of my son Beau, who proudly insisted on putting on that uniform and going with his unit to Iraq and giving up his spot as attorney general of the state of Delaware because he thought it was the right thing to do," he told reporters after his speech, before gesturing to the expanse of white tombstones memorializing other American service members, all glistening in the rain. "Look at them all."

Days later, I was speaking to a senior administration official about the rollout of the decision. It was understandably downbeat, I said, but it also had an air of resignation. It was like a former champion prizefighter coming to grips with the twilight of his career. "Yes," this person replied, "there's no question Afghanistan has humbled us."

The speech Biden wanted to give had to flick at that, the official continued. This was still America, the president wanted to convey, but those in charge had to be realistic about the extent of its power. No prolonged engagement, save for an indefinite influx of hundreds of thousands of troops, diplomatic personnel, and development professionals, was going to change the situation on the ground or turn Afghanistan into a Jeffersonian democracy. If the United States ever had the chance to create such a society, something Biden doubted, it had long passed.

Biden's decision was about ending a war that had outlived its sell-by date, but it was also about accepting America's limits. Better to focus on problems at home and the great powers of China and Russia than on trying to win a war beyond reach.

Biden had already dispatched Blinken and Austin to Brussels to tell European partners and NATO allies of the decision. "That was awkward," a senior U.S. official told me. The final call, after all, was unilateral—Biden's, and Biden's alone.

When word finally made it over to Europe, Jens Stoltenberg, the NATO secretary general, was livid. He told both of the president's aides that he strongly disagreed with the decision and felt that NATO's collective position hadn't been taken into account. The alliance went into Afghanistan after the attacks of 9/11, so Stoltenberg felt they deserved more courtesy than Biden stating that the United States was leaving, compelling allied forces to pack up because they relied so heavily on the Americans.

Both Blinken and Austin said they understood Stoltenberg's stance but that what was done was done. Now was a time to show that the alliance was stronger than any one decision by an American president, and that their collective commitment to Afghanistan would remain ironclad.

Stoltenberg complied. "We went into Afghanistan together, we have adjusted our posture together, and we are united in leaving together," he said at a press conference, flanked by the U.S. secretaries of defense and state. "This is not an easy decision, and it entails risks."

A reporter then asked Austin not how NATO as a whole felt about Biden's move but how America's top brass did. After all, they were adamant in their opposition throughout the entire process. His response hinted at their unease.

"In terms of the input of our senior military, I won't speak for them. What I can tell you is this was an inclusive process, and their voices were heard and their concerns taken into consideration as the president made his decision," the Pentagon chief said. "But now that the decision has been made, I call upon them to lead their forces, to lead their forces through this effort, through this transition. And knowing them all very well, as I do, I have every confidence that they will in fact lead their forces through this effort."

Privately, Blinken felt embarrassed. He agreed with Biden on the need to depart, but he had promised just a month earlier that no decision about the withdrawal would be made without Europe's input. They were consulted throughout the process, but not when the president was prepared to end it. *America was supposed to be back, be our friend,* he heard from fuming counterparts. It was not the foreign policy he'd hoped to run.

Maybe there was more homework the administration had to do on engaging with allies, Blinken told his aides.

Ross Wilson, the senior-most U.S. diplomat in Afghanistan, was a world away from the big-think issues of foreign policy. He had an immediate problem: a staff of people who soon might not be safe working in Kabul.

His first conversations with counterparts back at the State Department in D.C. about embassy security came on April 15, a day after Biden's speech. There were some people who didn't physically need to be at the embassy to perform their duties. Maybe it was best to get them far away from the Afghan capital before the situation got worse. The word from Washington came back: agreed.

On April 27, the mission in Kabul went on "ordered departure" status. That meant anyone who could and wanted to leave was welcome to do so. Wilson also had the authority to send someone away who wanted to stay if he felt their presence wasn't needed. Dozens of people left over the next few days, some of them scheduling their return flights. Once the embassy got word that some employees planned to return to Kabul, a message was sent to them individually: You're not coming back here. This is the beginning of the end.

Chapter 4

"More of Everything Is Not a Strategy"

April—May 2021

There's a story Joe Biden likes to tell anytime he speaks to an audience about Israel.

It's 1948, a matter of days before Israel's founding and three years after the end of World War II. Five-year-old Joey Biden is at the dinner table with his family, listening to his Catholic father wonder aloud why some people wouldn't want to recognize the state of Israel. That's when his dad uttered the words "Never again," making clear to young Joey that the existence of Israel was crucial to preventing another Holocaust.

Later, in 1973, during his first overseas trip as a senator from Delaware, the thirty-year-old Biden met with then Israeli prime minister Golda Meir. In their hour-long encounter, she chain-smoked while describing all the security threats her nation faced, using maps as aids, and detailed the devastation of the Six-Day War.

"She painted a bleak, bleak picture—scared the hell out of me, quite frankly, about the odds," Biden recounted over forty years later as vice president at the 67th Annual Israeli Independence Day Celebration in Washington, D.C. "She said, 'Senator, you look so worried.' I said, 'Well, my God, Madam Prime Minister,' and I turned to look at her. I said, 'The picture you paint.' She said, 'Oh, don't worry . . . we have a secret weapon in our conflict with the Arabs. You see, we have no place else to go.'"

The Arab–Israeli War started that same year. More than 2,500 Israelis were killed and another 7,500 were injured in the three-week fight that drew the United States in to defend its ally.

Biden would go on to say that his time with Meir was "one of the most consequential meetings I've ever had in my life."

With the words of his father and Meir echoing in his ears, Biden turned into a pro-Israel force in the Senate.

During the Reagan administration, Biden firmly opposed the sale of advanced weapons like F-15 warplanes to Saudi Arabia, arguing it would undercut Israel's military advantage in the region. "The Israeli Government now has recognized that Israel's military superiority and military-technology edge would be dangerously eroded by the arms package and could not be offset by any likely compensatory measures," he wrote in a 1981 *New York Times* op-ed.

Then, in June 1982, Biden joined colleagues for what *The New York Times* described as "a highly emotional confrontation" with then Israeli prime minister Menachem Begin in a closed session of the Senate Foreign Relations Committee. Israel had just invaded Lebanon—a maneuver known as "Operation Peace for Galilee"—to root out Palestinian guerrillas who attacked Israel from the country. American lawmakers weren't happy about it and were primed tell Begin off.

Except one senator. Biden said he wasn't critical of the Lebanon policy, with Begin later telling Israeli journalists the Delaware senator had "delivered a very impassioned speech . . . and he actually supported Operation Peace for the Galilee."

According to Begin, Biden "said he would go even further than Israel, adding that he'd forcefully fend off anyone who sought to invade his country, even if that meant killing women or children." The Israeli premier added, "I disassociated myself from these remarks. . . . According to our values, it is forbidden to hurt women and children, even in war."

Nearly eighteen thousand people were killed and another thirty thousand wounded in the invasion.

Biden did push back against Begin about one thing: settlements. The young lawmaker said if Israel continued to allow Israeli Jews to dispossess Palestinians of their homes, rancor in the U.S. toward Israel was likely to grow.

This would be a theme Biden returned to often in his career. Despite his rock-ribbed support for Israel's security, he felt settlements made the prospects of peace less likely, ruined Israel's image, and harmed Palestinians.

The issue of arms sales to Arab states in the Middle East came up again in 1986, reigniting debates about whether or not to block them so Israel could remain the predominant military force in the region. Biden, with a stern look and an impassioned voice, came to Israel's defense on the Senate floor.

"It's about time we stop . . . apologizing for our support for Israel, there's no apology to be made. None. It is the best three-billion-dollar investment we make," he said of the annual aid package to the country. "Were there not an Israel, the United States of America would have to invent an Israel to protect her interests in the region."

Biden's support continued. In the fall of 1991, President George H. W. Bush sought to put conditions on $10 billion in loan guarantees the United States was giving Israel to help the country welcome an influx of immigrants from the Soviet Union. To get the money, Israel would have to agree to end its settlements in Palestinian territories. Biden cosponsored a bill to make the assistance unconditional.

The following year, he gave a speech at the annual conference of the American Israel Public Affairs Committee (AIPAC)—a powerful pro-Israel group—to say that the U.S. shouldn't pressure Israel to make peace with Palestinians or other neighboring nations.

"We are now at the 'peace table,' quote unquote, with unclean hands, because there is a feeling abroad in this administration, among some in Congress, that somehow we owe an obligation to our Arab brethren to have Israel, quote, 'be reasonable,'" he said, claiming it was an "absurd notion that publicly vilifying Israel will somehow change its policy."

Biden's Israel support throughout his career was so fierce that he's said on more than one occasion: "I am a Zionist." Indeed, he believes you don't have to be a Jew to be a Zionist. Zionism is the ideology that holds that Judaism is a nationality as well as a religion, and that Jews deserve their own state in their ancestral homeland, Israel.

Biden tempered his outright support for Israel while serving as President Obama's number two. That had less to do with an evolution in his thinking and more to do with deferring to his boss's policy preferences, those who know him told me. Obama wasn't anti-Israel by any means, but he often took positions that irked the country's government—especially Prime Minister Benjamin "Bibi" Netanyahu—including seeking a nuclear deal with Iran, which the premier vehemently opposed.

That was awkward for Biden, who by then had a decades-long relationship with Netanyahu. He often got caught in the middle as the president and Netanyahu jousted, but he still came away with the reputation of being the "good cop" to Obama's "bad cop" on Israel.

It got tough for Biden almost right from the start.

Biden visited Israel on March 9, 2010, to reassure the country that it still had a partner in the United States and to restart peace talks between Israelis and Palestinians.

In a joint address, Netanyahu told the vice president that Israel had planted a circle of trees in Jerusalem as a "tribute" to Biden's mother, alongside a grove of trees rooted by foreign leaders to symbolize their friendship with Israel. Biden was touched. "My love for your country was watered by this Irish lady who was proudest of me when I was working with and for the security of Israel, so it's a great honor," he said.

But the trip turned sour when, just a few hours later, the Israeli government announced the construction of sixteen hundred new homes for Jews in East Jerusalem.

In 1948, Jerusalem—which both Israelis and Palestinians claim as their capital—was divided, with Israel controlling the western half and Jordan the eastern. But in 1967, after the Six-Day War, Israel controversially annexed East Jerusalem and since then has evicted some of the Arabs living there, making way for Israeli settlers.

The international community doesn't accept East Jerusalem as part of Israel, though, and views this settlement activity as detrimental to peace efforts. That was also the U.S. position at the time. So the Israeli government announcing the settlements while Biden was in the country, in part to try to restart peace talks, seemed like a slap in the face.

Netanyahu later claimed he knew nothing of the announcement, which was made by his Interior Ministry, but Biden had already taken offense. People who knew him at the time said the vice president was humiliated.

Biden released a statement expressing his displeasure that same day. "I condemn the decision by the government of Israel to advance planning for new housing units in East Jerusalem," he said. "The substance and timing of the announcement, particularly with the launching of proximity talks, is precisely the kind of step that undermines the trust we need right now and runs counter to the constructive discussions that I've had here in Israel." He continued, "Unilateral action taken by either party cannot prejudge the outcome of negotiations on permanent status issues."

Biden's aides recommended that he skip a dinner with Netanyahu, but the vice president said it was better he attend and discuss the matter delicately and privately with the Israeli premier.

That became a recurring theme during Biden's stint as Barack Obama's vice president. "Biden reserved his most strident criticism for Netanyahu for behind the scenes," an unnamed source close to Biden told *The Times of Israel* in 2020. "There was a lot less public drama involving Biden."

Still, Netanyahu knew Biden was a staunch supporter of Israel, even if they disagreed on a lot, which kept the vice president in the premier's good graces. "I hope you feel at home here in Israel because the people of Israel consider the Biden family part of our family," Netanyahu told Biden on his 2016 visit to Israel. "You're part of our mishpucha," he said, using the Hebrew word for "family."

The vice president responded with another story he tells often. Years after he and the Israeli leader became friends, Biden sent him a signed picture that jokingly read: "Bibi, I don't agree with a damn thing you say, but I love you."

Considering his long and close relationship with Netanyahu, it would have been safe to assume that once he became president, Biden would unapologetically stand by Israelis during a flare-up with Palestinians. No matter what was going on, Biden would drop all other important things and help Jerusalem as bombs and rockets traversed the skies between Israel and Gaza. That, after all, had been Biden's record.

But given a chance to act in the first big Israel drama of his presidency, Biden shrunk, contrary to how he'd dealt with regional violence in years past. It was indicative of a president who subdued his impulses in service of an American foreign policy that wouldn't get caught up in the smaller stuff.

It was a moment that showed how the old Biden had started to morph into President Biden. The United States had been dragged into the Middle East too many times before. There were bigger problems to solve than the intractable conflict roiling relations between Israelis and Palestinians. The U.S. could help from the sidelines without having to get directly involved. That path led only to lost time and effort.

The root of the crisis began when Israeli settlers and police clashed with Palestinian residents of the occupied East Jerusalem neighborhood of Sheikh Jarrah. Judicial rulings, prompted by U.S.-based settler organizations, led to the forced expulsion of eight Palestinian families from their homes. Palestinians from the neighborhood and surrounding areas flocked to Sheikh Jarrah to stage sit-ins and protests, clashing violently with Israeli authorities, who pushed to clear the areas.

Hundreds would be injured, some so badly they needed to be rushed to the hospital, inflaming tensions that only grew because of the timing: it was the month of Ramadan. Palestinians in East Jerusalem liked to gather outside the Old City's Damascus Gate to break the fast, but police put up barricades and other obstacles to stop the celebrations.

Then it got worse. A far-right Israeli group, Lehava, sent armed men through the streets of Palestinian neighborhoods on April 22. "Death to Arabs" rang out as they approached the Damascus Gate. Another fight soon followed—bottles and rocks flew from the side of the Israeli settlers and police to the Palestinians, and vice versa. More than a hundred Palestinians and twenty police officers were injured.

The crisis only grew. Two days after the march, thirty-five rockets from Gaza screamed into Israel, one of the largest regional violence spikes in months. Hamas, the terrorist group that controls Gaza, didn't launch the projectiles—it was another militant group—but Israel still responded ferociously by attacking Hamas positions in the Gaza Strip with fighter jets and attack helicopters.

The Biden administration didn't know how to react to the escalating violence, but they needed a strategy fast. Jake Sullivan was set to meet with Meir Ben-Shabbat, his counterpart, the Israeli national security adviser, on April 27. The thinking among the president's advisers was *this too shall pass*. The Democratic politics of U.S.–Israel ties were so fraught—with progressives wanting more support for Palestinian rights, and Biden's history on the issue so clear—that it made sense to show unyielding support for Israel at this time. Soon the skirmishes would go away and no damage would have been done to the relationship.

"The two sides also shared concerns about recent violent confrontations in Jerusalem and the U.S. officials welcomed Israel's recent calls for calm," the White House said in a statement after their meeting in Washington.

Even as clashes continued, the United States chose to mostly stay out of it. There were private conversations with Israeli and Palestinian counterparts, but other than that, the decision from the Oval Office was to monitor, not get involved. "We're going to let this go by," a U.S. official told me at the time.

The tipping point came on May 7, a Friday night and the last day of Ramadan. Israeli police moved in on thousands of worshippers at the al-Aqsa mosque, one of the holiest sites in Islam and Judaism; Jews call it the Temple Mount. The stun guns and grenades, which officials claimed they needed to use to stop the Palestinians from rioting, led to 163 injuries. The Palestinians, a mix of young and old celebrating the end of the holy month, fought back, injuring 17 Israeli police officers. As gunfire filled the night sky with noise and light, the mosque's loudspeaker called for calm: "Police must immediately stop firing stun grenades at worshippers, and the youth must calm down and be quiet!"

It was now undeniable that the weekslong clashes were growing in size, leading regional leaders to speak up. The ailing head of the Palestinian Authority, Mahmoud Abbas, said he held Israel "responsible for the dangerous developments and sinful attacks." Back in Washington, D.C., though, the administration was still treating the fighting as mainly a settler-versus-evictee issue. "It is critical to avoid unilateral steps that would exacerbate tensions or take us further away from peace, and that would include evictions, settlement activity, and home demolitions," State Department spokesperson Jalina Porter said on the day of the violence outside the mosque.

What to do? In the Oval Office, Sullivan recounted to the president that in 2012, then secretary of state Hillary Clinton traveled to Jerusalem and Egypt to broker a cease-fire between Hamas and Israel during a similar uptick in violence. The trip was visible, but the discussions were private. Speaking to the key players behind closed doors, and not stating key positions early in public, was the best way to stop the fighting before it spiraled out of control.

Biden was receptive to his national security adviser's advice. It fit his style perfectly: Biden loved nothing more than a one-on-one chat to get stuff done. Plus, the president told Sullivan, Netanyahu wasn't a man who wanted dirty laundry aired in public. The only way he had found success negotiating with the Israeli leader was methodically and quietly. If it worked in the past, it would work now.

In the meantime, Biden agreed that it made sense for U.S. officials throughout the government to contact their counterparts and deliver the same message: cool it. The highest-ranking person to make a call right now should be Sullivan, Biden said. Reach out to Ben-Shabbat, he ordered, and deliver the warning.

On their May 9 call, Sullivan expressed his "serious concerns" about the evictions, adding that "the launching of rocket attacks and incendiary balloons from Gaza towards Israel is unacceptable and must be condemned." One more thing: the U.S. encourages Israel "to pursue appropriate measures" to ensure that the celebrations for Jerusalem Day—which commemorates the unification of East and West Jerusalem following the 1967 war—could proceed without any problems.

But there would soon be problems—big ones.

Israeli police escalated their efforts to remove Palestinians from the area surrounding the mosque. They entered the holy grounds around 8:00 a.m. on May 10, once again carrying stun grenades and rubber bullets, faced by Palestinians armed with nothing but stones. It was the most brutal day of skirmishes yet. Around 330 Palestinians were injured, 250 of them hospitalized for their wounds. One person had been shot in the head with a rubber bullet, endangering their life. More than twenty Israeli police officers suffered injuries of their own.

Hamas took advantage of the mayhem. The group gave Israel an ultimatum to remove officials from the al-Aqsa mosque and Sheikh Jarrah that day. The government didn't give in to what was clearly a performative demand so that Hamas had an excuse to unleash hell. Minutes after the ultimatum passed on May 10, Hamas launched at least 150 rockets into

Israel, with one striking Jerusalem for the first time in seven years. Israel responded with thunderous airstrikes, killing twenty Palestinians, including nine children, per Palestinian authorities.

"We will not tolerate attacks on our territory, on our capital, on our citizens and on our soldiers. Whoever attacks us will pay a heavy price," Netanyahu said.

It was officially war.

Back at the White House, top administration officials realized the more hands-off approach hadn't worked. "We felt we had it under control until the rockets started," one of them told me.

Someone in close contact with senior U.S. figures couldn't believe the United States hadn't jumped in more forcefully and sooner. "They weren't prepared for this, exactly," this person told me on the phone. "They were kind of asleep at the switch until pretty late."

Why? I asked. Two reasons, the person responded, clearly angry: "They came in determined not to make the Middle East an issue, and we're really not going to get involved in Israel–Palestine." And the second reason? Look at who's on the National Security Council under Sullivan, they said. Brett McGurk, the top Middle East aide, and his deputy, Barbara Leaf, are experts in the Gulf. They're not experts on the Israeli–Palestinian issue. They're aware of the stakes, sure, but it's simply not a priority for them. They dismissed the growing crisis as a typical escalation in the decades-long conflict.

"They screwed up the run-up to this," the person concluded.

All right, Sullivan asked his team, *what are we going to do now?*

It was Tuesday, May 11, and the news out of the Middle East was only getting worse. A thirteen-story residential building in Gaza collapsed following an Israeli airstrike, which came in retaliation for rockets launched by Hamas and Islamic Jihad. The ground right off the eastern Mediterranean shook as explosives hit their targets and the sky lit up with the red-orange glow of fire. That day alone, thirty-two Palestinians and three Israelis died. It was the worst fighting seen in the region since the 2014 Israel–Hamas war in Gaza.

The decision came: It was time to follow a version of the president's plan. Telling Israel—the far stronger power—to calm down publicly would embarrass Netanyahu and open Biden to questions about whether he was pro-Israel enough. It was best, for the conflict and for politics, for the president to speak to Netanyahu privately. That way he could deliver a stern message that the violence needed to end before it got any worse. Meanwhile, the public messaging in readouts would state America's support for Israel. A little vinegar on the phone, honey in open statements.

The question was whether Netanyahu would listen. He had been in charge of Israel for years and knew that, eventually, the United States would look the other way if he didn't go too far in attacking Palestinians. But Netanyahu also didn't want to start off on the wrong foot with the new administration led by his longtime friend. Biden guessed that's how Netanyahu would be feeling and pushed on that any chance he got.

The two men spoke on May 12, two days into the most dangerous phase of the crisis. Biden told Netanyahu that the U.S. would stand with Jerusalem at this time. But, Biden pressed, if there's a chance to de-escalate, take it. In the meantime, both countries would remain in close contact as the fighting raged.

What the public saw, though, was a White House readout that said the president expressed "his unwavering support for Israel's security." Blinken, meanwhile, spoke to Abbas. The State Department said in a release that it "condemned the rocket attacks and emphasized the need to de-escalate tensions and bring the current violence to an end."

Speaking to reporters later that day, Biden said that his call with Netanyahu had gone well and that Israel needed to defend itself from "thousands of rockets"—a far higher number than were actually shot at Israel. The president still sounded upbeat: "My expectation and hope is that this will be closing down sooner than later."

Progressives were furious. "What the fuck," a left-leaning U.S. official told me in an interview at the time. "Here we go again." Biden was going to abandon standing up for human rights—those of the Palestinians—in order to stand more closely to Israel, this person contested. "This administration promised us change. This is more of the same." Progressives, this person said with an unmistakable break in their voice, were going to fight back.

A day after the Biden–Netanyahu chat, Rep. Rashida Tlaib, a Democrat from Michigan and the first Palestinian American in Congress, gave an impassioned speech on the House floor. Palestinians in Gaza and the West Bank were suffering, she said; that should be enough to end America's unconditional support for Israel at times like these.

"When I see the images and videos of destruction and death in Palestine, all I hear are the children screaming from pure fear and terror," she said, holding back tears. She read a statement from a Palestinian mother about putting her kids to bed during the bombings, which "broke me a little more because . . . my country's policies and funding will deny this mother's right to see her own children live without fear and to grow old without painful trauma and violence."

Then Sen. Bernie Sanders, the irascible Vermont independent who dragged the Democratic Party further to the left, piled on. A Jewish man, Sanders had long felt that the United States defended Israel too strongly when it used its overwhelming power to kill unarmed Palestinians. He was also trying to be the standard-bearer of a progressive foreign policy, one that centered on promoting human rights and moving away from relationships with strongmen-led governments.

Watching the events unfold in the news, Sanders wrote up his thoughts for a *New York Times* op-ed that captured the attention of official Washington—and the White House.

"In this moment of crisis, the United States should be urging an immediate cease-fire. We should also understand that, while Hamas firing rockets into Israeli communities is absolutely unacceptable, today's conflict did not begin with those rockets," he wrote on May 14, citing the controversy over the evictions in Sheikh Jarrah. "Further, we have seen Benjamin Netanyahu's government work to marginalize and demonize Palestinian citizens of Israel, pursue settlement policies designed to foreclose the possibility of a two-state solution and pass laws that entrench systemic inequality between Jewish and Palestinian citizens of Israel.

"None of this excuses the attacks by Hamas, which were an attempt to exploit the unrest in Jerusalem, or the failures of the corrupt and ineffective Palestinian Authority, which recently postponed long-overdue elections. But the fact of the matter is that Israel remains the one sovereign authority in the land of Israel and Palestine, and rather than preparing for peace and justice, it has been entrenching its unequal and undemocratic control," Sanders continued.

Something had clearly changed. For decades, lawmakers from both parties had steadfastly supported Israel in tough times. No one was saying they didn't back Israel or its right to defend itself, but the progressives *were* saying that support for Israel shouldn't come at the expense of Palestinian lives. That shift had come after years of Israel failing to seek a two-state solution and the introduction of more progressives in Congress.

The White House could no longer count on Democrats supporting their policy.

The administration's tone changed. Biden spoke to Netanyahu again, mostly rehashing what he had said three days earlier. This time, though, there was a new element: the United States had to stand with Palestinians too. "The President noted that this current period of conflict has tragically claimed the lives of Israeli and Palestinian civilians, including children," the White House said in a statement. "He expressed his support for steps to enable the Palestinian people to enjoy the dignity, security, freedom, and economic opportunity that they deserve and affirmed his support for a two-state solution."

"Well that's different," the same progressive told me in a text message. "Wasn't really expecting that."

Progressives didn't let up. They had the administration on the ropes. Rep. Alexandria Ocasio-Cortez, the prominent leftist from New York City, tweeted: "Apartheid states aren't democracies." Others from the infamous "Squad" in the House, including Tlaib, joined in support of her statement.

And in a shock, Sen. Robert Menendez, the New Jersey Democrat and Senate Foreign Relations Committee chief known for his staunch and unflinching support for Israel, said he was "deeply troubled" by what he was seeing—reports of dead innocents in Gaza as well as the bombing and destruction of a building that housed international media.

At the same time the administration was battling its own party, it was also battling perceptions about what it is to care about the Israeli–Palestinian conflict. John Kerry, when he was Barack Obama's secretary of state, rushed to the Middle East to broker a cease-fire in the 2014 Israel–Hamas war in Gaza. Once peace was reached, it became an article of faith in Washington that a secretary of state, or at least a top official, must follow Kerry's strategy when the next crisis arose.

But no top official went over. Instead, the president sent Hady Amr, the deputy assistant secretary of state for Israeli and Palestinian affairs. He arrived in Tel Aviv on May 14, set to meet with Israeli and Palestinian officials. Blinken didn't follow behind him. "If Blinken had gone [to the region], it actually would've slowed things down," said Dennis Ross, a distinguished fellow at the Washington Institute for Near East Policy.

There was an immediate and a longer-term reason, officials told me. The immediate issue was that sending a high-level official would increase the volume on what to that point was a quiet diplomatic approach. Expectations would be raised, increasing the political costs of a senior official returning home from the region empty-handed. Better to have Amr, a respected but low-profile State aide, do the dirty work and report back to Washington.

And then there was the grander thinking behind keeping top officials stateside: the administration didn't want to get bogged down in the Middle East. Kerry saw much of his time and his priorities derailed when he was secretary of state as he struggled against the weight of history in the Israeli–Palestinian conflict. Wading deeper into that mess would only complicate dealing with the pandemic, confronting Russia and China, and curbing climate change. The United States had spent too much time on the Middle East and on a peace process with little chance of success, many officials believed. If there was a way to make progress, then take it. But if no opening presented itself—and the middle of a war certainly wasn't an opening—it was best to avoid the quagmire.

At least one administration official, though, wished that Amr, as capable as he was, had some backup. Or as one official told me, "We should've been more hard out there."

Biden's rhetoric with Netanyahu did get tougher. On a May 17 call, he told the prime minister to do whatever he could to safeguard civilians as Israel's bombs continued to drop in Gaza in retaliation for rockets going the other way. He wanted a cease-fire, Biden reiterated, and he wanted it as soon as possible.

The comments, though, didn't seem to match the administration's actions. The United Nations Security Council met that same day to discuss approving a joint statement calling for a cease-fire. It was the third such meeting of the body on that issue, and for the third straight time the U.S. used its veto power to sink the measure. Progressives and human rights activists condemned the administration, saying Biden was just trying to protect Israel at the expense of suffering Palestinians.

Biden and his team, though, simply didn't want to embarrass Israel in public and in such a multinational way—arguably harsher than if the U.S. put out a critical statement on its own. "This was coming from the top," someone familiar with the administration's thinking told me at the time, even though the president and his chief advisers knew it was a bad look. The ends, which looked like a cease-fire that was painstakingly coming together, justified the means.

Democrats in Congress still weren't having it and sought more ways to express their disapproval. Rep. Gregory Meeks, the New York Democrat who chaired the House Foreign Affairs Committee, told members of his panel in a virtual session that he would send a letter to delay the impending passing of a $735 million arms deal for Israel. And during a May 18 visit to Detroit, where Biden went to tout his "Made in America" initiative at Ford Motor Company, the president found himself speaking to Tlaib on the tarmac for eight minutes.

Neither Biden nor Tlaib have yet detailed the true contents of that conversation. But what has leaked out from their aides is that Tlaib said Palestinian rights weren't something that could be easily traded as some part of an eventual deal to stop the fighting. Biden agreed, saying it was important for the United States to stand by Israel, and that he would do everything possible to improve the lives of Palestinians. But Hamas firing rockets helped no one, including Palestinians, he told the lawmaker, the eldest of fourteen kids of Palestinian immigrants, whose grandmother still lived in the region.

Michigan Democrat Rep. Debbie Dingell told *The New York Times* that the chat was "an important dialogue" and "a very compassionate honest discussion," but no more than that. "The president doesn't deal with these kinds of issues in public, and he doesn't negotiate in public." In a speech later that day, Biden praised Tlaib: "I admire your intellect, I admire your passion, and I admire your concern for so many other people," he said. "From my heart, I pray that your grandmom and family are well. I promise you, I'll do everything to see that they are."

It was vintage Biden: speaking candidly but kindly in private, making his own points but hearing the other side, and making commitments to find common ground. That was how Biden was conducting diplomacy with Netanyahu, and it was how he was dealing with his left flank at home.

• • •

If Biden acted with a sense of confidence in Detroit, Jake Sullivan was betraying the administration's nerves about the situation back in Washington. He met with a roundtable of experts at the White House about what to do. But first, he wanted to address some criticisms. The United States has tried to stop the flare-up, he said, putting pressure on the government in Jerusalem to stop the far-right parade that ended at the Damascus Gate. And while the U.S. stood by Israel, the president and his team weren't indifferent to the plight of Palestinians. "Of course we care about the people in Gaza and all Palestinians," Sullivan told the group, according to someone who attended the meeting. But he echoed the president: stop the killing first.

Then Sullivan, flanked by McGurk, Leaf, and his deputy, Jon Finer, spoke candidly about next steps. "It was a genuine conversation about what we do from here," another attendee told me. "It wasn't just a BS conversation about what they'd already done.... There was a recognition that they understood the administration wasn't dealing with the issue as they should have."

Collectively, the group said Biden's approach was generally working—better to keep the diplomacy private but increase the public pressure on Israel, as the stronger party, to agree to a cease-fire. Leverage Egypt on getting Hamas to accept.

Then the aperture opened in the conversation: What was the general policy for the region? Sullivan expressed the administration's thinking: minimize violence and "thread the needle" on the contradictions between promoting human rights and interests. Interests were paramount—improve America's relations with regional partners and ensure Israel's safety. But when there was room to maneuver, push partners to safeguard human rights and help civil society and minorities wherever possible.

One of the attendees left the meeting with this general takeaway: "You can lay out principles to guide you, but then you have problems that need to be solved. This is a group that's really geared to solving problems."

• • •

Pressure from congressional Democrats kept growing. The same day as Biden's talk with Tlaib in Detroit and Sullivan's meeting, Speaker of the House Nancy Pelosi called for a cease-fire. After some throat clearing about standing with Israel and how Hamas launched thousands of missiles, she said that the week of fighting made it "even more apparent that a cease-fire is necessary. There must be a serious effort on the part of both parties to end the violence and respect the rights of both the Israeli and Palestinian people."

Instead of being upset by Pelosi's comments, the White House and State Department were pleased. The pressure was no longer coming just from progressives but from Democratic leadership, at a time when Israel already was losing favor with the party. Biden could leverage Pelosi's statement to tell Netanyahu: "See, Bibi? It's time to stop this or you'll have only Republicans in Congress to talk to."

The next day, Biden was much more frank on the phone with Netanyahu, telling him that he expected the Israeli leaders to offer a plan to reach a cease-fire immediately. The White House put out a statement reflecting the conversation, showing that America's tone had turned from understanding Israel's defensive needs to urging the ally to end the bloodshed.

Perhaps Biden knew what was coming that day. In the House, Tlaib and Ocasio-Cortez joined a resolution to block the sale of the $735 million weapons package to Israel, which included a kit that turned so-called "dumb" bombs into precision-guided explosives. Selling that capability to Israel, especially after the events of the last week, seemed irresponsible to the Democratic lawmakers.

"The harsh truth is that these weapons are being sold by the United States to Israel with the clear understanding that the vast majority of them will be used to bomb Gaza. Approving this sale now, while failing to even try to use it as leverage for a ceasefire, sends a clear message to the world—the U.S. is not interested in peace, and does not care about the human rights and lives of Palestinians. You cannot claim to support human rights and peace on Earth and continue to back the extremist Netanyahu regime, it's that simple," Tlaib said at the time. Sanders the next day introduced a similar resolution in the Senate.

Israel, which had long had bipartisan support in both chambers, was watching its typical backing from the left wane in real time. And it had witnessed Biden, a decades-long supporter of the country, be more forceful in his criticism than ever. How much that contributed to the Israeli government accepting a cease-fire proposal on May 20—after eleven days of fighting that led to 232 Palestinians and 12 Israelis killed—remains unclear. But speak to progressives and they'll say their pressure saved lives.

"Progressives deserve a little credit for the cease-fire," Ben Rhodes, the National Security Action leader, told me at the time. "Biden was looking over his left shoulder and told Netanyahu, 'You have to move on this.'"

How the May 20 cease-fire came to be was an early window into how the Biden administration would handle a crisis: stay involved, stay quiet, stay the course—and keep an eye on the prize.

Officials made more than eighty calls to world leaders during the eleven days of fighting; Blinken made fifteen of them. The secretary decided that traveling to Europe for talks about the Arctic and climate change, and then a sit-down with his Russian counterpart ahead of Biden's summit with Vladimir Putin, was more important than jetting to the Middle East.

Part of that decision was fear: it was better not to go at all than to go all-in and potentially come home empty-handed. The administration voted with its feet, staying out of the region in favor of renewing ties with European allies to fend off the menace from Moscow.

The other takeaway is how small Biden and his team made the U.S.–Israel relationship, even when Biden had long made it a big part of his statesmanship. Officials said that was by design. "I find that in the current moment in Washington, although it's been true for a long time, the answer is to do more. Everyone wants more, more, we should be doing more," a senior State Department official told me. "Of course, more of everything is not a strategy."

This was an administration that didn't feel the need to "go big" solely for the showmanship. It was about getting results, even if the most effective play—in the administration's view—didn't win it any plaudits. Gone were the days of big boasts with little to show for them, a criticism Biden administration officials had of both the Obama and Trump eras. Better to underpromise and overdeliver.

Publicly, Biden said he was still pushing for the big deal. "There is no shift in my commitment and the commitment to the security of Israel, period. No shift. Not at all. But I'll tell you what there is a shift in: The shift is that we have to—we still need a two-state solution. It is the only answer. The only answer." Fine, people at the time told me. That's how he may feel. But how much time and interest has he put into brokering a two-state solution? Very little, or as an administration official put it: "Not a fucking second of effort."

The Biden administration was squaring the circle of going small on peripheral problems *and* trying to repair America's alliances *and* deter Russia *and* confront China across multiple domains. Biden, talking to *The New York Times*'s David Brooks on May 20, the day of the cease-fire, seemed to struggle with it. "The risk is not trying to go big," he said in the interview, speaking nominally about China but really his approach to the presidency. "If we stay small, I don't know how we change our international status and competitive capacity."

Four months into his first term, Biden seemed to be operating from a playbook developed over decades in the foreign policy world: core issues that challenge the world order or America's leadership get his full effort. Everything else, the United States will help if it can.

Biden would call that a realistic approach to foreign policy. Others perceived Biden as not taking his own advice, choosing not to "go big." As he spoke to Brooks, Biden was preparing to meet one of those people who thought the United States couldn't go big anymore—Putin—in Geneva.

Chapter 5

Frenemies

May–July 2021

If there was a theme to Joe Biden's early presidency, it was that the United States needed to show that its democracy could still deliver for its people. On the international stage, Biden went further: democracies needed to band together to deliver for the world. That meant steeling the liberal world order and curbing China's growing influence in the process. But it also meant keeping an increasingly aggressive Russia at bay.

Biden's long political career showed that the U.S. could find ways to cooperate with great powers. He ran for the Senate the same year President Richard Nixon visited China and Communist leader Mao Tse-tung, a face-to-face harbinger of the détente to come. And in Congress, Biden spent years working with Soviet counterparts to strike arms-control pacts even as the Cold War lingered. Countries didn't have to see eye to eye on everything to get stuff done, Biden believed.

Even dictators were willing to make deals. With Russian president Dmitri Medvedev, who was a puppet of the real leader, Vladimir Putin, Barack Obama was able to sign the New START arms-control agreement in 2010 to limit the number of deployable nuclear missiles and warheads. And with China's Xi Jinping, Obama announced, five years later, an "understanding" about how both nations would behave in cyberspace.

Biden also believed he could build rapport with strongmen. A prerequisite would be that he and his counterparts understood where the other was coming from. In 2011, then Vice President Biden met with Putin at the Kremlin. At one point, he got really close to the Russian's face and said, "I looked in your eyes and I don't think you have a soul." Putin shot back: "We understand one another."

Two years later, during a 2013 visit to China, Biden spoke about his "friendship" with Xi. "To strengthen dialogue and cooperation is the only right choice facing both countries. . . . Complex relationships call for sustained, high-level engagement," he said. "This new relationship requires practical cooperation to deliver concrete results."

Personal relationships were one thing. But the actions of leaders form the boundaries of a professional relationship. After Russia's invasion of Ukraine's Crimean Peninsula in 2014, its interference in the 2016 presidential election, and attempts to kill double agents and dissidents, the old Democratic hope of a "reset" with the country was dead. Now most in the Biden administration believed Russia needed to know that the West would unite against Moscow if Putin continued his provocations.

For Biden, Secretary of State Antony Blinken, and National Security Adviser Jake Sullivan, only reinvigorated alliances—and a stronger NATO—could lower Russia on the list of things to worry about. Better to focus on China, climate change, domestic economic renewal, and finally stamping out the COVID virus. After all, the United States and Russia extended the New START nuclear treaty in January—clearly, Russia could be reasoned with.

To show good faith, the White House ordered the Pentagon to delay a hypersonic missile test planned for about a week before Biden and Putin were to meet. It was important to send a signal that tensions really could be cooled down. The weapon could be tested later anyway. It was costless to postpone the launch, the White House thought, despite the pushback from the Pentagon.

Before going toe-to-toe with Putin, Biden needed to rebuild relationships with America's European allies. His first trip, then, had to be across the Atlantic. A meeting with the G7, a group of the world's top economies that once included Russia in an eight-nation configuration until it was expelled over Crimea, proved the perfect opportunity. Then the president would go to NATO headquarters in Brussels. Once there, he would reaffirm America's commitment to the Article 5 principle that an attack on one is an attack on all—a principle former president Donald Trump initially refused to support. Only after the U.S. strengthened its alliances in those June meetings would Biden have a one-on-one with Putin in Switzerland. There would be only two days between the NATO and Putin gatherings.

"This is an opportunity for democracies to show they can meet the challenges that people are facing—meet them and defeat them," a senior administration official told me ahead of the trip.

But the subtext was clear: Putin needed to know that he didn't face an America that was alone, isolated, declining. The United States still had friends and influence, and was blessed with immense power. Biden would rally the West against Russia if Putin crossed the figurative and literal line.

"Every component of the trip, including the timing, was intentional," a senior Biden administration official told me. It was important not to go too early because of the pandemic. The U.S. needed to show that it could get its own house in order, the official asserted, before going on a foreign excursion. In March, Biden signed the $1.9 trillion American Rescue Plan into law, hoping to alleviate economic suffering caused by COVID-19-related shutdowns. And in April, half of all U.S. states saw their cases drop, followed later by greater vaccine access for the general public. America, Biden hoped, was on the glide path to economic recovery—and revival.

First, Biden attended the G7 meeting in southwest England on June 12.

The U.S. got the other six nations to sign on to a Build Back Better World plan, providing $40 trillion to developing countries by 2035. It was a clear counter to China's Belt and Road Initiative—Beijing's way to ingratiate itself to poorer nations—even if Biden administration officials wouldn't admit it aloud. "This is not just about confronting or taking on China," a senior U.S. official said. "But until now we haven't offered a positive alternative that reflects our values, our standards, and our way of doing business."

Privately, Biden officials hoped that what they shorthanded as "B3W" signaled to America's autocratic rivals that democracies could work on big projects together. "Democracies can deliver" was no longer a slogan. It was reality. "We hoped Putin was paying attention," an official told me.

The official also referred to a Reuters article citing an unnamed person from a G7 government expressing gratitude for the Biden era. "It used to be complete chaos," the person said of the Trump years. "You can have a frank discussion without having to start it off by saying: 'No. Russia is not going to come back into the G7.'"

Interest in U.S.–Russia relations—and the upcoming Biden–Putin summit—remained high during the G7 meeting. Reporters—and officials, secretly—felt that the European trip was just a prelude to that event. At a news conference, a journalist asked if Biden thought Putin could be persuaded away from his years of antagonism. Sanctions didn't change his behavior—would performative gatherings with allies get him to stop?

"There's no guarantee you can change a person's behavior or the behavior of his country. Autocrats have enormous power and they don't have to answer to a public," Biden said. "And the fact is that it may very well be, if I respond in kind—which I will—that it doesn't dissuade him and he wants to keep going." Once again, Biden expressed his deep-seated fear about the limits of even America's influence: there's only so much a nation can do to dissuade a despot hell-bent on doing what he wants, even if the U.S. and its allies threaten punitive responses.

Sullivan added context to Biden's remarks during a chat with reporters on the plane ride to Brussels. "There are two fundamental elements to how we think about dealing with Russia. One is: Are there areas where, in our common interest, we can work together to produce outcomes that are—that work for the United States and for the American people? And the other is: How do we send a clear message about those harmful activities that we will not tolerate and to which we will respond?

"On the second: Of course, we can't make guarantees about what Russia will do, but we can make pledges about what America will do, which is we will respond if those harmful activities continue."

Questions about Russia continued at the NATO summit on June 14. The alliance's secretary general, Jens Stoltenberg, mentioned in his opening statement that NATO's relationship with Moscow was "at its lowest point since the end of the Cold War. This is due to Russia's pattern of aggressive actions." He stressed, however, that all thirty members should continue the "dual track approach," a cocktail of improving defenses while still engaging with Russia. It was a clear nod to the upcoming high-stakes meeting between Biden and Putin.

But as the NATO gathering got under way, China became a hotter topic than Russia. A lot hotter.

As Biden administration officials explained it to me in the lead-up to the summit, the United States couldn't take on China alone. The Trump administration had shown that was the case, imposing unilateral tariffs as part of a trade war that impacted the global market but did little to change Beijing's behavior. What could show that "America is back" more than not only reiterating the administration's support for the alliance and its desire to confront Russia but also convincing NATO members that they, too, had a role in confronting China?

Stoltenberg transitioned from the Russia section of his opening speech. "We will also address China," he said. "China's military buildup, growing influence, and coercive behavior also pose some challenges to our security. And we need to address them together as an alliance." For the first time in its history, NATO called China a threat to its security, writing it down in a new strategic concept that outlined the alliance's broad thinking for the next decade.

A joint communiqué went further: "China's stated ambitions and assertive behavior present systemic challenges to the rules-based international order and to areas relevant to Alliance security." U.S. administration officials, namely Sullivan and the National Security Council senior director for Western Europe, Amanda Sloat, pushed allies hard to adopt the language. Many nations were wary of China, but few wanted a statement that amounted to "it's us versus them."

China's own actions helped—like the forced internment of Uyghur Muslims and sales of telecommunications systems in the West that made it easy for authorities in Beijing to access private data—but it still required intensive behind-the-scenes diplomacy to convince allies of the new stance. "It wasn't a hard sell, but it wasn't the easiest either," an administration official told me.

As the sun set in the Belgian capital, attention quickly turned once more to the main event: Biden versus Putin.

The American president wasn't optimistic heading into the meeting, people around him told me. He'd never liked Putin and didn't think he could change. But the Russian president was a threat to America and, increasingly, the world. This meeting with him wasn't too soon or a concession, officials argued; it was all meant to be a warning. Biden said as much out loud: cooperate where possible, he stated during his NATO news conference, echoing the administration's talking point, but it's important to "make it clear what the red lines are." One of those red lines that had been growing redder, as Biden prepared to sit down with Putin, was the situation in Ukraine.

During May, as Biden and his team were preparing for the NATO summit, Ukrainian president Zelenskyy was beside himself. His aides told him that the United States was nearing a deal with Germany. The relationship between Washington and Berlin was in need of mending after Donald Trump left office. As a carrot, the U.S. would lift sanctions on a nearly built pipeline pumping energy into Germany from Russia called Nord Stream 2.

For Kyiv, the prospect of Nord Stream 2 coming online was a disaster. Russia would receive a financial windfall from its opening, not only from the sale of energy but from sanctions relief for the companies putting the last touches on the pipeline. The new 767-mile-long natural gas throughway, running under the Baltic Sea, was financed by Russian state-owned energy giant Gazprom and several European energy firms. Construction of the pipeline had started in 2011, to expand the Nord Stream 1 line and double annual capacity to 29,000 gallons. This new pipeline would also hurt Ukraine's economy. Once natural gas flowed through Nord Stream 2, Ukraine's older pipelines, which had also helped heat German homes in the winter, would be losing about $2.14 billion in annual payments.

"It was a betrayal. Ukraine clearly meant nothing to them," someone close to top officials in Kyiv said of the Biden administration. The Nord Stream 2 pipeline was not complete, but the deal made full construction a certainty. And the agreement happened after Biden had already held two calls with Putin, one perfunctory at the start of the administration and another with the offer of a summit, even as Russia was building up its military presence on the Ukrainian border. In contrast, Zelenskyy only had one conversation with Biden, which wasn't overly fruitful.

The final straw was when the Ukrainian president's aides brought him a May 19 news story: the United States was set to waive the sanctions on Nord Stream 2, thereby clearing the way for the U.S.–Germany deal. It was all but done, completed, finished. At some point soon, it wasn't clear when, Washington and Berlin would announce the move. They were surely just working out the details.

Zelenskyy was incensed. But he was more upset that no one in the Biden administration had called him or his staff to let them know ahead of time. Kyiv had been completely blindsided.

The lack of a phone call aside, Biden and his team felt they had no choice but to strike the deal with Germany. Berlin was an important ally that was still reeling from the Trump years. And while few in the U.S. actually wanted a Russian energy pipeline to deliver gas into the heart of Europe, there was little America could do about it. "We inherited a pipeline that was over ninety percent complete and so stopping it has always been a long shot," a State Department official said at the time. Kyiv, however, wanted the U.S. to maintain sanctions on the companies building the energy throughway. A 90 percent complete pipeline wasn't 100 percent complete, after all.

Zelenskyy was out of patience. From his perspective the first five months of the Biden administration featured mistreatment after mistreatment. It was time to go on the offensive. It was time to let the Americans know how he really felt.

The Ukrainian leader spoke on June 6 to *Axios*'s Jonathan Swan, whom the Ukrainians came to trust due to his leading coverage of the Trump administration. Zelenskyy used the opportunity to excoriate the Biden administration publicly.

He said he was "surprised" and "disappointed" at the pipeline decision. "This is a weapon, a real weapon . . . in the hands of the Russian Federation," he said. "It is not very understandable . . . that the bullets to this weapon can possibly be provided by such a great country as the United States." Zelenskyy also said openly that he learned about the move in the press, not from Washington.

The United States disputed that claim. "The State Department has regularly engaged with Ukrainian officials regarding Nord Stream 2. Prior to the transmission of the most recent report to Congress, the State Department notified the Ukrainian ambassador in Washington and senior officials in Kyiv, including the president's chief of staff, of the contents of the report," a State Department spokesperson told *Axios*.

Less noticed in the coverage of the interview was Zelenskyy's request to meet Biden before the Putin summit in about a week's time, saying he'd sit down with the American president "at any moment and at any spot on the planet." Biden's aides, including Sullivan, felt that organizing such an important meeting so hastily was a bad idea. But Biden could get on the phone with Zelenskyy as soon as the next day. Sullivan had his team work to make it happen.

Biden and Zelenskyy exchanged pleasantries during their June 7 phone call. The Ukrainian leader expressed his joy at speaking with Biden for the second time in his presidency, but lamented that he'd had to make harsh statements about U.S. policy to get him on the line. Biden said he understood where Zelenskyy was coming from, especially on Nord Stream 2, but promised that his administration would help to alleviate the economic pain caused by the agreement.

Zelenskyy wasn't convinced. The United States could be siding with Ukraine more strongly instead of handing Russia an economic win. Yes, the pipeline was nearly complete, but *nearly* wasn't done. Show the United States is a true friend of Ukraine and reverse the decision, Zelenskyy said. Biden didn't commit to that, but he did say that the two men should hash it out in person during a meeting later in the summer. Absolutely, the Ukrainian president agreed. In the meantime, Biden said, don't you worry about where America stands. She'll always be right by Ukraine's side.

The White House and State Department worked hand in glove to schedule the meeting that Biden promised. Kyiv was overjoyed to work on putting a summit on the books, but Ukrainian officials repeated a message over and over again: this better happen.

Villa La Grange, an eighteenth-century mansion, is surrounded by a park overlooking Lake Geneva in Switzerland. It was the perfect setting for the two leaders of great powers to meet on June 16. In fact, it was such a perfect venue that a couple was paid handsomely to move their wedding elsewhere so the United States and Russia could engage in high-stakes diplomacy.

The expectation was that the meeting between the two presidents would be chilly, even as the summer sun beat down on the villa's surrounding gardens. An air-conditioned tent was set up on the premises for American and Russian staffers to sit and work—separate from each other, of course. "Everyone took pains to stay off each other's turf," an American official at the summit told me.

Everyone was paranoid about security. No member of Biden's team carried their phone for fear that they might be used to listen in on conversations or get hacked. That provided the handful of aides both the enjoyment of spending time off their phones, able to ask their colleagues about what books they were reading, and the pain of not knowing what was going on in the world. In those panicky moments, it was helpful to read a sign on the fridge on the American side of the tent that reminded staffers to watch what they were saying. Someone could be listening in. The statement looked odd next to another sign that detailed the yummy contents inside: fresh-pressed juices and Popsicles.

A lot of planning had gone into the event, but it was widely felt inside the U.S. team that little of substance would get done in Geneva. "This is not about deliverables or shaking loose some grand agreement," a senior official told me in order to manage expectations.

Still, if the U.S. wanted to get anything done with Russia, then Biden had to talk to Putin. There was little sense in working up the chain of command. Putin was the whole chain.

The opening session between Biden and Putin, flanked solely by their respective top diplomats, Antony Blinken and Sergey Lavrov, set the frosty tone. There were some points of agreement: both leaders welcomed the extension of the New START arms-control agreement, saying it showed that there were ways to collaborate despite increasing tensions.

But then Putin went on a long tangent, blaming the United States for the decline in the relationship, calling Moscow a "scapegoat" for America's many problems. He rattled off a laundry list of complaints: Point one was that NATO kept expanding deeper into former Soviet territory and fomented a pro-Western revolt in Ukraine. Russia had to go in and quash that rebellion, Putin complained. The second was that Russia hadn't interfered in the United States' 2020 elections, so it was time for the U.S. to lift the relevant sanctions and the expulsions of ten Russian diplomats from the United States.

Biden responded that Russia was at fault for its new pariah status. The Russian government had exploited America's divisions to tilt the 2020 election in Donald Trump's favor, he said, adding that Russia had gained access to government agencies through the SolarWinds hack, in which Russia used at least a thousand engineers to infiltrate government and Fortune 500 company systems.

Biden was just getting rolling. The U.S. wouldn't stay silent about Russia's abuses of human rights, including jailing Putin's greatest political rival, Alexei Navalny, and would continue pressing for the release of Trevor Reed and Paul Whelan, two American hostages held by Russian authorities. He closed his rebuttal by promising Putin that America and its allies wouldn't stand by as Moscow attacked Western democracy, continued the war in Ukraine, or launched more cyberattacks.

"How would you feel if ransomware took on the pipelines from your oil fields?" Biden later said he asked Putin, using the example of the Colonial Pipeline, which was briefly taken offline by such an attack in May 2021. The Russian president responded that such an event would be of great concern to him.

Biden made it clear that the only thing that would end the sanctions on six cybersecurity companies and more than thirty individuals and entities, as well as the diplomatic freeze-out, was Russia changing its behavior. The ball, Biden said, was in Putin's court. The smaller meeting then adjourned for twenty minutes before an expanded session between the two countries.

Biden left the meetings telling his aides that he got his message through to Putin. The dictator now understood what to expect from the new administration—confrontation and competition where needed, cooperation where possible. As the day came to an end, the president's top aides were feeling upbeat about how it had all gone. There wouldn't be a new era of comity between Washington and Moscow, but at least there was a way forward in the relationship.

"Biden had come to Geneva to do what he needed to do," a senior staffer told me later on. "Now he could put Putin aside and deal with other issues," namely contending with China and climate change. The aide also said there was a sense that Russia might no longer be as major a cybersecurity threat. Biden's stern words, to a certain extent, deterred Putin. "That was the real success of the summit," the staffer told me.

After three hours of sessions, Biden held a news conference to detail the day's events. He spoke after Putin, who said there was "no hostility" during the talks, which he called "constructive." Biden agreed that the chat would ultimately prove helpful—it was good to get a measure of Putin's thinking. Biden always said that diplomacy was about understanding where the other person was coming from, even if there were profound disagreements. That was the only way to find common ground and move forward.

That mattered in this case, Biden argued, because it was important for the United States and Russia—guardians of nearly all the world's nuclear weapons—to have a "stable and predictable" relationship. "I wanted President Putin to understand why I say what I say and why I do what I do, and how we'll respond to specific kinds of actions that harm America's interests," Biden continued, saying out loud that he didn't expect much to change after the summit. But, the president surmised, "I don't think he's looking for a Cold War with the United States."

Still, reporters wanted to know: Did he trust Putin after all that? "This is not about trust; this is about self-interest and verification of self-interest. That's what it's about," Biden responded. "You know, as that old expression goes, 'The proof of the pudding is in the eating.' We're going to know shortly."

Biden would not have to wait long. On July 12, Putin released an aggressive manifesto. The document wasn't on how he planned to lead Russia in a tumultuous time or navigate a turbulent world or why his brand of leadership was best. It was about why Russians and Ukrainians were historically one people.

"I am confident that true sovereignty of Ukraine is possible only in partnership with Russia. Our spiritual, human, and civilizational ties formed for centuries and have their origins in the same sources, they have been hardened by common trials, achievements and victories. Our kinship has been transmitted from generation to generation. It is in the hearts and the memory of people living in modern Russia and Ukraine, in the blood ties that unite millions of our families. Together we have always been and will be many times stronger and more successful. For we are one people," he wrote.

It was exactly the kind of document a man who once decried the dissolution of the Soviet Union as the greatest geopolitical tragedy of the twentieth century would write.

Putin argued that Kyiv's estrangement from Moscow had little to do with his own actions, like the annexation of Crimea and the invasion in Ukraine's east. The West was to blame.

"I recall that long ago, well before 2014, the U.S. and EU countries systematically and consistently pushed Ukraine to curtail and limit economic cooperation with Russia. We, as the largest trade and economic partner of Ukraine, suggested discussing the emerging problems in the Ukraine–Russia–EU format. But every time we were told that Russia had nothing to do with it and that the issue concerned only the EU and Ukraine. De facto Western countries rejected Russia's repeated calls for dialogue," he lamented. "Step by step, Ukraine was dragged into a dangerous geopolitical game aimed at turning Ukraine into a barrier between Europe and Russia, a springboard against Russia. Inevitably, there came a time when the concept of 'Ukraine is not Russia' was no longer an option. There was a need for the 'anti-Russia' concept, which we will never accept."

Top NSC officials read the document. Sullivan in particular thought Putin was unhinged, the isolation during the pandemic having poisoned his mind to the point that he believed drastic measures were needed to keep Kyiv in Moscow's orbit. Did he really think that Ukraine, a country he invaded, and that had made clear its desire to align more closely to the West, was somehow yearning to be part of Russia? Was he truly that aggrieved, or was this a pretext for some future big play against Ukraine?

Sullivan and Finer posed this question to experts around the government. The answer they got back was unnerving—it wasn't clear why Putin put the article out into the world, and on the Russian president's official government page, no less. What everyone could agree on, though, was that Putin couldn't fabricate that deep-seated anger. He firmly believed Ukraine and Russia were one.

Was Putin planning to rectify his sense of a world-historical wrong? The possibility couldn't be counted out. But his language indicated that he viewed the U.S. and Europe as vulnerable enough for him take action. COVID and political divisions had the U.S. reeling, while Germany was going through an election season to replace longtime chancellor Angela Merkel. What better time to pounce?

Biden and his team knew that any efforts to counter Russian aggression would be stronger if the United States worked in tandem with a revitalized NATO that had a strengthened Germany at its core. When Biden conceived of what his foreign policy would look like, a key theme was to reverse Donald Trump's bashing of allies. Few had taken a harder hit than Germany, as Trump felt the U.S. spent too much to protect the strong European nation from Russia.

That was a bad deal, in the former president's mind, because Berlin at the same time sought to complete the Nord Stream 2 pipeline that would line Russia's pockets. Why, Trump said, should American taxpayers keep Germany safe from Russia when it was making deals with Moscow?

Trump's clear dislike of Germany angered leaders in Berlin, who felt their country had long proven itself a steadfast ally. It was an issue they brought up during meetings in the earliest days of the Biden administration. "We needed to feel the love," a senior German official told me of the message Berlin sent to Washington.

One way to show that love was to let Germany complete the pipeline. The issue would come to a head just a few weeks after Biden's Geneva summit with Putin and hot on the heels of Putin's call to bring Ukraine back into the Russian Federation. Senior White House and State Department officials rationalized letting Germany complete the pipeline because, well, it was nearly complete, and it would garner great favor with Berlin. A win-win is how aides sold it to Biden. Little did the president know that he'd just catalyzed a global firestorm.

The U.S. finalized an agreement with Germany on July 21 to allow the Nord Stream 2 pipeline to be completed and operate, bringing another needed source of energy into German homes and industry. The deal also included provisions to help Ukraine weather the economic hardship and, over time, transition to a greener energy sector.

Even senior administration officials stated openly that the move had its downsides. "Look, this is a bad situation and a bad pipeline," Victoria Nuland, the State Department's under secretary for policy, the number three position, told senators that same day. "But we need to help protect Ukraine. And I feel that we have made some significant steps in that direction with this agreement."

But Ukraine wasn't happy. Washington, D.C.–based lobbyists in touch with officials in Kyiv argued that the 767-mile pipeline arrangement amounted to America's abandonment of Ukraine. "It's an attack on Ukraine," one of the lobbyists told me at the time. The Biden administration, though, was telling the Ukrainians to keep their complaints to themselves.

In the run up to the announcement, Secretary of State Blinken and others were telling their counterparts to stay quiet. The deal was going to happen anyway, so Ukrainian leadership might as well stay in America's good graces by shutting up. A senior administration official at the time disputed that charge, saying there was more nuance in the way the private discussions were handled, but didn't provide any specific evidence to support the denial.

"It's unbalanced and unfair that Russia gets a huge reward and Ukraine is flogged over criticism," said Alina Polyakova, the president and CEO of the Center for European Policy Analysis in D.C. "It's 100 percent true that if Trump did this," everyone would go nuts, she added. Radek Sikorski, a former Polish foreign minister now serving in the country's Parliament, told me that the deal was viewed in Eastern Europe as a "betrayal."

American lawmakers, mainly Republicans, were also fuming. "This will be a generational geopolitical win for Putin and a catastrophe for the United States and our allies," Sen. Ted Cruz of Texas said in a written statement once reports of the deal surfaced. "Decades from now, Russian dictators will still be reaping billions from Biden's gift, and Europe will still be subject to Russian energy blackmail. We always knew Biden was in bed with Putin, now they're spooning."

Cruz was enraged by the deal and would tell any and all reporters about his dismay. "If it's ninety percent complete, then it's zero percent complete," he said. He would continue to block many of Biden's diplomatic nominees from confirmation unless and until the president reversed the deal with Germany.

It's always hard to know with politicians where conviction ends and ambition starts. Cruz was clearly eyeing a 2024 presidential run. Hitting Biden hard on Russia was one way to prepare for a campaign. But the Texan cared about the Nord Stream 2 issue even when Trump was in office, pushing to sanction the pipeline against some Democratic opponents who said the move would endanger relations with Germany.

"I believe, if they continue down this path, this will be on the order of magnitude of Jimmy Carter's giving away the Panama Canal. That, five decades later, remains a spectacular loss for U.S. foreign policy, because a Democratic president was too weak to stand up for our interests," he said in an interview. Biden's "decision on Nord Stream 2 is at that level of magnitude."

Biden's team knew that the Nord Stream 2 agreement would be unpopular both at home and in Ukraine. As a pact drew nearer, the State Department was hard at work scheduling the long-promised Biden–Zelenskyy meeting. Victoria Nuland worked alongside Counselor Derek Chollet to agree on a date and an agenda.

In messages to Andriy Yermak and Dmytro Kuleba, respectively a top aide to Zelenskyy and the foreign minister, the two offered dates in late June. Then, for unknown reasons, the proposed summit dates slipped to July. The only time the president could make it work was the end of August—when Congress was out of session and the capital was a ghost town. Kyiv pushed back. Having Zelenskyy in D.C. then would be an insult to him personally and to Ukraine as a whole. August was a no-go.

Nuland and Chollet relayed the message to the White House, but it quickly became clear that August was the soonest anything was going to happen. Kyiv worked with their lobbyists in Washington to make a final push for a non-August date, but the White House was immovable. Kyiv, reluctantly, agreed to the late August meeting.

"President Biden looks forward to welcoming President Volodymyr Zelenskyy of Ukraine to the White House on August 30, 2021. The visit will affirm the United States' unwavering support for Ukraine's sovereignty and territorial integrity in the face of Russia's ongoing aggression in the Donbas and Crimea, our close cooperation on energy security, and our backing for President Zelenskyy's efforts to tackle corruption and implement a reform agenda based on our shared democratic values," White House Press Secretary Jen Psaki said in a July 21 statement.

A person close to the government in Ukraine told me Zelenskyy was "personally offended" by the date of the White House meeting. Yermak thought the United States was "playing games." Questions about how seriously the Biden administration took Zelenskyy's and Ukraine's plight swirled around Kyiv. Ukraine needed the United States, but if Zelenskyy's team had a choice, "they would've told Biden, Sullivan, the lot of them to fuck off," the person said.

Disappointment with Biden was at an all-time high. It was getting to the point that "some in Kyiv wanted Trump back," the person said. "He at least believed in hospitality." Russia, for its part, continued to express deep satisfaction with the deal.

But mending fences with the Ukrainians would have to wait. The withdrawal from Afghanistan would consume Biden and his team for the remainder of the summer.

Part 2

The Great Humbling

Chapter 6

Return of the Taliban

June–July 2021

President Biden was pacing in the Oval Office on a hot June day, frustrated, perturbed, despondent. It was two months since he made the decision to withdraw the remaining twenty-five hundred U.S. troops from Afghanistan, and it didn't seem as if Kabul understood the gravity of what was about to happen. Perhaps it was a toxic cocktail of overconfidence and naivete. Maybe it was because the administration promised to continue supporting Afghanistan financially even as troops came home. Whatever the reason, he wanted to confront Afghan president Ashraf Ghani about it when he came to the White House in late June.

Ghani was annoyed with Biden too. For months he had pleaded with the United States to stay and help Afghan forces fight off the Taliban. The work wasn't done, and the former World Bank staffer had so many great ideas for developing his country's economy.

Both men expected the in-person meeting would turn testy as their calls had done in recent days. But first, they had to smile for the press. Biden said Ghani was among his "old friends"—more a function of time than true bonhomie—before mustering the warmest message possible for a public setting. "Afghans are going to have to decide their future of what they—what they want," he said in the Oval Office on June 25. All Ghani could say in response was "President Biden's decision has been historic. It has made everybody recalculate and reconsider. We are here to respect it and support it," adding that the decision proved a "new chapter in our relationship."

The president got down to brass tacks when the press shuffled out of the famed office. Biden's face contorted into a pointed stare, making the air feel heavy, cold. He left a pregnant pause before unloading. "Afghanistan's military strategy is a disaster—that's why the Taliban is starting to make gains," Biden told Ghani. "Your forces are all over the country trying to defend positions that are of no real strategic value to you. Defend your cities. Fight for everything your nation holds dear."

Ghani seemed hurt, even if he had expected the tongue-lashing. Afghan forces were doing what they needed to do, he shot back. The Taliban's advances were a temporary setback. A setback, Ghani made sure to note, brought on by Biden's decision to remove U.S. troops from the war.

Ghani then took the meeting in a direction few were expecting. The U.S. needs to invest more in Afghanistan. The country could be a technological hub, he said, especially if the U.S. helped connect the country's millions to the 5G network. Biden's face morphed again, this time expressing confusion, as if he were struggling to take in what he'd just heard. The American president's aides looked around at each other in disbelief. One thought quietly: *Ghani's country is in an existential crisis, and he's talking about 5G?!*

The Afghan leader, senior members of the Biden administration felt, had no time to waste. The Taliban had been preparing for the U.S.-led mission in Afghanistan to end for two decades, and there were signs that its forces could outmatch what Kabul had at its disposal.

One didn't need to be an intelligence officer to know that Afghanistan had a fight on its hands. The militants had about sixty thousand core fighters raring to go. They could coordinate with another ninety thousand local militias plus thousands of others willing to back their cause. That gave the Taliban a force much larger than the twenty thousand fighters the United States estimated it had in 2014. Even after years of war and thousands of deaths, the hardline Islamist group always found a way to bounce back.

Months before Biden made his decision, an article in *The New York Times* showed how the Taliban was already staging its members outside of cities and towns, ready for a quick assault. They captured outposts and bases with brutal force, artillery, and drones, even in winter's harsh fighting conditions. Taliban were sitting just outside Kandahar, after pushing their way in from the city's outskirts, prepared to pounce.

The good news was that U.S. intelligence showed that the Afghan National Defense and Security Forces, or ANDSF, and their 352,000 personnel could hold back the Taliban for about two years. In the meantime, the U.S. could quickly and safely remove its troops from the country, safeguard the embassy, and rebuild the system to process thousands of special immigrant visas, or SIVs, for Afghans who had allied with the American military during the war. There was much to do, but time to do it.

The last thing anyone wanted was a rushed American exit that echoed the scenes of Saigon thirty years earlier. The administration's nightmare was any image resembling the photo of CIA-flown helicopters parked atop a city roof to whisk evacuees to safety.

The pullout from Vietnam was chaotic. This military withdrawal would be orderly, the Biden administration planned. But one concern was that two years was hardly enough time to rebuild Afghan society to Ghani's satisfaction, especially in the middle of a war. Biden wanted his partner to get this message through his head: Fight now. Develop later.

For the White House, Ghani had already been moving too slowly. On May 1, the day all U.S. troops were supposed to be out of Afghanistan, the Taliban relaunched its paused offensive. But the militants didn't target Americans. Instead, they went after citizens and Afghan government facilities. In the first week of renewed hostilities, the Taliban bombed a school in Kabul, killing more than 50 people and injuring around 150 others, mostly female students. It was a deadly reminder of what life would be like for women and minorities under Taliban rule.

The group escalated its attacks in the roughly 50 to 70 percent of territory outside urban areas that it either controlled or contested. In some places, the much-vaunted Afghan military failed to put up a fight, leaving the Taliban to waltz in and seize land for itself. Slowly but surely, the Taliban was consuming Afghanistan. News of every recaptured town struck like a dagger at the heart of the Biden administration's plans. The intelligence was constantly revised as news of fallen town after fallen town rolled in, but the main assertion held: Afghan forces would eventually band together and reverse the Taliban's momentum.

The administration was readying itself for worst-case scenarios. The State Department worked overtime to fix the broken immigration system for Afghan SIV applicants. Planning was also under way on what to do about thousands of evacuees who were leaving their homes after the militants moved in.

One meeting on May 8 got heated. The Pentagon organized a rehearsal for how to conduct an evacuation operation with senior officials, including Lloyd Austin, Jake Sullivan, Deputy Secretary of State Wendy Sherman, General Milley, and General Miller. Once again, Pentagon and State Department officials tussled over whether it was necessary to close the U.S. embassy in Kabul as American troops left the country. The recommendation from Defense Department officials was that it would be too risky to operate as usual.

Brian McKeon, the deputy secretary of state for management and resources, said it was the diplomatic ethos to live with danger. "We at the State Department have a much higher risk tolerance than you guys," he said, according to three people in the room. All the uniformed personnel either stiffened or shifted uncomfortably in their seats. Milley nearly jumped out of his chair, but restrained himself from shouting how he and many serving in the armed forces had lost friends in war. Austin showed no signs of anger, but he later told colleagues that he was offended by McKeon's remark. That didn't change the matter at hand though: the U.S. still needed to prepare for hell.

Then hell came. The Taliban started capturing provincial capitals, moving in a manner that indicated Kabul was under threat much earlier than expected. On August 15, only eleven days after the start of the militants' offensive, they had overthrown the government America and its allies had spent billions of dollars and lost thousands of lives to support. The swift conquest caught the administration off guard, leading to a life-or-death scramble that embarrassed America on the world stage and damaged the president's argument that the adults were back in charge.

A senior administration official told me why the U.S. hadn't foreseen such a swift advance by the Taliban: "We were under the impression that the Taliban has made rapid territorial advances, but they may be at a stopping point" and ready to deal at the negotiating table. "Obviously that proved not to be the case, and the Taliban continued to go into Kabul unopposed. Everything changed pretty dramatically."

For an administration that felt America had to be humble about the limits of own power, the preparation for the fall of Kabul and Afghanistan was coated in hubris.

His nerves spiked. A bead of sweat dripped from his forehead. The clicking of his keyboard seemed to bother him more than usual, the *tap-tap-tap* echoing in his empty room. He assumed the anxiety was due to the news out of Afghanistan. Getting some answers might help.

Alex McCoy sat at his desk, his legs shaking, waiting for the Zoom call to begin. His organization, along with other progressive-leaning and pro-restraint groups supportive of the decision to leave Afghanistan, was about to join another private "kitchen cabinet" meeting with Biden's team. These meetings were always a give-and-take. *A slog,* McCoy thought to himself.

The White House wanted assurances that the groups would vocally support Biden's decision, echoing the argument that leaving Afghanistan was in America's national interest. Twenty years of war proved the United States and its allies couldn't win, and fighting there drained resources away from countering China and fending off Russia. Staying would also inexcusably leave American troops in danger.

The groups wanted to keep pressure on the president: *Don't back out now,* McCoy remembered thinking before the call. But he and his colleagues also wanted to stress that the administration needed to expedite the SIV process—friends of theirs were aching to leave, fearful that the Taliban would kill them as retribution for helping the U.S.

When the call started, Carlyn Reichel kicked off the July 7 meeting by saying how much the White House appreciated and needed the groups' support. Having Reichel deliver the message, someone who knew the president and his voice, gave it some weight. "It is a great concern for us as well, including at the very highest levels at the White House," Reichel said. The administration was working to ensure that the U.S. "was doing right by our Afghan allies" who were in harm's way as the Taliban made steady gains. Reichel didn't mention, though, that the president had only decided a day before the Ghani meeting in June to evacuate Afghan allies of the U.S.

Indeed, that decision came from mounting outside pressure. Lawmakers, including Democrats, had sent letters to the president urging him to mobilize government resources, including creating a task force, to get the SIV applicants out. These people had worked alongside the U.S. government during twenty years of war and knew some of the most sensitive details about American personnel and policies. Leaving them to the Taliban's wrath might expose government secrets, eventually get the SIVs killed, and weaken the argument that the U.S. stands with and by its allies.

But on July 5, just two days before McCoy joined the Zoom call, the U.S. military left Bagram Airfield in the middle of the night without so much as telling the Afghan commander, though senior Afghan officials were aware of the plan ahead of time. The U.S. had used that base, about thirty miles outside Kabul, as a main staging and training area during the war. Now it was a ghost town, left to the Afghans to use when fending off the Taliban assault.

The Pentagon defended the decision, insisting that withdrawing from Afghanistan required quick action. Retreat exposed the military; it was always more dangerous to leave a country, because troops were neither defending nor attacking—they were leaving. Speed, the administration argued, was safety. Still, the abandonment of the base led to questions about who would be left in Afghanistan to take the SIVs out with them.

Defenses of the decision hid some unease within the administration. Sullivan had called Austin and Milley on July 2 to ask if it didn't make sense to keep Bagram open a little longer. The symbolism of its closure would weaken Afghanistan's morale and prove a definitive symbol of America's departure. Maybe it was worth revisiting the timetable, Sullivan suggested. But both the defense secretary and the general made a passionate case that defending Bagram while trying to leave the country would prove too difficult and risky a task. It was a massive installation, after all, and defending it would suck people, resources, and time away from executing the withdrawal. Keeping it for longer would also open up troops defending Bagram to Taliban attacks.

Plus, the plan they had briefed Sullivan and others on weeks before detailed how Bagram needed to close on the July 4 weekend, as it would take weeks to properly hand over aspects of running the base, such as how to treat the sewage there. "We're too pregnant to stop it," Milley told Sullivan. The national security adviser heard the assessment, agreed, and relented.

By early July, the United States had effectively completed its military withdrawal "for all intents and purposes," per administration officials. Only a handful of troops remained, with most soldiers and Marines guarding the embassy in Kabul. The rest would go to the international airport to protect it against outside threats. General Miller and a handful of troops and logistical forces were the only others that needed a ride out of Afghanistan.

Back on the call, one of the participants expressed concern the SIV issue would be a "lightning rod for criticism." Choosing to leave without having streamlined the byzantine application process would make SIVs a major attack point for enemies during the withdrawal. (The process was complex because one step required the Afghan ally to prove they worked for the United States, even though records were barely kept by private contractors or the government.) Even those on the call who were happy with the decision to leave Afghanistan still raised an eyebrow about it.

McCoy's chance to speak came a few minutes later. He offered advice to the administration about how it could better message what it was doing. The narrative surrounding America's "over the horizon" counterterrorism capability—that is, using surveillance and other tools from a faraway place to track terrorist activity inside Afghanistan—wasn't a way to fight the war at arm's length but rather a way to fight terrorists that threatened the U.S.

Still, the former Marine wanted to know who, exactly, was in charge of getting all the SIVs home? This was going to be the new American fight. The U.S. had to win it—not for its own sake but for the countless people who helped Washington and its allies fight the Taliban for a better Afghanistan.

It grew more tense and quiet as McCoy asked what countries would serve as staging areas for evacuees. Would the U.S. military go around the country to evacuate SIVs in need, or would those Afghans have to get themselves to Kabul? Basically, McCoy asked, what's the plan?

The line crackled for a moment. Then Reichel broke through, but she didn't have a direct answer. "It is my hope that in the next twenty-four hours we will have a little bit more, something we can put on the bone for the president's remarks on this," the aide said, alluding to Biden's still-unknown plan to speak the next day on the withdrawal. "The problem is, there's a lot of contingency planning."

Some of that planning, she said, did include flying SIVs to a safe third country, but the administration was still "looking at a variety of options." The goal for the moment was moving the SIV situation from contingency planning to "operationalizing." Non-SIVs, Reichel continued, would likely have to work with refugee resettlement groups to get out—the U.S. wouldn't be providing a service for them.

McCoy, with his camera and microphone off, audibly sighed in resignation at the answer. People were dying in Afghanistan. Allies were in danger. They didn't have time to move from planning to an operation. The operation needed to be under way already. He understood that the Trump administration had abandoned the SIV program, leaving Biden's team to rebuild it during a complex time. But if that program was lagging, were other aspects of the withdrawal behind schedule? What were the contingencies the administration might've missed?

Another sigh, and then one word crossed his mind: *Fuck*.

This was not the address Biden wanted to give. The withdrawal from Afghanistan, the end of the war, was supposed to be a crowning achievement. Instead, it was threatening to be the noose around his presidency.

But Biden remained steadfast in his convictions. His late son, Beau, continued to influence his thinking. Beau had fought in Iraq, and his father believed that his son's brain cancer developed after exposure to burn pits. The Iraq War may not have directly killed Beau, but it may have contributed to his untimely passing in 2015 at the age of forty-six. Biden never again wanted to see American troops fighting somewhere they didn't have to be. He never again wanted a parent to suffer as he suffered.

So on July 8, Biden walked up to the White House podium, a dour look overcoming his face. His blue-and-yellow-striped tie stuck out, even with the American flag and the flags of the U.S. military services behind him. He wasn't the Uncle Joe of memes. He was somber, angry, and spoke defiantly against Republicans and some Democrats, including Senate Foreign Relations Committee Chair Bob Menendez of New Jersey, who questioned his decision to leave Afghanistan.

To those who thought he might reverse his decision, Biden said that U.S. troops would leave the country by August 31—not September 11, as originally planned. The withdrawal was going faster than expected, and his top military advisers repeated to him privately that a faster drawdown was better than a slower one.

The pace kept increasing and increasing, spurred by the Taliban's gains. The Pentagon was particularly worried about losing soldiers while closing a base, and some in the White House feared what such a tragedy would mean for the administration politically.

Biden proceeded: The United States would still support Afghanistan until the end of the mission and beyond. Antony Blinken and Zalmay Khalilzad would help Kabul and the Taliban reach a peace agreement. It was the end of America's military involvement but not the end of America's commitment. The U.S. would still provide military, economic, and development assistance after the troops had gone. The democratic push didn't have to end just because the war had.

Then the president turned to what the Alex McCoys of the world wanted to hear. "We're also going to continue to make sure that we take on the Afghan nationals who work side by side with U.S. forces, including interpreters and translators—since we're no longer going to have military there after this; we're not going to need them and they have no jobs—who are also going to be vital to our efforts so they—and they've been very vital—and so their families are not exposed to danger as well," he said. (*They're already exposed to danger*, McCoy thought to himself at the time.)

Around twenty-five hundred Special Immigrant Visa holders had been welcomed to the United States since his inauguration on January 20, Biden said, and more would come soon after the administration worked on legislation with Congress.

The president also had a message for the skeptics: The Afghan military could hold its own without twenty-five hundred U.S. service members behind them in support. "The Afghan troops have three hundred thousand well-equipped—as well-equipped as any army in the world—and an air force against something like seventy-five thousand Taliban. It is not inevitable" that the Taliban take over the country, Biden said, citing intelligence provided to him in daily morning briefings.

A White House aide working on Afghanistan texted after the speech to say he was confident the Afghan military could hold its own. Others in the administration weren't so sure. "It's smart not to be definitive when the Taliban is on the move," the aide said.

And they were moving. By the time Biden delivered his address, the Taliban had taken over a quarter of Afghanistan's 400 districts between May and June, moving at a faster clip than even some in the militants' loose leadership structure expected. The group wasn't preparing for governance, it was focusing on victory. And it was winning, putting U.S. troops and their Afghan allies in great danger.

Senior military and defense leaders at the Pentagon were fuming. They had warned against a withdrawal, specifically citing the Taliban's return as a reason for keeping a few thousand U.S. troops in the country. Gen. Frank McKenzie said internally that Afghan forces could now at best hold out through the winter before collapsing in the spring. The government would fall—the only question was when.

Listening to Biden's speech, Alex McCoy noticed that Biden hadn't offered any specifics on how the SIVs would be extracted safely from Afghanistan. His words amounted to little more than *we're working on it.* There was also the bit about needing Congress's approval to change immigration legislation—never an easy sell.

It's why McCoy and others grilled Jon Finer, the deputy national security adviser, about what the SIV plan was on another private call minutes after Biden's address. Finer told the group that there were weekly meetings at all levels of the National Security Council on the SIV issue alone, and that the president received at least a weekly update in the Oval Office on planning during his daily intelligence briefing.

"So what are we doing?" Finer continued. In the coming weeks, the SIVs will be moved out of Afghanistan while their applications are processed. "The exact numbers I don't have because we have not set an exact target or cap. We're going to begin moving the most vulnerable people out as soon as they're ready to be moved," he said.

But where would they go? That still wasn't decided, but there were three categories of places the administration was looking to send the SIV applicants. The first was U.S. territory, including places that had been used in the past. That was a clear nod to Guam, where the U.S. military relocated more than 110,000 Vietnamese refugees after the fall of Saigon. Activists closely tracking the SIV issue pushed strongly for the administration to send vulnerable Afghans there. The governor of the island supported the idea.

The second option was U.S. military installations overseas in countries like Qatar. That wasn't as easy as it sounded, Finer said. The host country had to agree to let the U.S. drop thousands of refugees in its sovereign territory, even if they were going to an American base. That required some diplomatic maneuvering that the administration was currently handling. And the final possibility was to send the SIVs to foreign countries that would agree to house, feed, and care for the refugees as they awaited processing. That was also a tall order, because some of the SIVs could be in the queue for months, "maybe even longer," Finer said.

The good news was the administration found the appropriate funds for evacuation flights and for the well-being of patient SIV applicants. If needed, the executive would turn to Congress in search of more money, but that for the moment wasn't necessary.

Finer then fielded a question he'd anticipated: Why not bring the SIV applicants to the continental United States directly? Wouldn't that be easier logistically in the long run, and more humane? The issue was security, the deputy said: "None of these people, at least very few of them, when they are initially moved, will have undergone security background checks." Sure, the United States trusted them to work in American government facilities and alongside the military, but they still wouldn't be fully vetted.

Finer, who had worked on the SIV program before, including while a top-ranking official at the State Department in the Obama administration, noted that a few of the applicants will have "derogatory information" pop up during the background-check process. "If we're talking about thousands and thousands of people, even a statistically small percentage is going to be a relatively significant number," he said. "We cannot take the risk of the security of the country, and of Americans, of bringing people into the country who've not been properly screened and vetted."

Holy shit, McCoy thought. Here's the deputy national security adviser outlining options, not saying, "Here's the plan." And the president just spoke about it! Plus, the Taliban was sweeping across the country as thousands of SIVs were still clamoring to get out. They were texting him, his friends, and other veterans they knew, hoping the Americans could call somebody—anybody—to clear their paperwork. These were desperate times, and the administration didn't seem desperate to fix the problem.

There was a reason for that. Multiple current and former Biden administration officials admitted that there just wasn't any political will to expedite improvements for the SIV process before the Taliban made its bid for power. Biden had other priorities to get through Congress, like COVID relief and the Build Back Better bill. Fighting with a fifty-fifty Senate over an immigration issue—"about bringing brown Muslims to America," as one person put it to me—would jeopardize that agenda. Rebuilding the SIV process that the Trump administration dismantled was important, sure, but not more important than those things.

There was also confidence within the administration, but not within the Pentagon, that Afghan forces would eventually slow the Taliban's progress. If Kabul was to fall, it would happen in the eighteen- to twenty-four-month time frame that officials kept touting internally. There was, as one senior U.S. official knowledgeable on Afghanistan discussions told me, "true belief."

• • •

On July 13, the State Department's dissent cable channel—where diplomats and other officials can disagree with a policy without fear of retribution—received another message. The cable, addressed to Secretary of State Antony Blinken and Policy Planning Director Salman Ahmed, warned that Afghanistan was likely to fall once American troops left the country. The twenty-three signees further called on State Department leaders to denounce the Taliban's human rights violations and prepare to evacuate people no later than August 1.

Blinken reviewed the cable but was unmoved. The administration was already forging ahead to secure Kabul and keep Americans safe. Just the next day, in fact, White House press secretary Jen Psaki was to announce a new SIV rescue plan.

"We are launching what we are calling 'Operation Allies Refuge' to support relocation flights for interested and eligible Afghan nationals and their families who have supported the United States and our partners in Afghanistan, and are in the SIV application pipeline," she said. She wouldn't get into numbers of people or available aircraft for security reasons, but Psaki did say flights would start in the last week of July, less than two weeks away. "Our objective is to get individuals who are eligible relocated out of the country in advance of the removal—of the withdrawal of troops at the end of August."

But there wasn't much excitement about the announcement. For one thing, the first flights were ages, in war terms, from taking off. That would give the Taliban plenty of time to hunt down perceived traitors. There was also the matter that only SIV applicants already in the pipeline would be allowed on evacuation flights. But surely, officials argued, there were thousands of Afghan allies not in the system who would risk life and limb to be rescued. And even if the interpreters and translators did understand what steps they needed to take, the burden of proof to be considered a serious applicant was so high that some eligible people couldn't even get their screening process started.

It was also a bad day to announce the mission. CNN reported on grainy images from videos showing the Taliban a month earlier executing twenty-two Afghan commandos. "Surrender, commandos, surrender," a militant said in Pashto, a local language, before the unarmed men appeared in frame. The Afghan government called the footage, now streaming worldwide, a "war crime."

A member of the "kitchen cabinet" asked Carlyn Reichel about it during another private call on July 14, this one organized only ten hours earlier to ensure the antiwar groups would back Operation Allies Refuge.

That atrocity, the person said, underscored the brutal way that the Taliban was winning the reinvigorated war. They were seizing outpost after outpost from Afghan troops, many of whom were ill-equipped, in terms of training and weaponry, to fend off the ferocious Taliban advance. Sometimes, the Afghan forces simply walked away from the fight, choosing to surrender instead of dying for their country. Shouldn't the administration come out and say such scenes were a result of the failure of the Afghan political leadership, not American troops coming home?

"That's a hard message for us to push," Reichel said. That would demoralize the Afghan National Defense and Security Forces and likely be viewed by critics as blame shifting. "We're going to have to continue our positive message"—that ANDSF are brave and capable fighters. Now is the time for them to prove it. It's their responsibility to defend their nation from threats.

McCoy also asked some questions of Reichel: Where were the flights leaving from, and who, specifically, would be welcomed on the planes? Reichel said that most, if not all, of the flights would depart from Hamid Karzai International Airport in Kabul. That still wasn't finalized, but it was the most logistically feasible way to get planes in and out safely. The capital was still in the government's hands. Every effort would be made to contact those eligible for the flights and tell them when and where to get on their plane.

In answer to McCoy's second question, Reichel said that there was no "minimum requirement" for an SIV applicant to hitch a ride out of Afghanistan. If someone was in the process, it didn't matter if it was Step 1 or Step 12—they could get on the aircraft. Of course, those earlier in the queue may be stuck at the way station far longer than those further along.

There was movement on the part of the administration, McCoy thought to himself. At least there was that.

After weeks of expressing unwavering confidence, the administration started to quiver in public.

Zalmay Khalilzad gave an interview in which he made the cardinal political sin of telling the truth: the Taliban was on the front foot. "Their position, given the developments of the past several weeks, is stronger than it was before," he said. By that point, July 19, the Taliban had captured around two hundred districts—many of them in the government's northern power center—since the start of May. "It's not surprising that with the reduction, or almost complete withdrawal of U.S. forces that were on the side of the Afghan government, that they would make some progress," Khalilzad continued. "They have made more progress, perhaps, with the reduction and withdrawal [than] one could have analytically predicted."

Diplomacy wasn't fully dead, Khalilzad assured, but it wasn't moving as quickly and effectively as he'd hoped. He was encouraged by statements that all sides hoped to find a diplomatic solution soon and that proposals had been put forward not just by Kabul and Washington but by the Taliban as well—even if those were mostly unsavory. The skeptics of the peace effort had the upper hand now, but, as Khalilzad had proved in the past, he would end up being right. He understood Afghanistan better than anyone in the U.S. government.

It was clear Washington and Kabul weren't on the same page. They took great pains to stay on message, but the cracks started to show as the Taliban moved nearer and nearer to overrunning Afghanistan.

Among the main interlocutors in Afghanistan was Hamdullah Mohib.

As a former ambassador to the United States, he was versed in the inner workings of Washington and was as comfortable in Afghanistan's tribal areas as at a glitzy D.C. dinner party. Mohib was the brains behind Ghani's war effort and the link to the United States. He spoke regularly with Sullivan, usually berating the administration for its decision to withdraw and begging Biden's team to reconsider. He delivered that message over and over, noting that the slim chances of brokering a peace were even more remote after Biden's decision to end America's involvement in the war.

"It definitely has made it harder to make peace with the Taliban because they believe in their own narrative, and their narrative is that of victory," he said. "But it has also created an opportunity for Afghans to take control of our own affairs in the way that is more sustainable to Afghanistan."

The Taliban, though, was still the Taliban. "We so far have not seen any concrete moves from the Taliban towards peace. They have wasted time. They've made excuses, they have used the peace process as a way to advance their military agenda. They have not delivered on substantial points that would get us closer to peace in Afghanistan."

Mohib remained optimistic about his nation's military chances. He said there was a "stalemate" on the battlefield, which was good since the Taliban was on the offensive. Once the Afghan government absorbed the initial blows and regrouped, it would be Afghanistan's forces on the attack.

That's not how U.S. officials at the embassy saw it. The district centers that were falling to the Taliban over the last few weeks weren't immediately curbing the government's hold on power, but they were making the Afghan forces' jobs much harder. Kabul's troops still held district capitals but lost control of many of the roads, stranding them in the territory they held. If they tried to travel away, including back to Kabul, they'd be putting their lives in severe danger.

The military's increasing isolation allowed the Taliban to capture border crossings to Tajikistan, Uzbekistan, Iran, and Pakistan. Now the militants controlled who or what went in and out of strategic points, effectively serving as the government in remote areas. Ghani, Mohib, and their colleagues were more and more living up to the Afghan refrain that the U.S.-backed government was really just the government of Kabul.

Ross Wilson, the de facto ambassador at the U.S. embassy, was worried about what he was seeing. It wouldn't be long before the Taliban grabbed district capitals and started making their way to Kabul. The diplomat continued to work on contingency options with his team. One idea was to shut down the chancery and move most of the embassy's staff out of the country. A rump team could work out of the airport to perform only the necessary duties. If the situation got so bad that their lives were in danger, it'd be easy to catch a plane and fly away.

Wilson hoped he never had to put that plan into action.

The administration's SIV planning was starting to bear fruit. In late July, the United States was in final talks with Qatar and Kuwait to have them authorize the evacuation of SIV applicants to American bases in those countries. Ned Price, the State Department's spokesperson since the start of the administration, said that the first twenty-five hundred people in the program would be flown to Fort Lee in Virginia. Those on the trip would be in the final stages of their application process. That was a good start for the roughly eighteen thousand awaiting a ride out of Afghanistan.

There was clearly movement, but privately there was concern that the administration had moved too slowly. The Taliban was gaining more and more territory, and the intelligence picture started to change. The intelligence community's initial estimate that it would be eighteen to twenty-four months until the Taliban took over Kabul had now, a senior administration official told me, shrunk to just a few weeks.

The "kitchen cabinet" of progressive and antiwar groups were losing their patience with the administration and, by extension, Biden. Where was the leadership, they wondered? During a July 21 call, meant to stay off the record, many of the organization's members asked if the White

House would prefer they stop blasting the U.S. for its handling of SIV evacuations.

No, Carlyn Reichel said, keep the pressure up, but know that the team is still working the issue intensively. "Everything is still on the table," she said: staging in Guam, U.S. military bases in Europe and Asia, and installations stateside. The problem is that government operations move slowly, she said. They require consensus-building and getting multiple agencies on board. There was also the issue of ensuring that everything the U.S. was doing was legal. Her main message: "We're not walking away yet."

The best-case scenario, of course, wasn't a fully democratic Afghanistan at peace. The best the U.S. and its allies could work toward, even as troops departed, was maintaining a secure-enough Afghanistan that allowed SIV applicants to get to Kabul for evacuation flights. How to do that was still in the works, Reichel said.

Experts watching all this unfold in real time noticed two key themes emerging from the Biden administration's scramble to save allied Afghans.

The first was how unprepared the United States was for the advance of the Taliban and the extraction of vulnerable Afghan allies.

Biden's team did have to drastically rebuild the SIV application process after its decimation during the Trump years. For example, the Trump administration issued slightly more than five hundred Afghan special immigrant visas between March and December 2020—even if Jake Sullivan said the number was zero. By the time August 2021 came around, about eight hundred SIV applications were approved a week. "I reject the idea that we didn't do all we could to help SIVs," a senior administration official told me. In a way that's true—the Biden State Department and Department of Homeland Security did yeoman's work to restart and rebuild the program.

Even so, it was all too late, leading to rushed planning within the administration and increased worries from Afghans who feared for their lives as the Taliban stormed across the country. "We should've done more to accelerate [the process] before the troops departed," former Rep. Tom

Malinowski, then a Democratic representative from New Jersey who had served in the Obama administration's State Department alongside many top Biden officials, told me.

What's more, administration officials didn't communicate some of the major decisions they'd already taken, even privately. The idea of sending refugees to Guam had been ruled out much earlier for fear of severe weather. Typhoon season in Guam is between late June and December, which meant there was the distinct possibility of a humanitarian and public relations crisis if a major storm hit the U.S. territory while thousands of refugees were there. Any scenes of SIV applicants and their families struggling to stay above water during a flood would make the administration look clueless and careless, and so the option was discarded early in the planning stage.

The second theme was how Reichel and other White House officials asked the groups over and over to just keep hitting the same main talking point: the United States needed to leave—it was time and it was in the national interest. All other arguments, including the ones about how slow the U.S. was on helping SIVs, distracted from that.

The administration was talking to these groups specifically to give them marching orders about what to say and how loudly to say it. But the White House didn't want to hear criticism. It didn't want to truly consider other options, or hear that it had moved too slowly in planning. It just wanted to say, effectively, *We failed in Afghanistan and staying hinders America's ability to help itself in other, more important areas.*

It was an exercise in narrative and expectations management for what America could now achieve after losing so much time, money, and prestige, not to mention so many lives, in Afghanistan. But it was also Bidenism in action. The U.S. had to be more humble about what its military could achieve, despite its strength. Resources to build, and in some cases rebuild, other elements of America's national power took precedence over unwinnable wars. Better to cut losses and run rather than continue sinking time and energy into a fight that would lead to only more bloodshed and body bags.

There was, as one person who dealt directly with administration officials on Afghanistan told me, "an arrogance in their humility." The problem, though, is that it would only get much, much worse. "I expected some turbulence," Alex McCoy said in an interview. "I didn't expect the chaos that came."

Chapter 7

Go Time

July–August 2021

The Hail Mary attempt to strike a last-minute peace deal between Afghanistan and the Taliban was faltering. The militants insisted that any agreement had to include the removal of President Ashraf Ghani, otherwise the fighting would continue. According to the militants, Ghani represented a corrupt government, and he refused to consider a power-sharing agreement. A new regime, one agreed to among all parties and that would include Taliban members, would need to be formed. The United States, of course, said any government needed to be democratically put together. Ghani, for all his imperfections, was the democratically elected leader of the country.

But the Taliban was increasingly in a position to make stronger demands. General Milley said during a July 21 Pentagon press conference that the Taliban had "strategic momentum"—another high-level nod to the darkening reality on the ground. And by that point in late July, roughly 95 percent of all American and NATO troops were already out of the country.

No one in the Biden administration believed a negotiated settlement was coming. But it was better to be caught trying than not, senior leadership believed. That way, if it all fell apart, as was widely expected, U.S. officials could claim they put their best foot forward. The failure would be the Taliban's, not America's or Kabul's. Suhail Shaheen, the top Taliban spokesperson, was bullish about the whole situation. In an interview, he effectively said that the militants were asking for everything they wanted because the Taliban would be in charge soon. "The ultimate outcome should be replacement of the current Kabul administration by an Islamic government acceptable to all Afghans," he said.

There was little incentive for the Taliban to make peace when their military advance was going so well. Not only were more and more districts falling under their control, but China's foreign minister had also met with high-level Taliban officials in Tianjin, a not-so-subtle indication that Beijing would support a new Taliban-run government. All the militants had left to do was take the country by storm.

The signals coming through special envoy Zalmay Khalilzad's office were that not much would be agreed upon before the August 31 withdrawal date Biden had set. Try as Khalilzad might, and as much as Biden, Jake Sullivan, and Antony Blinken wanted some sort of agreement done, he was never going to broker a grand bargain as the Taliban saw the backs of American troops.

As July wound down, the focus shifted to influencing the Taliban's behavior should they rise to power. It was a recognition that a peaceful end to the conflict—a win—was fully out of reach. "The Taliban says that it seeks international recognition, that it wants international support for Afghanistan," Blinken told reporters on July 28. "Presumably it wants its leaders to be able to travel freely in the world, sanctions lifted, et cetera," he said. "Taking over the country by force and abusing the rights of its people is not the path to achieve those objectives."

There was little faith the Taliban would heed those words. Two days after Blinken's remarks, the first plane of SIVs under Operation Allies Refuge arrived in Fort Lee, Virginia. No one on that aircraft was willing to sit and wait around in Afghanistan for a moderate Taliban. After the plane landed, a senior administration official told me that specific flight carrying evacuees exemplified how the United States was able to do multiple things at once: withdraw U.S. troops safely, continue the peace process, and protect those who had served alongside Americans. "We're fulfilling our promise," the person said. The tone of voice conveyed an overall message, "We're America, dammit."

At the beginning of August, the Taliban increased the pace of its operations. On August 3 alone, nine of ten districts outside the provincial capital of Lashkar Gah in Afghanistan's south changed hands. Residents were stunned by the speed of the near-total takeover as militants wandered openly in city streets that hours earlier were under the government's control. Provincial capitals in other regions were also under attack.

"The situation is very concerning," Khalilzad told a distinguished audience at the Aspen Security Forum that same day. He called on Kabul to get its "military bearings."

Khalilzad's worries weren't mirrored elsewhere in the Biden administration. Even as the Taliban captured its first provincial capital, Zaranj, near the border with Iran, on August 6, the administration projected calm. "It's probably nothing, but it is a bigger step," a senior U.S. official said at the time. Meanwhile, the administration continued to operate as if this were a minor setback, not a sign of things to come. After all, even *The New York Times* had labeled the taking of Zaranj a "symbolic victory."

I immediately texted Shaheen upon hearing the Zaranj news.

"You recently told me that the Taliban took the peace process seriously. But how can anyone believe you? Isn't the Taliban admitting its preference is to storm to power by taking town after town, city after city?"

When his reply finally came, I had to reread it several times to make sure I was understanding it correctly.

"We have to take it, return law and order," he said, brushing aside the

Taliban's storied history of brutal and repressive rule. "How can we [be] expected to just watch the city [as it's] facing a chaotic situation?" I replied that the fighting the Taliban reignited is what caused the chaos in the first place. Shaheen didn't respond.

The news of the horror unfolding in Afghanistan kept coming in. Over the next few days, the Taliban rolled up the cities of Shebergan, Kunduz, Aybak, and other provincial capitals. In each location, some members of Afghanistan's forces fought bravely, but the majority laid down their arms and either fled or flipped sides to help the Taliban seize power. The three-hundred-thousand-strong Afghan military that the United States had trained for two decades opted not to fight on behalf of a government that barely had authority outside Kabul. Those in the administration who had pushed Biden's inner circle to reconsider withdrawal started to say "I told you so."

"Anyone who knows how these things go knows Afghan forces wouldn't fight, it was obvious," an administration official who wanted to keep U.S. and Western forces in Afghanistan told me.

It started to sink in to the upper echelons of the Biden administration that its faith in the eighteen- to twenty-four-month timeline for a Taliban takeover was misplaced. Recriminations were happening in private conversations from the White House to the Pentagon. In one conversation that month between General McKenzie and subordinates at U.S. Central Command, they discussed why everything was going so wrong so quickly. "Why didn't anyone listen to the military? Why didn't anyone question the intelligence? Did we completely, as a government, miss how strong the Taliban was? Why did no one question the assumption that a takeover would take a long time?" one of the people in the room asked.

"Yeah," a senior military official said, "we fucked that up."

The administration now had to spring into action. On August 7, the Pentagon held a tabletop exercise—a simulation of how to deal with a crisis—on how to execute a noncombatant evacuation operation, known in the government as an NEO. The next day, homeland security adviser Elizabeth Sherwood-Randall hosted a call with colleagues from the Pentagon, State Department, and intelligence community to get input on whether to authorize the operation.

On August 9, Lloyd Austin met with Pentagon undersecretaries to discuss the situation in Afghanistan. He said the picture was becoming more challenging by the day. Soon he would attend a National Security Council meeting about whether to launch a NEO. Colin Kahl, the Defense Department's top policy official, said that the tabletop exercise showed the U.S. military could still pull off the operation down the road. The Taliban had yet to place pressure on Kabul, giving the U.S. and its allies more time to decide. Austin agreed, noting that any indication America was packing up and going home would unintentionally demoralize the Afghan government and military, possibly precipitating the Ghani administration's collapse.

Hours later, Sullivan held a Principals meeting with his counterparts, pushing them all to agree to the prepositioning of troops to help with a likely evacuation. It was time to take action as the timeline for a collapse of Kabul continued to shrink and shrink.

But the collective response was no. It was too early for such a drastic move. The administration had developed indicators to trigger action and none of them had yet been tripped. Sullivan was dumbfounded, and asked everyone again if they were sure. "The ability to move on Kabul relatively rapidly made sense," he said. But the officials around the table—Austin, Milley, Blinken, CIA director William Burns, and U.S. Agency for International Development administrator Samantha Power—all said not yet. There was still time to do evacuations and maybe even make some diplomatic progress, though the chance of that was dwindling fast. Fine, Sullivan said, "but I don't want us to look back and regret this."

A senior administration official told me that there were some internal regrets for believing Afghan forces could hold off the Taliban for so long. To his way of thinking, the intelligence community is great at a lot of things: assessing the size of a foreign military, its makeup, its capabilities, its leadership. The U.S. also had great insight into the Afghan forces because America had helped train them for two decades and served alongside them in intense combat.

What the U.S. intelligence community was bad at was assessing the will of a nation's military to fight. There were many brave Afghan soldiers giving their lives to fend off the Taliban, but others were giving up and going home. That, coupled with the Taliban's strength, increased the sense of panic inside the Biden administration.

Even then, Biden was determined to stay the course, urging the crumbling Afghan military to fend off the assault. "They've got to want to fight. They have outnumbered the Taliban," he said of the Afghan forces on August 10 during a news conference at the White House. "There's still a possibility" that they'll win. He concluded: "I do not regret my decision."

The defiant message was a true distillation of how Biden felt. From the Oval Office to the Situation Room, the president spoke both about the horrifying scenes in Afghanistan and also about how they showed he had made the right call. If the Afghans couldn't hold their own at this stage, two decades into America's involvement in the civil war, what was the point in staying? He didn't speak for everyone in the administration—senior officials in the Pentagon whispered privately that the withdrawal was a mistake and that Biden was reaping what he sowed—but he was the president. The decision was his. And it was final.

Biden delivered these comments about the will to fight on the same day he scored a major legislative victory: the passage of an infrastructure bill in the Senate that he believed would renew the American economy and help the country keep pace with Beijing's galloping economy. The split screen was precisely the kind of image Biden wanted his administration to project: he would cut the dead weight so America could be strong where it needed to be. The United States couldn't do it all.

Biden's bravado covered for the true fear of his own national security adviser. Sullivan retreated to his office, away from the celebration about the infrastructure deal, to call principals individually to ask them the same question about launching a NEO: "Do you really not think we should do this?"

The responses from senior officials made clear they still felt the situation was stable enough to keep watching and waiting, even as a new intelligence assessment showed Kabul could fall within ninety days, increasing the need to help get Americans and Afghan allies out. In the Oval Office, with Biden seated on one of the couches in the middle of the famed room, Sullivan let the president know about the unchanging attitudes and the new intelligence. Biden decided it was time for him to get directly involved in the action.

On Wednesday, August 11, the president decided to turn a previously scheduled national security meeting that evening into one focused solely on Afghanistan. The situation was getting worse by the minute, and the United States needed to respond—fast.

Ahead of that meeting, Austin held a policy discussion in his secure conference room at the Pentagon. His aides informed him that Taliban attacks had been reported at Bagram and in the south and southeast of Kabul. The militants had also seized nine provincial capitals and were releasing hundreds and hundreds of prisoners who could imminently or eventually join their ranks. Then the worst news came: the Taliban was closing in on Kabul from the east.

General McKenzie chimed in via secure video link. The Ghani "government is paralyzed," he said, and unable to make decisions as the Taliban descended upon the Afghan capital. Then Austin's aides briefed him on the prospects of launching a NEO. It would require a few thousand troops to pull off. Sending them to Kabul could take anywhere from twenty-four to ninety-six hours, so a decision needed to come soon.

That evening, Biden was joined around the Situation Room table by top members of his Cabinet and senior staff: Vice President Kamala Harris, Austin, Milley, Sullivan, Finer, Avril Haines, Ron Klain, CIA deputy director

David Cohen, and Elizabeth Sherwood-Randall. Blinken chimed in by phone. "It was a serious moment," a senior official recalled.

Events were growing so dire that the president ordered Austin and Milley to prepare a plan for deploying additional troops to the region, where they would reinforce those put on standby months earlier to evacuate American personnel.

Austin had grown so alarmed that he had already called the first of what was to become twice-daily meetings on Afghanistan in the Pentagon's third-floor secure video conference room, known as the secretary's "cables." The department's top civilian and military leaders attended; other top brass, such as General McKenzie and Rear Adm. Peter Vasely, the commander of forces on the ground in Afghanistan, called in via secure video.

In the Situation Room, Biden further directed the State Department to expand the evacuation of Afghan allies—those who had worked with the Americans were now in mortal danger—to include the use of military aircraft, not just chartered civilian planes. An emboldened Taliban would no doubt launch a search-and-kill mission for the Afghans who had helped the American military. Once they won the war, they would escalate their campaign to kill those they viewed as traitors.

Biden also asked his intelligence officials to prepare an up-to-date assessment on the situation in Afghanistan by the following morning. Everything at that moment was still on the table, including a full evacuation of the embassy in Kabul. After the meeting ended, a classified email was sent to pertinent staffers to convene at 7:30 a.m. the next day. The email went out so late that the Situation Room staff also started calling aides to Cabinet members to make sure their bosses would be on time Thursday morning.

Not everyone waited until daylight to weigh in on what should happen next. Milley received word that the Taliban had seized Ghazni, a provincial capital situated on the main road to Kabul to the south. The militants, it was clear, were sprinting toward the seat of power in Afghanistan. Moments after receiving the information, at 2:00 a.m. on August 12, Milley immediately called Jake Sullivan.

The call woke the national security adviser from a short nap. "They're in fucking Ghazni, Jake. Pull the fucking trigger, light the fucking fire," Milley said. "Call Blinken and tell him to start the NEO."

"I hear you, Mark," Sullivan replied. "We'll talk about it in a few hours."

Sullivan and other officials stumbled into the meeting, exhausted from a long night. "I remember how groggy everyone sounded," a senior administration official told me about the White House session. It wasn't ideal to be making decisions that could mean life or death to people in Kabul with little to no sleep.

The intelligence briefer kicked off the session. The situation was "fluid," the briefer relayed to Sullivan and the Cabinet officials on secure lines. Kabul could fall "within weeks or days."

"A lot of this moved more quickly than people expected," a senior U.S. official told me after the meeting. "You know it's not going well when my boss is on a seven thirty a.m. phone call with other members of the national security team."

Austin, who worked overnight to develop the options, recommended the commander in chief send troops into Afghanistan to evacuate the embassy in Kabul. Ghazni was only a three-hour drive from Kabul. Herat was teetering, and the prospects of an Afghan military victory in Kandahar were looking worse by the day. It was only a matter of time before the militants had control of the country and the capital. "The dominoes are about to fall," Austin said.

Ross Wilson said he was even less hopeful than Austin. The United States had little chance of keeping the Taliban out of Kabul, especially since the militants had effectively cut off Afghan forces from reaching the city.

Austin jumped back into the conversation, asking Blinken if he thought it was a good time to evacuate staff from the embassy in Kabul and close down the mission. Blinken said it was a good idea to take four hundred people out and downsize the staff to around sixteen hundred. In the meantime, diplomats were already destroying documents.

Sullivan asked if everyone else in the meeting agreed with Austin's recommendation and Blinken's acceptance: that it was time to send more U.S. troops into Kabul and begin closing the massive embassy. There was unanimous agreement. That was the "oh shit" moment, the senior official later told me.

Just before 10:00 a.m., Sullivan walked into the Oval Office to tell Biden what his team suggested he do. Biden then called Austin and told him to execute. "Yes, Mr. President," Austin responded. About three thousand U.S. troops were headed to Afghanistan—more than were in the country—to carry out the evacuation. It had to be completed by August 31, the last day of the U.S. military mission.

"The mood was extremely serious, professional, and mission focused," a senior administration official familiar with the meeting told me. "It was a serious moment and people behaved like it." Once the president opted to evacuate the embassy, many around the table realized that they'd misjudged the consequences of the withdrawal. "It all became pretty undeniable after the president's decision," the official lamented.

Sending additional troops to execute the embassy evacuation meant administration officials had to come face-to-face with the mistakes they'd made and start steeling themselves for what was to come. It got so bad that Khalilzad was begging the Taliban not to attack the embassy during the evacuation.

Biden was fearful of what would come next. In July, during a speech he gave to defend his withdrawal decision, the president said that "there's going to be no circumstance where you see people being lifted off the roof of an embassy of the United States from Afghanistan." It was a clear allusion to the scenes in Saigon, when a CIA officer atop a hotel near the U.S. mission reached to lift a Vietnamese citizen into a hovering helicopter during the evacuation. Biden had the failures of that war and the chaotic withdrawal on his mind. He was just two years into his first Senate term when that happened. Now, faced with having to evacuate the U.S. embassy in Kabul, Biden feared he would preside over similar scenes, tying his presidency to them forever.

Good foreign policy rarely made a presidency, but bad foreign policy moments could certainly break one. "Would we have done things differently if we had known we only had a few months from the April decision," when Biden ordered U.S. troops out of Afghanistan? "Yeah, probably so," a senior U.S. official said on the phone. The silence that followed lasted at least ten seconds. All I could hear was steady, heavy breathing.

Chapter 8

Hell

August—September 2021

Secretary of State Antony Blinken was dreading his call with Afghan president Ashraf Ghani. It was going to be a difficult conversation, as the Taliban had nearly surrounded Kabul and hours earlier took control of Afghanistan's second- and third-largest cities. He expected the Afghan leader to criticize the military withdrawal, as he often did, and blast the peace process that failed to produce even the smallest results.

During their August 14 conversation, Blinken asked Ghani outright: Are you going to stay in Afghanistan and fight for your government and country, even if the Taliban close in? Yes, Ghani replied. He was prepared to fight to the death. This was his country—he would war on, even if the United States no longer chose to.

Meanwhile, Gen. Frank McKenzie was on the August 15 plane to Doha, Qatar—where talks between the U.S. and Taliban had taken place for months—to make an ask of the advancing militants. Whatever you do, don't come into Kabul. The U.S. needs to evacuate thousands of Americans and at-risk Afghans from the country via Hamid Karzai International Airport.

We can't do that if you're taking over the capital at the same time. It'd be best for all involved if the Taliban stayed about eighteen miles away from it all.

The general thought he had a bit of time to make the deal. Only a week earlier, he and his team had written and sent to the top levels of the administration an intelligence assessment that said Kabul was going to fall. Not imminently, per the information, but the Taliban's presence would be enough to strangle the city and interfere with the evacuation operation. He'd hoped his assessment would be enough to give American troops and diplomats the physical and temporal space they needed to get everyone out as safely as possible.

But by the time McKenzie landed in Qatar on that scorching August 15 day, the Taliban had entered the presidential palace and taken control of Kabul. The Afghan government, propped up by the United States and NATO countries for twenty years, collapsed in a matter of hours. Ghani was nowhere to be seen. As the Taliban entered the capital, the Afghan leader, who the day before had told Blinken that he would fight to the death, was already on a plane to the United Arab Emirates, headed far from the country he no longer led.

Blinken never spoke to Ghani again.

The fate of Afghanistan changed in that instant. So did General McKenzie's calculus. The option for a relatively calm withdrawal was gone. A raucous one was now the best available play. Once in Doha, he devised a new proposal for the Taliban's cofounder, Mullah Abdul Ghani Baradar, without directly clueing the White House in: Let the evacuations proceed undisturbed. Once the U.S. extracts the people it needs to get out, Kabul—and the whole of Afghanistan—will be back under your command. "If you don't interfere with the evacuation, we won't strike," the general said.

Baradar had a proposal of his own. The U.S. should control and safeguard Kabul. The Taliban would remain outside until the last plane left Afghanistan. McKenzie didn't give Baradar's suggestion much thought. More American troops would have to stream into the city to properly secure it, and that wasn't feasible given everything else going on. And it wasn't clear that Baradar spoke for the entire Taliban, as the militants had their own factions, some more hardline than others. Even if he was speaking for the Taliban, how serious was his comment anyway?

McKenzie, beads of sweat pouring down his face, pushed back. No, the U.S. will control the airport and ensure the evacuation goes as smoothly as possible. America won't be securing Kabul anymore.

Ross Wilson watched in horror at the scenes unfolding around him and Afghanistan on August 15 as the Taliban entered Kabul. The noise of Kabul's bustling streets was replaced by gunfire, shots ringing out around the city. He was dismayed because top commanders for the militants promised they wouldn't work their way in. Whether they were lying or they didn't have as much command and control as they said they did, Wilson didn't know.

The United States had also recently obtained information that the Taliban was planning to seize two prisons near Kabul and release everyone inside. If true, and Wilson had no reason to doubt what he was hearing, that would mean a few thousand more Taliban fighters on the outskirts of the capital with little regard for following the orders of senior leadership. There were also ISIS members and common criminals in that mix—a profoundly dangerous situation.

Making matters worse, security personnel at the Green Zone, housing the U.S. embassy, had fled. Those inside the compound had fewer defenses with which to protect themselves against a possibly growing mob.

Wilson and Rear Adm. Peter Vasely, who led the evacuation efforts, got on the phone with Sullivan and Blinken around 9:30 a.m. Kabul time on August 16. It was time to close the embassy and move the smaller staff that remained to the airport, putting in action the contingency plan developed a month earlier. Without hesitation, the two top Biden aides agreed with their recommendation and said to execute.

The entire embassy staff was rushed into Chinook helicopters and airlifted nearly four miles to Hamid Karzai International Airport, known as

HKIA, by 2:30 p.m. that same day, with Wilson arriving on the last short flight. A small team stayed behind to destroy sensitive equipment and documents like passports belonging to Americans and foreigners awaiting visas. A few papers belonging to SIV applicants were in the mix, but not many, since most of that paperwork was digital.

Just like that, one of the United States' most important and largest embassies shuttered.

After stopping in Qatar, General McKenzie was supposed to make his way to Kabul on August 16 to help with the emergency evacuation. But he was getting reports and seeing video that the runway at Hamid Karzai International Airport wasn't clear—it was filled with thousands of people trying to flee Taliban rule. As a U.S. military aircraft lurched for takeoff, hundreds of people ran alongside it on the runway, desperately clinging to the wheels or anything they could grab to escape the horror befalling the country. The dramatic images were beamed across screens around the world. At least one person fell from a height after the plane took off, with local outlets showing the image of a dead body on a Kabul roof.

Planes got out that day, whisking hundreds of passengers away from the maelstrom. That wasn't enough to disabuse the impression, felt around the world, that the American decision to leave Afghanistan directly led to the scenes in Kabul. "Holy fuck," a U.S. official texted me that day. "We did this."

The moment was starting to weigh on President Joe Biden. The logic of the decision would pale in comparison to the scenes of large-scale human suffering in Kabul. That he ended the war wouldn't be his legacy. *How* he ended the war would.

Biden was briefed by his security team throughout the morning and evening of August 17. He, too, saw the mob surrounding the gray C-130 on the tarmac, the crush of people overwhelming the capacity of the modest airport. *Control the situation,* he told Sullivan. *Get control of the airport.*

The United States, working alongside Afghan commandos and the Taliban, wrested a semblance of order from the chaos after sixteen hours—but it came at a huge cost. Air traffic had to stop, as it was too unsafe to take off. Two armed men shot at U.S. forces. The troops shot back and killed them, unclear in the moment whether the assailants were Taliban or disgruntled civilians. The Taliban also maintained order in its own way, beating about four hundred people with sticks outside the airport. In America's attempt to end the fighting forever, more fighting ensued.

Questions immediately surfaced about the Biden administration's handling of the withdrawal. Sullivan told reporters that Biden would address the nation on Afghanistan "soon." The national security adviser and his team knew the president couldn't respond to the tumult at HKIA. Critics of ending the war would seize on the news and images to say the administration had bungled the initial decision and the withdrawal itself. It was time to go on a messaging offensive.

Against the usual backdrop of American flags, Biden walked up to the White House podium on August 16, looking clearly perturbed. He started his remarks with a defense of the decision: It had been twenty years of war with no end in sight, no realistic victory. The U.S. didn't go to Afghanistan after 9/11 to build a democracy there; it went to defeat al-Qaeda. The focus had to stay on counterterrorism, not an indefinite military presence for Kabul's sake.

"As President, I am adamant that we focus on the threats we face today in 2021—not yesterday's threat," Biden said. "I stand squarely behind my decision." Then the tone shifted. The fall of Afghanistan, the fall of Kabul, the violence at the airport ultimately were not the administration's fault. The Afghan government and military were to blame.

"We gave them every tool they could need. We paid their salaries, provided for the maintenance of their air force—something the Taliban doesn't have. Taliban does not have an air force. We provided close air support. We gave them every chance to determine their own future. What we could not provide them was the will to fight for that future," Biden said. "And here's what I believe to my core: it is wrong to order American troops to step up when Afghanistan's own armed forces would not. If the political leaders of Afghanistan were unable to come together for the good of their people, unable to negotiate for the future of their country when the chips were down, they would never have done so while U.S. troops remained in Afghanistan bearing the brunt of the fighting for them."

Alex McCoy, recalling his time in the Marines, was offended by what he heard from the president. Afghans had fought and died alongside Americans for two decades. Yes, some Afghans were abandoning their posts, but others were fighting for their country and had lost their lives.

His phone rang. Two people from the White House's Office of Public Engagement were on the line, asking McCoy what he thought of the speech. How'd it land? they asked. The activist unloaded on the same people who had listened to him in the lead-up to the withdrawal.

"Stop victim-blaming the Afghans," he said. Also, the blood of SIVs unable to get out of Afghanistan is on your hands. "Get your shit together now. People are dying. You can't shake this."

The administration, from the president on down, was trying to shake it.

On August 18, Biden sat down with ABC News's George Stephanopoulos. Biden had spoken to the former Clinton administration communications director-turned-journalist before, the tone usually friendly but always with a hint of combativeness. Stephanopoulos asked, on behalf of a veteran of the Afghanistan war, if there wasn't a way to extract all American troops and the at-risk Afghans in a more honorable way.

Biden wasn't having it: "What's the alternative? The alternative is why are we staying in Afghanistan? Why are we there? Don't you think that the one—you know who's most disappointed in us getting out? Russia and China. They'd love us to continue to have to—"

The anchor interrupted the president to ask if "this exit could've been handled better in any way? No mistakes?"

"No," Biden said. "The idea that somehow there's a way to have gotten out without chaos ensuing, I don't know how that happens."

So, Stephanopoulos asked, the scenes around Afghanistan, the scenes at the airport in Kabul, that was all baked into the decision?

"Yes," Biden replied before seemingly trying to walk back his answer. "Now, exactly what happened—is not priced in. But I knew that they're gonna have an enormous . . ." He stopped himself and then switched subjects to discuss the Taliban. They're cooperating to get Americans out, he said.

Stephanopoulos changed gears. The August 31 withdrawal deadline was coming up, and he wanted to know if everyone in Afghanistan who wanted to leave could do so by that date, less than two weeks away.

"We're gonna do everything in our power to get all Americans out and our allies out," Biden said.

The ABC News veteran pushed the veteran politician: "Are you committed to making sure that the troops stay until every American who wants to be out is out?" Biden said "yes" before Stephanopoulos finished his question. Once the journalist did, Biden said "yes" again to ensure he was heard.

There it was: A commitment from the president that no one would be left behind. The evacuation wouldn't end until everyone was safe. But what the president was saying was bravado. "There's no one here who thinks we can meet that promise," a senior White House official told me at the time.

Samuel Aronson felt his phone buzz. *Ugh*, he thought to himself, *work*. The State Department simply couldn't let him run around the Washington Mall in peace. He looked at his phone, seeing a number he expected would flash across his screen at some point. He answered, taking the call in the bright sunlight shining off Washington's monuments.

"Sam, can you get on a flight to Kabul tonight?" The airport was overrun with people forcing their way onto flights. The U.S. had only a few military and diplomatic personnel in the terminal working to process everyone, and the situation was growing more dangerous by the day. Young troops were stationed on the perimeter to keep order, but as the masses swelled, so, too, did the chance of a breakdown. Basically, Aronson's boss called because he—and the U.S. evacuation mission—was desperate. Aronson's experience working to process visas in African hot spots was exactly what was needed.

The foreign service officer arrived in Kabul on August 20, taking nearly two days to get there, first by commercial air and then by military aircraft. He was tired and cranky, damp and delirious. The trip made him miss the days of missed connections and long layovers in American airports.

But what he saw once he got off the plane in Kabul jolted him awake. One side of HKIA was the de facto U.S. embassy for Afghanistan, which had been evacuated in a hurry as the Taliban entered the city. The other side, run by the military, was where the evacuations took place. It wasn't much of an operation. At any given time, around ten Marines sat at a table equipped with a tablet and a computer to register the passengers. It was worse outside.

Bodies packed in tight around the airport, trying to show everyone, anyone, their paperwork to go through the gates. The dry air was thick with the smell of body odor and human waste. The dust kicked up by the shuffling of feet and vehicles made it hard to breathe and covered everything from bags to faces.

The scorching heat only made everything worse. Many didn't have enough food or water to withstand the long wait, which could last anywhere from two to three days before gaining entry. Fainting was a common occurrence, requiring a small medical team to go out into the crowd and care for the sick at great personal risk to themselves.

In the most severe cases, Aronson told me, he saw people die of heat exhaustion.

The only constant for Aronson and the small team of troops and diplomats running the evacuation was that there was no consistency. On any given day, at any given hour, the policy to get everyone out of Afghanistan would change. What was always true is that someone could get in if they waved a blue American passport. Second on the priority list were green-card holders. Third, and never higher, were SIV applicants with their visas stamped inside their passports. The problem was, sometimes a more senior official would tell Aronson and his team that they couldn't allow any SIVs in. Sometimes there weren't enough seats for them that day, or the priority was to ensure that the greatest number of natural-born and naturalized citizens could get out.

"The policies were kind of fucked up," Aronson told me about a year after the events.

But the policy changes were also handed down with a wink. At the end of the day, it was the U.S. official, out in the crowd in body armor and equipped with flashbang grenades, who could make the ultimate decision about who to let in and who to keep out. "I had no problem breaking those rules," Aronson said. No one would realize he was the one who let in the handful of SIVs who weren't supposed to get on a flight that day. They would still be put on the plane once they made it into the airport, after all.

Flouting the guidelines wasn't a straightforward process, though. Successful SIV applicants were allowed to travel with their families. But many arrived at HKIA not just with their spouse and kids, but with their uncles, grandparents, nieces, nephews, cousins, even distant relatives. That was their family, and they wouldn't leave home without them.

Aronson felt for them in those moments. He was grateful that his dark sunglasses hid the tears forming in his eyes, willing the droplets not to stream down his cheeks. But his sympathy couldn't override the job he was sent to do. He would tell the visa grantee that they had about five seconds to make a decision about who to bring and who to leave behind. If they couldn't, then he'd have to move on to the other people waiting in line. There were too many people to help to waste more than a few moments on each case.

Go, some family members would say, taking the pressure off their loved one. *I'll never see you again, but I know you'll be safe.* (When Aronson told me about this, he needed to pause. His breath slowed and got deeper on the phone.) Aronson would motion to the ones selected to go inside. They would make it out alive. The fate of their family members was far less assured.

As Aronson was on the front lines of the Kabul evacuation, Rep. Tom Malinowski was tracking the news about the evacuation from his home in New Jersey. Congress was in recess, as it usually was in August, but the fall of Afghanistan hadn't put the Democrat in a vacation mood. He'd spent his entire career working to defend human rights. Now he watched as his friends botched the withdrawal he'd opposed. He expected women and minorities to suffer with the Taliban in charge. But what he didn't expect, and what he was dumbfounded by, was the fall of Kabul and the trampling of human rights from the jump.

But even as a member of the powerful House Foreign Affairs Committee with senior people on speed dial, Malinowski was starting to feel a bit helpless. There was little he could do from his singular perch. He was only one of 535 members of Congress, after all.

That was Malinowski's sense until one of his constituents, the president of the New Jersey Chamber of Commerce, got in touch. He knew of an at-risk Afghan named Najeeb Monawari who was straining to escape the Taliban's clutches, but his paperwork still wasn't finalized. He was with his family, trying and failing at four different gates to get into the airport. Why don't you write a letter on the Monawaris' behalf on official letterhead, the constituent asked Malinowski. Surely no one at HKIA could ignore such a document. The letter might just be the golden ticket into the airport and onto a plane to safety.

"This is highly irregular and there's no precedent or procedure for doing it," Malinowski replied. "I'd be happy to write and sign it." It worked. Monawari and his family got into the airport, the U.S. soldier convinced by the letterhead he presented.

Hey, that did the trick, Malinowksi thought. *I should do more of these.*

He ordered his staff to draft many more for cases that came to their attention. Sending a PDF of a signed letter by a congressman and former top State Department official to an SIV applicant desperate to leave couldn't hurt. As Malinowski just saw, it could only help.

Actually, he realized as he signed more and more letters, doing that was far more impactful than getting his friends Jake Sullivan or Tony Blinken on the phone, not that they were picking up anyway. "Wouldn't have been useful even if they did," Malinowski told me. They were powerful people, but "feckless" when it came to the on-the-ground decision-making at HKIA. Better to contact people like Aronson or a Marine on the front lines directly. They were gods of the moment, choosing who lived or died.

Every day for a week, ever since he arrived on August 20, Aronson would wake up at 4:30 a.m. to put on his body armor for a minimum twelve-hour shift. He'd consider it a restful night if he was able to sleep for thirty-minute stretches without interruption. At most he could cobble together about two or three hours. The stress of the job, of the whole moment, had him wired. The throbbing in his head and the aching in his muscles didn't curb the omnipresent adrenaline rush.

His boss would relay the day's policy for who to let in. *Let's see how long this one lasts,* Aronson would think to himself. But he and his colleagues knew the general outline: American citizens and green-card holders get in, no questions asked. SIV applicants with visas printed in their passports also got in, after verifying it was all real, of course. Citizens of foreign countries with a valid passport could also make their way in—they had a government that would welcome them, after all. After that, it was essentially up to what Aronson assessed in his rapid-fire interviews.

Sometimes he'd see the letters that lawmakers like Malinowski signed and sent to the Afghans seeking refuge. They didn't matter to him at all, because the hierarchy of entrance to the airport gates is what determined who got in and who stayed out. When the letters didn't work, the Afghan with connections in the United States would get someone powerful to call Aronson on his personal phone. "It was ringing nonstop," he told me. If he told the current or former high-level U.S. official or foreign dignitary what they didn't want to hear, Aronson's superiors would see their phones light up and buzz.

There was the added complication that not all the flights leaving HKIA were run by the U.S. military. South Korea, the United Arab Emirates, and Qatar chartered their own planes, for example, and handled their own manifests. That led to some confusion for those U.S. officials on the front lines, like Aronson, who had to either usher someone through his gate or show them to someone else handling that specific evacuation flight. By comparison, all that chaos was easy. It was dealing with the outer perimeter of Taliban members that proved a challenge.

After the militants took the capital and overthrew the government, they established a first checkpoint outside the airport. They were looking for anyone the United States or other nations might try to sneak out of Afghanistan, and they would often exact retribution on the Afghans who'd helped America and NATO for so many years. The Taliban's physical positioning forced the U.S. to work closely with the group to evacuate as many refugees and Americans as possible.

"The Taliban was willing to deal with us because they wanted us out of there," Aronson told me.

That uneasy relationship led to some hard, unsavory decisions. Evacuees and their families were sometimes put on buses to make the dangerous journey to Kabul and the airport. To ensure that the vehicles could make it past the wall of Taliban members, the U.S. would have to provide the militants with lists of the passengers' exact names, passport numbers, and other identifying information. It bothered Aronson to do that, but there was no alternative—no one wanted to take the risk of the militants shooting up an entire bus of people. "We were in the land of bad options," he told me. "It was the least worst option and the right call."

News broke of the practice on August 26, with one U.S. defense official alleging that America was handing over a "kill list" to the Taliban. Hours later, a reporter asked Biden if the practice of handing over manifests to the Taliban was true. "Yes, there have been occasions like that," he said. "And to the best of my knowledge, in those cases, the bulk of that has occurred—they've been let through." However, Biden said he wasn't sure if there were any names on the provided lists.

Top administration officials immediately took to the airwaves to dispute the story. "The idea of what you just quoted from a Pentagon official is flat out not correct. There is no such 'kill list.' That is nonsense. It is irresponsible and unfounded reporting," Sullivan said during a CNN appearance. "The idea that we've done anything to put at further risk those that we're trying to help leave the country is simply wrong. And the idea that we shared lists of Americans or others with the Taliban is simply wrong," Blinken added while on NBC News's *Meet the Press*.

About a year later, Aronson told me those denials simply weren't credible. "Yes, of course we were giving names to the Taliban. That's how we got people through. Look who we were able to get out."

Some days, Aronson would marvel at how simple it was to work with the Taliban. There were some logistical pains, but otherwise they wanted America out, so the enemies ended up being colleagues of convenience. But there were instances when the militants showed their true colors.

He recalled a moment on August 23 when U.S. staff at the airport had American citizens meet at the old Interior Ministry building. The Taliban had the list of names, noticing that many of them were Afghan-born U.S. citizens. Almost immediately, a handful of militants began beating up the Americans, bruising their bodies and bloodying their faces. These were flashes of anger and brutality, a last doling out of Taliban justice before they ultimately let the Americans go free.

Aronson would have to console some of the injured when they arrived at the airport. The naturalized Americans knew why they were targeted, but they lamented being put in that position at all. "I'm sorry," Aronson would say, "but we'll get you out. Everything is going to be okay."

Aronson wanted to believe his own words—he really did—but the situation was dire enough that he knew he was likely offering false hope.

Every day since he arrived at HKIA from the embassy, Wilson hopped on a call with top administration officials in Washington. He and other top officials on the scene in Kabul provided updates on the evacuation effort and the security around the airport. Biden joined all of them.

"He was very, very engaged," a senior official in the discussions told me. He asked a lot of questions of the Kabul cohort. What was going on at the gates? How many forces are protecting embassy staff? The airport? Was the tarmac secure? Did they need anything that officials in Washington could provide?

Biden never missed an opportunity to remind everyone of the importance of what they were doing. Americans were counting on them to get them to safety. Do whatever it takes to bring them home. The CIA would chime in around those moments, discussing the secret gate—a dusty area the U.S. controlled, not really a portal—to the airport's north that they were using to bring in vulnerable Afghans and Americans. While the administration never said so publicly, U.S. officials—including Aronson—would leave HKIA to rescue people who couldn't find their way there.

On August 25, President Biden had a question for the chair of the Joint Chiefs of Staff: "What would happen if we stayed a little after August 31? Would we be fighting the Taliban again?" Gen. Mark Milley wasn't overly surprised to hear the question in the Oval Office. It was chaos at the airport and the evacuation operation was speeding along but could use more time. "I will assess and get you an answer soon," the four-star replied.

He immediately called all the Joint Chiefs to meet in the Tank, the storied conference room for the service's leaders. The question before them was straightforward: Was the risk of staying beyond August 31 worth it? They unanimously agreed that staying the course and executing the current plan was the best way forward. The number of American personnel was dwindling, and they would be in more danger if the U.S. overstayed its welcome. Making matters worse, all the risk factors were spiking, including the possibility of a terrorist attack. Incoming intelligence made clear that plots were under way to harm Western service members and diplomats in Kabul.

The president agreed with the recommendation, conveyed by Austin and Milley, not to push the operation into September.

The next day, Aronson received a message from a colleague: There was an active threat that intelligence had picked up on Abbey Gate. It was the last known way into the airport. Hundreds of people pushed toward the handful of U.S. troops and civilians manning the wide metal entrance, barely protected by rows of concertina wire. When a family received an authorization to enter, a Marine would crack the gate just wide enough for the people to stream in and then close it immediately once they were all through.

If the gate made a noise when opening and closing, those who manned it didn't know. "It was so loud between the yelling, crying, and airplanes taxiing and taking off right next to us. The tarmac was max fifty meters to the right," Aronson told me a year later.

Once someone passed through Abbey Gate and into the airport, what they saw didn't immediately look like salvation. The dusty road led to a gray stop sign above a red notice telling drivers their vehicles had to undergo a security sweep. Papers and clothes were strewn about. Cement walls towered above every huddled, tired, hungry group. But getting through Abbey Gate meant safety. Staying on the outside of it meant danger.

Chatter indicated that a terrorist would ram a vehicle through the crowd of people waiting to get into the airport and then detonate an explosive device. The danger was so real—and imminent—that Aronson and his colleagues got a radio message at 2:30 p.m. to leave the secret area and return to the Joint Operations Center, known as the JOC, about a block away from the passenger terminal. "Things are really fucking fluid and we've got to move fast," the colleague said in a matter-of-fact tone. If Aronson's colleague was scared, it wasn't evident in his voice.

As Aronson packed up, he saw CIA and Delta Force operatives prepare to leave alongside him. *Shit,* Aronson thought to himself. *When the CIA and Delta guys are being pulled off a secret mission, you know it's serious.* Aronson could see, as he looked over his shoulder, someone placing an armored personnel carrier in front of the gate.

"Sadly, it was a question of when, not if, something was going to happen," CIA director Bill Burns recalled later.

Aronson got back to the JOC a little after 5:00 p.m. local time. The building had a military side and an embassy side, separated by a double glass door. The military section had about six television screens, each showing different satellite images or drone footage. The embassy space featured couches for sleeping and sealed meals ready to eat for the famished.

Nothing had happened yet. There was still the same level of chaos around the airport. That meant nothing had changed. He could see on a television screen, beaming footage from an overhead drone, that the Marines remained at their posts at Abbey Gate. He assumed they were told to stay put even as a terrorist was soon expected to bomb the area they guarded. Perhaps a commander decided keeping them there both stopped the airport from being overrun and gave them a chance to shoot the attacker before the fireball?

Whatever the reason, Aronson felt something was coming. He just didn't know what. He lit a cigarette and blew out a plume of smoke. It commingled with the dust swirling around, darkening the gold hue of the sunlight surrounding him.

The feeling was prescient. At the same time, a man dressed in all black snaked his way through the throngs of people begging and pleading to be whisked out of the country. Once he got close enough to the Marines, he detonated an improvised explosive device.

At 5:11, Aronson heard a loud voice: "Attention in the JOC, reports of a blast at Abbey Gate, stand by for more information." The bustling rooms went quiet. All eyes turned to the television screens, which beamed drone footage of an unmistakable blast just outside Abbey Gate. The silence was interrupted by a driver honking the horn of his vehicle and shouting: "Move the fuck off the road. Get out of the way!"

It was panic and sensory overload for those near the blast. There was screaming, running, blood. Gunfire from the weapons of British and American troops rang out to control the crowd.

Ross Wilson's mind immediately went to the most horrifying possibility: a terrorist attack among the horde of people outside the airport. A Pentagon assessment had warned officials in Kabul that ISIS's franchise in Afghanistan was targeting HKIA and planes whisking away hundreds of passengers. Those concerns only grew as more than one hundred prisoners loyal to ISIS escaped two prisons near Kabul.

Perhaps this was the strike everyone was fearing.

Aronson could see the carnage from the grainy, gray drone feed streaming in the JOC. Bodies, contorted and dismembered, were strewn about Abbey Gate. It looked as if most of the dead were Afghans, but he and others around him could see that some of the Marines had been killed in the blast. His attention was diverted when the rocket detection system sounded: "INCOMING, INCOMING, INCOMING." A beat later: "Attention in the JOC, imminent rocket attack. Take cover." Aronson could feel and hear his heart pounding in his chest, sitting helplessly as he lived out what could have been his final moments.

Reports were also coming in about an attack at the Baron Hotel, just southeast of HKIA. Surveillance picked up a drone flying above the airport. Fear spread that it was carrying a bomb and would drop it on the Americans.

Aronson did what others around him were doing: texting their loved ones to say they were alive, at least for now. He got in touch with his brother but couldn't connect with his wife. He started frantically texting people he knew who worked in her office, hoping to speak with her one last time before he, too, perished in a blast. Nothing. He also tried someone who worked on the same computer network as his office, imploring the person to send her a direct, internal message to call her husband.

By the time she got in touch with him, the violence had subsided. The missile siren was a false alarm. There was no attack at the Baron Hotel. And the drone, it turned out, was friendly. The single suicide bombing was it. "We were in complete shock that it was the only one," Aronson told me later. "We thought it was a complex attack.... It turned out the overwhelming majority was just noise."

At the same time, on August 26, Blinken was in his daily 9:00 a.m. meeting with staff. He was going over his schedule for the day and getting updates on Afghanistan when someone walked into his office and handed a note to his chief of staff, Suzy George. She looked at it for a moment, stunned by what she was reading. Blinken asked what had her so upset. She said there had been an attack at Abbey Gate at HKIA. No American casualties had yet been confirmed, but that was likely to change.

The daily video call with the president proceeded as planned, starting about an hour after the lethal detonation. Everyone watched as General McKenzie routinely picked up a phone to hear the latest information about the attack. When McKenzie raised his hand, Sullivan, who led the meeting, called on him. "We can confirm it was an ISIS attack," he said in one of his early interjections. Some Afghans died in the bombing, though at that point it was unclear if any Americans were killed. The president then walked in. The meeting paused briefly as Sullivan got the boss up to speed. Time passed until McKenzie raised his hand again and Sullivan acknowledged him. Americans were confirmed dead, he said, but his staff was still working to get more details.

That sequence of events happened multiple times throughout the meeting, and in every instance the number of dead Afghans and Americans ticked upward. "The president became very emotional with the loss of life," someone in the meeting told me. He didn't cry, but it was clear the deaths of Americans on his watch—in part due to the decision he made—weighed on him.

Biden slumped in his chair, his head down, staring at his feet. The mood was heavy, tense. The silence piercing. Then the president spoke: "The worst that can happen has happened."

Biden, with the advice of aides, made some decisions in that meeting. It was time to shut the gates and prepare to leave imminently. Staying in Afghanistan under direct threat from the Taliban and ISIS was no longer an option. Orders then flowed downward that everyone had to have their bags packed—if they had a bag—and be ready to leave the country in roughly thirty-six hours. Bags had to be on a plane by 6:00 the following morning if they had expectations of ever seeing their belongings again. The troops helping to bring Afghan-born Americans from Afghanistan's Department of the Interior were to leave their rucksacks behind. It wasn't worth the risk of putting a bag on board that might have had a detonator placed inside it.

For the next few hours, all the official reports indicated that four American service members died in the attack. Wilson and his cohorts tried to account for all their people. Was anyone missing? If someone couldn't be found in the next few minutes, call them. Try anything to get in touch.

By the end of the accounting and subsequent investigations, the casualty count came to 13 U.S. troops and at least 170 Afghan civilians. "It was the worst day of our administration. Nothing else comes close," a senior U.S. official told me at the time. When I caught up with this person about a year later, they still felt the same. "It was such a difficult moment. Obviously I felt bad for the fallen and for their families. And then, thinking selfishly about what this meant for us, I wasn't sure we could recover from it. It was a failure. There's no way to spin it."

Later, as more news of dead Americans made its way to the Oval Office, Biden hung his head in silence while sitting behind the *Resolute* Desk. It seemed to those who witnessed the moment like part prayer and part moment of lament.

Biden recounted his own feelings to Chris Whipple two years later. "August twenty-sixth was one of the hardest of hard days," he said. "Those thirteen proud, patriotic American service members were beloved sons and daughters, brothers and sisters. They came from all over our country, each with a unique story and the dreams of loved ones who'd nurtured them, united by a common call to serve something greater than themselves. They were ultimate heroes, and each saved countless other lives as part of the largest airlift evacuation operation in our history."

Sullivan, meanwhile, had just suffered the greatest failure of his professional career. Always quick with an answer, this time he had fallen short, even though he knew an attack was coming. He was livid at the deaths, at the situation, at himself. His friends had never seen him so shaken, so lacking in confidence. "That wasn't the Jake we knew," one of them told me. "He was rocked."

The U.S. was out for revenge after Abbey Gate. "To those who carried out this attack, as well as anyone who wishes America harm, know this: We will not forgive. We will not forget. We will hunt you down and make you pay. I will defend our interests and our people with every measure at my command," Biden said in a White House address to the nation in the early evening of August 26.

Revenge would come swiftly. The next day, Zalmay Khalilzad asked a colleague to get in touch with senior Taliban representatives. The militants should know that the United States planned to "hold accountable those responsible for yesterday's strike which killed American Forces and Afghans," his military adviser wrote on his behalf to another staffer. "This act will not go unanswered. The U.S. will strike ISIS-K targets we know to exist. Our goal is to destroy those responsible with precision and without harming civilians or the Taliban." That message made its way to Suhail Shaheen, the Taliban's spokesperson, to relay to the group's leadership.

Later that day, at around 5:00 p.m. local time on August 27, almost exactly twenty-four hours after the attack, Rear Adm. Peter Vasely walked into the office of John Bass, the former U.S. ambassador to Afghanistan who was the leading civilian of the evacuation effort. A drone was tracking the bomb maker and planner of the ISIS strike. If there was a chance to take him out without civilian casualties, the U.S. was going to take the shot. Bass nodded and said he understood, and Vasely went back to the military-led side of the airport. Roughly seven hours later, U.S. forces announced that they had killed their target while he was in his car with an ISIS associate.

The threat wasn't over, and troops were on the lookout for any other menaces as the evacuation proceeded and wound down. That fear led to tragedy on August 29.

An American MQ-9 Reaper drone tracked the activity of a suspicious man throughout the capital, leading his trackers to assume he was a member of ISIS carrying a bomb and heading toward HKIA. When the white sedan pulled into a residential driveway, the decision was made to launch a Hellfire missile and destroy the driver, the vehicle, and its contents.

But the man wasn't a terrorist. His name was Zemari Ahmadi, and he worked for a U.S. aid organization in Afghanistan. He had spent the day not preparing to kill people but rather transporting colleagues to and from work and loading canisters of water into his trunk for his family to drink. When he arrived at his home near the end of the workday, Ahmadi sat in his car waiting for his kids and his family members to come out of the house and welcome him. That's when the missile hit its target—killing ten civilians, seven of them children. Days later, General Milley would call the decision a "righteous strike." It would take an investigation by *The New York Times* and, later, the Pentagon to realize the fatal error.

The Joint Chiefs chair was beside himself, first and foremost, because of the grave mistake on its own. He would also later tell aides that he regretted using the word *righteous* because of its religious undertone. What he should have said in the moment, he conceded, was that the strike was "legitimate," because the strike was based on the best information the U.S. military had at the time. "We, and I, should have done better," he told a confidant.

On August 30, it was clear: This would be the last day of the U.S. military mission in Afghanistan. There were few officials left, the remaining Americans who wanted to evacuate were hard to reach, and the dangers kept mounting. The final plane would leave that night.

Officials started to close the gate, with only a threadbare security presence outside. Afghan families desperate to leave were begging for the Americans to stay, to let them inside and take them onward to safety. "I'll never forget having to tell those people, 'No, we have to go. I pray you stay safe,'" a U.S. official told me.

Wilson wanted to ensure that his staff and everyone else got out before him. He was still the top diplomat there—their safety was his priority. As more and more personnel left, the noise above the airport grew louder and louder. Drones and helicopters were buzzing above HKIA, keeping an eye on any potential security threats as the last remnants of America's twenty-year war in Afghanistan prepared to leave. Among the security aircraft was a tiny one-man helicopter that, when the last plane was boarding, landed on the tarmac, got folded up, and was loaded onto the C-17.

Wilson, one of a handful of diplomats left, joined around a hundred troops on the last five planes out of Kabul. He had to climb over ropes and cords on his aircraft that tied down equipment, including the foldable helicopters. The last person to get on was Maj. Gen. Chris Donahue, a moment immortalized by a ghoulish green-and-black photograph of him walking toward the aircraft. He had just come from talking to a Taliban commander about what time the plane would take off. As the engines revved, Donahue, the last American service member out of Afghanistan, sent a final message

National Security Adviser Jake Sullivan briefs President Joe Biden en route to Poland on February 19, 2023, ahead of the surprise visit to Kyiv.

Secretary of State Antony Blinken delivers remarks on Russia's threats to Ukraine during a surprise appearance at the United Nations on February 17, 2022. Behind him (left) is Linda Thomas-Greenfield, the U.S. ambassador to the United Nations.

Defense Secretary Lloyd Austin answers questions during a press conference at the NATO defense ministerial meeting on October 13, 2022.

General Mark Milley, chair of the Joint Chiefs of Staff, was against the military withdrawal from Afghanistan, and helped provide the military assistance plans to President Joe Biden.

Director of National Intelligence Avril Haines briefs President Joe Biden during the daily briefing on January 24, 2022. Secretary of State Antony Blinken and National Security Adviser Jake Sullivan are in attendance.

President Joe Biden meets the "European Quad" leaders at the Rome G20 summit on October 30, 2021. From left to right: British prime minister Boris Johnson, French president Emmanuel Macron, German chancellor Angela Merkel, and Biden.

Sam Aronson on a hotwired school bus on the early afternoon of August 23, 2021, heading to Camp Alvarado in Afghanistan. He was on his way to meet American citizens at the Ministry of Interior Affairs to bring them to safety.

Sam Aronson just inside the east gate of Hamid Karzai International Airport on August 23, 2021. He climbed up a dirt mound to see over the gate, only to find hundreds of people hoping to be placed on an evacuation flight.

A U.S. Marine provides security outside Hamid Karzai International Airport in Kabul, Afghanistan, on August 18, 2021. In the background, hopeful escapees await their turn for a flight out.

Russia seized Antonov Airport in Hostomel, near Kyiv, within the war's first few days. But then Russian troops fanned out across the region, making it easier for Ukrainian troops to attack them. The Russians did destroy "Mriya" (the Dream), the world's largest airplane, its wreckage visible under the destroyed hangar.

Ukraine issued a postage stamp commemorating the "Russian warship, go fuck yourself!" quip by a Ukrainian soldier on Snake Island.

Ukrainian president Volodymyr Zelenskyy, flanked by his top aide, Andriy Yermak, observes the atrocities in the city of Bucha. Russian troops allegedly tortured and killed civilians there, leaving lifeless bodies in the street.

President Joe Biden meets with Ukrainian president Volodymyr Zelenskyy in Kyiv during a surprise visit on February 20, 2023, near the one-year anniversary of the war.

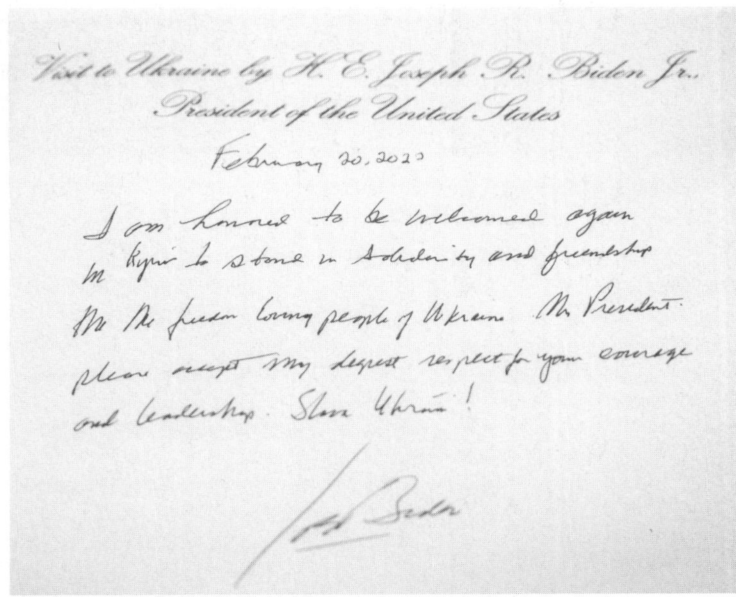

Visit to Ukraine by H. E. Joseph R. Biden Jr.,
President of the United States

February 20, 2023

I am honored to be welcomed again in Kyiv to stand in solidarity and friendship with the freedom loving people of Ukraine. Mr. President, please accept my deepest respect for your courage and leadership. Slava Ukraini!

Joe Biden

A note President Joe Biden wrote to Ukrainian president Volodymyr Zelenskyy during his surprise visit to Kyiv.

President Joe Biden holds a secure video call with his Russian counterpart, Vladimir Putin, on December 7, 2021. Biden told Putin that Russia would face severe economic punishments for invading Ukraine. Secretary of State Antony Blinken and National Security Adviser Jake Sullivan attend the call.

to his troops and others on board, many of whom had worked nearly twenty-four hours a day for about a month to safely escort thousands of people out of the country. "Job well done, I'm proud of you all."

Then everyone sat on the aircraft bound for Doha—bound for safety—in silence. Everyone knew they'd forever be bonded in trauma, and in knowing that they'd done the best they could do under trying circumstances. But those kinds of thoughts came later. On the plane, all anyone wanted to do was sleep.

The United States evacuated more than 124,000 people from Afghanistan and settled around 80,000 Afghans in America. In a statement on August 31, Defense Secretary Lloyd Austin said "no other military could have protected so many lives under such challenging circumstances in such a short amount of time—not just because of our airlift or our logistics capabilities, but most of all because of the immense compassion, skill, and dedication of American Service members." Everyone who was involved in the operation would receive the Meritorious Unit Commendation.

Aronson, a diplomat, got a hero's welcome when he landed at Washington's Dulles Airport on August 30. The Boeing 787 was nearly empty, with only about seventy of the more than two hundred seats taken by American officials making their way back from horrific nights in Kabul. When the plane landed and came to a stop, everyone gave one another a standing ovation.

The people mover drove directly up to the plane. It carried the passengers to the customs terminal, where the exhausted officials were met by top-level State Department figures led by Deputy Secretary of State for Management Brian McKeon. They applauded and hugged their colleagues, thanking them for their work.

Aronson could hear a murmur build into crowd noise within Dulles's packed customs hall. People were wondering what all the commotion on the platform above them was. Finally, it became clear: They were the people who had helped evacuate thousands from Kabul and brought them to safety. Suddenly, there was clapping. Cheering and whoops followed. Aronson wanted to appreciate it more than he did, but he was too tired to feel gratitude.

The seventy staffers were handed pamphlets on the other side of the customs line. The State Department was offering each of them a week off to recover from what they had just experienced. If they needed more time, all they had to do was speak with their career development officers, who would grant them all the time they needed. And if anyone wished to see a mental health professional, they should feel welcome to do so. Those visits wouldn't impact their security clearances.

Aronson already knew that he needed more than a week. Mentally he was drained, but physically he was also a shambles. The blisters on his feet got infected because he had been unable to change his socks in Kabul, leading him to walk with a limp. He had lost his voice; the most he could muster was a faint whisper. His nose bled roughly every two hours, either from malnutrition or from the dryness in the air back in Afghanistan.

Freshly returned to Washington, Aronson told his career officer he needed more time to recuperate, but he was told he couldn't have it. He was between overseas assignments and scheduled to head to the Middle East—another hardship post—and the government couldn't extend payments for his lodging and language training. Aronson also requested a nicer location for his next posting, hoping to avoid the rough-and-tumble and heat of the Middle East. No, he was also told, that couldn't change either. He was needed in the region.

The exhausted diplomat didn't blame any of what he considered mistreatment on Blinken. The secretary met with Aronson and thirty others about two weeks after they arrived back in the U.S. He said how impressed he was with each and every one of them. State Department leadership was at their disposal if they needed anything. The heroes of Kabul would get all the assistance they needed.

"He was very personable and down to earth," Aronson said about the meeting, noting that he had a short side chat with Blinken. The buck stopped with him, sure, but he couldn't possibly be aware of the administration issues far below him inside the department.

Aronson started to consider leaving State, fearing the agency wouldn't accommodate him. His department-provided therapist ultimately convinced him to leave, saying he was a rock star and, after all he'd been through, would have no problem finding a new job. It helped that the therapist made that case around the time Aronson was starting to get angry about the State Department failing to pay him the twelve thousand dollars he was owed for serving in Kabul.

After helping save thousands of lives—making the best of a terrible situation created by a decision made by administration leaders, including some in the State Department—Aronson chose to leave.

"I felt fucked with my assignment, [and] not getting paid on time wasn't working for me anymore. Another opportunity came about, and I took it," he told me. "I love adventure, and I was always picking the hardest assignments with the expectation that with these sacrifices, and with a good reputation, I could get what I needed when I called in favors. But that didn't happen—so I left."

On August 31, the first day America hadn't been at war in Afghanistan for two decades, Biden defended the withdrawal decision and the evacuation. "We were ready," he said in the State Dining Room of the White House. Unfortunately, he said, about one hundred to two hundred Americans who wanted to leave remained behind in Afghanistan. "Most of those who remain are dual citizens, long-time residents who had earlier decided to stay because of their family roots in Afghanistan." He then mistakenly said 90 percent of those who wanted out did leave—the real number was 98 percent—but the damage was done. The president had broken a promise: America left Americans behind.

Republicans were especially furious. "Hundreds of Americans and thousands of our Afghan allies have been left behind enemy lines. This is not a mission accomplished, this is a complete disgrace," said Wisconsin representative Mike Gallagher, who authored a bill that would have compelled U.S. forces to stay in Afghanistan until every willing evacuee got out. "America's last flight left Afghanistan, even though we still don't know the total number of Americans trapped behind enemy lines—it's unforgivable," added Montana senator Steve Daines.

That anger featured prominently in congressional hearings held in mid-September. Blinken drew the short straw of having to defend the withdrawal in front of lawmakers. Democrats and Republicans alike wanted answers, especially about the U.S. citizens, many of them dual nationals, who remained in Afghanistan.

"We're in constant contact with American citizens still in Afghanistan who have told us that they wish to leave. Each has been assigned a case management team to offer specific guidance and instruction," Blinken told the House Foreign Affairs Committee on September 13. "We'll continue to help them and we'll continue to help any American who still wants to leave and Afghans to whom we have a special commitment, just as we've done in other countries where we've evacuated our embassy and hundreds or even thousands of Americans remained behind."

How many remained behind, the House members wanted to know? "As of the end of last week, we had about one hundred American citizens in Afghanistan who told us that they wished to leave the country. And I want to emphasize that this is a snapshot in time," he responded.

Toward the end of September, it was the turn of Austin, Milley, and McKenzie to sit in front of Congress and answer their Afghanistan questions. Both the secretary and the general admitted for the first time in public that they had recommended keeping troops in Afghanistan, though Austin made the point that he'd never said the military mission should continue indefinitely. McKenzie agreed with that general position, telling lawmakers he thought a troop withdrawal would "lead inevitably to the collapse of the Afghan military forces, and, eventually, the Afghan government."

Milley, meanwhile, told Sen. Elizabeth Warren that U.S. troops should have stayed in Afghanistan indefinitely, even if it meant keeping them in harm's way. The mission was too important to pack up and leave. But in the end, Milley didn't blame the president or the Pentagon or the State Department or Congress or the media or anyone else that played a part in the failure of America's war. The failure left many culpable, he told the House Armed Services Committee.

"This is a twenty-year war," General Milley said. "It wasn't lost in the last twenty days or even twenty months for that matter. There is a cumulative effect from a series of decisions that go way back."

Administrations come and go. Once out of power, the people who made up Republican and Democratic teams tend to stick around Washington, D.C., hearing from former colleagues and friends about who's up and who's down on the inside. There are informal ways to glean insights, like who's invited to glamorous think tank–hosted award dinners or to speak at gala events. With time, these people develop a sense for when an administration has screwed up so badly that only a blood sacrifice will atone for the sin, the scandal, or the loss of international stature that the president has commissioned.

Such was the case in August 2021, when Republicans called for Biden to be impeached. A small handful of Democrats, including a former Obama administration official, were speaking privately and openly about pushing Jake Sullivan out too.

"President Biden needs to fire his national security adviser and several other senior leaders who oversaw the botched execution of our withdrawal from Afghanistan. He has to restructure how and with whom he is making major foreign policy decisions, allowing for more input from career experts,"

Brett Bruen, who served as a director of global engagement in the White House alongside Sullivan during the Obama administration, wrote in *USA Today* on August 16, right in the middle of the crisis.

Bruen wasn't the only one hoping heads would roll. Republican senator Marsha Blackburn of Tennessee said Blinken "needs to resign immediately" because he knew from the dissent cable that Kabul would fall soon after a military withdrawal. "Does Biden really think that the people advising him deserve to keep their jobs; do the people advising him really think the way he handled this is acceptable? *Really?*" center-right columnist Matt Lewis asked rhetorically.

There was never any serious reckoning inside the administration. Biden told his top aides, Sullivan included, that he stood by them and that they had done their best during a tough situation. They had served America and Americans nobly, and their jobs were safe. "There wasn't even a real possibility of a shakeup," a White House official told me at the time.

An abrupt career end would've hit differently for each member of Biden's tarnished A-Team. Blinken could have returned to WestExec and seen out the rest of his sunsetting career with a prestigious fellowship at a D.C.-area think tank. If Austin was the fall man, the general who had come out of retirement to be secretary of defense could easily go back on the motivational speaking circuit in retired life. He had already left public service once; there was no problem leaving it again.

Sullivan was the one with the most to lose at that moment. With at least two more decades of work ahead of him, his public service career might have ended the day Biden asked for his resignation. Any plans to be secretary of state or run for political office would assuredly have to be set aside for a career making money in the private sector. The lifelong believer in service would have to hang it up.

But no one offered to resign, in large part because the president didn't believe anyone had made a mistake. Leaving Afghanistan was always going to be messy. And none of the critics outside the administration could point to a single misstep along the way. Where was the negligence? Where was the wrong decision? What was the catastrophic error? Nobody could pinpoint any such moment to the satisfaction of senior leaders.

If some preferred that the United States stay in Afghanistan, then fine, that was their right. And could some decisions have been made sooner, like prepositioning U.S. forces days before their August 12 arrival to avoid the chaotic scenes at Kabul's airport? Sure. But did the Biden team make the right calls to airlift almost 125,000 people out of a collapsing nation? Absolutely.

Still, while Sullivan, Blinken, Austin, and others would keep their jobs, they all knew their reputations would take a huge hit. That would affect how people saw them as individuals and the administration as a whole. The A-Team, Biden's band of professionals, had for the time being become the B-Squad. They hadn't lived up to expectations when it mattered most. They were humbled on the national and world stage.

Sullivan asked colleagues if there was more he could have done to avoid the worst outcomes during the withdrawal. He wondered if there was anything he missed in the days leading to the tragic scenes in Kabul.

Austin strategized on how to convince the president that the Pentagon wasn't working to thwart Biden; they were trying to help him see that ending military involvements was always messier than planned. Blinken was left answering "I told you so" phone calls from angry allies. They had warned against a withdrawal and now the U.S.—the West's leader—looked weak.

Biden, distraught as he was after the events in Afghanistan, was confident the United States would soon be on a better path. Disentangled from Afghanistan, the nation he led could now refocus on climate change and pressing domestic concerns. The billions spent on the war would be reinvested in bridges, schools, and health care. It was not throwing good money after bad abroad if it could be used to good effect at home. Better to save the military for targeting terrorists and for the remote possibility of war with China.

Sometimes, it was worth a little short-term pain for long-term gain.

The press, which had unanimously been brutal on the administration's decision and execution, would eventually move on. The president knew this town and how it worked. Washington had become his adopted home over five decades. Even this, too, shall pass.

Few around the president had such confidence. The Biden administration was adrift. Approval ratings were tanking. Sullivan was at his lowest point, facing calls loud and quiet for his ouster. He, more than anyone, was looking to get the administration a much-needed win. The team needed to get back on its feet; America needed to get back on its feet.

"We didn't say this explicitly at the time, but later it became clear we were all thinking we needed a comeback," a senior official told me many months after the events. What that would even look like, though, no one knew. "I knew I wanted redemption, but what could be big enough to earn it after all that?"

Part 3

The Austin Powers Inspiration

Chapter 9

The Man from Ukraine

August–November 2021

Finally, Volodymyr Zelenskyy's day had arrived. After two years in office, all of it spent with Russia controlling swaths of his country, the Ukrainian president was getting his White House meeting. Zelenskyy's visit would signal back home that he had the respect of the United States government and its leader, and it would also broadcast Ukraine's plight and pain to a global audience.

Ukraine had undergone decades of turmoil and needed good news. More than 92 percent of Ukrainians voted for a declaration of independence from the Soviet Union in 1991, clearing the way for the country's sovereignty. Since then, much of the nation—generally split between a more European western side and a more Russia-friendly east—has sought to distance itself from Russia. That didn't happen.

In 2004, a candidate favored by Vladimir Putin won an allegedly fraudulent election. The challenger, Viktor Yushchenko, was poisoned with dioxin in a clear attempt to kill him. The election result and that assassination attempt led thousands to protest the new government in what became known as the Orange Revolution.

A decade later, now president Viktor Yanukovych abruptly reversed an agreement to more closely align Ukraine with the European Union. Thousands of pro-Western Ukrainians took to the country's streets. In February 2014, security forces, including snipers, killed around a hundred protesters in Kyiv's Maidan Square. A hotel was turned into an improvised hospital to deal with the casualties.

Russia invaded Crimea that same month, moving later to annex the peninsula. It was a physical manifestation of the control Russia still had over Ukraine's people and politics. Since 2014, Ukraine has had to exist as a country under siege. Its neighbor, with its vastly greater resources and military power, wanted to take Ukraine bite by bite, picking off Crimea and two eastern regions of the country. The Obama administration did little in response except to provide Ukraine with defensive weapons, sanction the Kremlin, and kick Russia out of the Group of Eight, turning the G8 into the G7.

The United States might have done more had Barack Obama's vice president, Joe Biden, been in charge. Russia should "pay in blood and money" for its actions, Biden told his boss as the 2014 invasion began. Obama disagreed, but he made Biden his effective ambassador to Ukraine during the crisis. The president told Biden not to overpromise anything to the Ukrainian government.

He made six visits to Ukraine as vice president, five of those coming after the 2014 Maidan protests. Alongside President Petro Poroshenko in Kyiv, just three days before Trump's inauguration on January 20, 2017, Biden committed the United States to supporting Ukraine in its continued fight for independence from Russia.

"Ukraine, like every country in Europe, has a right to determine its own path. Yet Russia seeks to deny that choice. And the international community must continue to stand as one against Russian aggression and coercion," he said. "It's no secret that Russia does not want you to succeed,"

Biden continued. "It's not just about Ukraine. It's about the future we have long sought of a Europe whole, free, and at peace—whole, free, and at peace—something that is in the vital national interest of both the United States and all Europeans."

That October, Antony Blinken, now writing op-eds for *The New York Times* and fresh off being the deputy secretary of state, was pushing for the Trump administration to go further than Barack Obama had in aiding Ukraine. In one column, he noted that the Obama administration debated lifting the ban on sending lethal aid to help Kyiv fight off Russian and Moscow-allied troops in the east. "President Barack Obama concluded that we should keep the focus where we had the advantage: on tough sanctions, economic aid to Ukraine, training for its troops, support for its reform efforts—especially combating endemic corruption—and determined diplomacy," Blinken wrote.

It was time for the Trump administration to right that wrong, he argued: "What might give Mr. Putin pause at turning up the temperature yet again within eastern Ukraine—or worse, taking another whole bite out of the country—is the knowledge his troops would be seriously bloodied in the doing."

So as Zelenskyy prepared to meet with his American colleague on August 30, 2021, he hoped to play off Biden's sense of not having been able to do the job he and his secretary of state had wanted to do years earlier.

As the day approached, world events pushed the meeting further back. First, Zelenskyy would have to wait just one more day to meet Biden, on August 31. The official reason, given by Ukrainian foreign minister Dmytro Kuleba during an August 19 briefing, was that Biden now wanted to expand the gathering by adding a one-on-one chat with Zelenskyy. Kuleba and Andriy Yermak, a top aide in Zelenskyy's office, worked out those details during their planning visits to Washington.

Then, just two days before the planned encounter, the White House asked if Zelenskyy could postpone the gathering for just another twenty-four hours. Biden was preoccupied with the last days of the withdrawal from Afghanistan. And as if that weren't enough, a Category 4 hurricane, Ida, was barreling toward New Orleans. Biden needed a bit more time to see the evacuation through and make sure that those affected by the storm in Louisiana and other southern states had everything they needed. That was no problem, Zelenskyy's team replied.

A senior administration official hopped on the phone with reporters to preview the September 1 encounter—a meeting months in the making. "Our strategic partnership has never been stronger than it is now," the official said. It would only grow stronger, the official continued, once the United States provided Ukraine with $60 million in security assistance, including Javelin anti-tank missiles alongside defensive and nonlethal equipment. Any disagreements in the past, like Zelenskyy's desire to meet with Biden in person before the Putin summit in Geneva, would not be a "point of contention."

If the two leaders were trying to signal to the world there was no underlying tension between them, they failed.

Biden spoke first in the Oval Office in front of cameras, removing his mask to tour a weapons package and other assistance—2 million COVID-19 vaccine doses and financial support for Ukraine's energy sector. He couldn't have sounded less excited to be in the room, though he spoke passionately about the long-standing relationship between Kyiv and Washington. He didn't have to like Zelenskyy to appreciate the need for a strong bond between their two countries.

It was Zelenskyy's turn to speak. Clean-shaven and donning a black tie, the fresh-faced Ukrainian president thanked Biden for his words and the help. But, with the cameras whirring, the former television star made his pitch to Biden and the world.

"We have to focus very much now on the security issue, which is the most important on this agenda. And security in Donbas—the Ukrainian Donbas, in the Ukrainian Crimea—temporarily, as we believe, occupied by the Russian Federation; security in the Black Sea and security in the Azov Sea region," Zelenskyy said. "And I would like to discuss with President

Biden here his vision, his government's vision of Ukraine's chances to join NATO and the timeframe for this accession, if it is possible; and the role the United States can play being involved in a peaceful settlement in Donbas that we would like to reach."

"Much to talk about," Biden agreed.

Indeed there was. Most of the private session between the two presidents was cordial enough, even on the subject of Nord Stream 2. But Zelenskyy brought up how he felt snubbed by the timing of the meeting—Congress was still out of session; many lawmakers wouldn't be returning to Washington until after Labor Day weekend—and that Biden seemed to have a lot more contact with the dictator in Moscow than the democratically elected president of Ukraine.

The message Zelenskyy wanted to get across, beyond Washington and Kyiv needing to form a closer partnership, was that Ukraine was fighting for its life. It would continue to defend itself, but it needed America's steadfast military and political support.

Biden committed as much, noting his years as a staunch transatlanticist and his record of supporting Ukraine during his time as vice president. But Zelenskyy was a bit perturbed by what he deemed Biden's lack of knowledge on the current Ukrainian situation.

The American president didn't seem to know about the aggressiveness of Russia's fleet in the Black Sea. That July, for example, a Russian ship made contact with an American destroyer engaged in live-fire exercises with Ukraine's navy, demanding that all parties leave and end the annual drills. Officers aboard the American vessel, the *Ross,* said they had a right to exercise in international waters. The conversation stopped there, though Russian warships and warplanes continued to patrol the area. Russia had also turned the Kerch Strait, the narrow waterway between Crimea and mainland Russia, into a flashpoint. In 2018, Russian forces shot at, and then captured, three Ukrainian ships along with twenty-four crew members. The incident made enough waves that the United States sent a warship from the Sixth Fleet into the Black Sea.

While Biden knew about the issue generally, Zelenskyy told his staff after the meeting that he had expected his American counterpart to know a lot more of the details. Perhaps Zelenskyy glommed on to that moment because he was nonplussed, and a little disappointed, with how the whole meeting had gone. He arrived in Washington with little pomp and circumstance and came away mainly with a pittance in security assistance. "We weren't talking about Stingers," someone familiar with Zelenskyy's thinking told me. "It wasn't a terrible visit, but not terribly successful either."

As Zelenskyy continued on his U.S. tour, he and his team felt the White House had organized the meeting just to say that it happened. A box to be ticked on Biden's diplomatic checklist. More about symbolism than substance. Symbolism had its place, but not when Russia was at war with Ukraine.

As September came and went, Ukraine was nowhere near the top of the administration's agenda. It was still dealing with the aftermath of the botched Afghanistan withdrawal. Secretary of State Antony Blinken and Defense Secretary Lloyd Austin were battling congressional Republicans in hearings about the evacuation and how many Americans had been left behind.

The administration was taking heat from both sides of the aisle: Blinken was almost always on the defensive during a testy five-hour session with the Democrat-led Senate Foreign Relations Committee. "There's no evidence that staying longer would have made the Afghan security forces or the Afghan government any more resilient or self-sustaining," he said. Blaming the Trump administration, Blinken thundered, "We inherited a deadline. We did not inherit a plan."

Rep. Michael McCaul, the Texan serving as the panel's top Republican, wasn't buying it: "The American people don't like to lose, especially not to the terrorists. But this is exactly what has happened."

Criticisms from the Hill weren't the only things plaguing the administration. North Korea was launching and testing new missiles again. Plans were under way for Boris Johnson to come to the White House following the annual United Nations General Assembly, known colloquially as UNGA. Even in the best of times, Johnson was not a Biden favorite. And completing the perfect shitstorm of bad press was the breaking news that the U.S., Britain, and Australia had made a secret nuclear-submarine deal that cut France out of a previous multibillion-dollar agreement with Australia, causing a weekslong diplomatic spat that led Paris to temporarily recall its ambassador to the United States.

Ukraine-related issues were so conspicuously absent that Chatham House, a prominent think tank in London, held a roundtable event titled "Where Is Ukraine in Biden's Agenda?" on September 15. Ukraine being an afterthought was confirmed when Biden's high-profile UN General Assembly address didn't feature the words "Ukraine," "Russia," or "Putin." He was instead, expectedly, focused on rallying the world to combat COVID-19 and climate change.

"This is the clear and urgent choice that we face here at the dawning of what must be a decisive decade for our world—a decade that will quite literally determine our futures. As a global community, we're challenged by urgent and looming crises wherein lie enormous opportunities if—if—we can summon the will and resolve to seize these opportunities," Biden said. How the world answered questions about those issues, as well as upholding human rights and the liberal international order under threat from China, "will reverberate for generations yet to come."

There was, however, some attention paid to Ukraine in D.C. The House Armed Services Committee's version of the fiscal 2022 defense policy bill included an amendment to send air-defense systems to Kyiv. Opponents of the provision said that the United States didn't have a big stockpile of those weapons; it could ill afford to send systems like Iron Dome to Ukraine, even if Kyiv was willing to open its checkbook to take them off America's hands.

The Biden administration also was keeping an eye on Russia's movements along Ukraine's border. Many of the troops and equipment that

Putin placed on the front earlier in the year remained. Around eighty thousand troops sat scattered on the border, equipped with trucks and armored vehicles that were never driven back. Few in the White House were thinking an invasion was imminent. They thought Putin was trying to show he could match forces with the U.S. and NATO, who were conducting massive joint exercises in southern and eastern Europe, including some countries that bordered Russia.

Russia was scheduled for a big exercise of its own in September: Zapad ("West") 2021. The weeklong drill alongside allies like Belarus served a double purpose: show that the Russian military was a force to be feared, even if it was inferior to NATO as a whole, and scare Washington and other Western capitals. It had two phases: a three-day defensive simulation against an attack from the West followed by a four-day counterattack to recoup lost lands. Around two hundred thousand troops would take part in the drills, far larger than the fifty thousand to seventy-five thousand that took part in the previous two iterations in 2013 and 2017. By the end of the week, Russia had participated in the largest military exercise in Europe in forty years.

The exercises had Europe worried. Some of the drill locations were too close to NATO territory for comfort. Poland declared a state of emergency on its border with Belarus in the east, while the Baltic states—Estonia, Latvia, and Lithuania—were already on high alert in case Russians rolled into their tiny nations. And Russia was showing off some new, sophisticated technologies, most notably unmanned ground vehicles that addressed part of a combat formation.

Moscow, in effect, was saying to the world that it was ready for a fight whenever a battle presented itself.

Analysts feared that Zapad 2021 was the great coming-out party for Russia's armed forces. Russia's military has "undergone a dramatic transformation over the past 15 years. They have gone from a ragged and resource-starved post-Soviet outfit that performed poorly in a war against Georgia in 2008 to a leaner, nimbler and more lethal organization with years of combat experience in Ukraine and Syria. The point of exercises like Zapad is not just to refine Russia's readiness for a big war, and its ability to wage it alongside Belarus, but also to show off that progress to would-be opponents," *The Economist* reported at the time.

White House officials were unfazed. "It's provocative but it's not a game changer," a senior White House aide told me during the exercises. Some members of Biden's staff were also snickering at the display in private. COVID-19 was ripping through Putin's inner circle at the Kremlin, forcing the dictator to self-isolate right in the middle of his major military exercise. "I mean, how threatening can Russia be, really?" the official said, the tone of ridicule unmissable.

"Sir, we have some information you should see."

A handful of the J-2 officers—the Joint Staff's intelligence directorate in the Pentagon—and other military intelligence analysts filed into Gen. Mark Milley's spacious office in late September. They carried with them papers and maps, splaying them across the Joint Chief chair's glass-topped side table. They showed Russia had amassed an unprecedented amount of troops and equipment along the border with Ukraine. As Milley peppered them with questions, he received information about Russia's plans for an order of battle, the decision to send colonels to the front, and the kinds of units.

By the end of the hour-long meeting, Milley, the top military adviser to the president, was alarmed. "I'm concerned this is really different" from a typical Russian military exercise, he told his staffers. "I need to brief the secretary."

Milley marched along the E-Ring corridor to Defense Secretary Lloyd Austin's office and relayed what he had just heard. He requested more information and admitted there were still some gaps in the intelligence. But, Milley said, he sensed this was no bluff. Russia was seriously preparing to invade Ukraine. "We need to speak with the president," Austin responded.

The Pentagon wasn't the only agency with the information. The intelligence had made its way, though not as comprehensively, into the President's Daily Brief around the same time. Jon Finer, the deputy national security adviser, had to blink a few times to assure himself that what he was reading was right. (Typically, he and other top officials reviewed the brief early in the morning before Biden saw it around 9:00 a.m.) If it was real, the entire course of the administration was about to change from that early October morning onward, and the former *Washington Post* reporter would be the one to deliver the news.

The document featured intelligence, reliably sourced, that said Putin wasn't planning to send those troops on the Ukraine border back to their barracks in Russia. He was seriously considering sending them into Ukraine to renew and revive his invasion from seven years earlier. Back then, Putin's aims were grander. He planned on taking the whole country by force. "If the information that came in was corroborated, it would occupy the rest of the administration," a senior U.S. official told me.

The intelligence seemed solid, but officials throughout the government deliberated about what it really showed, especially since what was missing was a silver bullet about intent.

The United States could see troops and the mounting equipment at the border, but Putin had made similar moves in April and hadn't given the invasion order. There was also some information about future military plans involving operations in Ukraine. That was provocative, but militaries planned for contingencies and what-ifs all the time—the Pentagon even had a plan to stop a zombie apocalypse. And then there were the second- and third-order motions that happened after something like an invasion order was given. For the moment, as the leaves were turning from green to shades of red and brown in Washington, nothing like that was happening.

Finer met with his boss, Jake Sullivan, in the national security adviser's corner office before Biden got briefed in his oval-shaped working quarters. They agreed the intelligence item in the document was troubling. It might not amount to anything, but it was worrying enough that the administration needed to prepare for the worst. "It was hard to believe the Russians would do it, but the intelligence was pretty unmistakable," another senior administration official told me.

After the briefing, Sullivan and Finer organized a daily meeting with relevant officials in Sullivan's office—filled with images of and real American flags, including one that flew on the U.S.S. *Constitution*—to develop the right response to the possibility of a new land war in Europe, one potentially far larger than any seen since World War II. The National Security Council staff typically invited included Eric Green, the Russia director; Amanda Sloat, who ran the Western Europe portfolio; and Daleep Singh and Peter Harrell, both high-ranking aides on the international economics team.

At the end of one of the first gatherings, they developed a provisional five-point plan.

The first and most obvious play was to create a list of sanctions with which to hit Russia, Sullivan suggested. This was crucial: the moment Russian forces streamed over the border, the U.S. and its allies needed to swiftly hit Moscow's elite and its defense-related industries hard with financial penalties. That was easier said than done, though. For starters, Russia was pretty integrated into the global economy, especially Europe's. What was the best way to punish Russia without harming its citizens and America's friends more than the Kremlin elite? The Office of Foreign Assets Control at the Treasury Department, which enforces sanctions against countries and individuals, would work with sanctions-focused officials at State. They would need time to figure it all out and coordinate with allies.

Second, Sullivan and Finer firmly believed the U.S. had to share the intelligence it had with European and NATO allies. This was an all-hands-on-deck situation. It wasn't time to sit on information and handle the crisis alone. America needed its friends to know what was happening and to prepare for the worst. The question was whether they'd help. France still felt burned by the submarine deal, and European capitals were still reeling from the abuse they suffered during the Trump years.

There was also the matter of getting the Europeans to believe the intelligence the U.S. would present to them. Some allies would surely be skeptical of the information—Russia didn't invade in the spring of 2021, after all, and why would it be dumb enough to try to take Ukraine by force now? But it was still worth the effort to convince them that what the Biden administration had was solid and required the world to mobilize quickly.

Third, the United States had to get its positioning of troops and weapons just right. Does the president want to send more American service members into Europe? How should NATO reorient itself, if at all? Was it worth putting some more warplanes and other military assets in the region, hopefully deterring Putin? And the question needed to be asked: Would Biden want to send U.S. forces *into* Ukraine, a non-NATO ally, if Russia did invade? Sullivan made a note to speak with the president about it.

Fourth, Ukraine needed more security assistance. The U.S. and its allies should send more weapons to Kyiv so it can defend itself against the new incursion. But questions needed to be asked about how well Ukrainian forces would comport themselves against a stronger Russian force. Would it be wise to dwindle America's stockpile of some of its most advanced weapons for a losing cause? Either way, what did Ukraine think it needed and where were there points of agreement? The Pentagon should write up a memo about what the U.S. military could part with over the next few months, Sullivan and Finer agreed.

Fifth, but no less important, there should be an effort to resolve the brewing crisis diplomatically. If Putin was dead set on invasion, there was little chance to stop him. But, Sullivan wondered aloud, might he be amenable to talks that put some of his grievances on the table? The chances of that were low, of course, but it was better if the world saw America trying to stop a war with diplomacy.

"Okay," Sullivan told his aides, "let's move."

The meetings in Sullivan's office with the core Russia–Ukraine team continued every morning, sometime between 9:00 and 10:00 a.m. They would discuss how best to handle multiple angles of the brewing crisis. What should the administration's messaging be? Which allies should know what the U.S. knows and when? How is the sanctions package coming along? When is the right time to announce security assistance to Ukraine and bolster NATO's eastern flank? And is the administration prepared for all contingencies?

The following days and weeks were full of interagency meetings on the five lines of effort with the mission of presenting Biden with options on what to do in case Putin went through with it. There were few options the president's team considered viable.

The diplomatic option was unlikely to work because what Putin wanted—the weakening of NATO—was a nonstarter. Sanctioning Russia early would remove a deterrent effect. Going to war was unpalatable on both sides of the Atlantic. Nothing the U.S. and its partners thought of seemed to have a real chance of success.

By mid-October, the grim intelligence picture only added to the growing sense of inevitability. CIA director William Burns and Director of National Intelligence Avril Haines thought what they were seeing was far different than previous information on Russia. This was specific: Putin was reviewing operational plans and giving orders on the best courses of action. This wasn't a drill. He was very likely going to start a war.

The trauma of allowing Vladimir Putin to invade Ukraine in 2014 was always on the A-Team's minds. That wasn't going to happen again. Not on this watch. "We were going to act. In Crimea, they created a *fait accompli* before the world had really fully woken up to what they had done. We wanted to make sure the world was wide awake," Sullivan recalled years later. The Obama-era modus operandi of risk aversion was gone.

The president was aware of the intelligence and that his team was preparing a large briefing for him on what they'd uncovered. Now it was time to present it all to him. Sullivan had Burns, Haines, General Milley, Blinken,

Austin, and others join Biden and Vice President Harris in the Oval Office for three sets of meetings in early October. The intelligence leaders laid out what they knew: this was the opening movement of a troop buildup. The stream of intelligence coming in showed Russia was gearing up for a military operation. "This is not just coercive diplomacy," Burns said.

In one of the briefings, Milley and Austin outlined for Biden what the Joint Chiefs chair had heard about a week earlier in his office. For two hours, Milley pointed to a large green map and flip charts on a tripod easel, detailing every element of the Kremlin's plot that the United States had uncovered. The session was in depth, arguably too in depth. Besides discussions of the major Ukrainian cities under threat and the discovered war plans, Milley walked through the minutiae of the terrain and the water table.

But his main point was unmistakable: "We're probably looking at a significant land invasion sometime in the coming months," he told the president. "The plan is to take down the country of Ukraine." It was Russia's version of "shock and awe," he said.

Once Putin gave the order, the Russians would enter Ukraine from the north, Milley explained, moving on either side of Kyiv. Some forces would advance east toward Chernihiv while others would go to Kyiv's west. It was likely that the troops would move during the cold winter months. The frozen ground made it easier for tanks to roll through Ukraine. Having surrounded the Ukrainian capital, regular Russian troops would attempt to take hold of Kyiv while special forces would look to capture Zelenskyy—and kill him if need be. In less than a week, Putin would have successfully decapitated, perhaps literally, the government of Ukraine.

Meanwhile, other Russian forces would come into Ukraine from the east, moving toward the Dnieper River. Troops stationed in Crimea, the annexed peninsula, would be charged with conquering Ukraine's south.

No one in the room doubted the reliability or the seriousness of the intelligence. The only question top U.S. officials had was: Why would Putin do this? Ukraine was a massive nation that for years was tilting westward. What made the Kremlin boss believe that he could somehow subjugate all Ukrainians with a force of about two hundred thousand? The ensuing discussion centered on the theme that Putin didn't necessarily have to do what made sense, just what he wanted to do. And as his summer essay claiming Ukraine wasn't even a country indicated, he might not be thinking about the prospects for war rationally.

The room was unanimous: Putin was going to do this. *All right,* Biden told them, *coordinate with America's allies. Let Putin see the West's resolve, and let's tell him what he'll face if he makes the final decision. If he goes through with it, the U.S. and Europe have to be ready and in lockstep.*

But Biden, not using any notes, told his team to keep some guiding principles in mind. The reason the administration was set to dive headfirst into intense preparations was to defend the rules-based international order. If Putin succeeded in wiping Ukraine off the map, the world America helped build would crumble on this administration's watch. The ultimate goal, then, had to be a sovereign Ukraine. To make that happen, NATO allies had to work together, Congress had to remain on Kyiv's side, the administration had to let Ukraine in on what it knew, and war with Russia had to be avoided at all costs. "We don't want World War III," the president said, his voice elevating.

The president dispatched Burns and Haines to different spots in Europe: the CIA boss to Moscow to meet with Russian officials; the intelligence chief to Brussels to tell the allies what America knew. Milley and Austin were to come back every week to update the president on the growing military mass on Ukraine's doorstep. Biden and Blinken, meanwhile, could brief their counterparts at the upcoming G20 in Rome.

Despite being set in the Eternal City, the annual gathering of the G20 had a pall over it from the outset. Previous meetings about financial cooperation or mitigating the effects of climate change showed how even adversaries could work together on common problems—but not this year. Putin and

Chinese leader Xi Jinping refused to attend in person, both citing the coronavirus outbreaks in their countries. As the October 31 meeting got under way, the feeling among the leaders of the remaining eighteen of the world's richest twenty nations was that Beijing and Moscow were moving away from the West. China had been doing that for years, and Russia—kicked out of the smaller group formerly known as the G8—was increasingly detaching itself from Western institutions.

The optics were bad, but Russia's absence meant it would be a little easier to talk openly with European counterparts about Putin's plans. Biden, Blinken, and Sullivan sat down with British prime minister Boris Johnson, French president Emmanuel Macron, and outgoing German chancellor Angela Merkel and her likely successor, Olaf Scholz, in a small side room at the grand event. Biden's team called this unique grouping of four countries the "European Quad."

The leaders sat around a table while each had a few advisers sitting right behind them. The U.S. president and secretary did a near carbon copy of the Oval Office briefings Biden received, emphasizing that the attack was likely to come in January—in other words, within months. Macron wondered if there was a way to reason with Putin. Merkel and Scholz were skeptical that Russia would do it, Merkel most of all. She grew up in East Germany and knew the Soviet mindset—Putin's mindset. He was threatening to test the West's limits and see if he could get something. He wasn't crazy. Scholz echoed Merkel's comments.

The overall response from the Europeans was "we hear you," but the invasion is not going to happen. Biden and Blinken understood where Europe's most powerful leaders were coming from. Still, they said, an invasion is likely going to happen, whether you want it to or not. It was time to prepare and, at a minimum, get sanctions packages lined up.

Blinken had another tough assignment soon after the G20, this time on the sidelines of a major climate change conference in Glasgow, Scotland. The secretary got a chance to meet with Zelenskyy one-on-one, once again laying out the intelligence picture the U.S. had and explaining why the administration was very convinced Russian troops would soon storm into Ukraine.

Zelenskyy was apprehensive. Russia had bluffed before—why wouldn't it be the same this time?

The intelligence Blinken briefed didn't seem all that different from what the U.S. shared with Ukraine during Russia's spring buildup. And if all this was true, then why wasn't America providing Kyiv with massive amounts of security assistance to defend itself? After all, Kyiv required Javelins, Stingers, and more training. That the United States wasn't fulfilling Ukraine's requests must mean that maybe, just maybe, the U.S. didn't take the situation *that* seriously, Zelenskyy said. Blinken remained calm and said he understood Zelenskyy's frustration.

The lack of an arms package aside, a storm was coming.

Burns showed up in Moscow tired and anxious. He had served in the Russian capital before as ambassador and, as such, was known in Washington and parts of Moscow as a seasoned Kremlinologist. Burns looking rattled showed just how dangerous the situation was. The career ambassador, the highest ranking in the diplomatic corps, equivalent to a four-star general, had long worried about what Russia might do to keep Ukraine in its fold.

"Ukrainian entry into NATO is the brightest of all redlines for the Russian elite (not just Putin)," the then ambassador to Russia wrote in a 2008 memo to then secretary of state Condoleezza Rice. "In more than two and a half years of conversations with key Russian players, from knuckle-draggers in the dark recesses of the Kremlin to Putin's sharpest liberal critics, I have yet to find anyone who views Ukraine in NATO as anything other than a direct challenge to Russian interests."

Burns didn't expect to have to be dealing with Russia and Ukraine so urgently again. During his February 2021 confirmation hearing to be the CIA director, he told lawmakers that his four priorities would be "China, technology, people, and partnerships." But if anyone understood and could get through to Putin, the president and his team felt confident the former diplomat, now spy chief, was the guy.

Burns grew up in a military and diplomatic family. His father, William, was a U.S. Army major general and served in the Reagan administration on arms-control and disarmament issues. Burns studied international relations at LaSalle University and Oxford, writing his thesis on American policy toward Egypt from 1955 to 1981. His conclusion was that economic support on its own couldn't foster U.S.-Egyptian cooperation, but it could smooth the pathway toward mutual work on areas of shared interest. When he wasn't working on his thesis, Burns played for the Oxford basketball team.

Burns joined the foreign service in 1982, rising through the ranks to become the U.S. ambassador to Jordan; ambassador to Russia; the top State Department official on Middle Eastern affairs; the under secretary of state for political affairs—arguably the number three job in the whole agency—and the deputy secretary of state. He was beloved by both Democrats and Republicans, viewed uniformly as a straight shooter with shrewd diplomatic and political instincts.

In the Obama administration, Burns grew close to Jake Sullivan, with whom he helped set the stage for the Iran nuclear deal negotiations, most famously meeting their counterparts in Oman five times. Once out of power, during the Trump years, the two men cowrote four op-eds—two in *The New York Times*, two in *The Atlantic*—all criticizing the Republican administration's handling of Tehran. Writing on Trump's decision to kill Iranian Revolutionary Guard Corps leader Qassem Soleimani in January 2020, Burns and Sullivan declared: "One of the iron laws of foreign policy is that just because you can do something, or just because it's morally defensible, doesn't make it a smart thing to do."

Burns now was trying to stop Putin from doing something stupid, and he understood better than most the tough task ahead of him.

For one thing, the Biden administration wasn't sure his visit would even work. The intelligence indicated that Putin couldn't be persuaded out of launching a war. Telling Putin what he would face if he went through with it—namely massive economic consequences—might get him to reconsider. But if Burns could let Putin know sanctions and export controls would hit Russia while the United States armed Ukraine and NATO increased the military presence on its eastern flank, that at least could halt an escalation down the line.

Then there was just dealing with the man himself. Putin, a former KGB man, could be wily and evasive in his conversations. Little was as it seemed when dealing with the Russian leader, but Burns could be sure of one thing: Putin's hatred of Ukraine ran bone deep. That, at least, was one fact both sides knew for sure was true. It could serve as an anchor in their conversation.

The problem was that Putin wasn't in Moscow when Burns walked through the Kremlin on November 2. He was in Sochi, the resort city on the Black Sea that hosted the Winter Olympics in 2014. The coronavirus was still tearing through much of the capital and Putin's own team. The dictator thought it best to work remotely until the internal pandemic calmed down.

Yuri Ushakov, the former Russian ambassador to the U.S. and current foreign policy adviser to Putin, welcomed Burns into his office. It was in that room that the CIA chief could speak with Putin over the phone. The phone crackled a bit as Burns and Putin exchanged pleasantries. The niceties didn't last long, though, as Burns explained precisely why he had come to town. The United States knew about Russia's war plans and the leader's inkling to renew the Ukraine invasion. "We see you" was the underlying message, according to someone familiar with the conversation.

Putin wasn't moved. He listed off his greatest hits of gripes with the West. NATO promised to stop expanding and it kept doing so, clearly threatening Russia's security each time the alliance's boundaries moved closer to Russia's borders. And the government of Ukraine was a sham, Zelenskyy a weak leader. The U.S. was supportive of a fake country led by dangerous people. As Burns told *The Washington Post* nearly a year after that conversation, "He was very dismissive of President Zelenskyy as a political leader."

Burns left a letter from Biden behind. In it, the American president explained what Russia could expect if it went forward with the invasion. But the CIA chief had little hope that the letter would change things. The warning had been delivered, but all he'd heard back was anti-West bile and views about Ukraine that were fueled by paranoia and hatred. The former diplomat had done what he came to Moscow to do, but he didn't return home with a better feeling about the situation. "My level of concern has gone up, not down," he later told Biden.

Meanwhile, at the Pentagon, Lloyd Austin met with a large group of senior civilian and military leaders in his secure conference room. It seemed like a storm was coming, and he wanted his team to get on the same page to begin preparations. The United States should have three goals, he told his aides: bolster NATO, support Ukraine, and avoid war with Russia. "We have to use everything we have in the inventory," he told me on November 1, "and some of that lies with our partners." More to the point, he tasked Pentagon staff to find the weapons and equipment the U.S. could spare to provide to Ukraine, and to identify what American allies had that Kyiv might find useful.

A few weeks later, on November 17, Avril Haines traveled to NATO headquarters in Brussels. It was cold, typical for northern Europe in the transition period from fall to winter. The early darkness outside reflected the darkening mood inside as she briefed the North Atlantic Council, the alliance's political decision-making body. She used the opportunity during the long-scheduled visit to update NATO's thirty allies on the intelligence the U.S. had obtained about Russia's plans and Putin's intentions.

Haines, the first woman to serve as America's top intelligence official, was a long way away from the judo mat she trained on or the bookstore she ran, made famous for the erotica reading nights it used to host. The Georgetown University graduate met her husband while taking flying lessons. But her unusual background never seeped into her professional work—Haines was always measured when discussing intelligence. It was best to be dispassionate.

As other Biden administration officials had done before her in other settings, she methodically went through the intelligence, this time adding a bit more detail: America believed Putin would put at least 125,000 troops on Ukraine's border, a number likely too large for the whole buildup to be a bluff. That meant NATO and the world could expect to see an increase of around 40,000 troops over the coming weeks.

Haines received the expected pushback: Putin wouldn't be so brash as to go all in. Zelenskyy, who certainly has a team that would know what Putin was up to, wasn't worried at all. It's a geopolitical message. It was best not to overreact, and to hear what he had to say. Some even wondered aloud if the United States was being too alarmist following the failure to anticipate the fall of Afghanistan in just eleven days. Maybe Haines and her team were too sensitive? There clearly wasn't the same confidence in America that there was in the weeks and months before Kabul fell. There just wasn't the same confidence in Biden's team anymore.

Haines, an intelligence official in a political decision-making space, refrained from offering her own views on actions. Her job was to lay out the facts as she knew them. By the end of the session in NATO's auditorium, Haines had only the UK and the three Baltic countries on her side; the rest were intrigued but weren't fully sold.

Around the same time, Milley was also encountering some resistance from his counterparts. He had organized the first-ever emergency meeting of NATO's chiefs of defense, the top officers or advisers in each allied nation, over teleconference. The Joint Chiefs chair went through his now well-rehearsed briefing about what Russia was planning, only this time the intelligence was more refined and precise. Using the map, he explained how Moscow planned to send its forces across Ukraine in one large sweep, and around when the invasion might start. But the Europeans on the line were skeptical that Putin would order something so risky.

The Ukrainian military chief, Gen. Valeryy Zaluzhnyy, was on the line and clearly unhappy. While Milley's intentions were good, he had effectively outlined a fever dream. The Ukrainians knew Russia, and the described plan was not something that the Kremlin would ever design, let alone authorize.

But on November 20, Ukraine's defense intelligence chief, Gen. Kyrylo Budavnov, said openly that Russia's roughly one hundred thousand troops would likely invade his country by late January 2022. The attacks would feature bombings from artillery and warplanes, tanks rolling in from the north and east, and amphibious assaults from the south. The weaponry already staged in Crimea and on Ukraine's border, plus the manpower, indicated a fight was coming—even if the harsh winter months were fast approaching. "It is no problem for us and the Russians," Budavnov said of fighting in the cold weather. He added that "Our evaluations are almost the same as our American colleagues."

CIA director Burns shared his read from the call with Putin upon arrival in Washington. Burns didn't mince words: He told the president that Putin was preparing to invade Ukraine. Nothing he heard during his Moscow sojourn gave him the impression that a ramping down of tensions was likely. Biden, who long touted the personal touches of diplomacy, believed what Burns was saying. There were no views he trusted more than those of people who had engaged in one-on-one interactions.

Biden, through Sullivan, directed his team to prepare for the worst. The United States couldn't give up—it was imperative to try to stop the war before it began. But since fighting was likely to happen, the goal was to stop Putin from shifting the blame for the war onto America and the broader West. He's going to say NATO expansion and U.S. support for Ukraine left him no choice but to invade. We can't cede that narrative ground to him, Biden ordered. At the same time, the U.S. had to coordinate the strongest possible response with its allies. This couldn't be just Washington versus

Moscow. The modern world had to stand united against the oncoming barbarism.

Sullivan told Finer, his deputy, that he had a scene from the movie *Austin Powers* playing and replaying in his head. Powers is riding a steamroller very slowly down a corridor, and a security guard is standing there screaming "Noooo!" even though the machine is far away. He inevitably gets rolled over. Sullivan didn't want the United States to be like that security guard. If the invasion starts, he told Finer, what would we have wished we'd done?

Sullivan asked Alex Bick, a National Security Council member with expertise in strategic planning, to lead what internally was called a "Tiger Team," an interagency group that would develop and test policy assumptions. The task was at once straightforward and complex: What should America and its allies do after Putin makes certain moves? To help, Bick corralled members of every agency that would have a hand to play: the Defense Department, Department of State, Treasury Department, Department of Energy, the U.S. Agency for International Development, and Homeland Security.

Sullivan wanted the Tiger Team up and running as soon as possible. Afghanistan hung over the brewing crisis: the administration was caught on its back foot as the Taliban stormed across the country; it had to be on the front foot in case a crisis erupted in Ukraine.

Bick was the perfect person to take it on. A historian by training, he had worked on Syria in Obama's National Security Council and on conflict resolution initiatives in Africa and Latin America led by former president Jimmy Carter. When Trump was in power, Bick spent time working on strategic planning studies at Johns Hopkins University.

The scenarios Bick worked on were as varied as they were dark. Say Putin just tried to capture and kill Zelenskyy: How should the West respond? What if Russia launches devastating cyberattacks on Ukraine before the fighting starts: Should America hack back? A war of any size would lead to a crush of refugees moving westward into Europe. What support should the U.S. provide to its allies taking in millions of people?

Some of the teams, nestled in the Eisenhower Executive Office Building next to the White House, had to consider the bleakest prospects: What if Russia used biological or chemical weapons? Or, even worse, what if Putin ordered nuclear strikes on Ukraine? "It was a very grim exercise," a senior administration official told me.

Making matters worse, no one could come up with a great response should Russia drop the bomb on Ukraine. A nuclear response in kind by the U.S. made little sense—it would only escalate the conflict and more than likely launch the world's first real tit-for-tat nuclear war. Getting major countries, including India and China, to cut off ties with Russia might be a smart long-term play, but politically it would play poorly in those countries. It also just didn't *feel* like a major reprimand. The president's opponents and much of the American public, surely, would push for more.

The group coalesced around conventional options, such as destroying Russia's Black Sea fleet or destroying key military targets inside Russia itself. But even those ideas were problematic. Bombing Russia would officially make the United States a party to the war and also entice the Kremlin to order a retaliation against America. Maybe a nuclear confrontation could be avoided, but still the U.S. would likely have to engage in a major war after just coming off a clear loss in Afghanistan.

"It was the ultimate Land of Bad Options," a person involved in the planning told me. "We kept looking for a good option, but it seemed like one of those things where every option was a bad option."

Whatever the options, the Tiger Team wrote in memos the moves and countermoves, the recommended administration messaging, diplomatic outreach, and possible military or cyber responses for every scenario. Those memos circulated widely in the government but were of most use to officials in the National Security Council, State Department, Pentagon, and intelligence community. Those documents would also inform war games and tabletop exercises held in other parts of the government.

"No one could blame us for not warning early and often," a senior official told me. But Biden and his team continued to ask themselves: "Are we doing enough?"

There was a relentless drive inside the administration. Staffers at the White House stayed at work later than usual, long beyond the hours when the White House mess closed at 8:00 p.m., which meant aides likely weren't going to get a meal until they got home. Meetings were organized deeper into the night than in months past. Some people went home only to shower and change their clothes before coming back to work. Others just worked through it all. "There were some smelly colleagues," a White House staffer told me.

The prospect of World War III was the top animating factor—it was enough to put anyone in the national security world into hyperdrive. But, a White House aide confessed to me, there was also something deeper at work: "This wasn't a do-over of Afghanistan. Nothing could be that. But this does help ensure that Afghanistan isn't the only thing this administration is remembered for. And it helps ensure that it won't be the only thing Jake and Tony are remembered for."

Chapter 10

Confrontation

December 2021

Vladimir Putin walked up to the podium inside the Kremlin's ornate Alexander Hall. The gold doors behind him glistened on-screen, a symbol of power that Putin wanted to display about his nation and himself. It made a nearly regal backdrop for the dictator, who arrived in the room on December 1 to receive the credentials of foreign ambassadors to Russia—among them the new envoys from Spain, Slovakia, Austria, and Italy. But that was the nominal reason for Putin's grand appearance. He had a message not just for the new envoys but for the world.

"In a dialogue with the United States and its allies we will insist on working out specific agreements that would exclude any further NATO moves eastward and the deployment of weapons systems that threaten us in close vicinity to the Russian territory," he said, adding that Moscow would seek "reliable and long-term security guarantees." Threats, he claimed, were mounting on Russia's western front. Only guarantees that NATO wouldn't expand any further, and especially that it would not allow Ukraine into the alliance, could resolve the geopolitical problem.

Putin knew that was a big ask. NATO has an "open door" policy, meaning that any country that wants to join the alliance can do so as long as it meets certain criteria. Ukraine's military was certainly capable enough to join, and Kyiv wanted in. But NATO requires that all thirty members agree to accession, and that was a tall order. France and Germany, among others, were likely to vote against Ukraine because it could anger Russia, and Paris and Berlin wanted to preserve their ties to Moscow. If Ukraine were in NATO, all members would be obligated to come to its defense if it was attacked. The most likely culprit for an assault, of course, was Russia.

Still, Putin didn't like that Ukraine had tilted westward in recent years, first choosing to move closer to the European Union and openly desiring to join NATO. These guarantees would reassure him that Kyiv wouldn't further tilt away from Moscow—or at least that's what he said.

Putin's comments came as Antony Blinken was in wintry, chilly Riga, Latvia, on December 1 to meet with officials in the former Soviet country. Latvia and its Baltic neighbors, Lithuania and Estonia, were the NATO allies most concerned about Russia's potential invasion. Blinken's visit to the Latvian capital gave him the chance to compare notes with the frontline state and then, separately, meet with other foreign ministers in the alliance. He came armed with a warning that he then shared during a news conference.

"We don't know whether President Putin has made the decision to invade. We do know that he is putting in place the capacity to do so in short order should he so decide," he said, noting for the first time in public that the United States believed an invasion could come at any moment. It was a message he didn't deliver lightly. It was coordinated with the White House, which was starting to develop ways to expose Putin's thinking and Russia's planning. That might shake the Kremlin's cage, but so could a public offer to de-escalate tensions. "There is a diplomatic path forward, and that is by far the preferred path. We are certainly not looking for conflict," Blinken said.

Asked about Putin's comments from the day before, the secretary of state took a jab at the Russian leader. "I saw the statement that you referred to, and quite frankly, it's perplexing because the idea that Ukraine represents a threat to Russia would be a bad joke if things weren't so serious," he said, noting that NATO "is a defensive alliance. We're not a threat to Russia. We don't have aggressive intent toward Russia. . . .

"The idea that Ukraine represents a threat to Russia or, for that matter, that NATO represents a threat to Russia is profoundly wrong and misguided," he asserted.

Unwittingly, those words became the opening gambits of a diplomatic dance between the U.S. and Russia. Moscow claimed it didn't want NATO to pose a threat anymore, and the U.S. wanted Russia not to pose a threat to Ukraine while allowing the alliance to operate as it had for decades. There was a large gulf in the positions, a senior official told me at the time, "but it's a start." There was no danger in having a dialogue even if it might prove futile. Or as one official noted, "Let's just get them talking and talking and talking. It'll either delay the inevitable, which gives us more time, or we miraculously find something that works.

Jake Sullivan huddled with Jon Finer in his corner West Wing office. The United States had told its allies what it knew. All parts of the government were planning for multiple what-if scenarios. There was an infinitesimal chance that diplomacy could work. Now it was time to let the Russians know what America knew, especially with a call between President Biden and Vladimir Putin coming soon. The question was: How?

The national security adviser and his deputy batted around some ideas. Maybe Biden could give a speech. He'd lay out the intelligence picture, and coming from him, the message would be strong. It would also be clear to Putin that Biden would be on the other end of the line with immense knowledge of the situation. Alternatively, maybe Blinken or Bill Burns could speak with their Russian counterparts privately and explain in vivid detail what information was in America's and Europe's possession. Neither of those were great ideas, they realized, and they both came with a significant amount of risk.

A speech by Biden or any U.S. official would put them out on a limb. If Putin eventually decided not to invade, which would be good, it would make them look foolish. The media would ask questions about whether the U.S. was too alarmist. The private conversation idea didn't make much sense either. Burns had already done his earlier, quiet mission to Moscow and had spoken directly with Putin. Plus, Russia wouldn't feel any public pressure if talks between Washington and Moscow remained a secret.

The group settled on a halfway option that the president had supported in previous meetings: leak intelligence to the press after downgrading it for public consumption. It was a decision that represented a change of course in communications strategy. The administration, for the first time, chose to release its current, real-time intelligence to the public. While the world saw the threatening posture on Ukraine's border, this would essentially be a direct communication from the White House to the free world *and* the Kremlin about what the United States believed it all meant. "It felt like a high-wire act to do that," a senior official said to me about the decision. "We wanted Putin, and the world, to know that we knew."

Sullivan asked Emily Horne, the NSC's communications chief, to pass the information along to a journalist. She chose Shane Harris of *The Washington Post,* an intelligence reporter trusted and respected throughout the capital. The administration provided him with a slide deck depicting where Russian troops were positioned and how many of them Putin would send into Ukraine. It looked like the real deal—and that was the point. "We wanted it to appear just like it would internally, with all the markings and everything," the official said.

Biden administration officials couldn't help but notice that the strategic leak was the kind of bold move they hadn't taken seven years earlier when Russian troops invaded Crimea. The U.S. was caught flat-footed during that advance, spending little to no time working to deter Putin from such a brash action. Sullivan, Finer, and many others in the White House didn't want to make the same mistake again. "We still felt burned by that whole situation," the senior aide said.

Harris, who would coauthor his *Washington Post* story with colleague Paul Sonne, told Horne he had all he needed to write. Horne communicated back to Sullivan and her team that the leak was done. All that was left to do was wait. And wait. And wait some more. "It was nerve-racking," a White House official told me. "We needed it to be exactly what we needed it to be. It had to work. Everyone was holding their breath until it came out."

Blinken, meanwhile, used his platform during a conference in Sweden to blast the Russians for their provocations.

For only the second time since he became secretary, Blinken met with Russian foreign minister Sergey Lavrov in a bilateral setting, a rare opportunity to deliver the administration's message to a prominent Kremlin official face-to-face. The American diplomat left nothing unsaid: Russia had to stand down and not invade Ukraine. If it did, the wrath of the West would fall upon Russia. Lavrov, per usual, deflected Blinken's comments. Russia had every right to move its own troops anywhere in its own territory. Any suggestion that an invasion was imminent was simply false. Blinken, of course, didn't buy that—and he also suspected that Lavrov wasn't fully clued in to Putin's thinking.

The half-hour meeting ended with no diplomatic progress, but Blinken suggested that he and Lavrov keep talking. "The best way to avert a crisis is through diplomacy," Blinken said during a news conference, seated right next to the Russian. "But, and again in the spirit of being clear and candid," he continued, "if Russia decides to pursue confrontation, there will be serious consequences." He also hinted that Biden and Putin would be speaking soon.

Lavrov couldn't let that comment stand on its own. "We, as President Putin has stated, do not want any conflicts," he said. "No one can guarantee their own security at the expense of the security of others. NATO's extension," Lavrov asserted, "will infringe on our security."

The talks did seem to bear some fruit. The U.S. and Russia struck a deal for American personnel working at the embassy in Moscow to get visas. It was an encouraging sign, as the shrinking American mission in Russia would get even smaller without the requisite approvals. That small dispute, overshadowed by the tensions over Ukraine, ended a monthslong drama that threatened to effectively shutter the American mission in Russia.

But the dispute also featured in a larger diplomatic game between both countries as they closed each other's consulates over allegations of spying. The closures and seizures of those outposts further tanked relations between the U.S. and Russia, lowering expectations that the two nations could ever solve a dispute diplomatically. The visa breakthrough suggested that there might be some hope for successful talks over Ukraine after all. "At least that's what we were hoping for, though no one was putting their money on it," a U.S. official told me.

Harris and Sonne's story was posted online at 7:00 p.m. on December 3 with the headline RUSSIA PLANNING MASSIVE MILITARY OFFENSIVE AGAINST UKRAINE INVOLVING 175,000 TROOPS, U.S. INTELLIGENCE WARNS. It began: "U.S. intelligence has found the Kremlin is planning a multi-front offensive as soon as early next year involving up to 175,000 troops." The administration offered up a senior official for an interview about what the intelligence indicated.

"The Russian plans call for a military offensive against Ukraine as soon as early 2022 with a scale of forces twice what we saw this past spring during Russia's snap exercise near Ukraine's borders," the aide said. "The plans involve extensive movement of 100 battalion tactical groups with an estimated 175,000 personnel, along with armor, artillery and equipment."

The White House couldn't have been more thrilled with how the story came out. Now, no one could claim that the U.S. failed to foresee what was coming. The decision to leak the intelligence was considered a rousing success inside the administration, and Sullivan decided it was a good idea for his team to release more intelligence to keep Putin on his toes. "It worked as intended," the national security adviser told his team, "so let's keep trying this."

The *Washington Post* story wasn't the only major administration communication. During a December 3 press briefing, on the November jobs report, a journalist asked Biden what he thought of the situation in Ukraine and what he was going to do about it. The president replied: "What I am doing is putting together what I believe to be, will be, the most comprehensive and meaningful set of initiatives to make it very, very difficult for Mr. Putin to go ahead and do what people are worried he may do."

For the president's team watching from the room, from their offices, or on their iPhones, they saw Biden raise the bar again. His goal was to make sure Putin would sweat before giving the invasion order, make him think twice. The boss's message to his aides was clear: There's more to do.

Time was running short for Biden's team to get on the same page ahead of his call with Putin, scheduled for December 7. He wanted the team's response nearly finalized and coordination with allies firmed up. When he spoke to Putin, Biden didn't want to speak to him just as the leader of the United States. He wanted to speak to him as the leader of the democratic world that would stand up to the autocrat.

Beneath Biden, the administration was buzzing. Conversations with allies were a near constant. The Pentagon was drawing up plans for any possible military contingency. And a list of sanctions, to be rolled out incrementally, was in the works. The White House was a flurry of activity as staffers whizzed back and forth between the West Wing and the adjacent Eisenhower Executive Office Building, braving the bitter cold during the short walk between them.

How hard to hit Putin should he give the order to invade was always the elephant in the room. Janet Yellen, the Treasury secretary, was constantly warning that the punishments on Russia would reverberate back onto the

American economy, namely in the form of rising energy and food prices. The president had campaigned on a foreign policy for the middle class and expanding financial opportunity for millions at home. Yes, an attempt to overthrow the government of Ukraine by force required a massive response. But the United States should think carefully about how quickly the sanctions are rolled out and how they might dovetail with the reprimands for other countries.

Eric Green, the NSC's Russia director, with decades of experience as a diplomat throughout Europe, also used every opportunity he could to remind his colleagues about the internal politics of the Kremlin. Backing Putin into a corner could backfire on the West. Invading Ukraine would be the greatest gamble of his roughly twenty years in power. Should it fail on its own or in part due to the response of America and its allies, then it was more than possible that the dictator could face a challenge to his leadership from within. That could lead him to act irrationally, not just domestically but also in Ukraine. It would be a world-historical disaster if the U.S. administration had to dust off the contingency plans for the days after Russia dropped a nuclear bomb on Ukraine.

Others didn't want to be more cautious; they wanted to be more aggressive. Victoria Nuland, the State Department's under secretary for policy, advocated for sanctions on Russia before an invasion. Notorious for her years as a staunch Russia hawk and her marriage to famous neoconservative scholar Robert Kagan, the Brown University graduate in Russian Studies argued in memos and in meetings that early penalties would show Putin that the U.S. and its allies were serious. In effect, a shot across the bow. What Putin was doing—threatening a sovereign country with invasion—was heinous enough. That behavior couldn't be tolerated, and the sanctions would make the West's disapproval crystal clear.

Nuland and others in her camp were in the minority. Sullivan, Blinken, and their cohort said sanctions were about deterrence. If Washington, Brussels, and other foreign capitals imposed those measures now, then Putin would have nothing to lose and would go on and invade Ukraine. It was better to keep the sanctions holstered until after Russian troops streak across the border. Plus, going early might spook Europeans into a "with us or against us" mindset. European countries, namely France and Germany, weren't ready to move on sanctions yet. It was better for Western countries to be united and move as one instead of the U.S. going first and hoping allies would follow.

These kinds of conversations fascinated Sullivan. The former debater consistently poked and prodded his colleagues about ideas for better ways to stop the war. What if there was another Biden–Putin summit? His aides shut the idea down, with Sullivan agreeing that wasn't smart. What if the U.S. signals early that it's willing to give in to some of Russia's demands. Might that change anything? The answer, again, was no. Sullivan also agreed. "His role was to coordinate the government's response," someone familiar with the national security adviser's halfhearted trial balloons told me. "But he also saw his role as pushing colleagues to find the right answers, even if that meant asking the wrong questions sometimes."

Biden and Putin spoke during a secure video call on December 7 as those deliberations continued behind the scenes. The two-hour discussion was as tense as any conversation Biden had had as president, and arguably ranked among the most high-stakes diplomatic encounters of his five decades in Washington.

The American president laid out, in stark detail, what Putin could expect if the enhanced invasion of Ukraine went forward. Sanctions, unlike any Russia had seen to date, would be imposed by the U.S. and its allies. NATO would be strengthened with a larger presence of multinational troops, including a beefed-up contingent nearer Russia's borders. More Western weaponry would flow into Ukraine. And Putin, who desperately wanted the world's respect, would become a global pariah overnight. Is that really what you want? Biden asked Putin.

The Russian leader didn't flinch. NATO had promised never to expand into former Soviet territory, but it could count the Baltics as members and was clearly trying to bring Ukraine into the fold. If Ukraine tilted further to the West, what was to stop America from placing missiles inside the country in a direct threat to the Russian homeland? The U.S. speaks of world order, but it was a bully on the world stage—and Moscow one of its victims.

It was vintage Putin, but he had an edge in his voice that those on the video call hadn't really heard before. This was more than the usual gamesmanship and whataboutism. His words came from a deep place, a place of hate. "We thought he was paranoid," someone on the call told me. "We came to realize he was very angry too."

Biden ended the Ukraine section, which dominated the call, by reiterating that his administration was willing to talk through Russia's security concerns in a diplomatic setting. But that offer stood only if Kremlin officials sat down to de-escalate tensions, not delay the inevitable escalation. Both men tasked their respective teams to start talking about sensitive European security matters. The first step toward diplomacy had been taken.

Biden spoke immediately afterward with the leaders of France, Germany, Italy, and the United Kingdom. He briefed them on what had just happened on the Putin call. He didn't seem willing to deal, Biden said. He had just spoken to a man seemingly dead set on invading Ukraine. That pained Emmanuel Macron and Angela Merkel to hear. Of course they didn't want war, but war wasn't inevitable. If only someone could engage him, hear him out, maybe he'd quit this foolishness.

Macron asked if anyone would object to him reaching out to Putin. Biden and everyone else on the line said to go for it—the more the merrier. But no one on the call, except maybe Macron, believed that outreach would work. "I could feel the collective eye roll from everyone on the call," a U.S. official told me.

Biden brought the call back to the issue at hand: If he does this, if Russia invades Ukraine, can the United States count on a commensurate response from its European allies? *Yes,* they all said. The call ended in agreement.

Sullivan briefed the press after both calls. A reporter asked him what punishments the U.S. was willing to do this time that the Obama administration—which Sullivan served in—didn't do. That clearly hit a nerve. "I will look you in the eye and tell you, as President Biden looked President Putin in the eye and told him today, that things we did not do in 2014 we are prepared to do now," Sullivan asserted, the irritation clear in his voice. This, one could sense, was the Obama cohort's chance at redemption.

Another reporter went for the jugular. Republicans were saying that Biden was a weak president, especially toward Putin. The decision to let Nord Stream 2 be completed and the Afghanistan withdrawal were cases in point. How did the administration—how did he—respond?

Three points, Sullivan said. First, Russia invaded the country of Georgia while the wars in Iraq and Afghanistan raged. Second, Nord Stream 2 still wasn't operational, which means the West had leverage over him. Finally, Biden had shown Putin no mercy when he committed atrocities on the world stage. "He said he would impose costs for Navalny, he said he would impose costs for SolarWinds; he did those things. And if Russia chooses to take these actions in Ukraine, he will do the same," Sullivan assured.

Sullivan referred to the sanctions on Russia for poisoning and later imprisoning Navalny, the administration's first sanctions on the Kremlin, followed by the financial punishment for the cyber intrusions into U.S. government and private networks. By reminding the reporter of these events, Sullivan didn't want the narrative to be that Biden's team was Obama's. It had many of the same people, but there was a different mentality now: act, and act fast.

Meanwhile, throughout the week, the White House was preparing for another tough call with Volodymyr Zelenskyy. Antony Blinken had set the table during a December 6 conversation, reminding the former comedian that the United States and its allies wouldn't make any decisions about Ukraine without Ukraine. This was a concerted and combined effort. The full force of the U.S. government stood behind Kyiv. Zelenskyy appreciated the chat, especially before Biden was scheduled to speak with Putin.

One of the preparations the administration had been considering was what to say about the potential for sending U.S. troops to Ukraine's defense. In private, Biden told his staff that he wasn't going to involve Americans in another war without end. Ukraine wasn't a NATO ally, and so the U.S. had no obligation to come to its defense. And that's not even accounting for the fact that Russia and the U.S. are by far the world's largest nuclear states. Pitting the two countries directly against each other could ignite World War III—this time featuring major nuclear powers.

The question was how to get that message out. One idea was to have Jen Psaki answer unequivocally during a news briefing that the U.S. would support Ukraine but not go to war for it. For Horne and Sullivan, though, that seemed like too small a moment for such a big announcement. Another option was to have Biden give a speech on the Russia–Ukraine tensions. He'd provide an update on how the administration saw Putin's threatening moves and, somewhere in the middle of the speech, mention that U.S. troops would stay home even if Putin launched an invasion. That was seen as too great an occasion. The goal was to lower tensions, and a big presidential address about a war that hadn't started yet was too much for Horne and Sullivan.

They made a decision: if Biden got a question about sending troops during one of his encounters with the press pool, most likely on his way to the Marine One presidential helicopter, then he'd deliver the talking point.

He got the question on December 8. "That is not on the table," he said before boarding the aircraft. "The idea the United States is going to unilaterally use force to confront Russia from invading Ukraine is not on—in the cards right now."

That proclamation, coming one day before Biden's call with Zelenskyy, had staff worried that their conversation could be more tense than expected. But it wasn't much of a slog at all. In fact, the ninety-minute chat was quite warm. Biden read out the details of his call with Putin and European partners. He also reassured Zelenskyy that any conversations between the U.S. and Russia about Ukraine would require representatives from Kyiv at the table. The double-barreled assurance from Blinken and Biden was meant to calm Zelenskyy. The West wasn't going to trade Ukrainian sovereignty for peace. That message reassured the Ukrainian leader.

After the call, a senior administration official spoke with the press about how it all went. The official made another push to remind the Russians that America was willing to talk, and potentially to deal. "We are always prepared to talk about security issues with Russia and, frankly, a large number of formats exist to be able to do that. That's why the NATO–Russia Council exists. It's why the OSCE [Organization for Security and Cooperation in Europe] exists. It's venues where the Russians can raise their concerns, and it's venues where we can raise our concerns. And so, we are, of course, prepared to talk to the Russians about this full set of issues," the official said.

A key theme arose as U.S. and European officials spoke to one another during those tense, frigid months: Putin was planning to invade not only because he hated Ukraine's existence but also because he sensed Western weakness. Putin, the ultimate geopolitical shark, smelled blood in the water.

For starters, twenty years of war in Iraq and Afghanistan ended with spectacular failures. China was growing in economic might, eating into the transatlantic stranglehold over world markets. European nations weren't investing in defense, and the United States was behind on missile technologies that the Russian military was perfecting. And, of course, the collective punishment for Russia following the annexation of Crimea had been very little.

Putin, these officials assessed, thought he could get away with it. That's why it was so important for the U.S. to encourage allies in Europe and the Indo-Pacific to stand up to a global bully and for democracy. Ukraine is fighting not only for itself but for "the whole of Europe" and "world order," said Radovan Javorčík, Slovakia's ambassador to the U.S. and previously his nation's envoy to NATO. Russia's designs on Ukraine turned out to be the true test of Biden's formulation that democracies could deliver. If they banded together to slow the rise of Putin's authoritarianism, now spilling out of Russia's borders, then democracies would once again be back on the rise.

Those kinds of statements—that Ukraine was now the front line for global democracy—started to creep out into the open by mid-December. "There is something even bigger at stake here, and it's the basic rules of the road of the international system, rules that say that one country can't change the borders of another by force; one country can't dictate to another country its choices, its decisions in its foreign policy, with whom it will associate; one country can't exert a sphere of influence over others," Blinken said on *Meet the Press* on December 12.

Blinken's statement was not hyperbole, at least for the Biden administration. The president had come into office saying that democracies had to prove that they could deliver for their people, that the authoritarian system was inferior to representative government. When he and his team developed that overarching theme for his candidacy and then presidency, they clearly had China in mind. Russia was part of the equation, sure, but no one expected Putin to hop over Xi Jinping as the poster child for the world's growing authoritarian movement. Now he was, and he needed to be stopped.

The Ukrainians weren't speaking in such lofty rhetoric, at least not yet. They were worried about the devastation that would occur if Putin gave the invasion order. "It will be Ukrainian blood, it will be Russian blood, and a lot of soldiers from Russia will come to home in coffins, and Facebook, Instagram, Telegram channels will show it. It will be a disaster," Ukrainian defense minister Oleksii Reznikov told *Politico*'s Paul McLeary in a memorable December 13 interview. Roughly five million of his countrymen would flee, seeking asylum in neighboring countries. "The war will come in Europe, not only in Ukraine," Reznikov said.

Putin, meanwhile, was still pushing for security guarantees that he must have known were no-gos for the West. He discussed those demands, namely the assurance that Ukraine would never be a part of NATO, in December 14 calls with France's Macron and Finnish president Sauli Niinistö. With the Finnish leader, Putin complained about Ukraine's tactics against Russian troops in the war he started seven years earlier and that negotiations with the U.S. and NATO needed to start right away. Both Niinistö and Macron, in their separate conversations, stressed that the continued threat of a hundred thousand troops on Ukraine's doorstep wasn't the way to get what Putin wanted. A war would all but guarantee he'd get nothing.

European allies, especially those closer to Russia, were concerned about the growing diplomatic rhetoric. They didn't want a war, but they didn't believe talking to Kremlin officials would lead anywhere either. Plus, why should Putin get a reward for throwing a temper tantrum and causing a crisis? Putin "is trying to present himself as a solution to this problem that he has created himself. And I think we shouldn't fall into that trap," Estonian prime minister Kaja Kallas said at the time. "I don't think that Russia has any right to say anything about who has the right and who doesn't have the right to join [the] European Union or NATO."

Biden administration officials were hearing this concern from many of its counterparts. But their response to colleagues in European capitals was: What's the alternative? Putin is unlikely to keep his gunpowder dry. Imposing sanctions now removes the deterrent. The only option is to give him an off-ramp through diplomacy. Russia—really, Putin—wins by getting a guarantee he didn't have before, and the West—mainly, Ukraine—wins by not engaging in a world-altering war.

The Kremlin put forward its demands in two draft treaties on December 17. If each were followed to the letter, they would fully change the entire security architecture in Europe by altering decades of postwar transatlantic policy.

The Kremlin insisted that Ukraine never be in NATO and that NATO's troops and weapons, like missiles, move away from the alliance's eastern front. In effect, NATO had to pull back to its 1997-era lines before it expanded further toward Russian territory and had to cease growing any larger. For Moscow, Ukraine was off limits.

The Kremlin also gave Russia a semi-veto over any NATO maneuvers in Eastern Europe. "The Parties shall refrain from deploying their armed forces and armaments, including in the framework of international organizations, military alliances or coalitions, in the areas where such deployment could be perceived by the other Party as a threat to its national security, with the exception of such deployment within the national territories of the Parties," read the document posted to the Russian Foreign Ministry's website. In other words, if Russia considered any U.S. moves as threatening to its territory, then the U.S. would have to back off.

Biden administration officials found these proposals laughable. "Are they serious?" senior National Security Council aide Amanda Sloat said upon hearing what the Russians had demanded. The demands were so one-sided, of course, that it couldn't be a serious offer. Some felt the treaty proposal was as much a declaration of war as anything. There was no way the Kremlin truly believed the United States and its allies would cave to those demands. It was basically Russia saying "we're going to invade Ukraine unless you give us everything we want." If anyone inside the administration wasn't convinced of what was to come, they were more convinced after the proposal went online.

In public, the Biden administration was laying down a marker of its own. Saying the administration had seen and reviewed the draft treaties, Jen Psaki said, "We will not compromise the key principles on which European security is built, including that all countries have the right to decide their own future and foreign policy free from the outside interference." Translation: No deal. Next.

The treaties led Sullivan to ask his staff a question he'd brought up often during previous meetings in the Situation Room and his office: Was it really worth having the discussion with the Russians if this is where they were coming from? *Yes*, was the overwhelming reply. Dictators had politics, too, and Putin had to show he was a tough negotiator. There was still a chance—a small one, but a chance—that this treaty was the maximalist offer. He might agree to some middle compromise. It was worth the shot.

By the end of the month, the U.S. announced that talks with Russia over the Ukraine situation would begin in the new year, on January 10. Few in the U.S. and Europe were confident about the prospects, but it was far better to talk than to war, officials would say, paraphrasing a famous Winston Churchill quote: "To jaw-jaw is better than to war-war."

The situation in Ukraine was still precarious, but it allowed officials to go home for the holidays with a little bit of hope. The grind would start up again when the calendar switched from 2021 to 2022. But before the emails slowed and the phones stopped ringing, Sullivan wanted to congratulate his team on what he described as one of the most challenging years not just in U.S. foreign policy history but in American history.

"It's a challenging world out there. But we face it with a sense of confidence and purpose in our strategy and policy as we approach the end of 2021," he told an audience at the Council on Foreign Relations, a centuries-old think tank, home to establishment U.S. foreign policy thinking in New York City and Washington, D.C., where Sullivan was once an intern. After a year in office, "I believe, fundamentally, that the United States is in a better strategic position than the day we took office, and that is because President Biden has set forth and then asked us to execute a vision of America's renewed role in the world, one that is measured to match our times, that really, fundamentally, is about both investing in ourselves here at home and then leveraging the force of alliances and partnerships globally to take on the great challenges of our time."

Sullivan, in effect, was praising Biden and the national security team he built for revitalizing NATO and America's standing in the world.

As for Russia, "meaningful progress at the negotiating table, of course, will have to take place in a context of de-escalation rather than escalation. . . . It's very difficult to see agreements getting consummated if we're continuing to see an escalatory cycle," Sullivan said, seemingly making that statement more for Kremlin officials than think tank audience members. "We should fundamentally be pursuing a combination of deterrence and diplomacy in an effort to see if we can produce exactly the de-escalation that we're all seeking."

Sullivan was exhibiting the confidence that the administration wanted to display in public, but he hid the internal terror over whether the United States could stop what was likely to come.

Chapter 11

Three-Ring Circus

January 2022

The Biden administration's most important week of diplomacy took place at the start of the New Year.

The United States would engage Russia three times starting on January 10: in a bilateral meeting in Geneva, and then separate engagements at the NATO–Russia Council and the Organization for Security and Cooperation in Europe in Brussels. The three meetings, which U.S. officials internally called the "three-ring circus," was where Washington and Moscow would chat seriously about their problems.

For Russia, the complaint was about NATO expansion and the alliance's growing presence on its eastern front. For the U.S., essentially representing the alliance, the aim was to compel Russia to move its hundred thousand troops off Ukraine's border, thus stopping a war before it started.

There was little doubt about who should lead America's negotiations: Deputy Secretary of State Wendy Sherman. One reason was just bureaucratic: it didn't make sense to send Secretary of State Antony Blinken until something concrete could be decided. But mainly she got the nod due to her decades as a seasoned negotiator who had a strong working relationship with her Russian counterpart, Deputy Foreign Minister Sergei Ryabkov. She had also proved instrumental in getting the 2015 Iran nuclear deal over the finish line and had experience negotiating with other unsavory nations, like North Korea, proving she could handle tough conversations.

"She was tailor made for that assignment," a senior administration official told me shortly after the meetings. "We didn't just send a starting player. We sent an all-star."

As she prepared to leave, though, another administration leak hit the wires on January 8. *The New York Times* detailed what kinds of sanctions the U.S. and its allies were preparing to slam Russia with should an invasion go forward. The timing was unmistakable: the Biden administration wanted the Kremlin to know what it would face if it didn't make a deal.

The plan included "cutting off Russia's largest financial institutions from global transactions, imposing an embargo on American-made or American-designed technology needed for defense-related and consumer industries, and arming insurgents in Ukraine, who would conduct what would amount to a guerrilla war against a Russian military occupation, if it comes to that," the *Times* reported, adding: "Such moves are rarely telegraphed in advance."

It was America's opening gambit, even before Sherman reached Europe.

Wearing masks, the ubiquitous symbol of the pandemic age, Sherman and Ryabkov posed for photos ahead of their high-profile meeting at the U.S. mission in Geneva. They stood far apart to stay safe as the coronavirus still traveled around the world morphing into variants, but it also reflected just how far the representatives were from reaching an agreement.

Over the course of eight grueling hours, Ryabkov reiterated Russia's position: Ukraine and Georgia could not be in NATO. The alliance had to guarantee that. The United States wouldn't budge on that point, but Sherman was willing to discuss the placement of American and allied missiles in Europe, especially since Moscow feared their movement further eastward, with the ultimate concern that they could be placed inside Ukraine itself. Sherman shot back that NATO's "Open Door" policy could never be closed, and especially not by force.

By the end of the meeting, the deputy secretary didn't sound sanguine about the prospects for a peaceful resolution to the crisis. "Today was a discussion, a better understanding of each other and each other's priorities and concerns. It was not what you would call a negotiation. We're not to a point where we're ready to set down text and begin to go back and forth," she told reporters roughly ninety minutes after her meeting with Ryabkov ended. "We are trying to have very serious, businesslike, candid, clear-eyed, straightforward conversations with each other to best understand each other's concerns and priorities."

To those outside the administration, especially Republicans, the Sherman–Ryabkov meeting was too little, too late. "Are you fucking kidding me?" a Republican Senate staffer texted me at the time. The Russians have a hundred thousand troops on the Ukrainian border and the administration isn't even having serious conversations with the Kremlin. "This is all theater."

In fairness, it mostly was. Even as top Biden officials continually said they wanted to strike a diplomatic deal with Russia, there was little optimism that one could be reached. The feeling inside the White House, State Department, and Pentagon was that Putin was likely to order an invasion by the end of January. One senior official told me the chances of a negotiated breakthrough that saw Russia end its threats were at 5 percent. Still, 5 percent was better than zero percent, and it was better for the West's legitimacy that it tried in good faith to broker an agreement. That way, if and when Russia turbocharged the war in Ukraine, few could question that the West sought only to punish Moscow.

Later that evening, news broke that the U.S. in December had secretly green-lighted another $200 million in security assistance to Ukraine. It was another sign that the Biden administration was preparing for the worst, even as the nation's second-highest diplomat was in Europe working on a deal. The small arms and ammunition, medical equipment, and other devices wouldn't necessarily turn the tide of any upcoming war, but they would bolster the needs of a Ukrainian military that could soon find itself in battle. It was smaller than a past package that had included Javelin missiles, but it was still significant.

Deputy Secretary of State Sherman then traveled to Brussels for a full day of meetings with NATO and European partners. She heard what she'd been hearing from allies for months. Russia wasn't going to invade. Putin was bluffing. But it was good to talk and calm tensions. Just in case, allies coordinated sanctions targets and export controls with Sherman, finalizing details so that the packages would be ready to go when the moment came.

During those meetings, U.S. officials were worried about European resolve. One person familiar with the discussions told me that it was unclear whether European leaders would actually pull the sanctions levers if Russian troops rushed over the border. Some of the continent's countries were close to Russia, or at least needed it for energy purposes. Plus, though Russia had already invaded Ukraine and annexed Crimea, relationships between Moscow and European capitals continued to blossom. It was possible, this person said, that governments in Western Europe could easily find an excuse to avoid joining the United States in punishing Putin's Russia.

Sherman strode into the NATO–Russia Council meeting in Brussels on January 12 with a sense of unease. This was the time for top officials from all thirty member states and Russia to hear one another out, and she couldn't count on all the allies around the table to stand up for the moment. She sat there for hours as Russia's Ryabkov rattled off his country's demands, followed by every NATO member's deputy foreign minister offering carrots and sticks. Some, like the British and Baltic leaders, talked tough. This was a time for the West to stand up for Ukraine and itself.

Others made references to understanding where Russia was coming from, though asserting it was a misunderstanding. NATO was a defense alliance. It wasn't designed to attack Russia or unsteady it. Russia could ensure NATO was never a threat to it if Russia was never a threat to NATO. A small group, namely representatives from Hungary and Turkey, flirted with siding with Russia. The alliance had failed to account for Russia's concerns over many years, saying that Moscow just had to grin and bear it. Maybe there was a way to scale back some of NATO's moves so Russia could feel comfortable again.

In another era, that argument might've carried more weight in the room, someone aware of the forum's discussion told me. But certainly not after Russia had invaded Ukraine and threatened to do so again. Putin showed who he was. It wasn't a time to back down.

Sherman watched and listened throughout the whole meeting, scribbling notes on her yellow pad as she witnessed counterpart after counterpart make their pitch. She used the notes to make concluding remarks, throwing her prepared comments aside.

"You could hear a pin drop in the room," a person familiar with her comments told me, especially as she addressed the Russians directly. "You've come as one to a room of thirty. We are thirty. But here at NATO, we are one." As she spoke, the Russians started passing notes and whispering among themselves. Seeing that, Sherman stopped her remarks and demanded the Russians pay attention to her. "The room again was silent," the person said.

The deputy secretary proceeded to weave in her family history, noting how her grandmother was from Russia—modern-day Ukraine—and her father served in the Marines during World War II, a war in which the U.S. and Soviet Union fought the Nazis. That was of particular resonance to Sherman, a Jewish American.

"There were tears in the eyes of some allies' representatives," this person told me.

Sherman still made sure to note that Russia would face severe consequences if it chose violence over diplomacy: "The secretary general of NATO has offered another and better path. The Polish chairman-in-office of the OSCE has offered another and better path. The French presidency of the Council of the European Union has offered another and better path. And so has the president of the United States." NATO secretary general Jens Stoltenberg got up from his seat after the meeting to praise Sherman's address. It was one of the most powerful speeches the NATO–Russia Council or, indeed, the alliance as a whole had ever heard.

That was Sherman's last act of the trip. The U.S. ambassador to the OSCE, Michael Carpenter, took over for that group's meeting on the crisis. Carpenter, a former foreign policy adviser to Vice President Biden and a senior Pentagon official for Russia policy, was tasked with delivering the United States' strongest rebuke to the Russians yet, coming after days of negotiations with the Russians and coordination with allies.

"We must decisively reject blackmail and never allow aggression and threats to be rewarded. We must resolutely defend, not dilute, our foundational principles and commitments," he said. "We must never stand for the flouting or erosion of our bedrock principles. That means no tolerance for overt or tacit spheres of influence, no restrictions on the sovereign right of nations to choose their own alliances, no privileging one state's security requirements over those of another."

A U.S. official spoke to me shortly after Carpenter's address about why it was so forward and direct. One reason was that Sherman had gone off script in Brussels and spoke with moral clarity about how America saw the moment. There was no use in dialing back the pressure after that. Another rationale was that the OSCE wasn't that prominent a group. It would be less high profile to have Carpenter deliver a broadside there than for Sherman in the heart of NATO.

But Carpenter didn't steal the show or the headlines. It was Polish foreign minister Zbigniew Rau, who chaired the meeting. "The risk of war in the OSCE area is now greater than ever before in the last thirty years," he said. "For several weeks we have been faced with a possibility of a major military escalation in Eastern Europe."

That quote made it into newspapers worldwide, showing just how seriously some in Europe, especially countries that were once aligned with the Soviet Union or had been invaded only decades ago, saw the situation.

The talks failed to reach a compromise, not that anyone in Washington thought that was possible. The Russians spoke with harsher tones after three days of diplomacy that yielded nothing. There were "no grounds" to continue talking, Ryabkov said, putting one nail in the coffin of a negotiated peace. The United States wanted to speak about matters that the Kremlin didn't care about, using the occasion for its purposes. Jake Sullivan, asked about the whirlwind week, said the U.S. heard "both hopeful signs and deeply pessimistic signs" from the Russians.

Carpenter was far less hopeful in a call with reporters after the OSCE meeting, taking a bit of the spotlight away from Poland's Rau: "The drumbeat of war is sounding loud, and the rhetoric has gotten rather shrill."

That sense of a drumbeat came from the intelligence Carpenter and his colleagues across the Biden administration were seeing. One piece that they shared with the press showed that Russia was planning a false-flag operation so Putin could use it as a pretext for war with Ukraine.

It was a dastardly plan. Russia would use a group of operatives "trained in urban warfare and in using explosives" in eastern Ukraine. The group then would "carry out acts of sabotage against Russia's own proxy-forces," using the footage to blame Ukraine for the attack. Putin could then go to his inner circle and the Russian people to say the threat emanating from Ukraine had to be wiped out. Such a plot could start within days to weeks from the January 14 reveal.

It was another successful instance of the administration "pre-bunking" Russian claims. The White House asked intelligence leaders at the CIA and Office of the Director of National Intelligence if the information could be downgraded and made public. The intelligence leaders had no problems doing so, as long as enough was stripped out that it wouldn't hurt sources and methods. It was the beginning of a standard operating procedure for an idea first hatched in December.

Meanwhile, Moscow wanted to show that days of talks hadn't changed its view. If anything, it had hardened the Kremlin position that negotiations wouldn't give Moscow the security guarantees it sought.

"We have run out of patience," Foreign Minister Sergey Lavrov said at a news conference the same day the U.S. intelligence was released. "The West has been driven by hubris and has exacerbated tensions in violation of its obligations and common sense."

He added: "They must understand that the key to everything is the guarantee that NATO will not expand eastward." If Russia didn't get what it wanted, "we will make a decision on how to ensure our security in a reliable way," including via "military-technical measures."

When the Lavrov quote hit the wires, a source noted, "Ha! They're just saying the quiet part out loud now."

American officials soon would do the same, taking their internal worries about a Russia invasion from the privacy of their offices out into the open. On just one day, January 18, administration figures made three separate statements about the prospects for invasion or peace. Safe to say it tilted heavily toward invasion.

"We're now at a stage where Russia could at any point launch an attack in Ukraine," Psaki said during her daily news briefing. Moscow's recent military moves "signal to us that Russia is looking at Ukraine in an aggressive way," Linda Thomas-Greenfield, the U.S. ambassador to the United Nations, told *The Washington Post*'s Jonathan Capehart. And chief Pentagon spokesperson John Kirby added in his own press conference that there's "no sign, no indication the Russians are willing to de-escalate."

It wasn't just members of the Democratic administration who feared for the future. Republicans got nervous too. "We're staring down an Afghanistan-in-Europe type of event with thousands dead, refugee floodgates opened, and U.S. credibility gutted. It's going to be horrible to watch," a House Republican aide texted me that same day.

It was clearer than ever that the U.S. government had fully switched from a sense of optimism to full-blown panic. The diplomatic process would continue, but it was all a smokescreen. War was coming, and it was coming soon.

On January 19, one day short of a full year in office, President Biden joined a group of reporters in the East Room of the White House. All he wanted to discuss was the advancements he said America had made under his leadership. But as he stood at the podium, his team knew that, at some point, questions about the possibility of war across the Atlantic Ocean would come up.

One did, after questions about the economy and the president's record over the last year. Bloomberg News's Jen Epstein wanted to know why Putin would be deterred by the threat of sanctions, especially since they hadn't stopped him from aggressive actions in the past and European countries weren't unified on a response.

Biden was bullish. "Well, because he's never seen sanctions like the ones I promised will be imposed if he moves," he said. "And the idea that NATO is not going to be united, I don't buy.

"I think what you're going to see is that Russia will be held accountable if it invades. And it depends on what it does. It's one thing if it's a minor incursion and then we end up having a fight about what to do and not do," he continued.

Wait a minute, another reporter followed up, might the West not respond if Russia does a "minor incursion"? Biden responded, saying that he didn't want to do anything that would split NATO. In other words, allies had to work in unison. Even if some countries wanted to do more, likely the United States, the UK, and the three Baltic states, it was best that NATO moved as one. "If it's a—something significantly short of a significant invasion—or not even significant, just major military forces coming across—for example, it's one thing to determine that if they continue to use cyber efforts, well, we can respond the same way, with cyber."

These statements caused a massive media uproar and headaches for Biden's White House aides. Biden had admitted that there was tension and disagreement on how to respond to Russia, despite weeks of assurances that the allies were in lockstep with one another. What's more, Biden seemed to suggest that there would be lower-level punishments for Russia if Putin ordered attacks that were less aggressive than a full-scale invasion.

It was unfortunate timing, especially since just one day earlier Russia and Belarus announced they would hold a joint military exercise on Ukraine's doorstep in February. The drill would revolve around fending off an external attack, which made U.S. and European officials worry that Russia was pre-staging troops ahead of an invasion and also practicing to fight NATO countries coming to Ukraine's aid. Some Russian troops had already arrived in Belarus, well in advance of the exercise.

Ukrainian officials were letting Biden have it for his "minor incursion" comment. "We want to remind the great powers that there are no minor incursions and small nations. Just as there are no minor casualties and little grief from the loss of loved ones," Zelenskyy tweeted. "Speaking of minor and full incursions or full invasion, you cannot be half-aggressive. You're either aggressive or you're not aggressive," Dmytro Kuleba told *The Wall Street Journal* on the record.

It forced Biden to clarify his comments the next day before an infrastructure meeting. By now, Washington had grown accustomed to having infrastructure policy upended by anything. "If any—any—assembled Russian units move across the Ukrainian border, that is an invasion," he said, noting he'd been clear with Putin about the consequences he faced.

A senior U.S. official was incredulous at how the press covered Biden's initial comment and Ukraine's response. "He was saying what was undeniably true," this person told me on the phone, unmistakable anger coming from the other end of the line. Say the Russians didn't try to swallow Ukraine whole but instead sent a few thousand more troops into the Donbas in Ukraine's east. "Is there any question that we or our allies would decide to go as far? Of course not."

But the damage was done. Experts and representatives for the Ukrainian government in Washington were telling any reporters who would listen about how Biden had in one moment shaken Kyiv's confidence in the administration. The president was signaling his reticence to get involved in supporting Ukraine since he's fearful of starting a war with Russia, they claimed. Ukraine was on its own. "They don't trust the admin," one of the representatives texted me. "They're beyond angry."

Zelenskyy made his anger known in a January 20 interview with *The Washington Post*, an outlet chosen to reach the president and D.C. policymakers directly. He blasted the administration's stance that sanctions should come after an invasion, not before. "I support imposing sanctions now," he said. "I asked one leader: 'Why do you support sanctions against Russia in case there is an invasion into Ukraine? Why do you need sanctions after we lose the whole territory of Ukraine?'" It was never clear if "the leader" was Biden, but I was told by a U.S. official that the Ukrainian leader and his team had made that point often to American officials.

Ukrainian officials and people close to them also kept telling reporters that they hated it when Biden administration figures said a Russian invasion was "imminent." Such suggestions were killing the Ukrainian economy and fomenting panic. Zelenskyy, whenever given a chance, fought back against America sounding the alarm bells. "I'm the president of Ukraine and I'm based here and I think I know the details better here," he told members of foreign media in Kyiv on January 28. His main point was that Ukraine had already been invaded. There was always a threat from Russia. The hundred thousand Russian soldiers on Ukraine's border, in addition to those training in Belarus, were part of a constant problem—not anything new.

"What the fuck is he doing?" a State Department official said to me. Ukraine is "about to get invaded" and Zelenskyy is acting "like nothing's wrong."

Everything Biden administration officials were saying publicly and privately was that something wicked this way comes. Zelenskyy, whether he believed it or not, was so nonchalant that it arguably bordered on dereliction of duty. There were whispers inside multiple government agencies that the former comedian simply wasn't up to the job. He was whistling past the graveyard before it filled up.

As Ukraine complained, the United States got to work. The winter was coming to an end, so if Putin planned to invade, he would do it soon.

The sanctions package was finally coming into full view. Russia's leading banks, major imports, and state-run companies would be the main targets of American and allied sanctions. But going after Russia's oil and gas exports, or moving to disconnect Russia from the SWIFT international banking system, still weren't serious options. European countries needed Russian energy to stay warm in the winter, and removing Russia from the infrastructure that connects global banks would effectively cut the country off from the world economy. That, for the moment, was a step too far.

In the meantime, the U.S. was preparing to send eighty-five hundred troops to Europe as part of a NATO operation in advance of an invasion. The intention was to bolster Europe's defenses, if need be, and signal to the Kremlin that the West was ready for anything. Except, as Biden told reporters that day, "we have no intention of putting American forces or NATO forces in Ukraine."

It was a stance the president felt deeply. This was the West's war, but not America's war. The U.S. would do what it could, but not so much that Russia would want to fight America and its NATO allies. That was how World War III could start.

Some European countries, mainly France and Germany, were still holding out hope that diplomacy could fend off the worst outcome. Emmanuel Macron kept speaking with Putin by phone, trying to broker some agreement. It was good that world leaders were engaging the Russian boss, Biden administration officials believed, but they were wary of their European counterparts pushing for a deal at any cost.

Meanwhile, Biden held a call with Volodymyr Zelenskyy on January 27. It didn't go well.

Biden emphasized that the war was coming to Ukraine. Kyiv needed to get ready. The Ukrainian leader balked at the suggestion. There was no war and the United States was inciting a global panic. But, Zelenskyy said, if the U.S. was truly serious, then Kyiv should expect a massive weapons and financial assistance package.

Zelenskyy was doing everything in his power to help Ukraine, asking for more weapons like the Javelin missiles that were in transit to the country. Biden tried to get his counterpart to focus. "Let's just press pause for a moment," Biden said. "They are coming for Kyiv." The president wanted Zelenskyy, on the call, to wrestle with and internalize the threat to his homeland. Zelenskyy bashed Biden's leadership again. The Ukrainian economy was cratering because of what the U.S. was saying. Biden again tried to center his colleague: "Are you listening to what I'm saying?" It was clear Zelenskyy was not.

Biden and his aides were stunned at Zelenskyy's intransigence. Sure, he didn't want to cause a panic and his economy to collapse by admitting that an invasion was a fait accompli. But Ukrainian intelligence was painting a different picture from what Biden was relaying. This was post-Afghanistan overreaction and overcaution, not serious analysis, Zelenskyy and his team believed.

Biden and his aides wondered if Zelenskyy really did know Russia better than America did, and invading Ukraine was simply not something Russia would do. It would be a crazy decision and out of character for the cold, calculating Putin. But Zelenskyy didn't have all the raw intelligence that made what was coming clear as day—and maybe without it, it was impossible to wrap one's head around the enormity of the oncoming storm.

When the call finally ended, the president clearly looked agitated and frustrated. He sat in his chair quietly for a beat before giving his team orders on what to do next.

The next day, Lavrov oddly offered some comments that made at least American ears perk up. In an interview with four Russian radio stations on January 28, he said he would soon send a letter to his Western counterparts to get a sense of how strongly they stood by their proposals of maintaining transatlantic unity. "We don't want wars," he said.

Was this a sign that Russia was willing to come back to the table for talks? Did the West's consistent statements of a unified response scare Putin off? Or was this another delay tactic? No one in the administration could be sure, including whether Lavrov was maybe freelancing without direct input from Putin. It didn't matter much, officials told me at the time, because the smart money was on Russia invading Ukraine at some point soon. It was just a matter of time.

"This sucks," one of the officials told me. "We're doing everything right and the Russians are probably going to invade anyway." That comment was about the administration's policy and handling of the crisis. But when I asked if it all meant something bigger—that America, even when everything was going well, couldn't stop major global crises anymore, the official paused for a moment, giving my question real thought. After what seemed like an eternity, I received a semisatisfying response: "Yeah, that's certainly part of the frustration."

The Biden administration, stewards of the world's preeminent power, was coming to terms with its inability to stop a war. A team that was formed to pull the world together had succeeded in doing so in service of a failed mission. But officials, from Biden on down, felt it wasn't wasted effort. If Putin were to do what he now seemed likely to do, the world would be united against him.

Either way, the administration's thinking went, the U.S.-led resistance and world order wins. Democracy wins. Russia and Putin's brand of authoritarianism, if not Putin himself, loses.

Chapter 12

War

February 2022

On the morning of February 1, Vladimir Putin was furious. The United States had delivered written responses to Russia's demands about security guarantees days earlier, but the answers weren't to his satisfaction.

Putin happened to be hosting Prime Minister Viktor Orbán of Hungary in Moscow, the two leaders toasting one another at opposite sides of a luxurious room. Putin, it appeared, was still scared of getting the coronavirus. The man threatening to upend the post–World War II order was too scared to embrace a like-minded colleague.

On paper, Orbán was a NATO ally, but in practice he shared a lot in common with the Russian leader, namely transforming their modern-day societies into conservative and xenophobic states.

Putin, inside the grand complex of the Kremlin, used their joint news conference to unload on the U.S. "Russian concerns were basically ignored. We didn't see an adequate response to our key concerns: non-expanse of

NATO, the refusal to deploy [an] offensive weapon next to the Russian borders and bringing back the military infrastructure of the alliance to the status quo of 1997, when the Russia–NATO treaty was signed," he said. "The United States, they don't care that much about Ukrainian security. Maybe they think about it. But it's a secondary priority for them. But their main job is to deter the development of Russia, to hinder the development of Russia. And in this sense, Ukraine is just a tool."

Other Russian officials had made those points before. But this was the first time Putin would make the case on the world stage. Either he was truly upset at the Biden administration's response or he was using it to bolster his case for war. Maybe a little of both.

White House officials watched as Putin essentially said a diplomatic deal wouldn't happen, at least not soon. It was expected, but still discouraging, that the path to war just became a little clearer.

Orbán, for his part, said that Putin's demands were reasonable and that sanctions on the Kremlin wouldn't work.

The diplomatic path also took a major hit. *El País,* a leading newspaper in Spain, got hold of NATO and America's responses to Russia's December 17 draft treaty. The NATO document encouraged Russia to make security agreements with the U.S., especially on the placement of missiles in Europe. And if Moscow wanted to improve ties with NATO allies, it had to remove troops right on Ukraine's border.

The Biden administration's response to Russia was the more important of the two documents. The U.S. said it would continue to support NATO's "Open Door" policy—thus potentially allowing Ukraine and Georgia to join the alliance at some future date—but was open to discussing a ban on ground-launched missile systems in Ukraine. "That one cost us nothing to give," a senior administration official told me later. "We were never planning to put missiles in Ukraine."

The response also came with a warning: Any further aggressions by Russia against Ukraine "will force the United States and our Allies to strengthen our defensive posture." In other words, attacking Ukraine meant Russia would have to deal with more NATO in Europe, not less.

Sullivan, Blinken, and other top administration officials were stunned at the leak. Biden's team was so close-knit and knew how important the diplomatic initiative was. A revelation of this magnitude could blow up whatever small chance remained of a peaceful end to the crisis. "It felt like a betrayal," a White House official told me at the time.

Feelings of betrayal were soon swept away by suspicion that Russia had leaked the documents. The Kremlin would show how NATO and the United States refused to concede even an inch to Russia's security concerns, leaving Putin no choice but to solve the problem with military might. Putin, in a sense, was giving himself a pretext for invasion.

Another theory, divined with Occam's razor, was that some Spanish official leaked the documents to the Spanish press. Spain, a NATO member, surely would have seen both documents, which were shared among allies before the Russians saw them. And it didn't make much sense that Russia, seeking to publicize the documents, chose a Spanish-language outlet as opposed to an English-speaking one in Britain or elsewhere.

Whatever the reason, the now-public documents meant there was less of a chance that diplomacy could work. The U.S. and its allies prepared more intensely for the other option.

The next day, Biden ordered three thousand U.S. troops to relocate to different parts of Europe. Around two thousand troops from the 82nd Airborne Division at Fort Bragg, North Carolina, would go to Poland and Germany while the other thousand, already in Germany, would go to Romania, where the U.S. had long enjoyed military access to bases near the Black Sea. This was in addition to the eighty-five hundred American service members the president put on standby to secure NATO if need be.

The president made the decision to bolster America's military presence in Europe on the recommendation of Austin and Milley. It would send both a deterrent message to Russia and a reassuring message to allies. This wouldn't be an invasion or a military buildup for war. It would be political language.

Should Russia invade, there was a concern, though not a large one, that Moscow's force might move farther westward and threaten NATO territory. But the deployment was meant to calm U.S. allies that America was with them and to put the Kremlin on notice. "A win-win move," a White House official texted me when asked about the decision.

And the need to simultaneously reassure the U.S.'s allies and deter Putin was desperately required. Milley had been quietly telling lawmakers in both chambers on February 2 and 3 that one possibility was that Kyiv could fall within seventy-two hours of Russia launching its invasion. Approximately fifteen thousand Ukrainian troops and five thousand Russian fighters would die in the struggle, he assessed. The administration was also working with European allies to assist with the expected influx of refugees soon after the war began.

The congressional members were stunned. "There was silence on the line," one of them who listened to a Milley briefing told me. But when the silence ended, some lawmakers, mainly Republicans, were livid. They questioned other officials at the briefing, namely Secretary of State Antony Blinken, Defense Secretary Lloyd Austin, and Director of National Intelligence Avril Haines, as to why the administration had failed to stop Putin from launching a major war in Europe, perhaps the largest the continent and the world had seen since World War II. First the collapse in Afghanistan, now this.

The general response was that there was little America or its allies could do to stop a renewed invasion. Only Putin could decide not to go down that path. The best the United States could do was catalyze the global response to the coming catastrophe and deny Putin the ability to set the narrative.

Surely Biden's top aides made these remarks with knowledge of what was to come. The administration again released downgraded intelligence that Moscow planned to film a video of a fake attack by Ukrainians on Russian territory or Russian-speaking people. "This video likely will depict graphic scenes of a staged false explosion with corpses, actors depicting mourners, and images of destroyed locations and military equipment," a senior administration official told the press on February 3. "We believe that the military equipment used in this fabricated attack will be made to look like it is Ukrainian or from allied nations."

What Biden's team was revealing was so gruesome, so made-for-TV, that it seemed farfetched. Reporters asked why the American and global public should believe the administration's fantastic claims. After all, America had a checkered history with intelligence. The George W. Bush administration, most notably, claimed shortly after the 9/11 terrorist attacks that Iraqi leader Saddam Hussein had weapons of mass destruction. The media at the time ate it up, failing in the emotional days after the horrendous scenes in New York City, Washington, D.C., and Shanksville, Pennsylvania, to question the Bush team's outlandish claims.

National Security Adviser Jake Sullivan expected these questions from journalists and critics and huddled with his staff on how best to respond. One of his communications advisers constructed a pithy formulation: The U.S. was using intelligence not to start a war but to prevent one. Sullivan's eyes lit up. "That's it," he said, his voice rising in excitement and relief. That would be the line he and other officials would use going forward whenever they had seemingly outrageous intelligence on Russia.

Such a moment of excitement was rare for Sullivan. He was, with each passing day, growing more and more worried about Russia's intentions. Internally he said it was time to level with the American people about what was to come and what to expect. The White House communications team agreed and they put him on the airwaves.

"We're in the window where something could happen that is a military escalation. An invasion of Ukraine could happen at any time. We believe that the Russians have put in place the capabilities to mount a significant military operation into Ukraine," he said on *Meet the Press* on February 6. He also expressed deep skepticism that Europe would take severe retaliatory measures against Russia's energy sector.

"We believe that the Europeans intend to step up and impose severe costs and consequences," he said, "because it is true that Europe has distance to travel when it comes to weaning themselves off of Russian gas and diversifying their energy supplies." That Sullivan made that comment just one day before German chancellor Olaf Scholz arrived at the White House for a meeting with Biden was no coincidence. Getting Germany to cancel Nord Stream 2 had dominated the president's agenda for weeks.

Conversations with German officials in the run-up to Scholz's meeting with Biden were heavily focused on what to do about Nord Stream 2, the Russia-to-Germany natural pipeline that Germany needed to warm homes and the Kremlin liked because it kept Europe dependent on its energy. The Biden administration, having previously advocated for the project's completion to ingratiate itself with Berlin, now opposed its completion.

Scholz and his officials, however, wouldn't commit publicly to scrapping the pipeline altogether. One senior German official I spoke with continued to say, even in private, that Scholz's coalition government would "take all steps" expected of it should Russia invade Ukraine. When pressed if that meant canceling the pipeline, the official would simply repeat the "take all steps" line.

Official discussions between the United States and Germany tracked along the same lines. Ahead of Scholz's visit, Sullivan told his counterpart that the newly minted chancellor needed to commit to killing Nord Stream 2. That was impossible, Sullivan heard back from Berlin, because that would complicate the new chancellor's already delicate relationship with German companies building the energy thruway and imperil his weak political position. He was the head of modern Germany's first-ever three-party coalition government. He had come to power only after months of wrangling, which hurt his ability to speak off the cuff about major policy pronouncements.

The Biden administration watched in exasperation as Scholz continually refused in media interviews to commit to killing the pipeline. "We are ready to take together with our allies all necessary steps. And we have a very clear agreement with the United States government on gas transit and energy sovereignty in Europe," he told *The Washington Post* on February 6, one day before his Biden summit.

The White House sent a warning to Scholz's team, sternly delivered by Sullivan and Blinken to their counterparts: He simply had to commit to ending Nord Stream 2 in the case of a Russian invasion. He would be tarnished mercilessly in the press and Germany's reputation would suffer not just in America, but around the world. "It wasn't survivable for Scholz to say nothing," a senior administration official told me, explaining what was relayed to Berlin. If Scholz didn't say it during the meeting or the news conference, Biden would have to address the discrepancy. The Germans responded that they understood the situation.

The two leaders got the question during their news conference in the East Room of the White House on February 7. Biden spoke first, saying that if Russian tanks or troops crossed over the Ukrainian border, "there will no longer be a Nord Stream 2. We will bring an end to it." How was still unclear, though U.S. officials told me at the time that the plan was to sanction the project so massively that it couldn't be completed. That, however, was a 180-degree turn from where the administration had been just a year earlier, when they said the project was nearly complete so there was no need to try to stop it anymore. Now Biden was saying there was a chance to keep it from operating entirely.

Then Scholz spoke. "We have intensively prepared everything to be ready with the necessary sanctions if there is a military aggression against Ukraine," he said before explaining why he wouldn't commit to the pipeline stoppage publicly. "It is part of this process that we do not spell out everything in public because Russia could understand that there might be even more to come. And, at the same time, it is very clear we are well prepared with far-reaching measures. We will take these measures together with our allies, with our partners, with the U.S., and we will take all necessary steps. You can be sure that there won't be any measures in which we have a differing approach. We will act together jointly."

U.S. officials were telling me that there was "no daylight" between the German and U.S. positions. Germany was going to scuttle the pipeline if Russia invaded Ukraine; the only differences were in public messaging. Plus, Scholz was preparing for a visit with Putin in a week's time. The Kremlin leader might cancel the visit if Scholz was so blatant about Nord Stream 2's future. He had to leave the issue ambiguous for that reason too.

Still, one State Department official told me that they thought the chances Germany would cancel the project "grew during this trip." That alone was a remarkable achievement. Germany, which only decades earlier had its eastern territory run as a Soviet satellite, was now contemplating working in concert with the United States to thwart Russian imperial designs. Sometimes history echoed, but it didn't rhyme.

The National Security Council was buzzing. At least once a day, either the Principals Committee, led by Jake Sullivan and featuring the top Cabinet-level officials, or the Deputies Committee, chaired by Jon Finer with his equivalents around the government, met in the Situation Room. They would discuss multiple aspects of what a U.S. response to Russia would look like. What sanctions should go first? What statements does the administration release, and with which allies? Do American troops need to be repositioned?

That was the question at hand during a February 10 meeting of the Principals Committee. Sullivan went around the room, asking Lloyd Austin and other officials what was needed to reassure allies and deter Russia. Suddenly, the door cracked open and an aide handed Sullivan a piece of paper. "We need to shift, the president is coming," the national security adviser said, the surprise evident in his voice.

Everyone moved down a chair or two, allowing Sullivan to vacate the head of the table in favor of a spot right next to it. About two minutes later, around 6:15 p.m., Joe Biden walked in. Sullivan caught him up on where they were in the discussion. Austin then spoke, saying the consensus was that putting more U.S. service members on NATO's eastern flank made sense as the next move.

Biden didn't hesitate. He slammed his hand down on the table. "Send them." An official in the room was surprised with "how swiftly the president made that decision."

Plans and assessments got written and rewritten. One was to have the 82nd Airborne stationed in Poland to help U.S. citizens get out of a war-torn Ukraine. The American troops weren't allowed to go inside Ukraine, but they could handle the logistics involved with safely evacuating and then housing fleeing U.S. citizens. Intelligence analysis also said that Ukrainian forces could last far longer against Russian troops than the Afghan government could against the Taliban. Russia would be able to seize certain territories, but the fighting would last for a long time. That assessment stood in stark contrast to the one Milley delivered to Congress that Kyiv could fall within three days.

In fact, the United States still hadn't fully pinpointed exactly how Russia would invade Ukraine. Intelligence and military officials identified nine routes Putin's troops could take into the country during a full-scale invasion. One scenario included an all-out effort to capture all of Ukraine's territory east of the Dnieper River, which bisects the country vertically. The other one was more aggressive, sending additional forces tasked with controlling the Ukrainian capital. In either case, Russia would open the invasion with artillery and missile strikes as well as bombing runs on key military targets.

It's why the U.S. and Europe had their eyes on Russia's joint military exercises with Belarus that began on February 10. The drills would feature thirty thousand troops, making them the largest of their kind since the Cold War. Tanks rolled in fields. Fighter jets screamed in the sky above. Air-defense missile systems were put into position. The size and timing of the exercises, perched on Belarus's western border with NATO allies Poland and Lithuania, made it all the more likely that this wasn't just any exercise. "This is the practice run before the invasion," a U.S. official told me at the time. "No one serious here"—that is, in the administration—"thinks it's anything else." The only way to know for sure was to see where the Russian troops would go after the drill was done: back home to Russia, or into Ukraine.

As the exercises proceeded, Milley spoke on the phone with Gen. Valery Gerasimov, his Russian counterpart. The Joint Chiefs chair laid out everything the U.S. knew about the pending invasion and told Gerasimov that it wasn't too late to change course. The Russian got heated. He replied in a stern voice that Russia was only exercising. Moscow never accused Washington of planning to invade Mexico when it conducted military drills near the southern border.

Milley couldn't contain himself. "That's dumb as dirt, Valery," he said. "We don't do exercises with one hundred and fifty thousand troops and blood bags."

He then offered his truest feelings about what would happen if Russia went through with it. "You're going to get in there in fourteen days, have to stay there for fourteen years, and body bags will be coming back to Moscow for a decade," he said. Ukraine had been a free country since 1991 and its people had no desire to be one with Russia again. "They'll fight you tooth and nail," the general boomed.

The line went silent.

The administration started to sound the alarm bells. The invasion "could begin during the Olympics" in China, ending on February 20, Sullivan told reporters from the White House podium, "despite a lot of speculation that it would only happen after the Olympics." A theory brewed inside and outside the government that Putin didn't want to ruin Chinese leader Xi Jinping's showcase event. The speculation was that Xi delivered that message to Putin directly in a face-to-face meeting in Beijing a week earlier.

Whether the Chinese premier endorsed the idea of an invasion or warned Putin against doing it was unclear, but few U.S. officials I spoke to at the time thought Xi was comfortable with the plan. Either way, Putin needed the support of Xi and the country he led, so he was likely to wait until the conclusion of the final Olympic ceremony. There was, however, intelligence floating around in the U.S. that Putin had already made the decision to invade and that it would start on February 16. Biden had briefed his counterparts on that intelligence, though of course nothing was set in stone when it came to the start date of Russia's invasion.

Biden and Putin spoke again on February 12, a conversation a U.S. official later described to me as a "come to Jesus" moment. Biden tried to discourage Putin from invading Ukraine. He told Putin that the United States knew from experience that military campaigns inevitably turn into long slogs that the invading country soon comes to regret. Putin was fighting against "historical physics" if he went forward with the "occupation," Biden said.

Putin went on another trademark diatribe. Russia was a nation accustomed to occupation, by Napoleon's France and later Nazi Germany. If any country had the DNA of occupation in its bones, it was Russia. Russia knew well how not to conduct an occupation and how to avoid its pitfalls. Biden raised an eyebrow, feeling that his counterpart wasn't making much sense. A U.S. official on the call said that conversation left no doubt about what was to come.

Even though it sounded as if Putin had made up his mind, he continued to signal that diplomacy was possible. He held a clearly choreographed meeting with Sergey Lavrov, his top diplomat, where he listened to the state of the negotiations. "I believe that our possibilities are far from exhausted," Lavrov said, adding: "I would propose continuing and intensifying them."

“Good,” Putin responded.

“That’s good theater,” a senior White House official told me at the time. No one was buying Putin’s suggestion that he was serious about diplomacy. “The Russians would show up to meetings and barely be there,” this official said.

The administration showed its deep concern about what was to come by closing the U.S. embassy in Kyiv and relocating diplomats to Lviv, a city near Ukraine’s border with Poland in the west. “We have taken note of his comments,” State Department spokesperson Ned Price responded to what Lavrov said in the staged meeting. “What we have not taken note of is any indication of de-escalation. We have not seen any tangible, any real sign of de-escalation.”

Sullivan and Blinken had spoken about the possibility for a long time. They felt their top priority was to protect American citizens and officials in Ukraine at all costs. And they didn’t want to see a repeat of what happened to the U.S. embassy in Kabul during the fall of Afghanistan. Once a new invasion seemed imminent, they both agreed that it was time to move the diplomats away from the center of danger. Austin and Milley agreed, and they detailed plans to assist with the evacuation.

Ukrainian officials were furious at the move. They thought it would panic the Ukrainian public and signal to other nations that it was time to leave. Zelenskyy told his aides to deliver a message to Washington: The invasion isn’t happening, and America is imperiling Ukraine’s future by panicking. “That’s his right,” a State Department official told me then. “It doesn’t change the reality of what’s coming.”

Russia started to play games.

On February 15, the Defense Ministry said that some Russian troops were withdrawing from the Ukrainian border. “That makes no sense,” a U.S. official texted me after the announcement. “We haven’t seen anything like that.”

Neither did NATO headquarters. "So far we have not seen any sign of de-escalation on the ground," the alliance's secretary general, Jens Stoltenberg, said that day. "Everything is now in place for a new attack." The Estonian government had also released intelligence that day noting that Russia was going to launch a full-scale invasion of Ukraine in the back half of February.

Putin seemed to convince Olaf Scholz that he was serious about diplomacy. During their February 15 meeting in Moscow, Putin again suggested he was open to talks and didn't want to push for a war. Scholz followed by telling reporters it made no sense to risk the next world war over NATO's Open Door policy, especially since Ukraine wasn't going to imminently join the alliance.

"The fact is that all involved know that NATO membership for Ukraine is not on the agenda. Everyone must step back a bit here and make it clear to themselves that we just can't have a possible military conflict over a question that is not on the agenda," Scholz said. Senior Biden officials agreed that Ukraine wouldn't join the alliance anytime soon, but such comments were unhelpful to make out in the open. Sullivan and Blinken quietly relayed their frustrations to their counterparts in Berlin.

Just as he said that, Russia's lower house of Parliament asked Putin to formally recognize the breakaway regions in Ukraine as part of Russia. It was a nonbinding resolution, but it gave Putin political cover to launch an invasion in supposed defense of the so-called Luhansk and Donetsk People's Republics. "Well, if that isn't a pretext, I don't know what is," a U.S. official told me in a call that day.

That afternoon, Biden chose to address the American public, and the world, about what his administration was seeing. It was a clear indicator that he and his team were nervous about where all the signs were pointing.

He outlined what he and Putin had discussed on a phone call three days prior, emphasizing his belief that there was a diplomatic way out of the situation. But "the fact remains," Biden continued, "right now, Russia has more than one hundred and fifty thousand troops encircling Ukraine in Belarus and along Ukraine's border. An invasion remains distinctly possible." The president then said what, other than stopping an unprovoked invasion of a sovereign country, motivated him and his team.

"This is about more than just Russia and Ukraine. It's about standing for what we believe in, for the future we want for our world, for liberty—for liberty, the right of countless countries to choose their own destiny, and the right of people to determine their own futures, for the principle that a country can't change its neighbor's borders by force. That's our vision. And toward that end, I'm confident that vision, that freedom will prevail," Biden proclaimed from the East Room of the White House. This wasn't just rhetoric for Biden. As one White House staffer told me, "Oh yeah. He feels it in his bones."

Biden knew that the only thing standing between a successful Russian invasion and a failed one was American involvement. A seized Ukraine might not affect the American middle class right away, but eventually it would. Pocketbooks would get thinner as energy and food prices rose. The U.S. government would have to further bolster military and economic support for allies in Europe. And an authoritarian power would gain more strength, potentially positioning itself for a move on NATO territory.

What happened in faraway lands wasn't an abstraction for Biden or the American people he led. Ukraine was a place for America and global democracy to defend their interests, to take a stand—and to win.

Over the next several days, Biden and his aides spoke with even more certainty that an invasion was close at hand. "Every indication we have is they're prepared to go into Ukraine, attack Ukraine," Biden told reporters before a February 17 trip to Cleveland. The next day, he said, "As of this moment, I'm convinced he's made the decision. We have reason to believe that." The president wasn't winging it: the United States had obtained intelligence that Putin had given the order to send his troops into Ukraine.

The intelligence prompted Defense Secretary Austin to demand a call with his Russian counterpart, Sergey Shoigu, on February 18. Austin was in Poland as part of a three-country swing, and the only time he could do the call was on the car ride from the Ministry of Defense in Warsaw to the airport on his way out. As a courtesy, Austin informed the Polish defense minister of the call on his soil.

The conversation turned tense from the start. Austin demanded that Shoigu order Russian forces away from Ukraine's border—he could help end the crisis right now. But Shoigu was unconvinced. The soldiers were there for "exercises," he told Austin. "Don't worry about it, the troops won't be there much longer."

After Austin hung up, he turned to his chief of staff and said, "Well, now we know." There was no doubt in the secretary's mind: Russia was about to invade Ukraine.

That coincided with news that Zelenskyy wanted to travel to the Munich Security Conference, the world's premier defense gathering, in a few short days. This was madness, Sullivan and his team believed. Russia might invade or take some other action while he was out of the country. It was possible that Zelenskyy might never be allowed to return to his homeland.

The Biden administration conveyed that message to Kyiv quietly, aiming to convince the Ukrainian president not to abandon his country at such a precarious time. The response was: Nonsense. Zelenskyy would be safe in Munich and could change his plans if anything happened. It was important for his people and the world to see him defying Russia at the preeminent conference on transatlantic security.

On February 19, Zelenskyy spoke to a group gathered at the Bayerischer Hof hotel with the clear intention of pushing the dignitaries in the audience to act more aggressively in Ukraine's defense. "We will defend our land with or without the support of partners. Whether they give us hundreds of modern weapons or five thousand helmets. We appreciate any help, but everyone should understand that these are not charitable contributions that Ukraine should ask for or remind of," he said. "These are not noble gestures for which Ukraine should bow low. This is your contribution to the security of Europe and the world."

That message, delivered in the same room where Vice President Kamala Harris gave her address on bolstering the transatlantic alliance, was met with great fanfare. But in the White House, there was a bit of heartburn. The U.S. and its allies had provided millions and millions in security assistance and would continue to do so. They'd spent months coordinating how to boost Ukraine's economy and crush Russia's. The notion that somehow the Biden administration didn't understand what was at stake was offensive to Biden and some of his top players, namely Sullivan. Still, they brushed it off. Wouldn't we say the same thing in his situation? they asked themselves.

There were bigger things to worry about anyway. Leaders in Ukraine's two breakaway regions started to evacuate millions of residents over trumped-up fears that Ukraine was going to attack them soon. Videos circulating online of the evacuation, however, showed that they were filmed days before their release. Russian state-run media also ran images of an explosion in the center of separatist-controlled Donetsk, though no government official or credible expert could verify their authenticity.

There it was—the long-suspected plot for a pretext for war. "This is what we've been warning about," a U.S. official told me then. The official sounded tired, resigned, almost defeated.

Russia had moved blood and medical materials to where its troops were perched on the Ukrainian border, as clear a sign as any of Putin's intentions. The diplomatic fountain had gone dry, no matter what Putin and his aides said. And gruesome Kremlin plans had been revealed, showing that Moscow had ambitions far beyond just seizing Ukrainian territory. Russia had drafted lists of political opponents and dissidents to capture or kill once the invasion started. Journalists, anti-corruption activists, and LGBTQI+ persons, among others, would also be targeted. The intelligence proved Russia didn't just want subjugation of dissidents. It wanted their annihilation.

In a call, Sullivan and Milley discussed the revelations: "We can't let this happen," Milley told the national security adviser. "Not on our watch," Sullivan replied.

Sitting at his desk, wearing a crisp white shirt and a maroon tie, Putin prepared to give one of the biggest announcements of his twenty years in power. Over the next fifty-five minutes on February 21, he addressed his nation about why Ukraine couldn't be a sovereign nation and why the two breakaway regions—Luhansk and Donetsk—should officially join Russia.

"I would like to emphasize again that Ukraine is not just a neighboring country for us. It is an inalienable part of our own history, culture, and spiritual space. These are our comrades, those dearest to us—not only colleagues, friends and people who once served together, but also relatives, people bound by blood, by family ties," he said. That made the "genocide" Ukraine was waging on those people, which Putin claimed without evidence, all the more heinous. The move to annex the two regions already run by Russian allies, he continued, was "a long overdue decision."

There was no doubt now that Putin was laying the groundwork and a pretext for invasion, even if it wasn't the precise pretext the Biden administration expected the Kremlin to use. It made Biden's call with Zelenskyy, which was ongoing during Putin's speech, all the more urgent, administration officials believed. Biden felt that way, at least, but not his counterpart.

Their eighty-minute conversation was a solemn occasion. Those listening on the call believed the invasion was hours to days away. Biden used the call to express his condolences ahead of what was to come and to assure the Ukrainian leader that America had the country's back. The relationship was rocky, Biden knew, but he always felt that there was a mutual respect between the two men.

Zelenskyy didn't want to hear Biden's words of encouragement and support. He once again chastised Biden for starting a panic. Putin hadn't made the decision to invade. There would be no invasion. It was impossible for Russia to take over Ukraine with only one hundred and fifty thousand troops. The country was too large and the people would fight back. Plus, if the invasion was so imminent, why hasn't the U.S. sent more weapons for Kyiv's forces to defend Ukraine?

Biden understood Zelenskyy's frustration, but he wasn't causing a panic unnecessarily. The invasion was going to happen, and it was going to happen soon. He needed to mobilize Ukraine's reserves and make real plans for the defense of the capital. If Zelenskyy needed help evacuating the country to run the government from exile, the U.S. would be willing to help.

No need, Zelenskyy said. Why run when there was nothing to run from?

"We thought Zelenskyy was living in La-La Land," someone on the call told me. "This guy was putting his country in immense danger."

The first real sign that the administration thought an invasion was under way came during a February 22 CNN interview with Jon Finer, the deputy national security adviser. CNN's Brianna Keilar asked Finer if the administration assessed that Putin was going through with it. "We think this is, yes, the beginning of an invasion, Russia's latest invasion into Ukraine," he replied. Keilar was visibly taken aback, surprised by what she heard. For emphasis, Finer made sure to repeat the point again later in the interview: "I don't know how much clearer I can be. This is the beginning of an invasion."

Keilar's surprise was understandable. Just a day earlier, White House officials avoided the i-word even as Putin sent his forces into the annexed regions of Luhansk and Donetsk, falsely claiming they were there for peacekeeping functions. "Russian troops moving into Donbas would not itself be a new step. Russia has had forces in the Donbas for the past eight years," a senior administration official told reporters.

The distinction was important: the deployment of an invasion would have triggered the prepared sanctions, kickstarting the U.S.-led rebuff of Russia by Western democracies. But European allies took action first. Germany canceled the Nord Stream 2 pipeline, ending the mystery about whether the controversial project would survive. Britain sanctioned five Russian banks and three oligarchs. The European Union targeted 351 members of Russia's Duma with financial penalties for recognizing the breakaway Ukrainian territories as official Russian land.

The United States had to move in lockstep with its allies. Later on February 22, the U.S. announced an executive order to impose sanctions on individuals and financial institutions that supported Putin's clear attempt to further control Luhansk and Donetsk. That, more than anything else, indicated that the Biden administration believed the invasion had truly and finally begun.

By moving Russian troops into Luhansk and Donetsk, Biden said on the afternoon of February 22, Putin is "setting up a rationale to take more territory by force, in my view," adding, "he's setting up a rationale to go much further.

"This," the president continued, "is the beginning of a Russian invasion of Ukraine."

Around the same time, Lloyd Austin was hosting Ukrainian foreign minister Dmytro Kuleba in his conference room at the Pentagon. Austin told the diplomat that American and Western weapons and ammunition would flow into Ukraine from Poland, and that Kuleba could expect steady, continued support from the Biden administration. Kuleba expressed his appreciation, quickly turning to his fear that if Russia succeeded in Ukraine, then Putin would turn his attention to the Baltic states.

The conversation then turned bleak. Austin asked Kuleba if there was a continuity of government plan in place. It was entirely possible that Russian forces would kill Zelenskyy or other senior officials in Kyiv. "You need a plan." But Kuleba said that wasn't something his administration was thinking about.

General Milley erupted. "You're going to get overrun," he said. Russia was set to move on Kyiv, and armored columns could be rolling down the streets of the Ukrainian capital only two to four days after the invasion was launched. "This could happen at lightning speed."

Kuleba and the Ukrainian delegation were stunned into silence. What wasn't clear is whether they were silenced by the gravity of the moment, Milley's outburst, or both.

Jake Sullivan was sitting in his West Wing office the next morning hosting his daily meeting with his aides on the escalating situation in Ukraine. The door opened and CIA director Bill Burns stuck his head in. His face was stoic, serious. If one of the nation's premier intelligence officials made an unscheduled visit to 1600 Pennsylvania Avenue, the news couldn't be good. Burns stood in the doorway for a minute until Sullivan caught his eye, then Sullivan scanned the top spy's face for clues about why he'd made the surprise trip. Burns's dour expression could mean only one thing.

"Bill, has it happened?" asked Sullivan.

Burns sighed, then nodded. Sullivan and his team now knew: February 23 was the day Russia would fully launch its all-out invasion of Ukraine.

That same day, Putin's regime released another video of the dictator sitting at his desk wearing a white shirt and maroon tie. It seemed that he had filmed his announcement at the same time as the earlier message announcing the supposed annexations. This address didn't hint at a coming invasion. It announced the war to come.

Without evidence again, Putin claimed that Ukraine was killing its own people and Russian speakers. Diplomacy that Russia seriously wanted to engage in wasn't working. NATO, led by the United States, showed no signs of ending its threat toward Russia.

And so, per Putin, "They did not leave us any other option for defending Russia and our people, other than the one we are forced to use today. In these circumstances, we have to take bold and immediate action," he said. "I made a decision to carry out a special military operation. The purpose of this operation is to protect people who, for eight years now, have been facing humiliation and genocide perpetrated by the Kiev regime. To this end, we will seek to demilitarize and denazify Ukraine, as well as bring to trial those who perpetrated numerous bloody crimes against civilians, including against citizens of the Russian Federation."

It was done. The Western effort to deter Russia had failed. Now it was just a matter of waiting to see when it would begin. White House officials who had gone home for the evening were called back into work, a sign that something major was afoot. Deputies of the various agencies were in the Situation Room for a ninety-minute meeting. The deputy director of national intelligence, Stacey Dixon, let her colleagues know that there were Russian planes headed toward the border with Ukraine. It was unclear whether they planned to cross into Ukraine and bomb the country or if they'd turn back. She promised to give them an update in roughly thirty minutes. But no update came to that meeting.

Since Putin's speech, Milley called Sullivan every twenty minutes with operations updates. "We're seeing some movement," he'd say, but nothing definitive. On about the fifth call, Milley said, "The bombers are in the air. This is it. It's starting."

Sullivan swore loudly. He would soon brief his team on what Milley just relayed, but NSC staff could see on the adviser's face that the war they worked so hard to stop had already begun.

Throughout the night, Sullivan and Jon Finer were in the Situation Room, calling the president in his residence about the earliest developments of the war. Ron Klain, the chief of staff, walked in and out to receive updates he could pass along personally to Biden. Late on the evening of the twenty-third, Biden asked to speak to Zelenskyy—it would be morning in Kyiv. They hopped on the phone soon after the president's request.

Unlike their previous conversations, full of acrimony and distrust, this discussion was personal, warm, even heartfelt. After vowing to help defend Ukraine, Biden told Zelenskyy that he was sorry Putin had forced the horrific situation on his country. But he knew the Ukrainian people, and they would resist Putin's assault. Zelenskyy expressed similar confidence, but then he paused. After a short sigh, the Ukrainian leader told Biden: "I don't know when I will be able to talk to you again." The president responded: "If you ever want to talk to me, I'm here."

"We felt a momentary, like, fuck," an NSC official told me about that moment. The administration had worked hard to avoid it, using American power and leverage to its maximum potential. And yet it didn't work. But then reality set in, and it was time to act.

"Here we go," the official said.

Chapter 13

"Kyiv Stands Strong"

February 2022–February 2023

Eric Green and Amanda Sloat watched on CNN as Russian tanks rolled into Ukraine and bombs streaked across the country, ripping through buildings and infrastructure, preparing the battlefield in Moscow's favor. The senior National Security Council officials for Russia and Western Europe had been planning for this moment for nearly a year. And now, standing in Room 393 of the Eisenhower Executive Office Building, they found it hard to breathe as the images beamed from the new war zone into the heart of the White House complex.

"It was tremendously stressful and tremendously distressing," another official in the room said. "It was a little numbing when we were standing there."

There was little time for reflection. It was war, and there was work to do.

In the months of preparations, President Biden's team developed what they called a "playbook" for how to respond to the invasion. The playbook, really an online document shared across the government, was honed during the Tiger Team process. It featured guidelines on the order of sanctions, talking points for statements, military positioning, ideas for intelligence downgrades, and acceptable security assistance for Ukraine. It became, in effect, the Bible for what to do. As Green and Sloat prepared documents for meetings in the Situation Room, including ones that Biden would lead, they often referred to the large digital packet.

"It basically was just putting into action a plan that we had rehearsed and prepared," an NSC official told me. "We knew exactly what we were going to do."

The first move was to have Biden speak to leaders of the G7, the world's seven largest economies. They reaffirmed a joint plan to strike at the heart of Russia's economy, sanctioning major banks and enforcing export controls to starve its industry and military of necessary components. The Biden administration on its own targeted two top Russian banks, including the country's largest, and ninety financial institutions, all accounting for roughly 80 percent of Russia's banking assets.

"We have now sanctioned Russian banks that together hold around one trillion dollars in assets," Biden said in a White House speech on the afternoon of February 24. With the addition of four more banks Biden vowed to sanction, "every asset they have in America will be frozen." The administration held off sanctioning Russia's energy sector. Senior administration officials explained the rationale: fewer energy supplies meant higher prices, putting more money in Russia's coffers. So sanctions against energy would have to wait.

Meanwhile, Biden assured the American people, neither the United States nor its NATO allies would send troops into Ukraine. But his administration would "defend every inch of NATO territory with the full force of American power." This was Biden's formulation, dictated to his top lieutenants. The red line was getting into a war with Russia, especially one that involved sending American troops into Ukraine or, even worse, Russia itself.

The alliance prepared to confer the following day, February 25, for an extraordinary virtual meeting of leaders.

Now that the fighting had begun, the once-skeptical Volodymyr Zelenskyy took on the mantle of wartime leader. Vladimir Putin wanted to erase his nation from the map, and there was no choice now but to defend Kyiv and his country—and stay alive. "The enemy has designated me as the target number one, and my family as the target number two," he said in a February 24 video address. A defiant Zelenskyy vowed to stay in Ukraine's capital city and direct the fight against Russia from there.

The Biden administration offered to whisk Zelenskyy to safety. Zelenskyy refused, saying he needed to stay in Kyiv. If he left, Zelenskyy and his aides conveyed to American counterparts, it would erode the military's will to fight. The other issue, though, was that an American-led extraction wouldn't be a guaranteed success. "We didn't have anyone in Kyiv from the United States government to be in a position to say to him, 'Hey, we can help facilitate your movement,'" Jake Sullivan said in an interview. "So we wouldn't have been in a position to do that even if we had wanted to."

As expected, Russian troops launched a full-out sprint to decapitate the Ukrainian government and seize Kyiv. Killing Zelenskyy, or at least forcing him into exile, would give Putin the chance to install a puppet leader and a new government more subservient to him. Plus, holding Kyiv would give Moscow greater leverage in any future negotiations over the war—or Ukraine's existence.

Central to the Kremlin's plan was to take Antonov Airport in Hostomel, about fifteen miles northwest of Kyiv, and use it as a logistics and supply hub for the capture of the capital city. Instead of waiting for airstrikes to soften up the battlefield, Russia sent armored columns of tanks, aircraft, and troops gushing into Ukraine, causing the equivalent of tank traffic jams along main routes, which made them vulnerable to attack by well-equipped and well-trained Ukrainian forces.

Moscow sent two hundred helicopters to take the Hostomel airfield. Kyiv's troops were able to down several of them, complicating the takeover mission. Still, Russia's heliborne troops fought their way in. En route to the capital, they met a Ukrainian resistance Moscow had failed to decimate. But the Russian forces were overwhelming at that early stage, and took the airport on February 25.

There were concerns within the Biden administration and European governments that Russia's capture of Antonov Airport might have compelled Zelenskyy to leave. Italian prime minister Mario Draghi openly feared the worst when Zelenskyy missed a planned phone call with him. Wanting to put negative rumors to bed, Zelenskyy filmed a video alongside his top aides with a dark Kyiv as his background. "We are here," he said in the video, among the first of his self-filmed speeches to the nation. "We are in Kyiv. We are protecting Ukraine."

Russia threw away any advantage it had at Hostomel. Instead of consolidating its gains at the airport, making it safe for supplies, equipment, and troops to flood in, Moscow's forces spread out into the nearby towns of Bucha and Irpin. The momentary awe of the airport takeover gave way to confusion. Troops, vehicles, and equipment were being destroyed, and Russian forces clearly had no idea when to expect an ambush and how to handle it when the Ukrainians launched one.

Instead of retreating, or seeking an alternative strategy, the Russians simply waited around for supplies and reinforcements largely delayed by a forty-mile-long convoy inching its way across Ukraine. Young service members, clueless about what to do, were easy prey for Ukrainians using drones and artillery to strike their positions. There was no order to advance into Kyiv or to retreat. It was an early indicator that Russia was far less prepared for the war than it seemed.

U.S. assessments about the strength and professionalism of Russia's military were off. Convinced by Putin's boast that its armed forces had modernized, the Biden administration had little doubt that, valiantly as the Ukrainians may fight, the Kremlin had developed a force too powerful to overcome. That, at least, is how it looked on the outside.

Internally, senior leaders in Moscow weren't communicating with the commanders on the ground. Troop morale was extremely low, and they were sent into battle with little food, training, or equipment to carry out their mission. In some cases, Russian troops were using maps that were decades out of date and making calls on unsecured phone lines, making it easy for Ukrainian and Western intelligence agencies to intercept their messages. And those were the lucky ones: Others didn't have maps or medical kits at all.

Russian troops effectively were given orders to sweep across Ukraine and take the capital city, but they were provided little tactical or strategic guidance to pull it off. "This isn't war," a Russian soldier named Mikhail told *The New York Times*. "It's the destruction of the Russian people by their own commanders."

But that gave little credit to the Ukrainian fighters who were confident despite the odds. On February 24, a Russian warship threatened to destroy a Ukrainian outpost on Snake Island in the Black Sea. "This is a military warship. This is a Russian military warship. I suggest you lay down your weapons and surrender to avoid bloodshed and needless casualties. Otherwise, you will be bombed," a Russian officer said.

One of the thirteen Ukrainians defending the tiny island responded with a quip that would become a rallying cry for his nation: "Russian warship, go fuck yourself."

Back in Washington, D.C., Jake Sullivan and his staff were surprised at the speed of the European response to Russia's invasion. The operating theory going into the conflict was that European countries would impose stringent and targeted sanctions at first, but then balk at escalating the pressure. Most of Europe, including the two most important countries on the continent, France and Germany, had long histories of interconnected ties with Russia. Berlin in particular heavily depended on Moscow for its energy, as evidenced by the construction of the Nord Stream 2 pipeline.

But European countries placed more sanctions and export controls on Russia than officials in the National Security Council expected. On February 25, the EU's second sanctions package targeted Russia's financial, technological, and energy sectors while banning travel for diplomats to the bloc. Then on February 28 and March 2, the EU excluded seven Russian banks from the SWIFT banking system—except those handling energy payments—majorly complicating Russia's ability to conduct everyday banking transactions. Two weeks later, the Europeans tightened the vise, prohibiting transactions with many state-owned firms, the import of luxury goods, and investments in Russia's energy sector.

Biden's Ukraine playbook expected that most of those moves would come months, not weeks, down the line. "We thought we had to drag the European Union along," a senior NSC official told me. "We were the victims of our own success in the first few days."

For Biden, Sullivan, Blinken, and Austin, what the world was witnessing was the power of cooperation with allies. It could be a burden to coordinate so broadly and so often, like straining to turn a massive cargo ship just a few degrees. But getting allies aboard the retribution plan gave it more legitimacy, strength, and impact. Alliances extended America's reach. This is what Donald Trump misunderstood about American power, and this is what Biden intuited in his bones.

The pleasant surprise at the speed with which NATO allies responded had the United States scrambling to devise new, more robust plans. The preplanned sanctions were quickly running out in the playbook, so Biden had Sullivan task the State Department and Treasury Department to come up with more severe punishments, but ones that European allies would still accept. In the meantime, Sullivan used his daily Ukraine meetings in his office to brainstorm next steps.

The national security adviser liked to think long term. Questions starting with "Should we be" or "Why wouldn't we" dominated the Ukraine meetings. "Should we be incentivizing greater defense production?" he'd ask, or "Why wouldn't we send long-range missiles and fighter jets to Ukraine?"

A real-time scenario arose to help Sullivan answer that last question. On February 27, the European Union's top foreign affairs official, Josep Borrell, surprisingly told reporters that the bloc planned to send fighter jets to Ukraine. That was music to Zelenskyy's ears: his administration was calling for more military support as Ukrainian forces continued to defy predictions and hold off Russia's advance. But it was uncomfortable for officials in European capitals and Washington to hear, as any talks about sending warplanes to Ukraine were to be kept under wraps. Borrell said the quiet part out loud.

Kyiv, however, ran with it, putting out official statements that Ukrainian forces would soon be provided with seventy Russian-made fighters by Poland, Slovakia, and Bulgaria. All three of those governments denied that was the case. In March Polish president Andrzej Duda unequivocally stated that there would be no Polish warplanes in Ukraine.

Antony Blinken videoed in from Moldova for an interview with CBS News's Margaret Brennan for the March 6 episode of *Face the Nation*. Brennan asked the secretary if the U.S. would oppose a nation wanting to send warplanes to Ukraine. "That gets a green light," he responded. "We're talking with our Polish friends right now about what we might be able to do to backfill their needs if, in fact, they choose to provide these fighter jets to the Ukrainians."

The message was heard loud and clear in Warsaw. Two days after those remarks, the Polish government reversed course in a surprise announcement. Duda's government said it was prepared to send twenty-eight MiG-29 fighter jets to Ukraine as long as the United States provided Warsaw with used jets with "corresponding capabilities." Warsaw's agreement came as a shock—the Polish government hadn't told the Biden administration about its statement in advance. Senior U.S. officials later quietly told their counterparts in the Polish ministries of foreign affairs and defense not to be so open about the arrangement. Putin, they feared, would use the deliveries to escalate the war.

Victoria Nuland expressed her surprise and concern to the Senate Foreign Relations Committee that same day. "To my knowledge, it wasn't preconsulted with us that they planned to give these planes to us" to transfer to Ukraine, she said. "I was in a meeting where I ought to have known about that just before I came," Nuland continued, "so I think that actually was a surprise move by the Poles."

Debate swirled within the administration about whether or not to go through with the plan. Blinken and the State Department argued it made sense to do so: the Poles were willing to send Soviet-made warplanes that Ukrainian pilots had trained on, and the U.S. would send its NATO ally more advanced fighter jets to replace them. It was a win-win. But the Defense Department, namely Lloyd Austin and Mark Milley, as well as the intelligence community, worried about the logistics of the transfer and too deeply involving the United States in the war. Plus, it would take months for the U.S. to remove sensitive technologies from the F-16s, so no deal could come together quickly anyway.

Biden, in a March 8 Oval Office meeting, sided with Milley and Austin. John Kirby, the Pentagon spokesperson, got the approval to release a statement quashing the deal. "We do not support the transfer of the fighters to the Ukrainian air force at this time and have no desire to see them in our custody either," he said. "We will continue to consult with Poland and our other NATO allies about this issue and the difficult logistical challenges it presents, but we do not believe Poland's proposal is a tenable one."

Also after the meeting, the president called Kamala Harris, who was already on her way to Poland to meet with Duda. Speaking to the vice president en route, Biden said that Duda had to scrap the deal his government had just announced. "Tell Duda it's my policy and that you're speaking for me," Biden instructed Harris. Harris delivered the message in person to the Polish leader on March 10: "We're not going to support the transfer of these planes."

Later that day, Duda and Harris appeared together at the Belweder Palace in Warsaw, a neoclassical residence for the Polish president, for a news conference. Duda, under pressure from its ally, backtracked in front of the world. "We wanted NATO as a whole to make a common decision so that Poland remains a credible member of NATO, not a country who decides on its own on important issues which impact the security of NATO as a whole," Duda said.

The first crack in the Western wall of resistance had been patched up.

The depth of Russia's military miscalculation was coming into full view. Just weeks into the war, Russian forces launched hypersonic missiles at Ukrainian targets, including a weapons depot in western Ukraine. Using such an advanced projectile so early could mean only one thing: Russia was already running low on precision-guided missiles after launching more than one thousand of them by mid-March. "It's really a significant sign of weakness," a Western official told me. "You only fire this thing if you're desperate."

On March 25, Russia's Ministry of Defense declared that the "first phase" of its war on Ukraine was over. Instead of a blitzkrieg to take Kyiv along with other major cities like Kharkiv and Mariupol, Russian forces would solely focus on the "liberation" of the Donbas region in eastern Ukraine. It was effectively an admission of failure: within a month, Russia lost between seven thousand and fifteen thousand troops and lost around two thousand vehicles, while Kyiv remained firmly under the Ukrainian government's control.

But Russia's bumbling and disastrous start initially masked a dark reality. In the town of Bucha, near the Antonov Airport and Kyiv, Russian troops tortured and killed civilians, in some cases leaving their corpses strewn about the city to rot. The body of twenty-one-year-old Dmytro Chaplyhin was found tied to a tripwire that would explode a mine. According to Human Rights Watch, an international watchdog group, "Russian forces committed a litany of apparent war crimes" while they occupied Bucha from March 4 to 31.

During that time, on March 16, Russia also attacked and destroyed the Donetsk Academic Regional Drama Theater in Mariupol, a city that was already darkened by a loss of power. The theater was Mariupol's largest bomb shelter, and a week before the strike the theater's set designer painted CHILDREN in Cyrillic on the pavement to spare the building from Moscow's aerial assault.

Around the same time, Russia attacked a maternity hospital just blocks away, leading some of the survivors to make their way to the bomb shelter. There they'd be safe. But Russian forces showed no mercy, compassion, or scruples. They launched an airstrike that killed six hundred people in and around the theater.

One day after Russia's Defense Ministry announced the change in plans, Biden spoke in front of a morose crowd outside the Royal Castle in Warsaw. It was a speech he had been preparing to deliver for weeks. A few days before the March 26 address, Jake Sullivan, Mark Milley, Lloyd Austin, and Mike Donilon, a senior adviser to the president, were debating in the Oval Office about what the president, who was listening attentively, should say.

Milley wasn't shy about offering his views. "This is your moment," the top general said directly to Biden. "This is your 'Mr. Gorbachev, tear down this wall' speech. You have to answer the question of why this war should matter to the American people and what the war is about."

"Okay, what is it about?" Biden asked.

"It's what you said months ago, sir: world order," Milley replied. "We have to preserve the order that has brought peace and stability to the world since the end of World War II. If Putin wins, the order goes *poof.* It would set the conditions for the next great war."

"That's good," Donilon said, jotting down notes. "I'll put that in there."

Now in Warsaw, speech in hand, the president who tried to avoid a war explained to the world why America and the West needed to see it through.

"This battle will not be won in days or months either. We need to steel ourselves for the long fight ahead," Biden said. "It's nothing less than a direct challenge to the rule-based international order established since the end of World War II."

Milley would later tell his staff, citing that portion of the speech, that the main message "reflected the essence of President Biden."

But Biden's effort to put the moment in context was overshadowed by an ad-libbed remark at the end of the speech, fueled by emotion at the atrocities unfolding across the border: "For God's sake, this man cannot remain in power."

Under intense scrutiny from reporters, the White House quickly clarified that Biden wasn't calling for Putin's ouster, or saying that his administration's policy was regime change. But the question remained: Was that how Biden truly felt? And if it was, then regime change was effectively the goal of the United States. The next day, when asked if removing Putin from power was his secret desire, Biden answered "no."

Back at the White House on March 28, the president moved to set the record straight. "I'm not walking anything back," he said. "I wasn't then, nor am I now, articulating a policy change. I was expressing the moral outrage that I feel, and I make no apologies for it."

The losses kept racking up for Vladimir Putin in April. Sweden and Finland signaled their clear intention to become NATO's thirty-first and thirty-second members. Ukrainian troops sank the *Moskva,* Russia's flagship in the Black Sea. Blinken and Austin visited Kyiv, the city that Putin expected to have under his thumb by then. Biden then asked Congress for $33 billion in aid for Ukraine, a substantial sum that showed the depth of his commitment to Kyiv's fight.

Despite the devastation, everything was looking up for Biden, his pro-democracy agenda, and Ukraine. "The United States is leading the way," a jubilant Biden said during a June NATO Summit in Spain.

Lloyd Austin had been working that NATO room and making calls, convincing allies that they needed to chip in weapons to help the Ukrainians fight. Kyiv stood a chance to remain in Ukrainian hands for a long time if the West could collectively serve as an arsenal for democracy. His work convinced once-skeptical nations to provide air defenses, artillery, munitions, and more for Ukrainian forces to use against their invaders.

Questions from within the United States, European allies, and Ukraine about Biden's commitment to Kyiv's cause and his pro-democracy bona fides arose in the summer.

Worried about China's increasing influence in the Middle East, Biden visited Israel and Saudi Arabia in July. The Israel visit was a pro forma stop: he had no big announcement to make or policy success to boast about. But for politics, he needed to spend time in Jerusalem—now under the leadership of freshly minted prime minister Yair Lapid—before heading to Jeddah to meet with Crown Prince Mohammed bin Salman (MBS).

During his campaign for president, Biden vowed to make Saudi Arabia a "pariah" after Mohammed bin Salman ordered the killing of U.S. resident and dissident Jamal Khashoggi. Now he was coming to the royal's summertime retreat, hat in hand, asking for the kingdom to produce more oil due to the energy crunch caused by Russia's invasion of Ukraine.

The visit was a clear success for MBS. As Biden exited the motorcade on July 15 into the sweltering heat, MBS waited to greet him, fist clenched and stretched outward toward the president. Biden met it with a fist of his own—a fist bump that officially ended Saudi Arabia's pariah status. Biden laughed off any criticism that he gave MBS and his nation far more than the U.S. got in return, even if Riyadh made no clear commitment to open the spigots.

Meanwhile, off-camera, Saudi officials were hounding reporters at their hotel in Jeddah, saying that Riyadh didn't commit to anything. Instead, the whole visit was a recognition by Biden that he needed to grovel to get back on the Saudis' good side, they said. Saudi minister of state for foreign affairs Adel al-Jubeir told me that it was shameful of the United States to blame his nation for human rights abuses when Washington was responsible for atrocities around the world.

Days later, Jake Sullivan spoke in front of an elite crowd in the ski resort town of Aspen, Colorado. It was the dead of summer on July 22, with golden sunbeams bouncing off the surrounding mountains as the Aspen Security Forum got under way. The annual event was usually one of the best times for administration officials to announce what they were planning to do—and what they would not do.

Sullivan, arriving in a business suit without a tie, spoke on a panel with moderator Jeffrey Goldberg of *The Atlantic*. The packed crowd, nibbling on fruit cups and sipping LaCroix fizzy waters, wanted to hear about Ukraine. The main point Sullivan wanted to get across was that the United States would provide Ukraine with whatever weapons it needed, but not the kinds that would deplete American stocks below a dangerous level or that could be used to strike deep in Russian territory.

"There are certain things that the president of the United States says he is not ready to transfer," namely the Army Tactical Missile System, known as ATACMS, with a range of 190 miles. Speaking of Biden, Sullivan said, "He believes that while the key goal of the United States is to do whatever is necessary to support and protect Ukraine, another key goal is to ensure that we don't get into a situation in which we are approaching the Third World War."

That statement wasn't taken well in Kyiv. Rep. Adam Smith, the Democrat from Washington State who chaired the House Armed Services Committee, had just returned from the Ukrainian capital city, where Zelenskyy said the U.S. needed to provide more weapons within weeks. "There's pressure mounting from a lot of people to try to get them to change their mind on that," Smith told me about the Biden administration.

By that point, the U.S. had provided more than $8 billion in military assistance since the start of the war. European allies, especially those in eastern Europe, demanded that the U.S. give more. "The price tag of aggression now is not high enough," Estonian foreign minister Urmas Reinsalu said during a visit to Kyiv in August, emphasizing that more sanctions and pressure on Russia would help. "We should make things more inconvenient for Russian society, the citizens of the aggressor state, so they know there is a certain price tag that they are accepting when they support a regime which is committing atrocities."

With Russia on the back foot, Ukraine saw its chance to go on the offensive.

An explosion rocked an ammunition depot on the Russia-controlled peninsula of Crimea. Unnamed Ukrainian officials took credit in the press for the strike, claiming their own special forces were responsible for the detonation that caused about three thousand people to evacuate the immediate area. The attack was part of a pattern. An attack by a drone on the port city of Sevastopol in Crimea led to the cancellation of Navy Day festivities and blasts destroyed munitions and other equipment of the Black Sea fleet's 43rd Naval Aviation Regiment.

The Biden administration debated internally about how to respond to the escalation. Biden had made clear to Sullivan, Blinken, Austin, and others that he didn't want to be seen as a direct participant in the war. Quietly, the United States told Zelenskyy's administration that avoiding escalation, after winning the war and the defense of Ukraine, was the ultimate goal.

But it became clear, in discussion between the State Department and the Pentagon, that the administration couldn't publicly dissuade Ukraine from targeting Crimea. The U.S. since the Obama years said that "Crimea was Ukraine," so in effect Kyiv's forces were choosing to attack Russian positions within its own sovereign territory. "We don't select targets, of course, and everything we've provided is for self-defense purposes. Any target they choose to pursue on sovereign Ukrainian soil is by definition self-defense," a senior administration official told me.

There was another opening. Vladimir Putin moved his troops to the southern Ukrainian city of Kherson to keep hold of it. With his forces dwindling, it left Kharkiv, Ukraine's second largest city, ripe for retaking. It was one of the best moments for Zelenskyy's troops to seize the momentum after Russia concentrated its efforts on taking Ukraine's south and east following the disastrous attempt on Kyiv.

For weeks, Ukrainian officials said openly that they were planning an offensive to bring Kherson back under their control. Now that they were armed with longer-range missiles and other advanced weapons that stalled Moscow's advances, it made sense to reclaim what had been wrongfully taken by the Russians.

But it was a head fake, a deception, an information operation. The Zelenskyy-approved plan wasn't to go after Kherson—Kharkiv was the target. Even the Biden administration was surprised, made aware of the plans only about a week before the offensive kicked off.

Using M270 multiple launch rocket systems, built by the United States, Ukrainian troops struck command posts, ammunition stocks, and other targets, startling their Russian enemies, who struggled to respond. Instead, they began to retreat.

"We broke through the front line, and the enemy started panicking," a Ukrainian soldier named Oleh told *The Washington Post* about the campaign. "They were panicking because we attacked all front-line positions at once—the entire front line itself was enormous—and everywhere there was a breakthrough." Some Russian troops stationed in the nearby town of Izyum, a key hub, surprisingly were fleeing their posts, encouraging the Ukrainians to recapture it too. Soon, the region would fall back to Ukraine.

The embarrassment of the Kharkiv-area offensive finally made Putin, on September 21, conscript three hundred thousand trained reservists to the invasion. It was a surprise to Jānis Garisons, the state secretary of Latvia's Ministry of Defense, whom I was updating on the address over breakfast in Riga by checking Twitter. There had been rumors that Putin would take such a step, but he was worried that announcement would make it seem like the war wasn't going to plan and would anger his base.

Perhaps wanting to look tough during a moment of weakness, Putin issued a thinly veiled nuclear threat: "To defend Russia and our people, we doubtlessly will use all weapons resources at our disposal," he said. "This is not a bluff."

Almost immediately, fighting-age men started to flee their country, fearful that they would be called into a war they didn't want to fight. "We are very scared. We want to run," Vladimir, a Russian twenty-year-old, said of himself and his two friends. "We are so young, we have so many plans, but the state thinks otherwise. We were promised that there would be no mobilization. We feel betrayed. The Kremlin lies, all the time. They look at us like toys."

Two weeks later, Putin once again showed that the war wasn't going his way. He named Gen. Sergey Surovikin, who was commanding troops in Ukraine's south and responsible for war crimes in Syria, as the leader of the "special military operation." His appointment indicated that Putin knew, even if he didn't admit it, that a full takeover of Ukraine wasn't possible with the fast-dropping numbers of troops and amount of equipment he had left. Instead, with Surovikin, he could beat Ukraine into submission by bombing more civilian targets ahead of a brutal winter.

It was a simple calculation: if this was a war of attrition, pounding apartments, critical infrastructure, schools, hospitals, and other targets would make Ukrainians surrender faster by breaking their will. Surovikin "knows how to fight with bombers and missiles—that's what he does," Gen. Kyrylo Budanov, head of Ukraine's military intelligence service, said that summer.

The move was met with shock inside the White House. A senior official said that the United States now expected even more devastation in Eastern Europe. It was a horrifying attempt to brutalize Ukraine even further because Putin had so grossly miscalculated at the start of the war. But if there was a silver lining, appointing Surovikin indicated just how desperate the Kremlin chief really was. "It's the most macabre good news," the official said.

Worse news came. Putin would attempt to capture by fiat what he could not capture in combat. On September 30, he announced that Russia had annexed four Ukrainian territories, all of them partially occupied. The people of Donetsk, Luhansk, Kherson, and Zaporizhia will be "our citizens forever," Putin claimed in a speech at St. George's Hall of the Kremlin, the nation's elites sitting before him. "We will defend our land with all our strength and all our means."

Sullivan and Blinken thought Putin was desperate. The announcement signaled that the Russian leader needed to claim he had control of parts of Ukraine to rally his own public. It was a brazen lie, but it was also an escalation. Did this mean Russia would consider attempts to control those regions as direct attacks on Russia? It wasn't clear, but the message from the Oval Office was: stay vigilant, but stay the course.

Biden had another problem on his hands: The bipartisan consensus on Capitol Hill was cracking apart. Some Republicans, particularly those with the same "America First" worldview as Donald Trump, questioned the billions in military and economic assistance the U.S. was providing to Kyiv. As midterm elections loomed in November, Rep. Kevin McCarthy, the California Republican who made no secret of his ambition to become Speaker of the House, had to walk a fine line keeping pro-Ukraine and Ukraine-skeptic Republicans in Congress happy.

Asked on October 18 about his spending priorities should Republicans take control of the lower chamber, McCarthy said, "I think people are gonna be sitting in a recession, and they're not going to write a blank check to Ukraine. They just won't do it." The Biden administration also had other issues to focus on, like cutting domestic spending and securing the southern border. "Ukraine is important, but at the same time it can't be the only thing they do and it can't be a blank check." Two days later, Biden said he was "worried" about what would happen to Ukraine aid if Republicans took control of the House.

Biden instructed his legislative affairs teams throughout the administration to work more closely with lawmakers and make the case for

Ukraine. It would be an uphill battle, the president surmised, as Republicans needed to find ways to differentiate themselves from Democrats and the White House. But Ukraine was worth the effort—and the president's legacy was on the line.

But the attitudes didn't change. They only hardened. Republican support for Ukraine declined in poll after poll, preferring that the U.S. focus on domestic problems instead of embroiling the country in a faraway war. "Is Ukraine now the fifty-first state of the United States of America? And what position does Zelenskyy have in our government?" Rep. Marjorie Taylor Greene, the pro-Trump Republican from Georgia, asked rhetorically during a November news conference.

Zelenskyy was worried, and a Republican victory in the House only added to his angst. He had to do something. In December, just weeks before McCarthy would likely take the gavel, the Ukrainian president decided to address Congress. He needed to keep the United States on Kyiv's side. Otherwise, his valiant troops would struggle against Russia's manpower and broader arsenal.

With Vice President Kamala Harris and Speaker of the House Nancy Pelosi behind him, Zelenskyy, dressed in the green military fatigues he wore throughout the conflict, made his pitch.

"Your money is not charity," Zelenskyy said on December 21, during his first known trip outside Ukraine since the invasion. "It's an investment in the global security and democracy that we handle in the most responsible way." Moments before Zelenskyy's arrival in a U.S. Air Force plane, the administration announced a new $1.8 billion security package for Ukraine, this one for the first time featuring Patriot surface-to-air missiles.

He then gifted a Ukrainian flag to Harris and Pelosi, signed by frontline fighters against Russia in Bakhmut, a city in eastern Ukraine. "This battle cannot be ignored, hoping that the ocean or something else will provide protection," Zelenskyy thundered, receiving rapturous applause in the House chamber.

• • •

Zelenskyy still needed more. Thanks to the United States and Europe, longer-range missiles, artillery, and missile defenses were flowing in from the West through Poland, Romania, and Slovakia. But as winter neared, what he wanted was new tanks to take on a regrouping Russia.

The Ukrainian government in November was in talks with their German counterparts about getting Leopard 2 main battle tanks. "We have reason to hope that the decision will be made to deliver the Leopard Two from Germany directly to Ukraine," Oleksii Makeiev, the new German ambassador in Ukraine, told local media outlets. "We need these tanks."

But quietly, the Germans were telling officials in Washington, D.C., and Kyiv that they didn't want to send the tanks. It would be too provocative, and there were opponents of the idea in Berlin who could threaten Chancellor Olaf Scholz's tenuous hold on power in a loosely aligned coalition government. The pacifist wing of Scholz's own party, the Social Democrats, would almost certainly revolt against him. But Jake Sullivan relayed to Jens Plötner, Scholz's foreign policy adviser, in October that Biden and the administration supported Germany's transfer of Leopard 2s to Ukraine, as well as Berlin greenlighting the transfer of the German-made tanks from other countries, like Poland and Slovakia, that used them.

Scholz had an idea to break the deadlock, which he asked Plötner to convey: Germany would send the Leopards if the U.S. sent M1A1 Abrams tanks at the same time. It would give him political top cover and also show that support for Ukraine remained a transatlantic priority. On January 19, 2023, the German chancellor told lawmakers at the World Economic Forum in Davos, Switzerland, of his plan.

The mood inside the room was uncomfortable. Sen. Chris Coons, the Democratic senator from Delaware who was close with Biden and had an uncanny resemblance to Scholz, said that the Pentagon didn't think it was a good idea. It would be hard to strip the Abrams of sensitive technologies, train Ukrainians to use them, and transfer them to the battlefield safely.

They also required jet fuel to run, meaning Ukraine would have to set up long supply and logistics lines that complicated their fight. The Leopards were much closer to the action and easier to operate, Coons told Scholz.

But inside a small meeting room on the bottom floor of the World Economic Forum's main hall, Scholz didn't relent. It was Abrams tanks for Leopards. There was no wiggle room. Scholz conveyed the message to the White House, but *Politico* broke the story of the private exchange, bringing the dispute out into the open.

The next day, at Ramstein Air Base in Germany, the hub for America's military presence in Europe, more than fifty nations met to broker some kind of agreement on the tanks. But Defense Secretary Lloyd Austin and his European counterparts couldn't get Germany to budge. That was frustrating to the Pentagon chief, who got more nations to give weapons to Ukraine than anyone else in the administration.

There needed to be a united delivery, or the Leopards would stay in Germany and in twelve other nations around Europe. Despite the failure, Austin told reporters that Berlin remained "a reliable ally, and they've been that way for a very, very long time."

Days later, Blinken and Sullivan were discussing the diplomatic dance over tanks with Biden in the Oval Office. Blinken offered an idea: What if the U.S. said it would send Abrams tanks to Ukraine in the future, especially because of all the logistical issues? "That might be enough to give the Germans what they need," Blinken said. Biden agreed with the plan. Sullivan presented the idea to Plötner, and Scholz liked it. On January 25, less than a week after the meeting in Davos and the failure at Ramstein, Scholz announced the deal. Leopards would soon be on their way to Ukraine.

Biden was pleased. Though he understood the Pentagon's objections, it was more important for him to maintain transatlantic unity at a time when it was severely tested. Military logistics were a second-order problem to maintaining strong relationships with key allies for the president. "We are united. America is united and so is the world. And [as] we approach the one-year mark of the Russian full-scale invasion of Ukraine, we remain as united and determined as ever in our conviction and our cause," Biden said in the White House's Roosevelt Room on January 25.

The war's anniversary was approaching, and Biden wanted to make the treacherous trip to Kyiv. Other world leaders, including British prime minister Boris Johnson, and members of his own administration had taken the journey, making the American president's absence in Ukraine more notable. There were good reasons why Biden couldn't go: The United States had no control over the war zone, posing a significant security risk. The route into Ukraine was a choice between the lesser of two evils—either Biden flew in on a military plane, opening up the possibility of the aircraft getting shot down, or he took a ten-hour train ride from Poland, where anything could go wrong.

But Biden knew the U.S.-led alliance needed to see the president of the United States in the city, as did Ukraine. It was the perfect moment for a visit. The president instructed his team to come up with a plan for him to make the trip, which Sullivan worked on for months with his Ukrainian counterpart, Andriy Yermak, before cautiously letting more people into the inner circle.

The plan they devised had him secretly traveling ahead of his scheduled departure for Europe and taking the eight-car train from Poland into Kyiv. The shades would be drawn the entire time so as to avoid snipers or being found out. The administration wouldn't confirm his visit until he was safely across the border back in Poland, even if images or video of Biden in Kyiv made their way onto social media.

There were risks, briefers from the Secret Service and the White House Military Office told the president in February, but this was the best way to make it all happen. "Let's do it," the president said in the Oval Office. The trip was a go.

On February 17, *The Wall Street Journal*'s Sabrina Siddiqui and the Associated Press's Evan Vucci were told to attend a private meeting at the White House. Waiting for them in the office of Communications Director Kate Bedingfield was Tamara Keith, the president of the White House Correspondents' Association. Right at the start, Bedingfield said that Biden was going to Kyiv and that they would be the only two reporters to travel with the president. They would receive an email the next day, with a subject line reading "Arrival instructions for the golf tourney," which would explain all the directions.

As instructed, Siddiqui and Vucci arrived at 2:15 a.m. outside Joint Base Andrews, about fifteen miles from the capital. Officials seized both their phones before getting on an Air Force C-32—not Air Force One. The plane was completely dark, had the shades drawn, and was parked off the tarmac. The C-32, a configured version of a Boeing 757 often used by the vice president or First Lady, took off at 4:15 a.m. Members of Biden's team, including Sullivan, went to the back of the plane to interact with the two reporters. But mostly they were still on call to work with Biden and catch some rest ahead of the historic visit.

As the C-32 hurtled eastward at six hundred miles per hour, the president who expected to make China his top priority was now making the most important trip of his administration to Europe. It was Bidenism in action: a show of resolve and commitment to a nation fighting for its democracy. America had to be by its side, assisting and cheering it on.

It was a departure from his predecessors. George W. Bush believed democracy building required the American military. Obama talked about diplomacy but revolutionized the use of covert power to keep military engagements off the front pages. Donald Trump ignored allies, preferring instead to wield American power solely for what he perceived to be in the nation's interests.

Biden was voting with his feet. By going to Ukraine, he wanted to show that America's commitment to allies and democracy didn't need to be demonstrated with force. It could be underscored with physical presence, engagement, and assistance. It was at once center stage and behind the scenes—and a throwback to his time as a young senator.

Back then, the prevailing wisdom of the era was that the United States would keep all its treaty commitments. It would provide a shield if a nuclear power threatened the freedom of a nation allied with us. In cases involving conventional aggression, the U.S. would furnish military and economic assistance when requested, but it would look to the nation directly threatened to assume the primary responsibility of providing the manpower for its defense.

America drifted away from that vision during President Ronald Reagan's time in office, evidenced by the invasion of Grenada and later George H. W. Bush's military campaign to push Iraq out of Kuwait. In the wake of the September 11, 2001, terrorist attacks, the calculus of when the U.S. engaged in military intervention changed again. And now with Biden, it was changing back: America would be internationalist without being interventionist.

How the Biden Doctrine played out in Ukraine would determine the president's legacy. Would he be remembered for the disastrous withdrawal from Kabul? Or as the statesman who reenergized NATO and held off Putin without putting boots on the ground?

The aircraft landed in Rzeszów-Jasionka Airport on the evening of February 19. It was the same place where, almost a year earlier, Biden visited with U.S. troops and humanitarian aid workers assisting Ukrainians before the start of the war. A motorcade of at least twenty cars streaked down an eastbound highway toward Przemyśl Główny train station, arriving around 9:15 p.m. Awaiting them was a mostly purple train with two large stripes on the bottom of the cars. Some were blue with a yellow stripe—the colors of the Ukrainian flag.

The station's offices were closed, but there were passengers on the other side of the tracks awaiting their train to a different destination. It didn't seem like they knew what was happening right across from them. The train started rolling, bound for Kyiv, and crossed into Ukraine just after 10:00 p.m. Streetlights, graffiti, and skinny trees dominated the landscape. The pastel colors of the mostly brick homes whipped by.

Biden couldn't sleep on the train. Neither could Sullivan. They worked the whole ride over, eating either peanut butter and jelly or ham and cheese sandwiches while going over security protocols and what they wanted to accomplish during their short time in Kyiv. They sat at a long, cherry-colored table beside a plush red sofa. Both men, still wearing their suits, plowed through papers as a single light allowed them to see what they were doing. The purple curtains were closed, hiding the president along the secret journey.

When the train pulled up at 8:00 a.m. local time on February 20, Sullivan stepped off about a minute before the president. Then Biden, appearing in his train car's open door, caught sight of Bridget Brink, the U.S. ambassador to Ukraine. "It's good to be back in Kyiv," Biden exclaimed.

A new motorcade whisked Biden to the Mariinskyy Palace, the president's residence, to meet with Zelenskyy. On the way, Biden was acting like a tour guide for Sullivan, pointing out landmarks and buildings where he had held engagements during previous visits to the Ukrainian city. Others in the car were surprised at how normal Kyiv felt: people were walking on the street, eating at restaurants, carrying on normal conversations. Ukraine was a nation at war but, at that moment, it was clear that a year's worth of American and Western support had allowed a sense of normality in Kyiv to persist.

Zelenskyy was waiting for Biden's arrival. "Thank you for coming," the Ukrainian president said. Biden later told him, "I thought it was critical that there not be any doubt, none whatsoever, about U.S. support for Ukraine in the war." Air-raid sirens blared as the two men walked through the city during Biden's five-hour stay. It was a reminder of the danger Ukraine still faced. Russia controlled about 20 percent of Ukraine's territory a year into the war, and Russia's missiles could reach anywhere in the country.

But Biden was still able to visit safely with Zelenskyy in the Ukraine capital, nearly twelve months after Putin expected to visit it himself as the leader of a Russian-controlled Kyiv. Instead, Biden used the moment to announce a new half-billion-dollar weapons package that included artillery ammunition and anti-armor systems like Howitzers and Javelins.

As Biden left Kyiv, the eighth time he had come and gone to Ukraine's capital during five decades of public service, he contemplated what his presence really meant. He had developed a doctrine of sorts over two years in office. Stand true with allies. Defend democracy. Avoid escalatory conflict. Work quietly, diligently. Preserve the rules-based order. His visit was the culmination of all that work.

The next day, Biden waited to speak to an excited crowd outside Warsaw's Royal Castle. He had been there a year earlier to mark the solemn moment: Russia had invaded despite the West's efforts. The U.S. and its allies had no choice but to help Ukraine stay on the map of the world.

Now, as thousands waved American, Ukrainian, and Polish flags, and crowds danced in a muddy field surrounding the compound to Twisted Sister and Earth, Wind, and Fire coming over the sound system, Biden was able to deliver a different message. Kyiv was still in Ukrainian control. Land seized by Russia in Ukraine's east was slowly returning to Ukrainian hands after a successful counteroffensive. Zelenskyy, despite months of skepticism that war was imminent, had turned into an iconic and effective wartime leader, Ukraine's answer to Winston Churchill. Germany had canceled the Nord Stream 2 pipeline. The Russian economy was reeling, and the country was losing friends at an astonishing clip, even if India and China were still chummy with Moscow.

In his speech, Biden wanted to prove that Bidenism worked—and the world just needed more of it.

He thundered from the podium: "Europe was being tested. America was being tested. NATO was being tested. All democracies were being tested. And the questions we faced were as simple as they were profound.

Would we respond or would we look the other way? Would we be strong or would we be weak? Would all of our allies be united or divided? One year later, we know the answer. We did respond. We would be strong. We would be united. And the world would not look the other way."

"Kyiv," Biden proclaimed, "stands strong, it stands proud, and it stands free."

Epilogue

April 27, 2023

The Brookings Institution, a Washington, D.C., think tank that for years has served as a beacon of Democratic establishment thinking, was about to be the site of a major reshaping. One of the party's leaders, Jake Sullivan, was about to challenge long-held beliefs and lay out a road map for the nation's ideological future. The times were changing, and America had to change with them.

Brookings is a legendary place, among the most famous think tanks in the world. It's the kind of institution presidents visited to give great speeches, senior officials went to for outside policy counsel, and the capital's elite waited out an opposing party's administration before itching to serve with a like-minded team. Now it would serve as the birthplace of a quiet revolution.

For weeks, Jake Sullivan and his team crafted an address that was nominally about the administration's views on economics. But it would really serve as a critique of orthodoxy in America's capital, a bludgeon to

U.S. foreign policy thinking that was so prominent in the gilded halls of Brookings and among Washington's well-heeled.

The contention was that globalization and free trade were an unalloyed good, growing economies and improving people's lives in the process. What was good for the stock market, in effect, was great for everybody. Given enough time, swelling wallets would produce a steady middle class, one that demands its political and human rights from its government. Even the most repressive regimes, the thinking went, would eventually crumble under the weight of inflowing capital. Consistent pressure via greenbacks did the most good for the most people.

Those theories had decades to prove themselves right after World War II. At Brookings, where that thinking took hold and was championed for years, Sullivan would assert that it was time to move on. It was time to adopt a new Bidenism.

On the surface, Sullivan was an unlikely candidate to deliver the message. Years earlier, while at law school at Yale, Sullivan sought out Strobe Talbott, who had recently been named the director of the university's Center for the Study of Globalization. Talbott—an archetypal patrician who had attended the best schools, campaigned for George McGovern, and was *Time* magazine's lead writer on Soviet-American relations before joining the State Department during his friend Bill Clinton's administration—became a mentor.

The two men shared an ideology that was mainstream among the Democratic and Republican parties. "Those were the heady days when the mainstream foreign policy consensus was that globalization was a force for good," Sullivan recalled in a 2017 interview. There was, of course, reason to think this. Capitalism helped keep the Soviet Union at bay, China still wasn't a major power, and building the economies of enemies turned them into friends. Globalization, per its champions, had the benefit of making many people rich while making the world safer in general and U.S. foreign policy less costly.

Talbott, one of those champions, would go on to lead and then serve as a distinguished fellow at Brookings. Whether Sullivan meant to distance himself from his beliefs during those "heady days" may have been intentional, or may have been a happy accident of the calendar.

As he strode up to the think tank, perched prominently on Massachusetts Avenue in downtown Washington, D.C., flanked by other prestigious institutions and embassies, Sullivan looked like any U.S. official at the upper echelons of power. His straw hair was matted down, swept to the right. He wore a typical dark-blue suit and a bright white shirt, muted by the gray tie hanging in front of it. The national security adviser looked like he was about to give a speech like any other, like thousands before it by D.C.'s elite. Not this time.

"After the Second World War, the United States led a fragmented world to build a new international economic order. It lifted hundreds of millions of people out of poverty. It sustained thrilling technological revolutions. And it helped the United States and many other nations around the world achieve new levels of prosperity. But the last few decades revealed cracks in those foundations," said Sullivan to a crowd that consisted of journalists, government officials, and well-known experts. In other words, the Marshall Plan and the tech boom during the 1990s were products of their time and place. They wouldn't necessarily have the desired effects in a modern context.

"A shifting global economy left many working Americans and their communities behind. A financial crisis shook the middle class. A pandemic exposed the fragility of our supply chains. A changing climate threatened lives and livelihoods. Russia's invasion of Ukraine underscored the risks of overdependence."

That was the problem. What was the solution? Instead of rampant globalization, Sullivan's pitch was that a reenergized American economy made the country stronger. It was time to remake the Rust Belt into a Cobalt Corridor, to establish industries that led not only to blue-collar work but to azure-collared careers. If that was done right, a strengthened America could act more capably around the globe.

"This moment demands that we forge a new consensus. That's why the United States, under President Biden, is pursuing a modern industrial and innovation strategy—both at home and with partners around the world," he said.

Sullivan would go on to list why America needed to take this new path. Manufacturing in the United States had lost out to cheaper labor abroad. Growth for growth's sake was inherently unequal, not benefiting everyone. The economic rise of other countries and their integration into the world economy didn't automatically make them more democratic—some, namely China, simultaneously grew more powerful and despotic. And the free market at home and globalization's effects wrought havoc on the climate while failing to incentivize greener means of production and industries.

Implicitly, Sullivan said the main assumptions undergirding America's foreign and economic policy had been wrong for decades. China, and the Washington belief that liberalized markets would eventually lead to democracy within the halls of power in Beijing, was the most glaring example.

"By the time President Biden came into office, we had to contend with the reality that a large non-market economy had been integrated into the international economic order in a way that posed considerable challenges," he said, citing China's large-scale subsidization of multiple sectors that crushed America's competitiveness across industries. Making matters worse, Sullivan continued, "economic integration didn't stop China from expanding its military ambitions." It also didn't stop countries like Russia from invading their neighbors.

Sullivan, the accomplished debater, was dismantling, point by point, the dominant worldview that Biden held for decades and that the national security adviser grew up believing until Donald Trump won the election in November 2016. He was, wittingly or not, offering a mea culpa for once being an acolyte of the foreign policy establishment. Now, cloaked in power, he was trying to right his perceived wrongs.

Righting wrongs was a through line during Sullivan's first two years at the helm alongside Biden, Secretary of State Antony Blinken, Defense Secretary Lloyd Austin, and the rest of the team. Withdrawing from Afghanistan, despite the deadly chaos, was the right decision. The war was unwinnable, and there were other priorities to pursue. But, having missed the warning signs leading up to the takeover of Kabul, and with the trauma of seeing Russia take Crimea and a bite out of eastern Ukraine in 2014 still fresh, Sullivan vowed not to be steps behind as the Kremlin plotted to seize the whole of Ukraine.

Standing in front of the esteemed audience, Sullivan was telling them he didn't want to be caught flat-footed as the global economy reshaped around them. The U.S. government would be proactive, prepared, and proud in search of an industrial strategy to undergird American power. Without saying the words, he was offering a plan to make America great again.

The speech served as the grandest example of the significant rethink that occurred in the Biden administration's first half of the first term. An "A-Team" came together to move beyond the Trump era, but in some ways they embraced elements of it. Not the nativist demagoguery, but the need to return to fundamentals: a healthy middle class powered by a humming industrial base, a humility about what the U.S. military alone can accomplish, a solid cadre of allies, attention to the most existential threats, and a refresh of the tenets that sustain American democracy. Sullivan proposed an old road map to a new future.

The speech reflected the journey Sullivan himself had been on for six years. Down and out after Trump's victory over Hillary Clinton, he sought to understand why the modern-day traditions of U.S. foreign policy weren't resonating with the kind of people he grew up with in Minnesota. He helped craft a new vision that took root among Democrats and formed the backbone of the Biden administration's thinking about the world after the scarring scenes of January 6, 2021.

And buoyed by the success of Washington's support for Kyiv, he now had confidence to offer a different vision for U.S. policy at home and abroad. It was Bidenism, fully embraced by the president, but a brainchild of the national security adviser who, due to his young age, could serve as an ideological leader within the Democratic Party for decades to come.

"This strategy will take resolve—it will take a dedicated commitment to overcoming the barriers that have kept this country and our partners from building rapidly, efficiently, and fairly as we were able to do in the past," Sullivan boomed assertively. "But it is the surest path to restoring the middle class, to producing a just and effective clean-energy transition, to securing critical supply chains, and, through all of this, to repairing faith in democracy itself."

America was ready for renewal. The world was there to remake. There were at least two more years to get it done.

Acknowledgments

I am the first to admit that this book isn't the entire history of Biden's first two years handling foreign policy. More could've been written about the three Cs: China/chips, climate change, and the coronavirus. But the intention was to write a story of a team that came in with immense confidence, lost it during the withdrawal from Afghanistan, and found their mojo again with the defense of Ukraine. There is more to write about these historic years of U.S. foreign policy, and I hope this serves as a helpful second draft of history for those seeking to go deeper.

In the meantime, I must thank the many people who were *my* A-Team during this process.

First, my thanks to Ethan Bassoff, agent extraordinaire, who took a chance on a young reporter at *Vox* who was eager to write a book. He helped conceive of this idea and was patient as its focus shifted along with world events. I hope he keeps me around.

My editor, Noah Schwartzberg, is a master of his craft. I couldn't have asked for anyone better to guide me through the toils and tribulations of writing one's first book. He is kind, caring, and absurdly smart. Working with him has been one of the joys of my professional life. However, the whole team at Portfolio has my thanks for their belief in this project and their tireless work to make it a reaiity.

John Brodie came in toward the end of the process like a knight in shining tweed. He took a book in need of polishing and did so much more. He gave it a beating heart and narrative flair. This book is more of a story thanks to his tireless efforts in the final stretches.

Many people who read this book improved it in ways I can't even describe. In no particular order, thank you to: David Bosco, Jim Goldgeier, Justin Logan, Jack Detsch, Kathy Gilsinan, Robbie Gramer, and Nahal Toosi. All errors and final writing decisions were my own. But if there were any triumphs throughout, they largely—or perhaps entirely—had a hand in it.

Jonathan Lemire, Peter Baker, and David Sanger offered their sage advice on book writing, reporting, and marketing. I am always well served by their journalistic example, day in and day out, and am lucky to consider them colleagues.

Matthew Kristoffersen was a brilliant fact-checker. He's thorough, kind, and whip smart. I look forward to fact-checking one of his books someday. Any errors in this work are on me, not Matt.

My family was incredibly supportive throughout this process, even as I wouldn't stop yammering about this book. To my parents, Esther and John, who asked me about how it was all going and offered encouragement when I needed it most. To my in-laws, Becky and Jeff, who let me work from their lovely home in Washington State during vacations and sent me a care package during the final writing stages.

To my grandma Ann, who first instilled in me (by force) a love of reading. To my uncles, aunts, and cousins in the U.S. and Europe: your support was incalculable. To my sister-in-law, Alisah, the best jockey of books, who promised me a spot on her overstuffed bookshelf and helped me send the first full draft of this work from her favorite bookstore.

I'd be remiss if I didn't mention beloved family members who are no longer with us: Jeffrey, Larry, Obdulio, Beatriz, Mai, Bonnie, and Ralph. They all had a hand in raising and teaching me along the way.

And, finally, to my wife, Christine. She took care of me and our new home while I was toiling away at a passion project. She is the greatest partner anyone could ask for, and a true love if there ever was one. She is my world.

Notes

Chapter 1: Relearning America

3 **"We can wait a little longer!":** Anne Gearan, "They Gathered in Hopes of Hearing Clinton's Victory Speech. The Night Ended in Sobs and the Sounds of TV Crews Moving On," *Washington Post*, November 9, 2016, www.washingtonpost.com/news/post-politics/wp/2016/11/09/they-gathered-in-hopes-of-hearing-clintons-victory-speech-the-night-ended-in-sobs-and-the-sounds-of-tv-crews-moving-on.

5 **flawlessly written assignments:** CBS News Minnesota, "Joe Biden Appoints Minneapolis Native Jake Sullivan as National Security Advisor," November 23, 2020, www.cbsnews.com/minnesota/news/joe-biden-appoints-minneapolis-native-jake-sullivan-as-national-security-advisor.

5 **debate tournaments and quiz bowls:** Tim Gehring, "'We Just Go to Jake': How a Southwest High Grad Became Hillary Clinton's Go-to Guy," *MinnPost*, February 9, 2016, www.minnpost.com/politics-policy/2016/02/we-just-go-jake-how-southwest-high-grad-became-hillary-clinton-s-go-guy.

5 **"I didn't think I would do it anywhere else":** Quoted in Gehring, "'We Just Go to Jake.'"

5 **"By the time I was 10 or 13, I'd learned the world capitals":** Quoted in Gehring, "'We Just Go to Jake.'"

5 **racing to the bottom of a pasta bowl:** Gehring, "'We Just Go to Jake.'"

5 **on frozen lakes:** Gehring, "'We Just Go to Jake.'"

5 **third in a national debate championship:** Gehring, "'We Just Go to Jake.'"

5 **top seed in the world debating championship:** Gehring, "'We Just Go to Jake.'"

5 **"I am a dyed-in-the-wool product":** Cited in Gehring, "'We Just Go to Jake.'"

6 ***Saved by the Bell* lines:** Gehring, "'We Just Go to Jake.'"

6 **Barack Obama's successful campaign:** Gehring, "'We Just Go to Jake.'"

6 **five other meetings alongside his colleagues:** Julie Pace, "Secret Talks with Iran Made Possible by Low-Key Obama Aide," Associated Press, December 23, 2013, www.timesofisrael.com/secret-talks-with-iran-made-possible-by-low-key-obama-aide.

6 **"He's essentially a once-in-a-generation talent":** Julie Paceap, "Vanishing Adviser Reappears as Iran Policy Player," Associated Press, December 23, 2013, https://apnews.com/article/07ab7ddd31c04d83be465dbf6bbfcbbc.

7 **the Letter of St. Paul to the Romans:** Kate Bennett, "Every Wedding Should Have a Hillary Clinton Bible Reading," *Politico*, June 11, 2015, www.politico.com/story/2015/06/every-wedding-should-have-a-hillary-clinton-bible-reading-118855.

7 **the Democratic foreign policy world:** Mark Leibovich, "Jake Sullivan, Biden's Adviser, a Figure of Fascination and Schadenfreude," *New York Times*, November 30, 2021, www.nytimes.com/2021/11/30/us/politics/jake-sullivan-biden.html.

7 **Obama called Sullivan from Air Force One:** Gehring, "'We Just Go to Jake.'"

7 **"Reject cynicism. Reject certitude":** Quoted in Jonathan Allen, "Meet Jake Sullivan, the Man Behind Hawkish Hillary Clinton's Foreign Policy," *Vox*, September 4, 2015, www.vox.com/2015/5/11/8569345/hillary-clinton-hawkish-foreign-policy.

8 **sided with the Republican candidate:** Caroline Freund and Dario Sidhu, "Manufacturing and the 2016 Election: An Analysis of US Presidential Election Data," Peterson Institute for International Economics," May 2017, www.piie.com/sites/default/files/documents/wp17-7.pdf.

8 **nearly five million manufacturing jobs:** Robert E. Scott, "We Can Reshore Manufacturing Jobs, but Trump Hasn't Done It," Economic Policy Institute, August 10, 2020, www.epi.org/publication/reshoring-manufacturing-jobs.

8 **said a close confidant:** AN AUTHOR'S NOTE ON SOURCING: Everything reported in this book is sourced, but not everything is attributed. Some people would only speak to me on deep background, meaning I could use the information provided but I couldn't cite from whom it came or someone's position, even vaguely. In those cases, I don't note where certain pieces of information originated. Still, to the best of my ability, I made sure to get at least a second confirmation for what I learned on deep background. I cite all other pieces of information in the endnotes, whether they are in the public record, an on-record interview, or a conversation on background.

10 **the ethnic cleansing of Rohingya Muslims:** Poppy McPherson, "Aung San Suu Kyi Says Myanmar Does Not Fear Scrutiny over Rohingya Crisis," *The Guardian*, September 19, 2017, www.theguardian.com/world/2017/sep/19/aung-san-suu-kyi-myanmar-rohingya-crisis-concerned.

10 **never any doubt that they would do it:** Interview with Ben Rhodes, February 11, 2023.

11 **"That was awkward," Rhodes said:** Interview with Ben Rhodes, July 9, 2021.

11 **spin them as "the blob":** All quoted in David Samuels, "The Aspiring Novelist Who Became Obama's Foreign-Policy Guru," *New York Times*, May 5, 2016, www.nytimes.com/2016/05/08/magazine/the-aspiring-novelist-who-became-obamas-foreign-policy-guru.html.

11 **He'd go on to be Hamilton's staffer:** Samuels, "The Aspiring Novelist Who Became Obama's Foreign-Policy Guru."

12 **Baltimore bookstore famous for its 1990s "erotica nights":** The Reliable Source, *Washington Post*, "Avril Haines, New CIA #2, Ran Indie Bookstore Remembered for '90s 'Erotica Nights,'" June 13, 2013, www.washingtonpost.com/news/reliable-source/wp/2013/06/13/avril-haines-new-cia-2-ran-indie-bookstore-remembered-for-90s-erotica-nights.

12 **his tweets attacking the Republican president:** Edward Price, "I Didn't Think I'd Ever Leave the CIA. But Because of Trump, I Quit," February 20, 2017, *Washington Post*, www.washingtonpost.com/opinions/i-didnt-think-id-ever-leave-the-cia-but-because-of-trump-i-quit/2017/02/20/fd7aac3e-f456-11e6-b9c9-e83fce42fb61_story.html.

12 **"why does he still have access to America's biggest secrets?":** Ned Price, "Why Does Jared Kushner Still Have a Security Clearance?," *Politico*, July 14, 2017, www.politico.com/magazine/story/2017/07/14/why-does-jared-kushner-still-have-a-security-clearance-215378.

13 **NatSec Action was ready:** I have since received permission from a NatSec Action staffer to recount the events of the meeting.

14 **winnowed down to seven:** Jessica Taylor, "7 Democrats Qualify for December Primary Debate," NPR, December 13, 2019, www.npr.org/2019/12/13/787476198/7-democrats-qualify-for-december-primary-debate.

18 **"it must conceive of its role in the world differently":** Edited by Salman Ahmed and Rozlyn Engel, "Making U.S. Foreign Policy Work for the Middle Class," Carnegie Endowment for International Peace, September 23, 2020, https://carnegieendowment.org/files/USFP_FinalReport_final1.pdf.

19 **"We no longer think in Cold War terms":** Quoted in Evan Osnos, "The Evolution of Joe Biden," *New Yorker*, July 20, 2014, www.newyorker.com/magazine/2014/07/28/biden-agenda.

19 **"I may be the most immoral":** Quoted in Annie Linskey, "From Saigon to Kabul: Biden's Response to Vietnam Echoes in His Views of Afghanistan Withdrawal," *Washington Post*, August 15, 2021, www.washingtonpost.com/politics/biden-vietnam-afghanistan/2021/08/15/fd155518-fdd5-11eb-ba7e-2cf966e88e93_story.html.

19 **"felt more strongly than I did about the immorality of the war":** Quoted in Greg Jaffe, "The War in Afghanistan Shattered Joe Biden's Faith in American Military Power," *Washington Post*, February 18, 2020, www.washingtonpost.com/politics/2020/02/18/biden-afghanistan-military-power/?itid=lk_inline_manual_15.

20 **both nations still adhered:** U.S. Department of State, "Strategic Arms Limitations Talks/Treaty (SALT) I and II," Office of the Historian, https://history.state.gov/milestones/1969-1976/salt.

20 **"I think the prospects":** Quoted in Andrew Roth, "How Joe Biden's Cold War Experience Will Shape His Approach to Russia," *The Guardian*, December 29, 2020, www.theguardian.com/us-news/2020/dec/29/how-joe-biden-cold-war-experience-will-shape-approach-to-russia.

20 **at the behest of President Ronald Reagan:** Roth, "How Joe Biden's Cold War Experience Will Shape His Approach to Russia."

20 **a stronger candidate than the others:** Howard Kurtz, "Sen Biden May Try to Talk His Way into the White House," *Washington Post*, July 28, 1986, www.washingtonpost

.com/archive/politics/1986/07/28/sen-biden-may-try-to-talk-his-way-into-the-white-house/a19e4497-0d36-4536-95b7-abb38cc17888.

20 **he asked rhetorically about the proposed campaign:** Quoted in Murtaza Hussein and Jeremy Scahill, "1991: Iraq Gulf War," *The Intercept*, April 27, 2021, https://theintercept.com/empire-politician/biden-1991-iraq-gulf-war.

20 **"has allowed us to take on 95 percent of the sacrifice across the board":** Quoted in Adam Clymer, "Confrontation in the Gulf; Congress Acts to Authorize War in Gulf; Margins Are 5 Votes in Senate, 67 in House," *New York Times*, January 13, 1991, www.nytimes.com/1991/01/13/world/confrontation-gulf-congress-acts-authorize-war-gulf-margins-are-5-votes-senate.html.

20 **"more than 116,000 combat air sorties":** Charles Pope, "30 Years Later, Desert Storm Remains a Powerful Influence on Air, Space Forces," February 23, 2021, www.af.mil/News/Article-Display/Article/2512938/30-years-later-desert-storm-remains-a-powerful-influence-on-air-space-forces.

20 **"I think I was proven to be wrong":** Quoted in Murtaza Hussein, "1991: Biden Begins Walking Back His Opposition to Gulf War," *The Intercept*, https://theintercept.com/empire-politician/biden-walks-back-opposition-gulf-war.

20 **to depose Iraq's Saddam Hussein was a "fundamental mistake":** Quoted in Hussein, "1991: Biden Begins Walking Back His Opposition to Gulf War."

21 **"We have turned our backs on conscience":** Quoted in Jaffe, "The War in Afghanistan Shattered Joe Biden's Faith in American Military Power."

21 **"will we respond to aggression then? Or anywhere else?":** Joseph R. Biden, Jr., "More U.N. Appeasement on Bosnia," *New York Times*, June 7, 1983, www.nytimes.com/1993/06/07/opinion/more-un-appeasement-on-bosnia.html.

21 **"blow up all of the bridges on the Drina":** U.S. Government Printing Office, "The Crisis in Kosovo," May 6 and June 24, 1988, www.govinfo.gov/content/pkg/CHRG-105shrg49265/html/CHRG-105shrg49265.htm.

21 **began dropping bombs on Serbian nationalist forces in 1994:** Chuck Sudetic, "Conflict in the Balkans: The Overview; U.S. Planes Bomb Serbian Position for a Second Day," *New York Times*, April 12, 1994, www.nytimes.com/1994/04/12/world/conflict-balkans-overview-us-planes-bomb-serbian-position-for-second-day.html.

22 **"a view many in Congress share":** Quoted in Tara Golshan and Alex Ward, "This Is Joe Biden's Checkered Iraq History," *Vox*, October 15, 2019, www.vox.com/policy-and-politics/2019/10/15/20849072/joe-biden-iraq-history-democrats-election-2020.

22 **"likely to enhance the prospects that war would occur":** Quoted in Golshan and Ward, "This Is Joe Biden's Checkered Iraq History."

22 **"under funded and under manned":** "Iraq Up Close: Senators Joseph Biden and Chuck Hagel," PBS *NewsHour*, June 25, 2003, www.pbs.org/newshour/show/iraq-up-close-senators-joseph-biden-and-chuck-hagel.

22 **"what we were going to do in the aftermath":** "Iraq Up Close."

22 **mass destruction and saw 4,500 Americans die:** U.S. Department of Defense, "Casualty Status," February 6, 2023, www.defense.gov/casualty.pdf.

23 **"means repairing and reinvigorating":** Democracy in Action, "Remarks as Prepared for Delivery by Vice President Joe Biden in New York City, New York," July 11, 2019, www.democracyinaction.us/2020/biden/bidenpolicy071119foreignpolicy.html.

26 **"We can make America, once again":** Joseph R. Biden, Jr., "Inaugural Address" (speech), January 20, 2021, www.whitehouse.gov/briefing-room/speeches-remarks/2021/01/20/inaugural-address-by-president-joseph-r-biden-jr.

Chapter 2: Great-Power Competition

28 **"Will this make life better":** All quotes from this event are from CSPAN, "Biden Foreign Policy and National Security Team Announcement," November 24, 2020, www.c-span.org/video/?478351-1/biden-foreign-policy-national-security-team-announcement.

31 **"an irreversible one-state reality":** John Kerry, "Remarks on Middle East Peace," U.S. Department of State, December 28, 2016, https://2009-2017.state.gov/secretary/remarks/2016/12/266119.htm.

31 **"Yes, the United States should stand firm":** Thomas Wright, "The Risk of John Kerry Following His Own China Policy," *The Atlantic*, December 22, 2020, www.theatlantic.com/ideas/archive/2020/12/risk-john-kerry-following-his-own-china-policy/617459.

31 **"Obviously we have serious differences":** White House, "Press Briefing by Press Secretary Jen Psaki, Special Presidential Envoy for Climate John Kerry, and National Climate Advisor Gina McCarthy, January 27, 2021," www.whitehouse.gov/briefing-room/press-briefings/2021/01/27/press-briefing-by-press-secretary-jen-psaki-special-presidential-envoy-for-climate-john-kerry-and-national-climate-advisor-gina-mccarthy-january-27-2021.

33 **China's and Russia's increased aggressions:** For a good read on the reemergence of great power competition, read Uri Friedman, "The New Concept Everyone in Washington Is Talking About," *The Atlantic*, August 6, 2019, www.theatlantic.com/politics/archive/2019/08/what-genesis-great-power-competition/595405.

33 **"primary concern in U.S. national security":** U.S. Department of Defense, "2018 National Defense Strategy of the United States of America," January 19, 2018, https://dod.defense.gov/Portals/1/Documents/pubs/2018-National-Defense-Strategy-Summary.pdf.

33 **as it promoted human rights:** Nahal Toosi, "How Tony Blinken's Stepfather Changed the World—and Him," *Politico*, January 19, 2021, www.politico.com/news/magazine/2021/01/19/samuel-pisar-tony-blinken-secretary-of-state-460155.

34 **"he has to worry today about poison gas":** Quoted in Jason Horowitz, "Antony Blinken Steps into the Spotlight with Obama Administration Role," *Washington Post*, September 15, 2013, www.washingtonpost.com/lifestyle/style/antony-blinken-steps-into-the-spotlight-with-obama-administration-role/2013/09/15/7484a5c0-1e20-11e3-94a2-6c66b668ea55_story.html.

34 **Building closer ties:** Toosi, "How Tony Blinken's Stepfather Changed the World."

34 **Philip Gordon, a colleague of Blinken's:** Quoted in Toosi, "How Tony Blinken's Stepfather Changed the World."

34 **"The Nicaraguan's arguments":** Antony J. Blinken, "The Trouble with Nicaragua," *Harvard Crimson*, April 23, 1983, www.thecrimson.com/article/1983/4/23/the-trouble-with-nicaragua-piin-1979. See also Jesús A. Rodriguez, "The World According to Tony Blinken—in the 1980s," *Politico*, January 11, 2021, www.politico.com/news/magazine

/2021/01/11/tony-blinken-secretary-state-harvard-crimson-college-writing-new-republic-columns-world-view-456699.

35 **"superpowers don't bluff":** Quoted in Adam Entous, "Behind Obama's About-Face on Syria," *Wall Street Journal*, June 15, 2013, www.wsj.com/articles/SB10001424127887324049504578545772906542466.

35 **"American leadership still matters":** Quoted in Matthew Lee, "Senate Confirmed Antony Blinken as 71st Secretary of State," Associated Press, January 26, 2021, https://apnews.com/article/joe-biden-donald-trump-biden-cabinet-antony-blinken-cabinets-d74929057a9e8e5f74e0ee553a6baced.

35 **he had around $10 million in the bank:** Dan Alexander, "Inside the $10 Million Fortune of Antony Blinken, Biden's Secretary of State," *Forbes*, June 17, 2021, www.forbes.com/sites/danalexander/2021/06/17/inside-the-10-million-fortune-of-antony-blinken-bidens-secretary-of-state/?sh=4b2e66925376.

36 **"The thread that runs throughout my life":** David Browne, "Antony Blinken's Rock & Roll Heart," *Rolling Stone*, June 8, 2021, www.rollingstone.com/music/music-features/antony-blinken-interview-rock-music-eric-clapton-ablinken-1176319.

36 **It was a call Putin himself asked for:** Franklin Foer, *The Last Politician: Inside Joe Biden's White House and the Struggle for America's Future* (New York: Penguin Press, 2023), 22–23.

37 **"have their teams work urgently":** White House, "Readout of President Joseph R. Biden, Jr. Call with President Vladimir Putin of Russia," January 26, 2021, www.whitehouse.gov/briefing-room/statements-releases/2021/01/26/readout-of-president-joseph-r-biden-jr-call-with-president-vladimir-putin-of-russia.

37 **"An unconstrained nuclear competition":** U.S. Department of State, "On the Extension of the New START Treaty with the Russian Federation," February 3, 2021, www.state.gov/on-the-extension-of-the-new-start-treaty-with-the-russian-federation.

38 **"The message I want the world to hear today":** White House, "Remarks by President Biden on America's Place in the World," February 4, 2021, www.whitehouse.gov/briefing-room/speeches-remarks/2021/02/04/remarks-by-president-biden-on-americas-place-in-the-world.

39 **"China is the only country":** U.S. Department of State, "A Foreign Policy for the American People," March 3, 2021, www.state.gov/a-foreign-policy-for-the-american-people.

40 **"They had the right speech":** Susan Glasser, "National Security Team Blindsided by NATO Speech," *Politico*, June 5, 2017, www.politico.com/magazine/story/2017/06/05/trump-nato-speech-national-security-team-215227.

40 **"We face many threats":** Susan Glasser, "The 27 Words Trump Wouldn't Say," *Politico*, June 6, 2017, www.politico.com/magazine/story/2017/06/06/trump-nato-speech-27-words-commitment-215231.

41 **"I'm committing the United States to Article 5":** Alex Ward, "Trump Just Committed to NATO's Article 5. Finally," *Vox*, June 9, 2017, www.vox.com/world/2017/6/9/15772292/trump-article-5-nato-commit.

41 **the Russian leader had ordered the meddling:** Office of the Director of National Intelligence, "Assessing Russian Activities and Intentions in Recent U.S. Elections," January 6, 2017, www.dni.gov/files/documents/ICA_2017_01.pdf.

41 **"exaggerating" the extent of Russia's election interference:** Alex Ward, "Putin 1,

Trump 0," *Vox*, July 7, 2017, www.vox.com/world/2017/7/7/15937784/trump-putin-g20-meeting-outcome-syria-election.

41 **a conversation the administration didn't disclose for over a week:** Eli Watkins and Jeremy Diamond, "Trump, Putin Met for Nearly an Hour in Second G20 Meeting," CNN, July 19, 2017, www.cnn.com/2017/07/18/politics/trump-putin-g20/index.html.

41 **"While smaller pull-aside meetings are common":** Watkins and Diamond, "Trump, Putin Met for Nearly an Hour in Second G20 Meeting."

41 **"How stupid can you be?":** Quoted in Jake Nevins, "Late-Night Hosts Blast Trump's Second Putin Meeting: 'How Stupid Can You Be?'," *The Guardian*, July 20, 2017, www.theguardian.com/culture/2017/jul/20/late-night-tv-trump-putin-meeting-voter-fraud-commission.

42 **hinged on world leaders treating Trump nicely:** Julian Borger and Anne Perkins, "G7 in Disarray after Trump Rejects Communique and Attacks 'Weak' Trudeau," *The Guardian*, June 10, 2018, www.theguardian.com/world/2018/jun/10/g7-in-disarray-after-trump-rejects-communique-and-attacks-weak-trudeau.

42 **"We looked at what the Trump administration did":** Ben Gittleson, "Biden Speaks with China's Xi for 1st Time as President," ABC News, February 10, 2021, https://abcnews.go.com/Politics/biden-speaks-chinas-xi-time-president/story?id=75817231.

43 **cost the United States around 245,000 jobs:** Oxford Economics and the U.S.–China Business Council, "The U.S.–China Economic Relationship," January 2021, www.uschina.org/sites/default/files/the_us-china_economic_relationship_-_a_crucial_partnership_at_a_critical_juncture.pdf.

43 **trade deficits with China and much of the world also grew higher:** Michael Pettis, "How Trump's Tariffs Really Affected the U.S. Job Market," Carnegie Endowment for International Peace, January 28, 2021, https://carnegieendowment.org/chinafinancialmarkets/83746.

43 **"equivalent to one of the largest tax increases":** Emily York, "Tracking the Economic Impact of U.S. Tariffs and Retaliatory Actions," Tax Foundation, April 1, 2022, https://taxfoundation.org/tariffs-trump-trade-war.

44 **$1.9 trillion COVID-19 relief package:** Kate Sullivan, "Biden Signs Historic $1.9 Trillion Covid-19 Relief Law," CNN, March 11, 2021, www.cnn.com/2021/03/11/politics/biden-sign-covid-bill/index.html.

44 **"As I stand here tonight":** White House, "Remarks by President Biden on the Anniversary of the Covid-19 Shutdown," March 11, 2021, www.whitehouse.gov/briefing-room/speeches-remarks/2021/03/11/remarks-by-president-biden-on-the-anniversary-of-the-covid-19-shutdown.

45 **sanctioning twenty-four Chinese officials:** Lara Jakes, Steven Lee Myers, and Austin Ramzy, "U.S. Punishes 24 Chinese Officials on Eve of First Talks under Biden," *New York Times*, March 17, 2021, www.nytimes.com/2021/03/17/world/asia/us-china-biden.html.

45 **"The challenges facing the United States":** State Department, "Secretary Antony J. Blinken, National Security Advisor Jake Sullivan, Director Yang and State Councilor Wang at the Top of Their Meeting," March 18, 2021, www.state.gov/secretary-antony-j-blinken-national-security-advisor-jake-sullivan-chinese-director-of-the-office-of-the-central-commission-for-foreign-affairs-yang-jiechi-and-chinese-state-councilor-wang-yi-at-th.

47 **required the United States to place restrictions:** U.S. Department of State, "U.S.

Sanctions and Other Measures Imposed on Russia in Response to Russia's Use of Chemical Weapons," March 2, 2021, www.state.gov/u-s-sanctions-and-other-measures-imposed-on-russia-in-response-to-russias-use-of-chemical-weapons.

47 **"Foreign Threats to the 2020 US Federal Elections":** U.S. National Intelligence Council, "Foreign Threats to the 2020 US Federal Elections," March 10, 2021, www.dni.gov/files/ODNI/documents/assessments/ICA-declass-16MAR21.pdf.

48 **"That is a deep concern not only to Ukraine":** Quoted in Alexander Smith and Matthew Bodner, "Russia Amasses Troops Near U.S. Ally Ukraine. But What Is Putin's Goal?," NBC News, April 14, 2021, www.nbcnews.com/news/world/russia-amasses-troops-near-u-s-ally-ukraine-what-putin-n1263894.

48 **"That was deeply alarming":** Quoted in Erin Banco, Garrett M. Graff, Lara Seligman, Nahal Toosi, and Alexander Ward, "'Something Was Badly Wrong': When Washington Realized Russia Was Actually Invading Ukraine," *Politico*, February 24, 2023, www.politico.com/news/magazine/2023/02/24/russia-ukraine-war-oral-history-00083757.

48 **Blinken reaffirmed America's "unwavering support":** U.S. Department of State, "Secretary Blinken's Call with Ukrainian Foreign Minister Kuleba," March 31, 2021, www.state.gov/secretary-blinkens-call-with-ukrainian-foreign-minister-kuleba.

48 **four thousand armed Russian troops:** Oren Liebermann and Barbara Starr, "Top US National Security Officials Call Counterparts as Russia–Ukrainian Tensions Rise," CNN, March 31, 2021, www.cnn.com/2021/03/31/politics/us-russia-ukraine-calls/index.html.

49 **NATO had to scramble:** Barbara Starr, "NATO Scrambles Jets 10 Times to Track Russian Military Planes Across Europe," CNN, March 30, 2021, www.cnn.com/2021/03/30/politics/nato-russia-jets/index.html.

49 **"Bizarrely, President Biden has still not spoken":** Jonathan Swan (@jonathanvwan), Twitter post, April 1, 2021, 4:28 p.m., https://twitter.com/jonathanvswan/status/1377719573743611911, and April 1, 2021, 4:41 p.m., https://twitter.com/jonathanvswan/status/1377722766301011975.

49 **Polls showed that in March 2021:** International Republican Institute, "Public Opinion Survey of Residents of Ukraine, March 13–21, 2021," March 2021, www.iri.org/wp-content/uploads/2021/05/public_-_03.2021_national_eng-_public.pdf.

50 **"I would like us to enter a new phase":** Office of the President of Ukraine, "Interview of the President of Ukraine for the Axios Program Broadcast on the HBO Platform," February 1, 2021, www.president.gov.ua/en/news/intervyu-prezidenta-ukrayini-programi-axios-sho-vihodit-na-p-66313.

50 **Biden tried to talk Putin down:** White House, "Readout of President Joseph R. Biden, Jr. Call with President Vladimir Putin of Russia," April 13, 2021, www.whitehouse.gov/briefing-room/statements-releases/2021/04/13/readout-of-president-joseph-r-biden-jr-call-with-president-vladimir-putin-of-russia-4-13.

51 **you suffer the consequences:** White House, "FACT SHEET: Imposing Costs for Harmful Activities by the Russian Government," April 15, 2021, www.whitehouse.gov/briefing-room/statements-releases/2021/04/15/fact-sheet-imposing-costs-for-harmful-foreign-activities-by-the-russian-government.

52 **The escalation led U.S. European Command:** Andrew Kramer, "Fighting Escalates in

Eastern Ukraine, Signaling the End to Another Cease-Fire," *New York Times,* March 30, 2021, www.nytimes.com/2021/03/30/world/europe/ukraine-russia-fighting.html.

Chapter 3: Ending the Forever War

54 **"We have not thought through our strategic goals!":** Bob Woodward, *Obama's Wars* (New York: Simon & Schuster, 2010), 80.

55 **September 13 National Security Council meeting:** Woodward, *Obama's Wars,* 163.

55 **The first point was that:** Woodward, *Obama's Wars,* 309–10.

55 **for Obama to read:** Greg Jaffe, "The War in Afghanistan Shattered Joe Biden's Faith in American Power," *Washington Post,* February 18, 2020, www.washingtonpost.com/politics/2020/02/18/biden-afghanistan-military-power.

55 **thirty thousand more troops to Afghanistan:** Obama White House, "Remarks by the President in Address to the Nation on the Way Forward in Afghanistan and Pakistan," December 1, 2009, https://obamawhitehouse.archives.gov/the-press-office/remarks-president-address-nation-way-forward-afghanistan-and-pakistan.

55 **Biden warned the president:** Fred Kaplan, "We Now Know Why Biden Was in a Hurry to Exit Afghanistan," *Slate,* September 29, 2021, https://slate.com/news-and-politics/2021/09/biden-afghanistan-exit-troops-milley.html.

55 **the White House privately seethed:** Rosa Brooks, "Obama vs. the Generals," *Politico,* November 2013, www.politico.com/magazine/story/2013/11/obama-vs-the-generals-099379.

55 **McChrystal's request made it into the hands:** Bob Woodward, "McChrystal: More Forces or 'Mission Failure,'" *Washington Post,* September 21, 2009, www.washingtonpost.com/wp-dyn/content/article/2009/09/20/AR2009092002920.html.

56 **"When he came back":** Chris Whipple, *The Fight of His Life: Inside Joe Biden's White House* (New York: Scribner, 2023), 77–78.

56 **"I would bring American combat troops":** Council on Foreign Relations, "The Presidential Candidates on the War in Afghanistan," July 30, 2019, www.cfr.org/article/presidential-candidates-war-afghanistan.

56 **The United States would withdraw:** U.S. Department of State, "Agreement for Bringing Peace to Afghanistan between the Islamic Emirate of Afghanistan Which Is Not Recognized by the United States as a State and Is Known as the Taliban and the United States of America," February 29, 2020, www.state.gov/wp-content/uploads/2020/02/Agreement-For-Bringing-Peace-to-Afghanistan-02.29.20.pdf.

58 **"It was an absolute joke":** Alex Ward, "Biden Wants America to Trust the Process Again," *Vox,* February 10, 2021, www.vox.com/22272240/biden-trump-national-security-council-yemen-myanmar.

61 **"if you go to zero, they collapse":** Lara Seligman, "The Afghanistan Deal That Never Happened," *Politico,* August 11, 2022, www.politico.com/news/magazine/2022/08/11/the-afghanistan-deal-00050916.

61 **"will go back to the Stone Age":** Interviews, and Alex Ward, "An 'Emotional' Moment at an NSC Meeting Shows Why Withdrawing from Afghanistan Is So Hard," *Vox,* March 4, 2021, www.vox.com/2021/3/4/22313380/afghanistan-nsc-milley-austin-biden.

62 **"We're not going to make decisions":** Interviews, and Ward, "An 'Emotional' Moment at an NSC Meeting Shows Why Withdrawing from Afghanistan Is So Hard."

62 **Austin later checked in:** Interviews, and Ward, "An 'Emotional' Moment at an NSC Meeting Shows Why Withdrawing from Afghanistan Is So Hard."

62 **gotten to know Biden's son Beau:** Dan Lamothe, "Gen. Lloyd Austin, Defense Secretary Nominee, Brings Deep Combat Experience and a Connection with Biden," *Washington Post,* December 8, 2020, www.washingtonpost.com/national-security/lloyd-austin-biden-defense-secretary/2020/12/08/dd937584-396e-11eb-8328-a36a109900c2_story.html.

63 **"That will happen":** Interviews, and Ward, "An 'Emotional' Moment at an NSC Meeting Shows Why Withdrawing from Afghanistan Is So Hard."

68 **"Although we have not yet completed our review":** TOLOnews, "Blinken Proposes New Steps to Peace, Keeps May 1st Pullout Option," March 7, 2021, https://tolonews.com/afghanistan-170509.

69 **"I'm in the process":** ABC News, "Transcript: ABC News' George Stephanopoulos Interviews President Joe Biden," March 17, 2021, https://abcnews.go.com/Politics/transcript-abc-news-george-stephanopoulos-interviews-president-joe/story?id=76509669.

71 **"We don't have to hang on":** Associated Press, "Germany: Tie Afghanistan Troop Pullout to Talks' Progress," February 2, 2021, https://apnews.com/article/joe-biden-afghanistan-kabul-germany-taliban-31c802b38730d3a960bc14d89f117988.

71 **"Austin recommended that the United States withdraw":** Bob Woodward and Robert Costa, *Peril* (New York: Simon and Schuster, 2021), 376.

72 **"I was astonished":** Zalmay Khalilzad, *The Envoy* (New York: St. Martin's Press, 2016), 50.

72 **"my views were considered alarmist":** Khalilzad, *The Envoy.*

72 **"Once the Soviets are in, they will not go out":** Quoted in Khalilzad, *The Envoy.*

74 **"I can't picture that being the case":** White House, "Remarks by President Biden in Press Conference," March 25, 2021, www.whitehouse.gov/briefing-room/speeches-remarks/2021/03/25/remarks-by-president-biden-in-press-conference.

76 **the boss's side is the coin of the realm:** Also reported in Woodward and Costa, *Peril,* 384.

76 **"It's time to bring the troops home":** Interviews with U.S. officials; Helene Cooper, Eric Schmitt, and David E. Sanger, "Debating Exit from Afghanistan, Biden Rejected Generals' Views," *New York Times,* April 17, 2021, www.nytimes.com/2021/04/17/us/politics/biden-afghanistan-withdrawal.html.

76 **"I didn't become president to do the easy thing":** Quoted in Woodward and Costa, *Peril,* 385.

78 **"I have concluded that it's time":** White House, "Remarks by President Biden on the Way Forward in Afghanistan," April 14, 2021, www.whitehouse.gov/briefing-room/speeches-remarks/2021/04/14/remarks-by-president-biden-on-the-way-forward-in-afghanistan.

79 **"I have trouble these days":** White House, "Remarks by President Biden After Wreath Laying at Section 60 of Arlington National Cemetery," April 14, 2021, www.whitehouse.gov/briefing-room/speeches-remarks/2021/04/14/remarks-by-president-biden-after-wreath-laying-at-section-60-of-arlington-national-cemetery.

80 **"We went into Afghanistan together":** U.S. Department of State, "Secretary Antony J.

Blinken, Secretary of Defense Lloyd J. Austin, and NATO Secretary General Jens Stoltenberg at a Joint Press Availability," April 14, 2021, www.state.gov/secretary-antony-j-blinken-secretary-of-defense-lloyd-j-austin-and-nato-secretary-general-jens-stoltenberg-at-a-joint-press-availability.

80 **"In terms of the input":** U.S. Department of State, "Secretary Antony J. Blinken, Secretary of Defense Lloyd J. Austin, and NATO Secretary General Jens Stoltenberg at a Joint Press Availability."

Chapter 4: "More of Everything Is Not a Strategy"

83 **"She painted a bleak, bleak picture":** White House, "Remarks by Vice President Joe Biden the 67th Annual Israeli Independence Day Celebration," April 23, 2015, https://obamawhitehouse.archives.gov/the-press-office/2015/04/23/remarks-vice-president-joe-biden-67th-annual-israeli-independence-day-ce.

84 **"The Israeli Government now has recognized":** Joseph R. Biden, Jr., "Stop Arms for Saudis," *New York Times*, April 15, 1981, www.nytimes.com/1981/04/15/opinion/stop-arms-for-saudis.html.

84 **"a highly emotional confrontation":** Bernard Gwertzman, "Mood Is 'Angry' as Begin Meets Panel of Senate," *New York Times*, June 23, 1982, www.nytimes.com/1982/06/23/us/mood-is-angry-as-begin-meets-panel-of-senate.html.

84 **"delivered a very impassioned speech":** Raphael Ahren, "Biden a Veteran Friend of Israel, Settlement Critic, May Be at Odds over Iran," *Times of Israel*, November 7, 2020, www.timesofisrael.com/biden-a-longtime-friend-israel-critic-of-settlements-may-be-at-odds-over-iran.

85 **"It's about time we stop . . . apologizing":** "Joe Biden says if Israel didn't exist, the US would have to invent one to protect US interests," YouTube, uploaded by Candidate Research (@candidateresearch5694), March 3, 2019, https://www.youtube.com/watch?v=FYLNCcLfIkM.

86 **"We are now at the 'peace table'":** Murtaza Hussain, "1990S: Israel and AIPAC," *The Intercept*, April 27, 2021, https://theintercept.com/2021/04/27/biden-israel-aipac.

86 **"My love for your country":** Israeli Prime Minister's Office, "Statements of PM Netanyahu and Vice President Joe Biden," September 3, 2010, www.gov.il/en/departments/news/speechpress090310.

87 **"I condemn the decision":** White House, "Statement by Vice President Joseph R. Biden, Jr.," March 9, 2010, https://obamawhitehouse.archives.gov/realitycheck/the-press-office/statement-vice-president-joseph-r-biden-jr.

87 **"Biden reserved his most strident criticism":** Ron Kampeas, "'The Good Cop': Joe Biden and Israel During the Obama Years," *Times of Israel*, October 30, 2020, www.timesofisrael.com/the-good-cop-joe-biden-and-israel-during-the-obama-years.

88 **"I hope you feel at home":** Israeli Prime Minister's Office, "PM Netanyahu and Vice President Joe Biden in a Joint Statement," September 3, 2016, www.gov.il/en/departments/news/eventbiden090316.

88 **"Bibi, I don't agree with a damn thing you say":** Excerpted from Alex Ward, "Why Biden Won't Push Israel Harder on Gaza Ceasefire," *Vox*, May 20, 2021, www.vox.com/22442000/biden-israel-gaza-hamas-history-policy.

89 **"Death to Arabs":** Dana El Kurd, "Young People Are Leading the Palestinian Protests

in Jerusalem. And They Aren't Going Away," *Washington Post,* May 12, 2021, www.washingtonpost.com/politics/2021/05/12/young-people-are-leading-palestinian-protests-israel-they-arent-going-away.

89 **bottles and rocks flew:** BBC, "East Jerusalem Clashes Leave over 100 Injured," April 23, 2021, www.bbc.com/news/world-middle-east-56854275.

89 **one of the largest regional violence spikes:** Oliver Holmes, "Gaza Militants Fire Rockets after Clashes Flare in Jerusalem," April 24, 2021, www.theguardian.com/world/2021/apr/24/gaza-militants-fire-rockets-after-clashes-flare-in-jerusalem.

89 **"The two sides also shared concerns":** White House, "Readout of Jake Sullivan's Bilateral Meeting with Israeli NSA Meir Ben-Shabbat," April 27, 2021, www.whitehouse.gov/briefing-room/presidential-actions/2021/04/27/readout-of-jake-sullivans-bilateral-meeting-with-israeli-nsa-meir-ben-shabbat.

90 **"Police must immediately stop":** BBC, "Al-Aqsa Mosque: Dozens Hurt in Jerusalem Clashes," May 8, 2021, www.bbc.com/news/world-middle-east-57034237.

90 **"responsible for the dangerous developments":** BBC, "Al-Aqsa Mosque: Dozens Hurt in Jerusalem Clashes."

90 **"It is critical to avoid":** U.S. Department of State, "Department Press Briefing—May 7, 2021," www.state.gov/briefings/department-press-briefing-may-7-2021/#post-241755-ISRAEL.

91 **On their May 9 call:** White House, "Emily Horne on National Security Advisor Jake Sullivan's Call with Israeli National Security Advisor Meir Ben-Shabbat Regarding the Situation in Jerusalem," May 9, 2021, www.whitehouse.gov/briefing-room/statements-releases/2021/05/09/readout-from-nsc-spokesperson-emily-horne-on-national-security-advisor-jake-sullivans-call-with-israeli-national-security-advisor-meir-ben-shabbat-regarding-the-situation-in-jerusalem.

91 **Israeli police escalated their efforts:** Patrick Kingsley and Isabel Kershner, "After Raid on Aqsa Mosque, Rockets from Gaza and Israeli Airstrikes," *New York Times,* May 10, 2021, www.nytimes.com/2021/05/10/world/middleeast/jerusalem-protests-aqsa-palestinians.html.

91 **Minutes after the ultimatum passed:** Kingsley and Kershner, "After Raid on Aqsa Mosque, Rockets from Gaza and Israeli Airstrikes."

92 **"We will not tolerate attacks":** Kingsley and Kershner, "After Raid on Aqsa Mosque, Rockets from Gaza and Israeli Airstrikes."

92 **a thirteen-story residential building:** Nidal al-Mugrahbi, Stephen Farrell, and Jeffrey Heller, "Dozens Dead as Israel and Hamas Escalate Aerial Bombardments," Reuters, May 11, 2021, www.reuters.com/world/middle-east/palestinian-rocket-fire-israeli-air-strikes-gaza-2021-05-11.

93 **"his unwavering support for Israel's security":** White House, "Readout of President Joseph R. Biden, Jr. Call with Prime Minister Benjamin Netanyahu of Israel," May 12, 2021, www.whitehouse.gov/briefing-room/statements-releases/2021/05/12/readout-of-president-joseph-r-biden-jr-call-with-prime-minister-benjamin-netanyahu-of-israel-2.

93 **"condemned the rocket attacks":** U.S. Department of State, "Secretary Blinken's Call with Palestinian Authority President Abbas," May 12, 2021, www.state.gov/secretary-blinkens-call-with-palestinian-authority-president-abbas.

93 **"My expectation and hope":** White House, "Remarks by President Biden on the COVID-19 Response and the Vaccination Program," May 12, 2021, www.whitehouse.gov

/briefing-room/speeches-remarks/2021/05/12/remarks-by-president-biden-on-the-covid-19-response-and-the-vaccination-program-2.

94 **impassioned speech on the House floor:** As seen on Middle East Eye, "Rashida Tlaib in Emotional Plea to US Congress for Palestinian Rights," YouTube, uploaded May 14, 2021, www.youtube.com/watch?v=41h8WFxQE2o.

94 **"In this moment of crisis":** Bernie Sanders, "Bernie Sanders: The U.S. Must Stop Being an Apologist for the Netanyahu Government," *New York Times,* May 14, 2021, www.nytimes.com/2021/05/14/opinion/bernie-sanders-israel-palestine-gaza.html.

95 **"affirmed his support for a two-state solution":** White House, "Readout of President Joseph R. Biden, Jr. Call with Prime Minister Benjamin Netanyahu of Israel," May 15, 2021, www.whitehouse.gov/briefing-room/statements-releases/2021/05/15/readout-of-president-joseph-r-biden-jr-call-with-prime-minister-benjamin-netanyahu-of-israel-3.

96 **"Apartheid states aren't democracies":** Alexandria Ocasio-Cortez (@AOC), "Apartheid states aren't democracies," Twitter post, May 15, 2021, 5:04 p.m., https://twitter.com/AOC/status/1393673695433043976.

96 **he was "deeply troubled":** U.S. Senate Committee on Foreign Relations, "Chairman Menendez Statement on Violence Across Israel and Gaza," May 15, 2021, www.foreign.senate.gov/press/chair/release/chairman-menendez-statement-on-violence-across-israel-and-gaza.

96 **"If Blinken had gone":** Quoted in Alex Ward, "Why Biden's Team Didn't Go All-In on Israel-Gaza," *Vox,* May 27, 2021, www.vox.com/22453241/biden-blinken-israel-gaza-ceasefire.

97 **He wanted a cease-fire:** Interviews, and White House, "Readout of President Joseph R. Biden, Jr. Call with Prime Minister Benjamin Netanyahu of Israel," May 17, 2021, www.whitehouse.gov/briefing-room/statements-releases/2021/05/17/readout-of-president-joseph-r-biden-jr-call-with-prime-minister-benjamin-netanyahu-of-israel-4.

97 **the U.S. used its veto power:** Al Jazeera, "Israel-Palestine: US Blocks UN Statement for Third Time in a Week," May 17, 2021, www.aljazeera.com/news/2021/5/17/no-us-action-after-third-unsc-meeting-on-israel-palestine.

98 **"an important dialogue":** Luke Broadwater and Nicholas Fandos, "On Tarmac in Detroit, Representative Rashida Tlaib Confronted Biden on U.S. Support for Israel," *New York Times,* May 18, 2021, www.nytimes.com/live/2021/05/18/us/joe-biden-news-today#tlaib-biden-palestine-israel.

98 **"I admire your intellect":** Quoted in Broadwater and Fandos, "On Tarmac in Detroit, Representative Rashida Tlaib Confronted Biden on U.S. Support for Israel."

100 **"respect the rights of both the Israeli and Palestinian people":** Office of Speaker Nancy Pelosi, "Pelosi Statement Calling for Ceasefire in Israel-Hamas Conflict," May 18, 2021, https://pelosi.house.gov/news/press-releases/pelosi-statement-calling-for-ceasefire-in-israel-hamas-conflict.

100 **The White House put out a statement:** White House, "Readout of President Joseph R. Biden, Jr. Call with Prime Minister Benjamin Netanyahu of Israel," May 19, 2021, www.whitehouse.gov/briefing-room/statements-releases/2021/05/19/readout-of-president-joseph-r-biden-jr-call-with-prime-minister-benjamin-netanyahu-of-israel-5.

100 **"The harsh truth":** Office of Rep. Alexandria Ocasio-Cortez, "Ocasio-Cortez, Pocan & Tlaib Lead Joint Resolution to Block Weapon Sales to Netanyahu," May 19, 2021,

https://ocasio-cortez.house.gov/media/press-releases/ocasio-cortez-pocan-tlaib-lead-joint-resolution-block-weapon-sales-netanyahu.

101 **Sanders the next day introduced a similar resolution:** Office of Sen. Bernie Sanders, "NEWS: Sanders Moves to Block Weapons Sale to Israel," May 19, 2021, www.sanders.senate.gov/press-releases/news-sanders-moves-to-block-weapons-sale-to-israel.

101 **"'You have to move on this'":** Alex Ward, "The Progressive Foreign Policy Moment Has Arrived," *Vox*, May 26, 2021, www.vox.com/2021/5/26/22445895/israel-gaza-progressive-democrats-sanders-cortez.

102 **"more of everything is not a strategy":** Ward, "Why Biden's Team Didn't Go All-In on Israel-Gaza."

102 **"There is no shift in my commitment":** White House, "Remarks by President Biden and H. E. Moon Jae-in, President of the Republic of Korea at Press Conference," May 21, 2021, www.whitehouse.gov/briefing-room/speeches-remarks/2021/05/21/remarks-by-president-biden-and-h-e-moon-jae-in-president-of-the-republic-of-korea-at-press-conference.

102 **"The risk is not trying to go big":** David Brooks, "Has Biden Changed? He Tells Us," *New York Times*, May 20, 2021, www.nytimes.com/2021/05/20/opinion/joe-biden-david-brooks-interview.html.

Chapter 5: Frenemies

104 **"I looked in your eyes":** "Joe Biden ABC Interview Transcript March 16," Rev, March 16, 2021, www.rev.com/blog/transcripts/joe-biden-abc-interview-transcript-march-17. See also Talia Lakritz, "Biden Once Told Putin 'I Don't Think You Have a Soul.' He Responded, 'We Understand One Another,'" *Business Insider*, March 11, 2022, www.businessinsider.in/politics/world/news/biden-once-told-putin-i-dont-think-you-have-a-soul-he-responded-we-understand-one-another-/articleshow/90145310.cms.

104 **"To strengthen dialogue":** Obama White House, "Remarks by Vice President Joe Biden and President Xi Jinping of the People's Republic of China," December 4, 2013, https://obamawhitehouse.archives.gov/the-press-office/2013/12/04/remarks-vice-president-joe-biden-and-president-xi-jinping-peoples-republ.

104 **delay a hypersonic missile test:** Alexander Ward and Quint Forgey, "White House Had Pentagon Delay a Hypersonic Missile Test Before Biden-Putin Summit," *Politico*, October 28, 2021, www.politico.com/newsletters/national-security-daily/2021/10/28/white-house-had-pentagon-delay-a-hypersonic-missile-test-before-biden-putin-summit-494891.

106 **"This is not just about":** Quoted in Steve Holland and Guy Faulconbridge, "G7 Rivals China with Grand Infrastructure Plan," Reuters, June 13, 2021, www.reuters.com/world/g7-counter-chinas-belt-road-with-infrastructure-project-senior-us-official-2021-06-12.

106 **"It used to be complete chaos":** Guy Faulconbridge, "G7 Source Praises Biden after 'Complete Chaos' of Trump," June 12, 2021, www.reuters.com/world/us/g7-source-praises-biden-after-complete-chaos-trump-2021-06-12.

106 **"There's no guarantee":** White House, "Remarks by President Biden in Press Confer-

ence," June 13, 2021, www.whitehouse.gov/briefing-room/speeches-remarks/2021/06/13/remarks-by-president-biden-in-press-conference-2.

107 **"There are two fundamental elements":** White House, "Press Gaggle by Press Secretary Jen Psaki and National Security Advisor Jake Sullivan En Route Brussels, Belgium," June 13, 2021, www.whitehouse.gov/briefing-room/press-briefings/2021/06/13/press-gaggle-by-press-secretary-jen-psaki-and-national-security-advisor-jake-sullivan-en-route-brussels-belgium.

107 **"lowest point since the end of the Cold War":** Jens Stoltenberg, "Doorstep Statement," NATO, June 14, 2021, www.nato.int/cps/en/natohq/opinions_184960.htm.

108 **"China's stated ambitions":** NATO, "Brussels Summit Communiqué," June 14, 2021, www.nato.int/cps/en/natohq/news_185000.htm?selectedLocale=en.

108 **"make it clear what the red lines are":** White House, "Remarks by President Biden in Press Conference," June 14, 2021, www.whitehouse.gov/briefing-room/speeches-remarks/2021/06/14/remarks-by-president-biden-in-press-conference-3.

109 **The new 767-mile-long natural gas:** Nikolaus J. Kurmayer, "Ukraine Gets Compensation in Exchange for US-Germany Deal on Nord Stream 2," Euractiv, July 22, 2021, www.euractiv.com/section/energy-environment/news/ukraine-gets-compensation-in-exchange-for-us-germany-deal-on-nord-stream-2.

109 **clearing the way for the U.S.–Germany deal:** Andrea Shalal, Timothy Gardner, and Steve Holland, "U.S. Waives Sanctions on Nord Stream 2 as Biden Seeks to Mend Europe Ties," Reuters, May 19, 2021, www.reuters.com/business/energy/us-waive-sanctions-firm-ceo-behind-russias-nord-stream-2-pipeline-source-2021-05-19.

110 **"We inherited a pipeline":** Quoted in Shalal, Gardner, and Holland, "U.S. Waives Sanctions on Nord Stream 2 as Biden Seeks to Mend Europe Ties."

110 **"This is a weapon":** Jonathan Swan and Dave Lawler, "Ukraine's Zelenskyy 'Surprised' and 'Disappointed' by Biden Pipeline Move," *Axios*, June 6, 2021, www.axios.com/2021/06/06/zelensky-biden-ukraine-russia-nord-stream-pipeline.

110 **"The State Department has regularly engaged":** Quoted in Swan and Lawler, "Ukraine's Zelenskyy 'Surprised' and 'Disappointed' by Biden Pipeline Move."

110 **"at any moment and at any spot on the planet":** Swan and Lawler, "Ukraine's Zelenskyy 'Surprised' and 'Disappointed' by Biden Pipeline Move."

113 **"How would you feel if ransomware":** White House, "Remarks by President Biden in Press Conference," June 16, 2021, www.whitehouse.gov/briefing-room/speeches-remarks/2021/06/16/remarks-by-president-biden-in-press-conference-4.

114 **"We're going to know shortly":** White House, "Remarks by President Biden in Press Conference," June 16, 2021.

115 **"For we are one people":** Vladimir Putin, "On the Historical Unity of Russians and Ukrainians," Office of the President of Russia, July 12, 2021, http://en.kremlin.ru/events/president/news/66181.

115 **"I recall that long ago":** Putin, "On the Historical Unity of Russians and Ukrainians."

117 **"Look, this is a bad situation":** Quoted in John Hudson, "U.S., Germany Reach Agreement on Russian Gas Pipeline, Ending Dispute Between Allies," *Washington Post*, July 21, 2021, www.washingtonpost.com/national-security/nord-stream-pipeline-germany-russia/2021/07/21/c8788eda-ea4b-11eb-84a2-d93bc0b50294_story.html.

118 **evidence to support the denial:** Betsy Woodruff Swan, Alexander Ward, and Andrew

Desiderio, "U.S. Urges Ukraine to Stay Quiet on Russian Pipeline," *Politico*, July 20, 2021, www.politico.com/news/2021/07/20/us-ukraine-russia-pipeline-500334.

118 **"It's unbalanced and unfair":** Swan, Ward, and Desiderio, "U.S. Urges Ukraine to Stay Quiet on Russian Pipeline."

118 **"This will be a generational geopolitical win":** Office of Sen. Ted Cruz, "Sen. Cruz: Reports of Deal to Finish Nord Stream 2 Pipeline a 'Catastrophe for the US and Our Allies,'" July 20, 2021, www.cruz.senate.gov/newsroom/press-releases/sen-cruz-reports-of-deal-to-finish-nord-stream-2-pipeline-a-and-145catastrophe-for-the-us-and-our-allies-and-146.

118 **Biden's "decision on Nord Stream 2":** Alexander Ward, "Ted Talks: What Cruz Wants from Biden on Nord Stream 2," *Politico*, July 22, 2021, www.politico.com/newsletters/national-security-daily/2021/07/22/ted-talks-what-cruz-wants-from-biden-on-nord-stream-2-493697.

119 **"President Biden looks forward":** White House, "Statement by White House Press Secretary Jen Psaki on the Visit of President Volodymyr Zelenskyy of Ukraine," July 21, 2021, www.whitehouse.gov/briefing-room/statements-releases/2021/07/21/statement-by-white-house-press-secretary-jen-psaki-on-the-visit-of-president-volodymyr-zelenskyy-of-ukraine.

Chapter 6: Return of the Taliban

124 **"new chapter in our relationship":** White House, "Remarks by President Biden and President Mohammad Ashraf Ghani of the Islamic Republic of Afghanistan Before Bilateral Meeting," June 25, 2021, www.whitehouse.gov/briefing-room/speeches-remarks/2021/06/25/remarks-by-president-biden-and-president-mohammad-ashraf-ghani-of-the-islamic-republic-of-afghanistan-before-bilateral-meeting.

125 **a way to bounce back:** Jonathan Schroden, "Afghanistan Security Forces Versus the Taliban: A Net Assessment," *CTC Sentinel* 14, no. 1 (January 2021), https://ctc.usma.edu/afghanistans-security-forces-versus-the-taliban-a-net-assessment.

125 **the Taliban was already staging its members:** Thomas Gibbons-Neff and Taimoor Shah, "The Taliban Close In on Afghanistan, Pushing Country to the Brink," *New York Times*, February 15, 2021, www.nytimes.com/2021/02/15/world/asia/taliban-afghanistan.html.

126 **The group escalated its attacks:** Ruchi Kumar, "Afghan Military under Fire as 'Tactical Retreats' Hand Territory to Taliban," *The National*, June 23, 2021, www.thenationalnews.com/world/asia/afghan-military-under-fire-as-tactical-retreats-hand-territory-to-taliban-1.1246062.

128 **the Ghani meeting in June to evacuate Afghan allies of the U.S.:** Dan DeLuce and Mike Memoli, "The Biden Administration Says It Will Evacuate Afghans Who Worked with U.S. Troops," NBC News, June 24, 2021, www.nbcnews.com/news/world/biden-administration-says-it-will-evacuate-afghans-who-worked-u-n1272265.

128 **to get the SIV applicants out:** Lara Seligman, "Lawmakers Urge Biden to Evacuate Afghan Allies 'Immediately,'" *Politico*, June 4, 2021, www.politico.com/news/2021/06/04/lawmakers-urge-biden-to-evacuate-afghan-allies-immediately-491899.

128 **senior Afghan officials were aware of the plan ahead of time:** Interviews, and Kathy

Gannon, "US Left Afghan Airfield at Night, Didn't Tell New Commander," Associated Press, July 6, 2021, https://apnews.com/article/bagram-afghanistan-airfield-us-troops-f3614828364f567593251aaaa167e623.

129 **needed a ride out of Afghanistan:** Lara Seligman, "Sources: U.S. Troops Withdrawal from Afghanistan Complete 'For All Intents and Purposes,'" *Politico*, July 7, 2021, www.politico.com/news/2021/07/07/us-troop-withdrawal-afghanistan-498671.

131 **his decision to leave Afghanistan:** Alex Ward, "Top Senate Democrat Says Biden Should 'Reconsider' May 1 Afghanistan Troop Withdrawal," *Vox*, March 9, 2021, www.vox.com/2021/3/9/22321740/biden-afghanistan-menendez-troop-withdrawal-trump.

132 **"The Afghan troops have three hundred thousand":** White House, "Remarks by President Biden on the Drawdown of U.S. Forces in Afghanistan," July 8, 2021, www.whitehouse.gov/briefing-room/speeches-remarks/2021/07/08/remarks-by-president-biden-on-the-drawdown-of-u-s-forces-in-afghanistan.

133 **the Taliban had taken over a quarter:** Kate Clark and Obaid Ali, "A Quarter of Afghanistan's Districts Fall to the Taleban amid Calls for a 'Second Resistance,'" Afghanistan Analysts Network, July 2, 2021, www.afghanistan-analysts.org/en/reports/war-and-peace/a-quarter-of-afghanistans-districts-fall-to-the-taleban-amid-calls-for-a-second-resistance.

136 **denounce the Taliban's human rights violations and prepare to evacuate people:** Vivian Salama, "Internal State Department Cable Warned of Kabul Collapse," *Wall Street Journal*, August 19, 2021, www.wsj.com/articles/confidential-state-department-cable-in-july-warned-of-afghanistans-collapse-11629406993.

136 **"We are launching":** White House, "Press Briefing by Press Secretary Jen Psaki, July 14, 2021," www.whitehouse.gov/briefing-room/press-briefings/2021/07/14/press-briefing-by-press-secretary-jen-psaki-july-14-2021.

137 **called the footage, now streaming worldwide, a "war crime":** Anna Coren, Sandi Sidhu, Tim Lister, and Abdul Basir Bina, "Taliban Fighters Execute 22 Afghan Commandos as They Try to Surrender," CNN, July 14, 2021, www.cnn.com/2021/07/13/asia/afghanistan-taliban-commandos-killed-intl-hnk/index.html.

138 **"Their position, given the developments":** Alexander Ward, "Khalilzad: Taliban in 'Stronger Position than It Was Before' after Military Gains," *Politico*, July 19, 2021, www.politico.com/newsletters/national-security-daily/2021/07/19/khalilzad-taliban-in-stronger-position-than-it-was-before-after-military-gains-493639.

138 **those were mostly unsavory:** Ward, "Khalilzad: Taliban in 'Stronger Position than It Was Before' after Military Gains."

139 **"It definitely has made it harder":** Ward, "Khalilzad: Taliban in 'Stronger Position than It Was Before' after Military Gains."

140 **authorize the evacuation of SIV applicants:** Lara Seligman and Andrew Desiderio, "U.S. in Final Talks to House Afghan Interpreters at Qatar, Kuwait Military Bases," *Politico*, July 20, 2021, www.politico.com/news/2021/07/20/us-afghan-interpreters-qatar-kuwait-military-bases-500275.

140 **Those on the trip would be in the final stages:** Seligman and Desiderio, "U.S. in Final Talks to House Afghan Interpreters at Qatar, Kuwait Military Bases."

142 **Typhoon season in Guam:** Andersen Air Force Base, "Typhoon Season Is Around the

Corner: It's Time to Get Ready Again," www.andersen.af.mil/News/Photos/igphoto/2000614766.

Chapter 7: Go Time

145 **the Taliban had "strategic momentum":** U.S. Department of Defense, "Secretary of Defense Austin and Chairman of the Joint Chiefs of Staff Gen. Milley Press Briefing," July 21, 2021, www.defense.gov/News/Transcripts/Transcript/Article/2702966/secretary-of-defense-austin-and-chairman-of-the-joint-chiefs-of-staff-gen-mille.

145 **American and NATO troops were already out of the country:** Kathy Gannon, "To Reach a Peace Deal, Taliban Say Afghan President Must Go," Associated Press, July 23, 2021, https://apnews.com/article/middle-east-only-on-ap-taliban-ffbce635cf19ce4874700fd2d81a0f39.

146 **"an Islamic government acceptable to all Afghans":** Quoted in Alexander Ward, "Easy Access to Guns Makes Domestic Terror Attacks Harder to Stop, NSC Official Says," *Politico*, July 23, 2021, www.politico.com/newsletters/national-security-daily/2021/07/23/easy-access-to-guns-makes-domestic-terror-attacks-harder-to-stop-nsc-official-says-493714.

146 **"The Taliban says":** U.S. Department of State, "Secretary Antony J. Blinken and Indian External Affairs Minister Dr. Subrahmanyam Jaishankar at a Joint Press Availability," July 28, 2021, www.state.gov/secretary-antony-j-blinken-and-indian-external-affairs-minister-dr-subrahmanyam-jaishankar-at-a-joint-press-availability.

146 **the first plane of SIVs:** U.S. Department of State, "Arrival of First Flight of Operation Allies Refuge," July 30, 2021, www.state.gov/arrival-of-first-flight-of-operation-allies-refuge.

147 **provincial capital of Lashkar Gah:** Tameem Akghar and Rahim Faiez, "Taliban Take Much of Provincial Capital in South Afghanistan," Associated Press, August 3, 2021, https://apnews.com/article/middle-east-afghanistan-united-nations-taliban-fa64aa119c0daadd55fd44e42ab223c2.

147 **"The situation is very concerning":** Aspen Security Forum, "A Conversation with Ambassador Zalmay Khalilzad," YouTube, August 3, 2021, www.youtube.com/watch?v=AQey-jvtbtY.

147 **the administration projected calm:** Adam Nossiter, Taimoor Shah, and Fahim Abed, "Taliban Capture Zaranj, an Afghanistan Provincial Capital, in a Symbolic Victory," *New York Times*, August 6, 2021, www.nytimes.com/2021/08/06/world/asia/taliban-afghanistan-capital-zaranj.html.

147 **the taking of Zaranj a "symbolic victory":** Nossiter, Shah, and Abed, "Taliban Capture Zaranj, an Afghanistan Provincial Capital, in a Symbolic Victory."

147 **"We have to take it":** Alexander Ward and Quint Forgey, "Taliban on Afghan Provincial Capital Capture: 'We Have to Take It,'" *Politico*, August 6, 2021, www.politico.com/newsletters/national-security-daily/2021/08/06/taliban-on-afghan-provincial-capital-capture-we-have-to-take-it-493889.

148 **the Taliban rolled up the cities of Shebergan, Kunduz, Aybak:** Ruby Mellen, "The Shocking Speed of the Taliban's Advance: A Visual Timeline," *Washington Post*, August 16, 2021, www.washingtonpost.com/world/2021/08/16/taliban-timeline.

150 **"They've got to want to fight":** White House, "Remarks by President Biden on the Senate Passage of the Bipartisan Infrastructure Investment and Jobs Act," August 10, 2021, www.whitehouse.gov/briefing-room/speeches-remarks/2021/08/10/remarks-by-president-biden-on-the-senate-passage-of-the-bipartisan-infrastructure-investment-and-jobs-act.

151 **Kabul could fall within ninety days:** Dan Lamothe, John Hudson, Shane Harris, and Anne Gearan, "U.S. Officials Warn Collapse of Afghan Capital Could Come Sooner than Expected," *Washington Post,* August 10, 2021, www.washingtonpost.com/national-security/2021/08/10/afghanistan-intelligence-assessment.

152 **make sure their bosses would be on time Thursday morning:** Adapted from Bryan Bender, Alexander Ward, Lara Seligman, Andrew Desiderio, and Alex Thompson, "'This Is Really Happening,'" *Politico,* August 20, 2021, www.politico.com/news/magazine/2021/08/20/biden-afghanistan-kabul-chaos-taliban-evacuation-505600.

154 **Biden then called Austin:** Bender, Ward, Seligman, Desiderio, and Thompson, "'This Is Really Happening,'"

154 **"there's going to be no circumstance":** White House, "Remarks by President Biden on the Drawdown of U.S. Forces in Afghanistan," July 8, 2021, www.whitehouse.gov/briefing-room/speeches-remarks/2021/07/08/remarks-by-president-biden-on-the-drawdown-of-u-s-forces-in-afghanistan.

Chapter 8: Hell

157 **Afghanistan's second- and third-largest cities:** Tameem Akhgar, Rahim Faiez, and Joseph Krauss, "Taliban Sweep Across Afghanistan's South, Take 4 More Cities," Associated Press, August 13, 2021, https://apnews.com/article/middle-east-taliban-c6c8d4a41c554f36031a8131538d1402.

157 **Blinken asked Ghani outright:** Interviews, and TOLOnews, "US Sec. Blinken: Relations 'Will Depend' on Taliban Actions," September 8, 2021, https://tolonews.com/afghanistan-174571.

157 **Whatever you do, don't come into Kabul:** Lara Seligman, "The Afghanistan Deal That Never Happened," *Politico,* August 11, 2021, www.politico.com/news/magazine/2022/08/11/the-afghanistan-deal-00050916.

158 **"If you don't interfere with the evacuation":** Interviews, and Seligman, "The Afghanistan Deal That Never Happened."

158 **Baradar had a proposal:** Interviews, and Seligman, "The Afghanistan Deal That Never Happened."

160 **thousands of people trying to flee Taliban rule:** Seligman, "The Afghanistan Deal That Never Happened."

160 **the image of a dead body on a Kabul roof:** Susannah George, Adam Taylor, Dan Lamothe, and Jennifer Hassan, "Scenes of Deadly Chaos Unfold at Kabul Airport after Taliban's Return," *Washington Post,* August 16, 2021, www.washingtonpost.com/world/2021/08/16/afghan-kabul-airport.

161 **beating about four hundred people with sticks:** Seligman, "The Afghanistan Deal That Never Happened."

161 **He started his remarks:** White House, "Remarks by President Biden on Afghanistan," August 16, 2021, www.whitehouse.gov/briefing-room/speeches-remarks/2021/08/16/remarks-by-president-biden-on-afghanistan.

162 **"What's the alternative?":** All quotes from ABC News, "Full Transcript of ABC News' George Stephanopoulos' Interview with President Joe Biden," https://abcnews.go.com/Politics/full-transcript-abc-news-george-stephanopoulos-interview-president/story?id=79535643.

166 **at-risk Afghan named Najeeb Monawari:** George Packer, "The Betrayal," *The Atlantic*, January 31, 2021, www.theatlantic.com/magazine/archive/2022/03/biden-afghanistan-exit-american-allies-abandoned/621307.

166 **"This is highly irregular":** The quote here is written as Malinowski told me in an interview. A similar quote first appeared in Packer, "The Betrayal."

166 **the U.S. soldier convinced by the letterhead he presented:** Malinowski interview, and Packer, "The Betrayal."

167 **choosing who lived or died:** Malinowski made a similar point in Packer, "The Betrayal."

169 **America was handing over a "kill list":** Lara Seligman, Alexander Ward, and Andrew Desiderio, "U.S. Officials Provided Taliban with Names of Americans, Afghan Allies to Evacuate," *Politico*, August 26, 2021, www.politico.com/news/2021/08/26/us-officials-provided-taliban-with-names-of-americans-afghan-allies-to-evacuate-506957.

169 **"Yes, there have been occasions like that":** White House, "Remarks by President Biden on the Terror Attack at Hamid Karzai International Airport," August 26, 2021, www.whitehouse.gov/briefing-room/speeches-remarks/2021/08/26/remarks-by-president-biden-on-the-terror-attack-at-hamid-karzai-international-airport.

169 **"There is no such 'kill list.' That is nonsense":** CNN, "Transcripts, *State of the Union*," August 29, 2021, https://transcripts.cnn.com/show/sotu/date/2021-08-29/segment/01.

169 **"The idea that we've done anything":** U.S. Department of State, "Secretary Antony J. Blinken with Chuck Todd of NBC's *Meet the Press*," August 29, 2021, www.state.gov/secretary-antony-j-blinken-with-chuck-todd-of-nbcs-meet-the-press-2.

170 **rescue people who couldn't find their way there:** Jessica Donati, "A Secret CIA Gate at Kabul Airport Became an Escape Path for Afghans," *Wall Street Journal*, October 14, 2021, www.wsj.com/articles/a-secret-cia-gate-at-kabul-airport-became-an-escape-path-for-afghans-11633545417.

172 **"Sadly, it was a question of when":** Chris Whipple, *The Fight of His Life: Inside Joe Biden's White House* (New York: Scribner, 2023), 96–97.

172 **he detonated an improvised explosive device:** U.S. Department of Defense, "General Kenneth F. McKenzie, Jr., Commander, U.S. Central Command, Holds a Press Briefing," February 4, 2022, www.defense.gov/News/Transcripts/Transcript/Article/2924617/general-kenneth-f-mckenzie-jr-commander-us-central-command-holds-a-press-briefi.

173 **"Move the fuck off the road":** Sam Aronson digital diary, obtained by author.

173 **There was screaming, running, blood:** Aronson diary.

173 **ISIS's franchise in Afghanistan was targeting HKIA:** Lara Seligman, Andrew Desiderio, and Alexander Ward, "ISIS Terrorist Threats Jeopardize Afghanistan Evacuation, Pentagon Assessment Warns," *Politico*, August 24, 2021, www.politico.com/news/2021/08/24/isis-terrorist-threats-afghanistan-kabul-evacuation-506807.

173 **more than one hundred prisoners loyal to ISIS:** Jim Sciutto and Tim Lister, "US Concerned about 'Very Specific Threat Stream from ISIS-K Against Crowds Outside Airport," CNN, August 25, 2021, www.cnn.com/2021/08/25/politics/isis-k-concerns-kabul-airport/index.html.

175 **"The worst that can happen has happened":** Interviews, and Whipple, *The Fight of His Life*, 98.

175 **the casualty count:** U.S. Department of Defense, "General Kenneth F. McKenzie, Jr., Commander, U.S. Central Command, Holds a Press Briefing," February 4, 2022, www.defense.gov/News/Transcripts/Transcript/Article/2924617/general-kenneth-f-mckenzie-jr-commander-us-central-command-holds-a-press-briefi.

176 **"the largest airlift evacuation":** Whipple, *The Fight of His Life*, 100.

176 **"He was rocked":** Interviews, and Whipple, *The Fight of His Life*, 99.

176 **"To those who carried out this attack":** White House, "Remarks by President Biden on the Terror Attack at Hamid Karzai International Airport," August 26, 2021, www.whitehouse.gov/briefing-room/speeches-remarks/2021/08/26/remarks-by-president-biden-on-the-terror-attack-at-hamid-karzai-international-airport.

177 **they had killed their target:** Idrees Ali, "U.S. Strikes Islamic State in Afghanistan after Deadly Kabul Attack," Reuters, August 27, 2021, www.reuters.com/world/asia-pacific/us-drone-strike-targets-islamic-state-planner-afghanistan-2021-08-28.

177 **Ahmadi sat in his car:** Matthieu Aikins, Christoph Koettl, Evan Hill, Eric Schmitt, Ainara Tiefenthäler, and Drew Jordan, "In US Drone Strike, Evidence Suggests No ISIS Bomb," *New York Times*, September 10, 2021, www.nytimes.com/2021/09/10/world/asia/us-air-strike-drone-kabul-afghanistan-isis.html.

177 **a "righteous strike":** U.S. Department of Defense, "Secretary of Defense Austin and Chairman of the Joint Chiefs of Staff Gen. Milley Press Briefing on the End of the U.S. War in Afghanistan," September 1, 2021, www.defense.gov/News/Transcripts/Transcript/Article/2762169/secretary-of-defense-austin-and-chairman-of-the-joint-chiefs-of-staff-gen-mille.

179 **"Job well done, I'm proud of you all":** Tara Copp, "Inside the Final Hours at Kabul Airport," Defense One, August 30, 2021, www.defenseone.com/threats/2021/08/inside-final-hours-kabul-airport/184975.

179 **evacuated more than 124,000 people:** U.S. Department of Defense, "Statement by Secretary of Defense Lloyd J. Austin III," August 31, 2021, www.defense.gov/News/Releases/Release/Article/3145780/statement-by-secretary-of-defense-lloyd-j-austin-iii.

179 **receive the Meritorious Unit Commendation:** U.S. Department of Defense, "Statement by Secretary of Defense Lloyd J. Austin III."

181 **"We were ready":** White House, "Remarks by President Biden on the End of the War in Afghanistan," August 31, 2021, www.whitehouse.gov/briefing-room/speeches-remarks/2021/08/31/remarks-by-president-biden-on-the-end-of-the-war-in-afghanistan.

182 **"America's last flight left Afghanistan":** "'It's Unforgivable: Lawmakers Furious U.S. Citizens Stranded in Afghanistan," *Politico*, August 31, 2021, www.politico.com/newsletters/national-security-daily/2021/08/31/its-unforgivable-lawmakers-furious-us-citizens-stranded-in-afghanistan-494185.

182 **"We're in constant contact":** Quoted in Meg Wagner, Melissa Macaya, Melissa Mahtani, and Mike Hayes, "Secretary of State Testifies on Afghanistan Withdrawal,"

CNN, September 13, 2021, www.cnn.com/politics/live-news/blinken-hearing-congress-afghanistan/h_1ea2c0d9099878e713392461fe05249c.

183 **"collapse of the Afghan military forces":** Quoted in Helene Cooper and Eric Schmitt, "Defense Chief Says He Advised Against Staying in Afghanistan 'Forever,'" *New York Times*, September 29, 2021, www.nytimes.com/2021/09/29/us/politics/house-hearing-milley-austin-afghanistan.html.

183 **U.S. troops should have stayed:** Sen. Elizabeth Warren, "At Armed Services Hearing, Gen. Milley Concedes That Outcome in Afghanistan Would Have Been the Same No Matter When Troops Were Withdrawn," press release, September 28, 2021, www.warren.senate.gov/newsroom/press-releases/at-armed-services-hearing-gen-milley-concedes-that-outcome-in-afghanistan-would-have-been-the-same-no-matter-when-troops-were-withdrawn. See also: Alexander Ward and Quint Forgey, "Milley's Most Important Admission," *Politico*, September 29, 2021, www.politico.com/newsletters/national-security-daily/2021/09/29/milleys-most-important-admission-494519.

183 **"This is a twenty-year war":** Quoted in Cooper and Schmitt, "Defense Chief Says He Advised Against Staying in Afghanistan 'Forever.'"

183 **Republicans called for Biden to be impeached:** Olivia Beavers, "The I-Word Looms: McCarthy Faces Internal Pressure to Go Harder at Biden on Afghanistan," *Politico*, August 31, 2021, www.politico.com/news/2021/08/31/mccarthy-biden-afghanistan-impeachment-507831.

183 **"President Biden needs to fire":** Brett Bruen, "Afghanistan Disaster: Why Biden's Foreign Policy Team Failed America," *USA Today*, August 16, 2021, www.usatoday.com/story/opinion/2021/08/16/afghanistan-disaster-why-bidens-foreign-policy-team-failed-america/8145997002.

184 **Blinken "needs to resign immediately":** Sen. Marsha Blackburn (@MarshaBlackburn), Twitter post, August 18, 2021, 6:18 p.m., https://twitter.com/MarshaBlackburn/status/1428481581702950916?s=20.

184 **"Does Biden really think":** Matt Lewis, "The Buck Stops with No One after Biden's Afghanistan Debacle," *Daily Beast*, August 19, 2021, www.thedailybeast.com/the-buck-stops-with-no-one-after-bidens-afghanistan-debacle.

Chapter 9: The Man from Ukraine

190 **Thousands of pro-Western Ukrainians:** Ian Traynor, "Ukraine's Bloodiest Day: Dozens Dead as Kiev Protesters Regain Territory from Police," *The Guardian*, February 21, 2014, www.theguardian.com/world/2014/feb/20/ukraine-dead-protesters-police.

190 **"pay in blood and money":** Quoted in Glenn Thrush and Kenneth P. Vogel, "What Joe Biden Actually Did in Ukraine," *New York Times*, November 10, 2019, www.nytimes.com/2019/11/10/us/politics/joe-biden-ukraine.html.

190 **"Ukraine, like every country in Europe":** Obama White House, "Remarks by Vice President Joe Biden with Ukrainian President Petro Poroshenko," January 17, 2021, https://obamawhitehouse.archives.gov/the-press-office/2017/01/17/remarks-vice-president-joe-biden-ukrainian-president-petro-poroshenko.

191 **"What might give Mr. Putin pause":** Antony J. Blinken, "Time for the Trump Adminis-

tration to Arm Ukraine," *New York Times*, October 4, 2017, www.nytimes.com/2017/10/04/opinion/trump-ukraine-russia.html.

191 **worked out those details during their planning visits to Washington:** Daria Derevianchuk, "Zelensky and Biden's Meeting Postponed to Aug. 31," *Kyiv Post*, August 19, 2021, www.kyivpost.com/ukraine-politics/zelensky-and-bidens-meeting-postponed-to-aug-31.html.

192 **"Our strategic partnership":** White House, "Background Press Call by Senior Administration Officials on the President's Upcoming Meeting with President Zelenskyy of Ukraine," September 1, 2021, www.whitehouse.gov/briefing-room/press-briefings/2021/09/01/background-press-call-by-senior-administration-officials-on-the-presidents-upcoming-meeting-with-president-zelenskyy-of-ukraine.

192 **"We have to focus very much":** White House, "Remarks by President Biden and President Zelenskyy Before Bilateral Meeting," September 1, 2021, www.whitehouse.gov/briefing-room/speeches-remarks/2021/09/01/remarks-by-president-biden-and-president-zelenskyy-of-ukraine-before-bilateral-meeting.

193 **a Russian ship made contact:** Megan Eckstein, "Tension on the Black Sea: What Great Power Competition Looks Like from the Deckplates," *Navy Times*, August 10, 2021, www.navytimes.com/news/your-navy/2021/08/10/tension-on-the-black-sea-what-great-power-competition-looks-like-from-the-deckplates.

193 **three Ukranian ships along with twenty-four crew members:** Megan Eckstein, "After 2014 Decimation, Ukrainian Navy Rebuilds to Fend Off Russia," *Defense News*, August 9, 2021, www.defensenews.com/naval/2021/08/09/after-2014-decimation-ukrainian-navy-rebuilds-to-fend-off-russia.

193 **the United States sent a warship from the Sixth Fleet:** David B. Larter, "After a Kerch Strait Confrontation, the US Beefs Up Ukraine's Maritime Force," *Defense News*, July 2, 2020, www.defensenews.com/naval/2020/07/02/after-the-kerch-strait-confrontation-the-us-moves-to-beef-up-ukraines-maritime-forces.

194 **"There's no evidence":** U.S. Department of State, "Opening Remarks by Secretary Antony J. Blinken Before the Senate Foreign Relations Committee," September 14, 2021, www.state.gov/opening-remarks-by-secretary-antony-j-blinken-before-the-senate-foreign-relations-committee.

195 **"Where Is Ukraine in Biden's Agenda?":** Chatham House, "Where Is Ukraine in Biden's Agenda?," September 15, 2021, www.chathamhouse.org/events/all/research-event/where-ukraine-bidens-agenda.

195 **"This is the clear and urgent choice":** White House, "Remarks by President Biden Before the 76th Session of the United Nations General Assembly," September 21, 2021, www.whitehouse.gov/briefing-room/speeches-remarks/2021/09/21/remarks-by-president-biden-before-the-76th-session-of-the-united-nations-general-assembly.

195 **send air-defense systems to Kyiv:** Paul McLeary, "The U.S. Army's Iron Dome Could Be Headed to Ukraine," *Politico*, September 14, 2021, www.politico.com/news/2021/09/14/us-army-iron-dome-weapons-ukraine-511787.

196 **Around eighty thousand troops:** Helene Cooper and Julian Barnes, "80,000 Russian Troops Remain at Ukraine Border as U.S. and NATO Hold Exercises," *New York Times*, May 5, 2021, updated September 1, 2021, www.nytimes.com/2021/05/05/us/politics/biden-putin-russia-ukraine.html.

196 **conducting massive joint enterprises:** Cooper and Barnes, "80,000 Russian Troops Remain at Ukraine Border as U.S. and NATO Hold Exercises."

196 **It had two phases:** Capt. Chris Bott, "ZAPAD 2021 Brief," U.S. Naval Institute, *Proceedings* 147 (September 2021), www.usni.org/magazines/proceedings/2021/september/zapad-2021-brief.

196 **Around two hundred thousand troops:** Eugene Rumer, "Even a Major Military Exercise Like Zapad Can't Fix Some of the Biggest Security Challenges Facing Russia," Carnegie Endowment for International Peace, September 21, 2021, https://carnegieendowment.org/2021/09/21/even-major-military-exercise-like-zapad-can-t-fix-some-of-biggest-security-challenges-facing-russia-pub-85397.

196 **the largest military exercise in Europe:** "Russia Holds the Largest Military Exercise in Europe for 40 Years," *The Economist*, September 13, 2021, www.economist.com/europe/2021/09/13/russia-holds-the-largest-military-exercise-in-europe-for-40-years.

196 **Poland declared a state of emergency:** Amy Mackinnon, "Moscow Expands Its Military Footprint on NATO's Borders," *Foreign Policy*, September 16, 2021, https://foreignpolicy.com/2021/09/16/russia-expand-military-footprint-nato-border.

196 **Russia was showing off:** Mackinnon, "Moscow Expands Its Military Footprint on NATO's Borders."

196 **"undergone a dramatic transformation":** "Russia Holds the Largest Military Exercise in Europe for 40 Years."

197 **forcing the dictator to self-isolate:** CBS News, "Putin Forced to Self-Isolate as COVID Hits His Inner Circle," September 14, 2021, www.cbsnews.com/news/putin-covid-coronavirus-russia-self-isolate.

198 **a plan to stop a zombie apocalypse:** Gordon Lubold, "Exclusive: The Pentagon Has a Plan to Stop the Zombie Apocalypse. Seriously," *Foreign Policy*, May 13, 2014, https://foreignpolicy.com/2014/05/13/exclusive-the-pentagon-has-a-plan-to-stop-the-zombie-apocalypse-seriously.

201 **"We were going to act":** Erin Banco, Garrett M. Graff, Lara Seligman, Nahal Toosi, and Alexander Ward, "'Something Was Badly Wrong': When Washington Realized Russia Was Actually Invading Ukraine," *Politico*, February 24, 2023, www.politico.com/news/magazine/2023/02/24/russia-ukraine-war-oral-history-00083757.

202 **three sets of meetings in early October:** Interviews, and Shane Harris, Karen DeYoung, Isabelle Khurshudyan, Ashley Parker, and Liz Sly, "Road to War: U.S. Struggled to Convince Allies, and Zelensky, of Risk of Invasion," *Washington Post*, August 16, 2022, www.washingtonpost.com/national-security/interactive/2022/ukraine-road-to-war.

202 **Russia's version of "shock and awe":** Interviews, and Harris, DeYoung, Khurshudyan, Parker, and Sly, "Road to War: U.S. Struggled to Convince Allies, and Zelensky, of Risk of Invasion."

202 **and kill him if need be:** Harris et al., "Road to War: U.S. Struggled to Convince Allies, and Zelensky, of Risk of Invasion."

202 **Troops stationed in Crimea:** Harris et al., "Road to War: U.S. Struggled to Convince Allies, and Zelensky, of Risk of Invasion."

205 **"Ukrainian entry into NATO":** Quoted in Peter Beinart, "Biden's CIA Director Doesn't Believe Biden's Story about Ukraine," Beinart Notebook, February 7, 2022,

https://peterbeinart.substack.com/p/bidens-cia-director-doesnt-believe?utm_source=url.

205 **"China, technology, people, and partnerships":** William J. Burns, "Statement for the Record Senate Select Committee on Intelligence," February 24, 2021, www.intelligence.senate.gov/sites/default/files/documents/os-wburns-022421.pdf.

206 **meeting their counterparts in Oman five times:** Arshad Mohammed, "The Invisible Man: Bill Burns and the Secret Iran Talks," Reuters, January 1, 2014, www.reuters.com/article/us-iran-nuclear-burns/the-invisible-man-bill-burns-and-the-secret-iran-talks-idUSBREA000AD20140101.

206 **"One of the iron laws of foreign policy":** William J. Burns and Jake Sullivan, "Soleimani's Ultimate Revenge," *The Atlantic*, January 6, 2020, www.theatlantic.com/ideas/archive/2020/01/soleimanis-ultimate-revenge/604471.

208 **"He was very dismissive of President Zelenskyy":** Quoted in Harris et al., "Road to War: U.S. Struggled to Convince Allies, and Zelensky, of Risk of Invasion."

208 **"My level of concern has gone up, not down":** Quoted in Harris et al., "Road to War: U.S. Struggled to Convince Allies, and Zelensky, of Risk of Invasion."

208 **Haines, the first woman to serve:** Anagha Srikanth, "Meet the Very Unusual, Judo-Trained, Erotica-Hosting First Female Top Spy," The Hill, January 27, 2021, https://thehill.com/changing-america/respect/equality/536088-meet-the-very-unusual-judo-trained-and-erotica-hosting.

209 **Haines had only the UK and the three Baltic:** Quoted in Harris et al., "Road to War: U.S. Struggled to Convince Allies, and Zelensky, of Risk of Invasion."

210 **"Our evaluations are almost the same":** Howard Altman, "Russia Preparing to Attack Ukraine by Late January: Ukraine Defense Intelligence Agency Chief," Military Times, November 20, 2021, www.militarytimes.com/flashpoints/2021/11/20/russia-preparing-to-attack-ukraine-by-late-january-ukraine-defense-intelligence-agency-chief.

211 **Sullivan didn't want the United States to be like that security guard:** Banco et al., "Something Was Badly Wrong."

211 **Bick corralled members of every agency:** Interviews, and Ellen Nakashima and Ashley Parker, "Inside White House Preparations for a Russian Invasion of Ukraine," *Washington Post*, February 14, 2022, www.washingtonpost.com/national-security/2022/02/14/white-house-prepares-russian-invasion.

Chapter 10: Confrontation

215 **the new envoys from Spain, Slovakia, Austria, and Italy:** Office of the President of Russia, "Ceremony for Presenting Foreign Ambassadors' Letters of Credence," December 1, 2021, http://en.kremlin.ru/events/president/news/67250.

215 **"In a dialogue with the United States":** Quoted in Vladimir Isachenkov, "Putin Demands NATO Guarantees Not to Expand Eastward," Associated Press, December 1, 2021, https://apnews.com/article/business-russia-ukraine-moscow-sergey-lavrov-90d7347e8f25bea1ddb2c7b3dc1687c0.

215 **not allow Ukraine into the alliance:** Isachenkov, "Putin Demands NATO Guarantees Not to Expand Eastward."

216 **"We don't know whether President Putin":** U.S. Department of State, "Secretary Antony J. Blinken at a Press Availability at the NATO Ministerial," December 1, 2021,

www.state.gov/secretary-antony-j-blinken-at-a-press-availability-at-the-nato-ministerial.

217 **"The idea that Ukraine represents a threat to Russia":** U.S. Department of State, "Secretary Antony J. Blinken at a Press Availability at the NATO Ministerial."

219 **"The best way to avert a crisis":** Quoted in Missy Ryan and Isabelle Khurshudyan, "Top U.S., Russian Diplomats Trade Blame in Talks over Ukraine," *Washington Post,* December 2, 2021, www.washingtonpost.com/national-security/blinken-lavrov-talks-ukraine/2021/12/02/a865c9fa-5341-11ec-8ad5-b5c50c1fb4d9_story.html.

220 **American personnel working at the embassy in Moscow to get visas:** Isabelle Khurshudyan and John Hudson, "Russia, U.S. Make Breakthrough on Staffing at Moscow Embassy," *Washington Post,* December 3, 2021, www.washingtonpost.com/world/europe/russia-us-moscow-embassy/2021/12/03/2a459f56-49fe-11ec-beca-3cc7103bd814_story.html.

220 **"U.S. intelligence has found":** Shane Harris and Paul Sonne, "Russia Planning Massive Military Offensive Against Ukraine Involving 175,000 Troops, U.S. Intelligence Warns," *Washington Post,* December 3, 2021, www.washingtonpost.com/national-security/russia-ukraine-invasion/2021/12/03/98a3760e-546b-11ec-8769-2f4ecdf7a2ad_story.html.

221 **"What I am doing is putting together":** White House, "Remarks by President Biden on the November Jobs Report," December 3, 2021, www.whitehouse.gov/briefing-room/speeches-remarks/2021/12/03/remarks-by-president-biden-on-the-november-jobs-report.

225 **"I will look you in the eye":** White House, "Press Briefing by Press Secretary Jen Psaki and National Security Advisor Jake Sullivan, December 7, 2021," www.whitehouse.gov/briefing-room/press-briefings/2021/12/07/press-briefing-by-press-secretary-jen-psaki-and-national-security-advisor-jake-sullivan-december-7-2021.

225 **"He said he would impose costs":** White House, "Press Briefing by Press Secretary Jen Psaki and National Security Advisor Jake Sullivan, December 7, 2021."

226 **"That is not on the table":** White House, "Remarks by President Biden Before Marine One Departure," December 8, 2021, www.whitehouse.gov/briefing-room/speeches-remarks/2021/12/08/remarks-by-president-biden-before-marine-one-departure-10.

226 **the ninety-minute chat was quite warm:** White House, "Background Press Call by a Senior Administration Official on President Biden's Calls with President Zelenskyy of Ukraine and European Leaders," December 9, 2021, www.whitehouse.gov/briefing-room/press-briefings/2021/12/09/background-press-call-by-a-senior-administration-official-on-president-bidens-calls-with-president-zelenskyy-of-ukraine-and-european-leaders.

227 **"We are always prepared to talk":** White House, "Background Press Call by a Senior Administration Official on President Biden's Calls with President Zelenskyy of Ukraine and European Leaders."

227 **for "the whole of Europe":** Quoted in Alexander Ward, Matt Berg, and Lawrence Ukenye, "Slovakia's U.S. Ambassador: 'Crazy' for Putin to Drop Nuke," *Politico,* October 5, 2022, www.politico.com/newsletters/national-security-daily/2022/10/05/slovakias-u-s-ambassador-crazy-for-putin-to-drop-nuke-00060440.

228 **"the basic rules of the road":** U.S. Department of State, "Secretary of State Antony J.

Blinken with Chuck Todd of NBC Meet the Press," December 12, 2021, www.state.gov/secretary-antony-j-blinken-with-chuck-todd-of-nbc-meet-the-press.

228 **"It will be Ukrainian blood":** Paul McLeary, Alexander Ward, and Quint Forgey, "'It Will Be Ukrainian Blood, It Will Be Russian Blood,'" *Politico*, December 13, 2021, www.politico.com/newsletters/national-security-daily/2021/12/13/it-will-be-ukrainian-blood-it-will-be-russian-blood-495446.

229 **A war would all but guarantee he'd get nothing:** Dasha Litvinova, "Putin Discusses Ukraine Tensions with Macron, Niinistö," Associated Press, December 14, 2021, https://apnews.com/article/joe-biden-russia-ukraine-europe-vladimir-putin-00adcb233374676d39175b6342e4e1ef.

229 **Putin "is trying to present himself as a solution":** Jacopo Barigazzi, "Don't Fall into Putin's trap, Estonian PM Warns the West," *Politico* Europe, December 15, 2021, www.politico.eu/article/estonia-pm-eu-nato-putin-influence.

229 **The Kremlin put forward its demands:** Andrew Roth, "Russia Issues List of Demands It Says Must Be Met to Lower Tensions in Europe," *The Guardian*, December 17, 2021, www.theguardian.com/world/2021/dec/17/russia-issues-list-demands-tensions-europe-ukraine-nato.

230 **"The Parties shall refrain from deploying":** Russian Foreign Ministry, "Treaty Between the United States of America and the Russian Federation on Security Guarantees," December 17, 2021, https://mid.ru/ru/foreign_policy/rso/nato/1790818/?lang=en; and Russian Foreign Ministry, "Agreement on Measures to Ensure the Security of the Russian Federation and Member States of the North Atlantic Treaty Organization," December 17, 2021, https://mid.ru/ru/foreign_policy/rso/nato/1790803/?lang=en.

230 **"We will not compromise":** White House, "Press Gaggle by Press Secretary Jen Psaki en Route to Orangeburg, SC," December 17, 2021, www.whitehouse.gov/briefing-room/press-briefings/2021/12/17/press-gaggle-by-press-secretary-jen-psaki-en-route-orangeburg-sc.

231 **talks with Russia over the Ukraine situation:** David Sanger, "U.S. and Russia Agree to Talks Amid Growing Tensions over Ukraine," *New York Times*, December 28, 2021, www.nytimes.com/2021/12/28/us/politics/nato-russia-ukrain-us.html.

231 **"It's a challenging world out there":** "A Conversation with Jake Sullivan," Council on Foreign Relations, December 17, 2021, www.cfr.org/event/conversation-jake-sullivan.

Chapter 11: Three-Ring Circus

234 **"cutting off Russia's largest financial institutions":** David Sanger and Eric Schmitt, "U.S. Details Costs of a Russian Invasion of Ukraine," *New York Times*, January 8, 2022, www.nytimes.com/2022/01/08/us/politics/us-sanctions-russia-ukraine.html.

235 **"Today was a discussion":** U.S. Department of State, "Briefing with Deputy Secretary Wendy R. Sherman on the U.S.–Russia Strategic Stability Dialogue," January 10, 2022, www.state.gov/briefing-with-deputy-secretary-wendy-r-sherman-on-the-u-s-russia-strategic-stability-dialogue.

235 **$200 million in security assistance:** Jennifer Hansler, Jeremy Herb, Kylie Atwood, Natasha Bertrand, and Rob Picheta, "US Says No Breakthrough in 'Frank and Forthright' Talks with Russia over Ukraine Border Crisis," CNN, January 10, 2022, www.cnn.com/2022/01/10/politics/us-russia-ukraine-meetings-geneva-intl/index.html.

237 **"You've come as one to a room of thirty":** Details on the meeting and speech in Alexander Ward and Quint Forgey, "The Dueling Lobbying Campaigns on Cruz's NS2 Bill," *Politico,* January 12, 2022, www.politico.com/newsletters/national-security-daily/2022/01/12/the-dueling-lobbying-campaigns-on-cruzs-ns2-bill-495703.

238 **"We must decisively reject blackmail":** Organization for Security and Cooperation in Europe, "Response to the Opening Address by the OSCE Chairperson-in-Office and Minister for Foreign Affairs of Poland Zbigniew Rau," January 13, 2022, www.osce.org/files/f/documents/4/4/512197.pdf.

238 **"The risk of war in the OSCE area":** Organization for Security and Cooperation in Europe, "Polish OSCE Chairmanship 2022 Address by Minister of Foreign Affairs H. E. Zbigniew Rau at the OSCE Permanent Council, Vienna, 13 January 2022," January 13, 2022, www.osce.org/files/f/documents/7/d/509900.pdf.

239 **There were "no grounds":** Robyn Dixon and Paul Sonne, "A Flurry of Talks in Europe This Week Has Failed to Resolve a Mounting Security Crisis over Ukraine," *Washington Post,* January 13, 2021, www.washingtonpost.com/world/2022/01/13/europe-osce-russia-ukraine.

239 **"both hopeful signs and deeply pessimistic signs":** White House, "Press Briefing by Press Secretary Jen Psaki and National Security Advisor Jake Sullivan, January 13, 2021," www.whitehouse.gov/briefing-room/press-briefings/2022/01/13/press-briefing-by-press-secretary-jen-psaki-and-national-security-advisor-jake-sullivan-january-13-2022.

239 **"The drumbeat of war":** Thomas Escritt and Tom Balmforth, "Russia Says Ukraine Talks Hit 'Dead End,' Poland Warns of Risk of War," Reuters, January 13, 2022, www.reuters.com/world/europe/russia-says-us-nato-talks-so-far-unsuccessful-2022-01-13.

239 **"trained in urban warfare":** Alexander Ward, "U.S. Intel Suggests Russia Is Planning a False-Flag Operation," *Politico,* January 14, 2022, www.politico.com/news/2022/01/14/us-intel-russia-false-flag-operation-527112.

240 **"We have run out of patience":** Vladimir Isachenkov, "Russia Demands US, NATO Response Next Week on Ukraine," Associated Press, January 14, 2022, https://apnews.com/article/europe-russia-ukraine-moscow-sergey-lavrov-9b6c7c17bd462c02cfb9420463057188.

240 **administration figures made three separate statements:** All quoted in Alexander Ward and Quint Forgey, "Psaki: 'Russia Could at Any Point Launch an Attack in Ukraine,'" *Politico,* January 18, 2022, www.politico.com/newsletters/national-security-daily/2022/01/18/psaki-russia-could-at-any-point-launch-an-attack-in-ukraine-495761.

240 **"an Afghanistan-in-Europe type of event":** Quoted in Ward and Forgey, "Psaki: 'Russia Could at Any Point Launch an Attack in Ukraine.'"

241 **"he's never seen sanctions like the ones":** White House, "Remarks by President Biden in Press Conference," January 19, 2022, www.whitehouse.gov/briefing-room/speeches-remarks/2022/01/19/remarks-by-president-biden-in-press-conference-6.

242 **Some Russian troops had already arrived in Belarus:** "Russia Moves Troops to Belarus for Joint Drills amid Ukraine Invasion Fears," Reuters, January 18, 2022, www.nbcnews.com/news/world/russia-moves-troops-belarus-joint-drills-ukraine-invasion-fears-rcna12533.

242 **"We want to remind the great powers":** Volodymyr Zelenskyy (@ZelenskyyUa), Twitter post, January 20, 2022, 9:29 a.m, https://twitter.com/ZelenskyyUa/status/1484171183264129025?s=20.

242 **"Speaking of minor and full incursions":** Vivian Salama, James Marson, and Alex Leary, "Biden Seeks to Reassure Ukraine, Vowing a Strong Response to Russia and Transferring Weapons," *Wall Street Journal,* January 20, 2022, www.wsj.com/articles/ukraines-foreign-minister-says-bidens-minor-incursion-comment-invites-russian-attack-11642686159.

242 **"If any—any—assembled Russian units":** White House, "Remarks by President Biden Before Meeting with the Infrastructure Implementation Task Force," January 20, 2022, www.whitehouse.gov/briefing-room/speeches-remarks/2022/01/20/remarks-by-president-biden-before-meeting-with-the-infrastructure-implementation-task-force.

243 **Zelenskyy made his anger known:** Lally Weymouth, "Volodomyr Zelensky: 'Everyone Will Lose' If Russia Invades Ukraine," *Washington Post,* January 20, 2022, www.washingtonpost.com/outlook/2022/01/20/ukraine-russia-zelensky-interview.

243 **a Russian invasion was "imminent":** Alexander Ward and Quint Forgey, "Why 'Imminent' Pisses Zelenskyy Off," *Politico,* January 28, 2022, www.politico.com/newsletters/national-security-daily/2022/01/28/why-imminent-pisses-zelensky-off-00003339.

243 **"I'm the president of Ukraine":** Christopher Miller (@ChristopherJM), Twitter post, January 28, 2022, 10:10 a.m., https://twitter.com/ChristopherJM/status/1487080558610071562.

244 **The sanctions package was:** Ian Talley and Brett Forrest, "Biden's Sanctions Plan Targets Russian Banks, Companies and Imports If Ukraine Is Attacked," *Wall Street Journal,* January 28, 2022, www.wsj.com/articles/biden-sanctions-plan-targets-russian-banks-companies-and-imports-if-ukraine-is-attacked-11643387219.

244 **"we have no intention of putting American forces":** White House, "Remarks by President Biden in Press Gaggle," January 25, 2022, www.whitehouse.gov/briefing-room/speeches-remarks/2022/01/25/remarks-by-president-biden-in-press-gaggle-4.

245 **Biden held a call with Volodymyr Zelenskyy:** White House, "Readout of President Biden's Call with President Zelenskyy of Ukraine," January 27, 2022, www.whitehouse.gov/briefing-room/statements-releases/2022/01/27/readout-of-president-bidens-call-with-president-zelenskyy-of-ukraine-2.

246 **"We don't want wars":** David M. Herszenhorn, "Sergey Lavrov Says He Wants Clarifications from Western Powers on Security," *Politico* Europe, January 28, 2022, www.politico.eu/article/russia-sergey-lavrov-wants-clarifications-from-western-powers-nato-ukraine.

Chapter 12: War

247 **"Russian concerns were basically ignored":** Alexander Ward and Quint Forgey, "Putin Seethes Publicly, Lavrov Rants Quietly," *Politico,* February 1, 2022, www.politico.com/newsletters/national-security-daily/2022/02/01/putin-seethes-publicly-lavrov-rants-quietly-00004290.

248 **"will force the United States and our Allies":** Hibai Arbide Aza and Miguel González,

"US Offered Disarmament Measures to Russia in Exchange for De-escalation of Military Threat in Ukraine," *El País*, February 2, 2022, https://english.elpais.com/usa/2022-02-02/us-offers-disarmament-measures-to-russia-in-exchange-for-a-deescalation-of-military-threat-in-ukraine.html.

250 **Kyiv could fall within seventy-two hours:** Jacqui Heinrich and Adam Sabes, "Gen. Milley Says Kyiv Could Fall Within 72 Hours If Russia Decides to Invade Ukraine: Sources," Fox News, February 5, 2022, www.foxnews.com/us/gen-milley-says-kyiv-could-fall-within-72-hours-if-russia-decides-to-invade-ukraine-sources.

251 **"This video likely will depict":** Alexander Ward and Quint Forgey, "U.S. Alleges Russia Weighing Fake Video as Pretext for War," *Politico*, February 3, 2022, www.politico.com/newsletters/national-security-daily/2022/02/03/u-s-alleges-russia-weighing-fake-video-as-pretext-for-war-00005376.

251 **"We're in the window":** NBC News, "*Meet the Press*—February 6, 2022," www.nbcnews.com/meet-the-press/news/meet-press-february-6-2022-n1288711.

253 **"We are ready to take together":** Souad Mekhennet, "Scholz Says Response to Russia Will Be 'United and Decisive' If Ukraine Is Invaded," *Washington Post*, February 6, 2022, www.washingtonpost.com/national-security/2022/02/06/scholz-interview-germany-ukraine.

253 **"there will no longer be a Nord Stream 2":** White House, "Remarks by President Biden and Chancellor Scholz of the Federal Republic of Germany at Press Conference," February 7, 2022, www.whitehouse.gov/briefing-room/statements-releases/2022/02/07/remarks-by-president-biden-and-chancellor-scholz-of-the-federal-republic-of-germany-at-press-conference.

255 **housing fleeing U.S. citizens:** Gordon Lubold and Nancy A. Youssef, "Biden Approves Pentagon Plan to Help Americans Fleeing Ukraine If Russia Invades," *Wall Street Journal*, February 9, 2022, www.wsj.com/articles/white-house-approves-plan-to-help-americans-leaving-ukraine-if-russia-attacks-11644413069.

255 **the fighting would last for a long time:** Lubold and Youssef, "Biden Approves Pentagon Plan to Help Americans Fleeing Ukraine If Russia Invades."

255 **nine routes Putin's troops could take:** Courtney Kube, "U.S. Intel: Nine Probable Russian Routes into Ukraine in Full-Scale Invasion," NBC News, February 10, 2022, www.nbcnews.com/news/world/u-s-intel-nine-probable-russian-routes-ukraine-full-scale-n1288922.

255 **Russia's joint military exercises with Belarus:** Evan Gershkovich, "Russia's Massive Military Drills on Ukraine Border Stir Invasion Fears," *Wall Street Journal*, February 10, 2022, www.wsj.com/articles/massive-russian-military-drills-on-ukraine-border-ratchet-up-threat-11644496231.

256 **"could begin during the Olympics":** White House, "Press Briefing by Press Secretary Jen Psaki and National Security Advisor Jake Sullivan, February 11, 2022," www.whitehouse.gov/briefing-room/press-briefings/2022/02/11/press-briefing-by-press-secretary-jen-psaki-and-national-security-advisor-jake-sullivan-february-11-2022.

257 **a face-to-face meeting in Beijing:** Ministry of Foreign Affairs of the People's Republic of China, "President Xi Jinping Held Talks with Russian President Vladimir Putin," February 4, 2022, www.fmprc.gov.cn/mfa_eng/zxxx_662805/202202/t20220204_10638923.html.

257 **the start date of Russia's invasion:** Quint Forgey and Myah Ward, "White House Warns Russian Invasion 'Threat Is Immediate,'" *Politico,* February 11, 2022, www.politico.com/news/2022/02/11/white-house-warns-russian-invasion-threat-is-immediate-00008299.

257 **a "come to Jesus" moment:** White House, "Readout of President Biden's Call with President Vladimir Putin of Russia," February 12, 2022, www.whitehouse.gov/briefing-room/statements-releases/2022/02/12/readout-of-president-bidens-call-with-president-vladimir-putin-of-russia.

257 **"I believe that our possibilities":** Alexander Ward and Quint Forgey, "Inside Jake Sullivan's Private House Call on Ukraine," *Politico,* February 14, 2022, www.politico.com/newsletters/national-security-daily/2022/02/14/inside-jake-sullivans-private-house-call-on-ukraine-00008672.

258 **"We have taken note of his comments":** U.S. Department of State, "Department Press Briefing—February 14, 2022," www.state.gov/briefings/department-press-briefing-february-14-2022.

258 **withdrawing from the Ukrainian border:** Tucker Reals, "Russia Says Some Troops Pulling Back from Ukraine Border," CBS News, February 15, 2022, www.cbsnews.com/news/russia-ukraine-news-moscow-says-troops-pulling-back-from-border.

259 **"So far we have not seen any sign":** North Atlantic Treaty Organization, "Pre-Ministerial Press Conference," February 15, 2022, www.nato.int/cps/en/natohq/opinions_191832.htm?selectedLocale=en.

259 **The Estonian government had also released intelligence:** Estonian Foreign Intelligence Service, "Russia Is Ready for War," February 15, 2022, https://raport.valisluureamet.ee/en/russian-armed-forces/russia-is-ready-for-war.

259 **"The fact is that all involved":** Alexander Ward and Quint Forgey, "The Most Chaotic Day Yet of the Russia–Ukraine Crisis," *Politico,* February 15, 2022, www.politico.com/newsletters/national-security-daily/2022/02/15/the-most-chaotic-day-yet-of-the-russia-ukraine-crisis-00009135.

259 **formally recognize the breakaway regions:** Felix Light, "Russian Parliament Backs Plan to Recognize Breakaway Ukrainian Regions," *Moscow Times,* February 15, 2022, www.themoscowtimes.com/2022/02/15/russian-parliament-backs-plan-to-recognize-breakaway-ukrainian-regions-a76381.

259 **But "the fact remains":** White House, "Remarks by President Biden Providing an Update on Russia and Ukraine," February 15, 2022, www.whitehouse.gov/briefing-room/speeches-remarks/2022/02/15/remarks-by-president-biden-providing-an-update-on-russia-and-ukraine.

260 **"Every indication we have":** White House, "Remarks by President Biden Before Marine One Departure," February 17, 2022, www.whitehouse.gov/briefing-room/statements-releases/2022/02/17/remarks-by-president-biden-before-marine-one-departure-14.

260 **"As of this moment, I'm convinced":** White House, "Remarks by President Biden Providing an Update on Russia and Ukraine," February 18, 2022, www.whitehouse.gov/briefing-room/speeches-remarks/2022/02/18/remarks-by-president-biden-providing-an-update-on-russia-and-ukraine-2.

261 **"We will defend our land with or without":** "Zelensky's Full Speech at Munich Security Conference," *Kyiv Independent,* February 19, 2022, https://kyivindependent.com/national/zelenskys-full-speech-at-munich-security-conference.

262 **Russia had moved blood:** Phil Stewart, "Russia Moves Blood Supplies Near Ukraine, Adding to U.S. Concern, Officials Say," Reuters, January 29, 2022, www.reuters.com/world/europe/exclusive-russia-moves-blood-supplies-near-ukraine-adding-us-concern-officials-2022-01-28.

262 **Russia had drafted lists:** Amy Mackinnon, Robbie Gramer, and Jack Detsch, "Russia Planning Post-Invasion Arrest and Assassination Campaign in Ukraine, U.S. Officials Say," *Foreign Policy,* February 18, 2022, https://foreignpolicy.com/2022/02/18/russia-ukraine-arrest-assassination-invasion.

263 **"I would like to emphasize again":** Office of the President of Russia, "Address by the President of the Russian Federation," February 21, 2022, http://en.kremlin.ru/events/president/news/67828.

264 **"This is the beginning of an invasion":** CNN interview with Jonathan Finer, February 22, 2022, available at: Jackson Richman, "CNN's Brianna Keilar Gets National Security Official to Say Russian Incursion Into Ukraine is an 'Invasion' After Relentless Grilling," *Mediaite,* February 22, 2022, www.mediaite.com/tv/cnns-brianna-keilar-gets-national-security-official-to-say-russian-incursion-into-ukraine-is-an-invasion-after-relentless-grilling.

264 **"Russian troops moving into Donbas":** Paul McLeary and Andrew Desiderio, "As Putin Sends Troops into Donbas, White House Avoids the 'I' Word," *Politico,* February 21, 2022, www.politico.com/news/2022/02/21/putin-sends-troops-breakaway-territories-00010447.

264 **Germany canceled the Nord Stream 2:** Alexander Ward and Quint Forgey, "The Economic War on Russia Has Begun," *Politico,* February 22, 2022, www.politico.com/newsletters/national-security-daily/2022/02/22/the-economic-war-on-russia-has-begun-00010755.

265 **"setting up a rationale":** White House, "Remarks by President Biden Announcing Response to Russian Actions in Ukraine," February 22, 2022, www.whitehouse.gov/briefing-room/speeches-remarks/2022/02/22/remarks-by-president-biden-announcing-response-to-russian-actions-in-ukraine.

266 **"They did not leave us any other option":** Bloomberg News, "Transcript: Vladimir Putin's Televised Address on Ukraine," February 24, 2022, www.bloomberg.com/news/articles/2022-02-24/full-transcript-vladimir-putin-s-televised-address-to-russia-on-ukraine-feb-24?leadSource=uverify%20wall.

268 **"If you ever want to talk to me, I'm here":** Quoted in Erin Banco, Garrett M. Graff, Lara Seligman, Nahal Toosi, and Alexander Ward, "'Something Was Badly Wrong': When Washington Realized Russia Was Actually Invading Ukraine," *Politico,* February 24, 2023, www.politico.com/news/magazine/2023/02/24/russia-ukraine-war-oral-history-00083757.

Chapter 13: "Kyiv Stands Strong"

270 **80 percent of Russia's banking assets:** U.S. Department of the Treasury, "U.S. Treasury Announces Unprecedented & Expansive Sanctions Against Russia, Imposing Swift and Severe Economic Costs," February 24, 2023, https://home.treasury.gov/news/press-releases/jy0608.

270 **"defend every inch of NATO territory":** White House, "Remarks by President Biden

on Russia's Unprovoked and Unjustified Attack on Ukraine," February 24, 2022, www.whitehouse.gov/briefing-room/speeches-remarks/2022/02/24/remarks-by-president-biden-on-russias-unprovoked-and-unjustified-attack-on-ukraine.

271 **"The enemy has designated me":** BBC, "As It Happened: Ukraine Deaths as Battles Rage on Day One of Russian Invasion," February 24, 2022, www.bbc.com/news/live/world-europe-60454795.

271 **"We didn't have anyone in Kyiv":** From an unpublished section of an interview with Jake Sullivan, for Erin Banco, Garrett M. Graff, Lara Seligman, Nahal Toosi, and Alexander Ward, "'Something Was Badly Wrong': When Washington Realized Russia Was Actually Invading Ukraine," *Politico,* February 24, 2023, www.politico.com/news/magazine/2023/02/24/russia-ukraine-war-oral-history-00083757.

271 **take Antonov Airport in Hostomel:** Patrick J. McDonnell, "Russia Lost the Battle for Kyiv with Its Hasty Assault on a Ukrainian Airport," *Los Angeles Times,* April 10, 2022, www.latimes.com/world-nation/story/2022-04-10/battered-ukraine-air-field-was-key-to-russian-plan-to-take-the-capital-the-airport-fell-but-resistance-continued.

272 **Moscow sent two hundred helicopters:** McDonnell, "Russia Lost the Battle for Kyiv with Its Hasty Assault on a Ukrainian Airport."

272 **"We are in Kyiv. We are protecting Ukraine":** Quoted in Valerie Hopkins, "In Video, a Defiant Zelensky Says, 'We Are Here,'" *New York Times,* February 25, 2022, www.nytimes.com/2022/02/25/world/europe/zelensky-speech-video.html.

272 **Moscow's forces spread out:** Stijn Mitzer and Joost Oliemans, "Destination Disaster: Russia's Failure at Hostomel Airport," Oryx, April 13, 2022, www.oryxspioenkop.com/2022/04/destination-disaster-russias-failure-at.html.

272 **The momentary awe of the airport takeover gave way:** Mitzer and Oliemans, "Destination Disaster: Russia's Failure at Hostomel Airport."

272 **There was no order to advance:** Mitzer and Oliemans, "Destination Disaster: Russia's Failure at Hostomel Airport."

273 **Others didn't have maps or medical kits at all:** Michael Schwirtz, Anton Troianovski, Yousur Al-Hlou, Masha Froliak, Adam Entous, and Thomas Gibbons-Neff, "Putin's War," *New York Times,* December 16, 2022, www.nytimes.com/interactive/2022/12/16/world/europe/russia-putin-war-failures-ukraine.html.

273 **"This isn't war":** Quoted in Schwirtz, Troianovski, Al-Hlou, Froliak, Entous, and Gibbons-Neff, "Putin's War."

273 **"Russian warship, go fuck yourself":** Quoted in Brad Lendon, Tim Lister, and Josh Pennington, "Soldiers on Snake Island Reacted with Defiant Words to Threats from Russian Warship," CNN, February 28, 2022, www.cnn.com/2022/02/25/europe/ukraine-russia-snake-island-attack-intl-hnk-ml/index.html.

275 **there would be no Polish warplanes in Ukraine:** Paul McLeary, Alexander Ward, and Betsy Woodruff Swan, "Shot Down: How Biden Scuttled the Deal to Get MiGs to Ukraine," *Politico,* March 10, 2022, www.politico.com/news/2022/03/10/poland-fighter-jet-deal-ukraine-russia-00016038.

275 **"That gets a green light":** U.S. Department of State, "Secretary Blinken with Margaret Brennan of CBS News," March 6, 2022, www.state.gov/secretary-antony-j-blinken-on-cbs-face-the-nation-with-margaret-brennan.

275 **jets with "corresponding capabilities":** Paul McLeary and Alexander Ward, "'Surprise Move': U.S. Stunned by Poland's Fighter Jet Offer," *Politico,* March 8, 2022, www.politico

.com/news/2022/03/08/poland-transfers-mig-fighters-to-the-us-as-ukraine-asks-for-help-00015259.

276 **Putin, they feared, would use the deliveries to escalate the war:** McLeary and Ward, "'Surprise Move': U.S. Stunned by Poland's Fighter Jet Offer."

276 **"that actually was a surprise move by the Poles":** Quoted in McLeary and Ward, "'Surprise Move': U.S. Stunned by Poland's Fighter Jet Offer."

276 **sided with Milley and Austin:** Chris Whipple, *The Fight of His Life: Inside Joe Biden's White House* (New York: Scribner, 2023), 264.

276 **"We do not support the transfer":** Quoted in McLeary, Ward, and Woodruff Swan, "Shot Down: How Biden Scuttled the Deal to Get MiGs to Ukraine."

276 **"Tell Duda it's my policy":** Interviews, and quoted in Whipple, *The Fight of His Life*, 265.

277 **"We're not going to support the transfer of these planes":** Interviews, and Whipple, *The Fight of His Life*.

277 **"We wanted NATO as a whole":** White House, "Remarks by Vice President Harris and President Andrzej Duda of Poland in Joint Press Conference," March 10, 2022, www.whitehouse.gov/briefing-room/speeches-remarks/2022/03/10/remarks-by-vice-president-harris-and-president-andrzej-duda-of-poland-in-joint-press-conference.

277 **"You only fire this thing if you're desperate":** Quoted in Alexander Ward, "Russia Launched Hypersonic Missiles Due to a Low Stockpile, Sources Say," *Politico*, March 22, 2022, www.politico.com/news/2022/03/22/russia-hypersonic-missiles-low-stockpile-00019358.

277 **the "first phase" of its war":** BBC, "Russia Targets East Ukraine, Says First Phase Over," March 26, 2022, www.bbc.com/news/world-europe-60872358.

277 **It was effectively an admission:** Justin Bronk, "Russia Has Effectively Admitted Defeat in Ukraine," *Al Jazeera*, March 30, 2022, www.aljazeera.com/opinions/2022/3/30/russia-has-effectively-admitted-defeat-in-ukraine.

277 **In the town of Bucha:** Max Bearak and Louisa Loveluck, "In Bucha, the Scope of Russian Barbarity Is Coming into Focus," *Washington Post*, April 6, 2022, www.washingtonpost.com/world/2022/04/06/bucha-barbarism-atrocities-russian-soldiers.

277 **"Russian forces committed a litany of apparent war crimes":** Human Rights Watch, "Ukraine: Russian Forces' Trail of Death in Bucha," April 21, 2022, www.hrw.org/news/2022/04/21/ukraine-russian-forces-trail-death-bucha.

277 **destroyed the Donetsk Academic Regional Drama Theater:** Lori Hinnant, Mstyslav Chervnov, and Vasilisa Stepanenko, "AP Evidence Points to 600 Dead in Mariupol Theater Strike," Associated Press, May 4, 2022, https://apnews.com/article/Russia-ukraine-war-mariupol-theater-c321a196fbd568899841b506afcac7a1.

277 **killed six hundred people in and around the theater:** Hinnant, Chervnov, and Stepanenko, "AP Evidence Points to 600 Dead in Mariupol Theater Strike."

279 **"This battle will not be won":** White House, "Remarks by President Biden on the United Efforts of the Free World to Support the People of Ukraine," March 26, 2022, www.whitehouse.gov/briefing-room/speeches-remarks/2022/03/26/remarks-by-president-biden-on-the-united-efforts-of-the-free-world-to-support-the-people-of-ukraine.

279 **removing Putin from power was his secret desire:** Phil Stewart, Breandan O'Brien,

and Humeyra Pamuk, "Biden Says He Is Not Calling for Regime Change in Russia," Reuters, March 27, 2022, www.reuters.com/world/europe/us-envoy-nato-no-american-policy-regime-change-russia-2022-03-27.

279 **"I'm not walking anything back":** White House, "Remarks by President Biden Announcing the Fiscal Year 2023 Budget," March 28, 2022, www.whitehouse.gov/briefing-room/speeches-remarks/2022/03/28/remarks-by-president-biden-announcing-the-fiscal-year-2023-budget.

279 **"The United States is leading the way":** White House, "Remarks by President Biden in Press Conference, Madrid, Spain," June 30, 2022, www.whitehouse.gov/briefing-room/speeches-remarks/2022/06/30/remarks-by-president-biden-in-press-conference-madrid-spain.

280 **the killing of U.S. resident and dissident Jamal Khashoggi:** Alex Emmons, Aída Chavez, and Akela Lacy, "Joe Biden, in Departure from Obama Policy, Says He Would Make Saudi Arabia a 'Pariah,'" *The Intercept*, November 21, 2019, https://theintercept.com/2019/11/21/democratic-debate-joe-biden-saudi-arabia.

280 **off-camera, Saudi officials:** Alexander Ward and Jonathan Lemire, "Biden's Middle East Expedition: Reputation Dinged, Interests Secured?," *Politico*, July 16, 2022, www.politico.com/news/2022/07/16/bidens-middle-east-reputation-00046214.

281 **"we are approaching the Third World War":** "White House Not Ready to Send Long-Range Missiles to Ukraine," New Voice of Ukraine, July 23, https://english.nv.ua/nation/us-will-not-send-ukraine-long-range-missiles-for-himars-russia-ukraine-war-50258417.html.

281 **"get them to change their mind on that":** Alexander Ward and Quint Forgey, "HASC Chair Smith: Ukraine Needs Urgent Help Next 3–6 Weeks," *Politico*, July 25, 2022, www.politico.com/newsletters/national-security-daily/2022/07/25/hasc-chair-smith-ukraine-needs-urgent-help-next-3-6-weeks-00047662.

282 **"The price tag of aggression":** Christopher Miller and Alexander Ward, "'Not Enough': Estonia's FM Wants More Support for Ukraine," *Politico*, August 3, 2022, www.politico.com/newsletters/national-security-daily/2022/08/03/not-enough-estonias-fm-wants-more-support-for-ukraine-00049563.

282 **three thousand people to evacuate:** Michael Schwirtz and Anton Troianovski, "Ukraine Strikes Again in Crimea, Posing a New Challenge for Putin," *New York Times*, August 16, 2022, www.nytimes.com/2022/08/16/world/europe/crimea-russia-ukraine-explosions.html.

282 **the Black Sea fleet's 43rd Naval Aviation Regiment:** Schwirtz and Troianovski, "Ukraine Strikes Again in Crimea, Posing a New Challenge for Putin."

282 **"by definition self-defense":** Alexander Ward, "U.S. Approves of Ukraine Striking Russian-Occupied Crimea," *Politico*, August 17, 2022, www.politico.com/newsletters/national-security-daily/2022/08/17/u-s-approves-of-ukraine-striking-russian-occupied-crimea-00052364.

283 **Russian enemies, who struggled to respond:** Isabelle Khurshudyan, Paul Sonne, Serhiy Morgunov, and Kamila Hrabchuk, "Inside the Ukrainian Counteroffensive That Shocked Putin and Reshaped the War," *Washington Post*, December 29, 2022, www.washingtonpost.com/world/2022/12/29/ukraine-offensive-kharkiv-kherson-donetsk.

283 **"everywhere there was a breakthrough":** Quoted in Khurshudyan, Sonne, Morgunov, and Hrabchuk, "Inside the Ukrainian Counteroffensive That Shocked Putin and Reshaped the War."

283 **encouraging the Ukrainians to recapture it too:** Khurshudyan, Sonne, Morgunov, and Hrabchuk, "Inside the Ukrainian Counteroffensive That Shocked Putin and Reshaped the War."

283 **conscript three hundred thousand trained reservists:** Zoya Sheftalovich, "Putin Calls Up 300,000 Reservists, Makes Nuclear Threat," *Politico,* September 21, 2022, www.politico.eu/article/putin-announces-partial-mobilization-russian-reservists-nuclear-threat-conscription-ukraine.

284 **"This is not a bluff":** Quoted in Sheftalovich, "Putin Calls Up 300,000 Reservists, Makes Nuclear Threat."

284 **"We are very scared. We want to run":** Quoted in Jedidajah Otte, "'We're Scared, We Want to Run': The Russian Men Fleeing Conscription," *The Guardian,* September 27, 2022, www.theguardian.com/world/2022/sep/27/we-want-to-run-russian-men-fleeing-conscription.

284 **"knows how to fight with bombers and missiles":** Quoted in Aleksandra Klitina, "'All in Good Time'—Head of Ukrainian Military Intelligence Speaks Out," *Kyiv Post,* July 5, 2022, www.kyivpost.com/post/2369.

285 **"our citizens forever":** *Al Jazeera,* "Putin Announces Russian Annexation of Four Ukrainian Regions," September 30, 2022, www.aljazeera.com/news/2022/9/30/putin-announces-russian-annexation-of-four-ukrainian-regions.

285 **"it can't be a blank check":** Quoted in Punchbowl News, "McCarthy on Debt Limit, Immigration and Ukraine," October 18, 2022, https://punchbowl.news/archive/101822-punchbowl-news-am.

285 **if Republicans took control of the House:** Andrea Shalal and Steve Holland, "Biden Is 'Worried' about Ukraine Aid If Republicans Win Congress," Reuters, October 20, 2022, www.reuters.com/world/biden-is-worried-about-ukraine-aid-if-republicans-win-congress-2022-10-20.

286 **"Is Ukraine now the fifty-first state?":** Quoted in Andrew Desiderio, "GOP Downplays Its Trump Wing on the World Stage," *Politico,* November 22, 2022, www.politico.com/news/2022/11/22/gop-ukraine-aid-halifax-00069709.

286 **"Your money is not charity":** Quoted in Zeke Miller, Lisa Mascaro, and E. Eduardo Castillo, "Zelenskyy Thanks 'Every American,' Sees 'Turning Point,'" Associated Press, December 21, 2022, https://apnews.com/article/zelenskyy-biden-68c65b3274e552f36f16853f24fedbb9.

286 **featuring Patriot surface-to-air missiles:** Miller, Mascaro, and Castillo, "Zelenskyy Thanks 'Every American,' Sees 'Turning Point.'"

287 **"We need these tanks":** "Ukraine Updates: 'We Need These Tanks,' Kyiv Tells Berlin," Deutsche Welle, November 5, 2022, www.dw.com/en/ukraine-updates-we-need-these-tanks-kyiv-envoy-tells-germany/a-63658775.

288 **The Leopards were much closer to the action:** Interviews with U.S. officials, and Alexander Ward, Lara Seligman, and Paul McLeary, "U.S., Allies Ramp Up Pressure on Germany to Send Tanks to Ukraine," *Politico,* January 19, 2023, www.politico.com/news/2023/01/19/german-tanks-ukraine-scholz-davos-00078503.

288 **Scholz conveyed the message:** Ward, Seligman, and McLeary, "U.S., Allies Ramp Up Pressure on Germany to Send Tanks to Ukraine."

288 **the Leopards would stay in Germany:** Erika Solomon, "Allies Fail to Agree on Sending Tanks to Ukraine," *New York Times*, January 20, 2023, www.nytimes.com/2023/01/20/world/europe/ukraine-germany-us-tanks.html.

288 **"a reliable ally":** Quoted in Solomon, "Allies Fail to Agree on Sending Tanks to Ukraine."

288 **"give the Germans what they need":** John Hudson, "The Ukraine War Is Antony Blinken's Defining Moment," *Washington Post*, March 16, 2023, www.washingtonpost.com/national-security/2023/03/16/antony-blinken-ukraine-russia.

288 **Leopards would soon be on their way to Ukraine:** Rob Schmitz, Charles Maynes, and Joanna Kakissis, "Germany Agrees to Send Its Leopard Battle Tanks to Ukraine after Weeks of Pressure," NPR, January 25, 2023, www.npr.org/2023/01/25/1150759498/germany-leopard-2-tanks-ukraine.

288 **"We are united. America":** White House, "Remarks by President Biden on Continued Support for Ukraine," January 25, 2023, www.whitehouse.gov/briefing-room/speeches-remarks/2023/01/25/remarks-by-president-biden-on-continued-support-for-ukraine.

291 **The train started rolling:** All these details came from Siddiqui's brilliant White House travel pool report.

292 **"Thank you for coming":** Quoted in Alexander Ward and Jonathan Lemire, "Biden Visits Kyiv Ahead of Anniversary of Russia's Invasion," *Politico*, February 20, 2023, www.politico.com/news/2023/02/20/biden-ukraine-traveling-00083597.

293 **anti-armor systems like Howitzers and Javelins:** Ward and Lemire, "Biden Visits Kyiv Ahead of Anniversary of Russia's Invasion."

294 **"stands strong, it stands proud, and it stands free":** White House, "Remarks by President Biden Ahead of the One-Year Anniversary of Russia's Brutal and Unprovoked Invasion of Ukraine," February 21, 2023, www.whitehouse.gov/briefing-room/speeches-remarks/2023/02/21/remarks-by-president-biden-ahead-of-the-one-year-anniversary-of-russias-brutal-and-unprovoked-invasion-of-ukraine.

Epilogue

296 **"mainstream foreign policy consensus":** Greg Jaffe, "Lessons in Disaster: A Top Clinton Adviser Searches for Meaning in a Shocking Loss," *Washington Post*, July 14, 2017, www.washingtonpost.com/world/national-security/lessons-in-disaster-a-top-clinton-adviser-searches-for-meaning-in-a-shocking-loss/2017/06/30/6ca81022-5453-11e7-b38e-35fd8e0c288f_story.html.

298 **a modern industrial and innovation strategy:** This quote, like all others from the speech, from White House, "Remarks by National Security Advisor Jake Sullivan on Renewing American Economic Leadership at the Brookings Institution," April 27, 2023, www.whitehouse.gov/briefing-room/speeches-remarks/2023/04/27/remarks-by-national-security-advisor-jake-sullivan-on-renewing-american-economic-leadership-at-the-brookings-institution.

Image Credits

Insert page 1: Official White House Photo by Adam Schultz

Insert page 2: (top) USUN photo; (middle) DoD photo by Chad J. McNeeley (via CC BY 2.0); (bottom) DoD photo by Lisa Ferdinando (via CC BY 2.0)

Insert page 3: (top) Official White House Photo by Adam Schultz; (bottom) State Department photo by Ron Przysucha

Insert page 4: photos used with permission of Sam Aronson

Insert page 5: (top) U.S. Marine Corps photo by Sgt. Isaiah Campbell via DVIDS; (bottom) Photo by Kyiv City State Administration, Oleksii Samsonov (via CC BY 4.0)

Insert page 6: (top) stamp by Boris Groh; (bottom) from the website of the President of Ukraine (via CC BY 4.0)

Insert page 7: (top) White House photo; (bottom) White House photo (@POTUS)

Insert page 8: White House photo (@WhiteHouse)

Index

Index

Index

Index

Index

Index

Index